# The World's Greatest Literature

THE Masterpieces of the World's Greatest Authors in *History, Biography, Philosophy, Economics, Politics*; Epic and Dramatic Literature, History of English Literature, Oriental Literature (*Sacred and Profane*), Orations, Essays. Sixty-one Crown Octavo Volumes  ::  ::  ::

ILLUSTRATED WITH FRONTISPIECES, EACH A MASTER WORK OF ART IN PORTRAITURE OR HISTORIC PAINTING

## Editors

### LIBRARY COMMITTEE

JUSTIN McCARTHY, M.P.
*Historian and Journalist*

TIMOTHY DWIGHT, D.D., LL.D.
*Ex-President Yale University*

RICHARD HENRY STODDARD
*Author and Critic*

PAUL VAN DYKE, D.D.
*Princeton University*

ALBERT ELLERY BERGH
*Managing Editor*

### ADVISORY COMMITTEE

JOHN T. MORGAN
*United States Senate*

FREDERIC R. COUDERT, LL.D.
*New York Bar*

EDWARD EVERETT HALE
*Author and Editor*

MAURICE FRANCIS EGAN, LL.D.
*Catholic University of America*

JULIAN HAWTHORNE
*Literary Editor*

# Voltaire

*Photogravure from the original painting by Largillière*

FRANCOIS MARIE AROUET DE VOLTAIRE, the foremost man of letters in his time (he was styled "King Voltaire"), was born at Châtenay, France, on February 20, 1694, and died on May 30, 1778—from excitement, it is said, induced by his tumultuous reception by the Parisians on his visit to the capital after an absence of many years. His "Charles XII," written in 1731, is admitted to be the best of his histories. Justin McCarthy says of it that "it has all the living fascination which is to be found in the stirring romances of the elder Dumas."

# CHRONICLES
## OF ENGLAND, FRANCE, SPAIN

### AND THE ADJOINING COUNTRIES

FROM THE LATTER PART OF THE REIGN OF EDWARD II TO
THE CORONATION OF HENRY IV

BY
SIR JOHN FROISSART

TRANSLATED FROM THE FRENCH BY
THOMAS JOHNES

REVISED EDITION

*VOLUME II*

NEW YORK
P. F. COLLIER & SON

Copyright, 1901
By THE COLONIAL PRESS

# CHRONICLES
VOLUME TWO

# CONTENTS

### CHAPTER I

The Free Companies—Duke of Gueldres Challenges King of France and Obtains Aid from England—Preparations of the King of France for Invading Guelderland............................  1

### CHAPTER II

Scots Invade England During her International Troubles—Meeting of Earl Douglas and Sir Henry Percy; the Famous Battle of Otterbourne................................................  32

### CHAPTER III

The King of France Visits the Pope at Avignon—A Field of Arms at Calais—Invasion of Africa and a Challenge from the Saracens....................................................  53

### CHAPTER IV

Tournament at Smithfield—Death of the Count de Foix—The King of France Declares War on Brittany—Derangement of the King  75

### CHAPTER V

Negotiations for Peace—Dukes of Berry and Burgundy Govern France—Death of the Pope at Avignon—Froissart Visits England and Presents a Book to King Richard...................  105

### CHAPTER VI

Reconciliation of Sir Oliver de Clisson and the Duke of Brittany—The King of Hungary Makes War against Turkey—De Coucy Defeats the Turks—Hainault at War with Friesland..........  131

### CHAPTER VII

The Kings of England and France have an Interview—Bajazet Defeats the Christian Army and Takes many Prisoners—Duke of Gloucester Excites Rebellion in England.....................  154

## CONTENTS

### CHAPTER VIII

Death of De Coucy and of Artois—Magnificence of Bajazet—The Knights of Rhodes—King Richard and the Duke of Gloucester—Execution of the Earl of Arundel .......................... 173

### CHAPTER IX

Palm Sunday at Eltham Palace—Schism in the Church—The Pope and his Cardinals—Lord Derby's Return from Banishment—Coronation of Henry........................................ 189

# THE CHRONICLES

## CHAPTER I

Count d'Armagnac and the Free Companies—Hostility Between the Houses of Brabant and Gueldres, and the Cause of It—Death of the King of Navarre—Garrison of Ventadour—Forty Bold Companions Set Out from Chaluçet in Search of Adventure—Bonne-lance and the Lady of Montferrant—Perrot le Béarnois Ransoms Geronnet de Maudurant—Insolent Challenge of the Duke of Gueldres to the King of France—The English Send Troops Over to Brittany to Assist the Duke—The Duke of Berry Proposes to Marry the Daughter of the Duke of Lancaster—The King of Castille Endeavors to Break Off This Alliance, and Requests the Lady for His Own Son—The Duke of Brittany Comes to Paris to Do Homage to the King—La Rochelle—Preparations of the King of France for Invading Guelderland.

AT this period the Count d'Armagnac resided in Auvergne, and was negotiating with such free companies as held forts in Auvergne, Quercy, and Limousin; from his attachment to France he took great pains to make the leaders of these garrisons, who did much mischief to the country, surrender them up, and depart to other places. All the captains except Geoffry Tête-noire, who held Ventadour, seemed willing to accept his terms, and received in one sum 250,000 francs; on payment of which sum they were all to quit the country, which would gladly have seen them depart, for the inhabitants could neither till the earth nor carry on trade for fear of these pillagers, unless they had entered into composition with them according to their wealth and rank; and these compositions amounted in the year to as much as was now demanded for the evacuation of the forts. The dukes of Berry and Burgundy were informed of the arrangement on the part of the Count d'Armagnac, and were greatly desirous of seeing it accomplished; however, the matter was attended with much difficulty, for when commissaries were sent by the count to parley with Perrot le Béarnois, Amerigot Marcel, and others, those captains could never agree as to terms, since when one party agreed to it one week, the next it was refused; for being of different countries, they had various opinions. Those from Armagnac, who were a sort of retainers to the count, readily assented to what he offered; but the greater part and the most determined of these pillagers were from Béarn and Foix. I do not mean that the Count de Foix ever wished anything but what was honorable and advantageous to France; but when he first heard of these negotiations with the captains of the free companies he was desirous to know upon what terms they were made, and the reason the Count d'Armagnac was so busy in the matter, also where the captains intended to fix themselves when they left their present position. To these inquiries he was answered that it was the intention of the Count d'Armagnac to lead these men-at-arms to Lombardy, where his brother-in-law was employed in defending his inheritance.[a]

The Count de Foix made no reply when he heard this; he was not, however, the less thoughtful on the subject, and determined secretly to prevent any of these treaties being concluded, which he did. But I must now leave these matters, and speak of what was passing in my own country, from the peace which was granted to the Ghent men, on the conclusion of the war, by the Duke and Duchess of Burgundy, who signed and sealed it in the noble city of Tournay. To add strength to my history, I must also tell what was passing in Gueldres and Brabant: for the King of France and the Duke of Burgundy were much affected by the events that happened in those countries, and took great part in the war that ensued.

There had been for some time hatred between the houses of Brabant and Gueldres, whose countries border on each other. The origin of this hatred was the town of Grave, which the Duke of Gueldres had taken possession of, and held by force. Of this the Brabanters complained, as the town is situated on their side of the river Meuse; and though many conferences were held on the subject, the hatred was not abated, and the people of Gueldres complained that the Duke of Bra-

[a] Froissart says this brother-in-law had married the widow of the count's son.

bant had in revenge seized on three castles,[b] on their side of the same river. This quarrel between the two dukes was frequently embittered; but it was the opinion of many able knights and squires, that if the Lord Edward of Gueldres (who was unfortunately slain by an arrow from an archer of the dukes of Luxembourg and Brabant, at the battle of Juliers) [c] had survived and gained the victory, he was so valiant, that he would have reconquered these three castles. Duke Reginald of Gueldres, cousin-german to the Prince of Wales, had mortgaged these castles for a sum of florins to a great baron of Germany, called the Count de Mours, who kept possession of them for a time; and when no intention was shown of paying back the money he had lent, the Count de Mours offered the castles for the money for which they were mortgaged, to the Duke of Brabant, who eagerly accepted the proposal, as they were on the confines of the territory of Fanquemonts, of which he was lord; he took possession of them accordingly, and placed in them, as governor, the Lord de Kale. When on the death of Duke Reginald the Lord Edward succeeded to the duchy of Gueldres, he sent ambassadors to the Duke of Brabant, requesting that he might have the castles for the same money that had been paid for them; but the duke, not having purchased them for this end, returned a positive refusal; at which the Duke of Gueldres was highly indignant, and in consequence was hard upon his sister-in-law, the widow of the Lord Reginald and younger sister to the Duchess of Brabant, by preventing her from receiving her dower. The lady, upon this, went to the Duke of Brabant, and laid before him and the duchess the vexations the Duke of Gueldres was occasioning her; who, on account of the long-subsisting hatred between the Brabanters and those of Gueldres, for the seizure of Grave, were well inclined to aid the lady by force of arms. Twelve hundred spears were at once collected, who advanced to Bois-le-Duc, and as the Duke of Gueldres likewise assembled his forces, it was generally thought a battle would have been the result; but the Duke Albert, the Count de Mours, and the Count de Juliers, this time interfered, and they separated without coming to blows.

The quarrel, however, still continued, and on the death of

[b] The names of the three castles were, Gambet, Buct, and Mille.   [c] A.D. 1372.

Duke Winceslaus the young Duke of Gueldres began to take measures for the regaining of these three castles, which had created such hatred between Brabant and his uncle, the Lord Edward of Gueldres; he, therefore, sent persons properly authorized to treat for the surrender: but the Duchess of Brabant, to whom they belonged, replied, "that they were now legally in her possession, and that she intended to keep them for herself and her heirs;" adding, "that if the duke were in earnest in his professions of friendship to Brabant, he should prove it by yielding up the town of Grave, which he unjustly detained." The Duke of Gueldres, on hearing this, was much piqued, but did not give up his plans; for he now attempted to gain over to his interest Sir John Gosset, the governor of these castles; but in this he could not succeed.

Affairs remained for some time in this state, and the mutual hatred between the Brabanters and those of Gueldres was continued. The Duke of Gueldres crossed the sea to England, to visit his cousin, King Richard, and his other relations, the dukes of Lancaster, York, and Gloucester, who were at that time at home. He entered into an alliance with the King; and, although he had not hitherto received anything from him to induce him to become his liegeman, he now accepted a pension of 1,000 marks, on the King of England's treasury, which, according to the value of the coin, was equal to 4,000 francs, ready money. He was advised to renew his claims on Brabant, and was promised effectual assistance from England, in return for which he swore to be ever loyal in his services to the English Crown. When this treaty was concluded, he took leave of the King and his barons, and returned to Gueldres. The Duke of Juliers, his father, remonstrated with him on the step he had taken, declaring that his alliance with England was an imprudent one, and that it would never turn out to his advantage; but the Duke of Gueldres paid little attention to what his father said, for he was young and rash, and preferred war to peace.

The Duchess of Brabant, who resided at Brussels, was well informed of everything that was passing, and was very fearful lest the Duke of Gueldres should put his threat of war into execution. She, therefore, assembled her council, who, when she demanded their advice, said, "We advise, lady, that you send ambassadors to the King of France and the Duke of Burgundy for assistance." The duchess did so; and her ambassadors received from the duke the following answer: "You will return to our fair aunt, and salute her many times in my name; give her these letters from the King and myself; and tell her that we consider her affairs as our own, and desire her not to be alarmed at anything: for she shall speedily have aid. Tell her, also, that the Count of Brabant shall not in any way be injured." This reply was, of course, deemed very agreeable, and the duchess was much pleased when she heard it.

About this time died a king who has supplied ample materials for many parts of this history; you may readily guess that I mean the King of Navarre. It is a well-known truth that nothing is more certain than death. I mention this because the King of Navarre, when he died, did not think his end so near. Had he thought it, he would no doubt have taken more care of himself. He was residing in the city of Pampeluna, when he took it into his head that he could raise 200,000 florins by a tax on his country, and his council could not contradict him. At the news of this heavy tax, however, the whole country was in great consternation, and unanimous in declaring that they could not bear this additional burden; at which the King was greatly enraged, and went so far as to behead three persons who were most determined in their opposition to the tax. Just at this moment an extraordinary event happened at Pampeluna, which seemed like a judgment from God. I will relate it as it was told me at Foix by several persons from Pampeluna. "The King had passed the night with his mistress, when, returning to his own chamber, he said to one of his varlets, ' Prepare my bed, for I want to lie down.' He undressed himself and went to bed; but he had no sooner laid down than he began to shake and could not possibly get warm. He was now about sixty years of age, and for a long time had been accustomed to have his bed well warmed with heated air. As usual, therefore, he ordered his servant to warm his bed; but this time it turned out very unfortunately, for the flames somehow set fire to the sheets and it could not be extinguished before they were destroyed, and the King, who was wrapped in them, was horribly burned. He did not die immediately, but lingered on fifteen days in great misery and pain."

Such was the end of the King of Navarre,[d] whose death freed his subjects from the tax he would have laid on them. He was succeeded by his son Charles, who, soon after his father's obsequies, was crowned at Pampeluna.

You have heard of the treaties which the Count d'Armagnac attempted to make with the captains of the free companies, and how the Count de Foix determined to oppose him; also, that Geoffry Tête-noire, who held the castle of Ventadour, on the borders of Auvergne and Bourbonnois, refused to surrender for any sum of money. He considered the castle as his own inheritance, and had forced all the surrounding country to enter into composition with him to avoid being plundered, by which means he was enabled to keep up the state of a great baron. He was a cruel man, and very ferocious in his anger. You must know that when the tax for the redemption of these castles was first raised the inhabitants of Auvergne, imagining that Ventadour would be surrendered to the Duke of Berry and the country delivered from the oppressions of the garrison, very cheerfully paid their quota; but when they saw that of all the garrisons which continued their inroads, Ventadour was the most daring, they were very disconsolate, and considered that the tax had been thrown away. Moreover, they declared, that until the garrison was prevented from overrunning the country, they would never pay one farthing of any future tax. When this was reported to the Duke of Berry, he resolved to besiege Ventadour, which he

---

[d] Charles, King of Navarre, died in 1387, aged fifty-five years. His death was worthy of his life. He was wrapped up in cloths that had been dipped in spirits of wine and sulphur, to reanimate the chill in his limbs, caused by his debaucheries, and to cure his leprosy. By some accident they caught fire, as they were securing them about him, and burned the flesh off his bones. It is thus that all the French historians relate the death of Charles; but in the letter of the Bishop of Dax, his principal minister, to the Queen Blanche, the sister of this prince, and widow of Philip de Valois, there is not one word said of this horrid accident, but only of the great pains he suffered in his last illness, and the resignation with which he bore them. Voltaire pretends that Charles was not worse than many other princes. Ferreras had said before him, "that the French surnamed him Charles the Bad, on account of the troubles he had fomented in the kingdom; but that, if his actions were examined, he would be found not sufficiently wicked to deserve such a surname." It is, however, precisely his actions that have caused it. "He was," says Father Daniel, "treacherous, cruel, and the sole cause of the ruin of France." Father Daniel speaks exactly like Mariana, who has painted with energy his cruelties, his infamous debaucheries, and his treasons. Our best historians have done the same.—" Nouveau Dictionnaire Historique."

did, and so saved the country the large sums which they used to pay as composition money.

This same year, about the middle of May, forty bold companions set out from Chaluçet, which was in the possession of Perrot le Béarnois, to seek adventures in Auvergne under command of a squire from Gascony called Geronnet de Maudurant, an able man-at-arms.

On account of the dread which the country and the borders of the Bourbonnois had of these people, the Duke of Bourbon had appointed for its defence one of his knights, a valiant man-at-arms, called Sir John Bonne-lance, courteous, amorous, and eager to display his courage. When he heard that these companions were abroad, he asked how many they might be; and when told about forty, he replied, " As for forty lances, we have no fear of that number. I will take as many to meet them." As soon as he had got his men together, they set out and came to a pass which they imagined the enemy must cross; and so it was, for they had not been there more than half an hour when the enemy appeared, no way suspecting this meeting. Bonne-lance and his party, with their spears in their rests, charged them, shouting their cry as they were descending the mountain. When they found they must fight they put a good face upon it, and prepared for their defence, Geronnet, who was a stout squire, setting them a good example. At the first onset many were beaten down on both sides; but, to say the truth, the French were far better men-at-arms than the adventurers, twenty-two of whom were made prisoners, and sixteen left dead upon the field, while the leader surrendered himself to Bonne-lance. The victorious party set out on their return, taking their prisoners with them. On the road Bonne-lance recollected that about a month ago, when at Montferrant, in Auvergne, a lady who was much in his good graces expressed a desire to see an Englishman, adding, " I have often heard that they are most determined and expert men-at-arms, and indeed they prove it by their gallantry, and by taking from us towns and castles." " Fair lady," replied Bonne-lance, " if I have the good fortune to make one of them prisoner you shall see him."

Bonne-lance, remembering this conversation, took the road to Montferrant, and he and his people dismounted at the hotel.

The ladies and damsels assembled, when Bonne-lance, addressing the lady who was so anxious to see an Englishman, said, "Lady, I come to acquit myself of the promise I made to you about a month since. Through the grace of God I have this day fallen in with a party of valiant Englishmen; not, indeed, real Englishmen, but Gascons who wage war under that name; you may view them at your leisure, for, out of love to you, I shall leave them in this town until they have paid me their ransom." The ladies laughed and expressed their obligation to him: during his stay in Montferrant, Bonne-lance well entertained Maudurant and his companions, and on leaving said that Maudurant must remain as a hostage, while some of his companions went to seek for the ransom, and that as soon as the money was paid, they would all be set at liberty. When the captain of Chaluçet heard of the ill-success of Geronnet de Maudurant, he was very indifferent about it, and said to those who brought him the news, "You are come, I suppose, to seek for money to pay his and your ransom." "Yes," they replied. "Well," said the captain, "you will get nothing from me; I did not send you on this excursion—it was your own free choice to seek an adventure. I will not ransom any man unless he be taken when in my company." This was all the answer they could get: when they reported it to Maudurant and the rest of the companions, they were extremely vexed, and after a time resolved to send again to Perrot le Béarnois, and tell him that if he would pay the ransom, they would, within one month after their deliverance, lead him to such a place that it would be his own fault if he did not gain 100,000 francs from it.

When this message was delivered to Perrot le Béarnois, he mused upon it awhile, and then ordered a large coffer to be opened, which contained upward of 40,000 francs—money acquired from pillage you must understand, and not the rent of his estates, for the town wherein he was born had in it but twelve houses and belongs to the Count de Foix. Perrot le Béarnois had counted out before him two-and-twenty hundred francs, and one hundred for their expenses, which he put into a purse, and calling to him the three companions who had returned from Montferrant, said, "I give you three-and-twenty hundred francs; a friend in need is a friend indeed;

I shall risk this for Geronnet's freedom: he is able to regain for me, if he pleases, as much again, if not more." Geronnet, on learning that his ransom was obtained, was much pleased, and immediately paid the sum to those who had been appointed to receive it. On gaining his liberty he returned to Chaluçet, when Perrot le Béarnois called him and said, " Geronnet, you are obliged to the fair offers you sent me for your freedom, and to them alone; I was not in any way bound to pay your ransom—you must, therefore, now prove the truth of your offers; otherwise we shall be upon bad terms." " Captain," replied Geronnet, " I now offer to put you in possession of Montferrant within fifteen days, if you be willing to undertake it; in this town there is great wealth, and wherewithal to plunder, for, besides its riches in silk and merchandise, many of the inhabitants have much money; besides, the town is one of the weakest and worst guarded in the realm." " It is well said," answered Perrot, " I accept it; you know all the outlets of the town; will it require many men?" " Three or four hundred spears," said Geronnet, " will do the business."

Perrot immediately got himself in readiness and sent information of his intention to the captains of the forts in the neighborhood, fixing their rendezvous at the castle of Donzac,*e* of which place Olim Barbe, a Gascon and famous pillager, was captain. On the day appointed the companions from seven forts, to the number of 400 lances, well mounted, met at Donzac; of these Perrot le Béarnois, to show he was chief of the expedition, was the first to arrive. Geronnet, with eleven companions, dressed themselves in coats of frieze, like traders, and each leading a horse well laden, according to the custom of the country, set out from Donzac before day, and arrived about noon in the town of Montferrant. No one made inquiries as to who they were, never suspecting them to be any but traders or carriers, as their dresses indicated, and supposing that they were come to purchase draperies and linens at the fair: Geronnet and his company put up their horses at the Crown Inn, where they remained in quiet, not venturing abroad in the town lest their plan should be discovered. Toward evening they took a great deal of care of their horses,

*e* A village in Armagnac, diocese and generality of Auch.

giving the host and hostess to understand that, as they came from afar off, it was necessary they should be well attended to. They had no inclination to retire to rest, but kept drinking in their chamber, and the host and hostess noticing the merry life they led, and not having the slightest suspicion of them, went to bed.

The same day, toward evening, Perrot le Béarnois and his companions left Donzac, and in their way were obliged to pass under the walls of Clermont; when within a league of this place they fell in with Amerigot Marcel, governor of Alose, with about 100 spears; they were much rejoiced at meeting, and mutually asked whither they were going in such bad weather, and what were the objects of their being abroad. Amerigot Marcel said, " I came from my castle of Alose, and am going to Carlat." " In God's name," replied the two captains of Carlat, the bourg Anglois, and the bourg de Copane, who were of Perrot's company, " here we are, if you have anything to say to us." " Yes," said he, " you have some prisoners who belong to the Dauphin d'Auvergne, and I wish to have them in exchange for some others who are in my fort; but where are you going?" asked Amerigot. " By my faith, brother soldier, we are going straight to Montferrant, which town is to be delivered to me to-night." " Perrot," replied Amerigot, " this is very wrong; you know we have entered into a treaty with the Count d'Armagnac, and you will act very ill if you break the treaty." On my troth, I shall never keep any treaties," said Perrot, " as long as I am master of the field. Come with us; you have nothing to do at Carlat, as the captains are here." " No, no," replied Amerigot, " I shall return to my own castle." The parties then separated, and Perrot continued his road toward Montferrant. It was eleven o'clock when they arrived at the place, and Perrot said to his companions, " Do you wait here while I go by those ditches, and see if I can learn anything of Geronnet, who has brought us hither." On this Perrot le Béarnois, with three others, went away. It was so dark that they could scarcely see an acre before them, and it rained, snowed, and blew most unmercifully. Geronnet was at this hour on the walls impatiently awaiting their arrival, and as soon as he thought he could discover them he began to whistle. He was heard by

Perrot, who advanced farther into the ditch, and Geronnet said, " Who is there ? " Perrot knew him from his Gascon pronunciation, and in return said, " Is that you, Geronnet ? " " Yes," replied he; " and if you are ready you shall enter the town at this place, for the inhabitants are all in bed." " At this place! " said Perrot, " God forbid; if I enter it shall be through the gate." " Then you will not enter at all," replied Geronnet in a passion; " it is impossible to enter by the gate, as it is closed and guarded." While they were thus talking, some of Perrot's men came near the ditch to hear if anybody was stirring.

Near where they were talking was a small house adjoining the walls in which lived a poor tailor, who, having been hard at work until that hour, was just going to bed, when fancying he heard voices, he left his house in order to make further examination, and seeing Perrot's men walking about, he cried out, " Treason! Treason! " One of Geronnet's party, however, seized him by the throat and kept him quiet. Geronnet then addressing Perrot, said, " Return to your men, and when you hear the inner gate open, attack the outward one with axes in order to gain admittance." He then told him the use he meant to make of the tailor. Perrot upon this returned and related what he had heard; and as soon as he was gone Geronnet told the tailor that he must go with him to the gate of the town, awaken the porter, and tell him that the governor had sent him to give orders that the gates were to be opened to admit some merchants who were coming from Montpellier. The poor man, seeing nothing but instant death unless he complied, did as he was ordered; and on asking for the keys at the gate, one of the porters arose, opened a small window, and gave them to him. The moment after Geronnet snatched them from him, and luckily opened the lock with the first key he put into it; he then went to the outward gate, thinking to do the same there, but in vain. Perrot and his companions were on the outside waiting its opening, and as Geronnet's endeavors with the key were fruitless, they provided themselves with axes and wedges, and forced an entrance. The porters gave an alarm, crying out, " Treason! Treason! " which aroused the whole town; many fled to the castle, but few were allowed to enter it; for when the governor heard that the enemy had surprised the place, he would not lower the drawbridge, but made his preparations for defence in case the castle should be attacked. The captain with his companions now marched into the town without opposition, and went through it to ascertain whether any bodies of men were collecting to resist them; they found only a few, who were soon either slain or made prisoners.

But why should I make a long story of it? The town of Montferrant was thus surprised on February 13th, and when Perrot le Béarnois and his accomplices saw themselves masters of the place they took up their lodgings at different hotels, without doing violence to anyone: for Perrot had ordered under pain of death that neither women nor damsels should be injured; that no houses should be burned, nor any prisoners made without his knowledge; and that no one under the same penalty should hurt church or churchman, nor take anything away from them: the whole town was put in possession of himself and his captains, and on Friday morning all the inhabitants were tied together, so that no one should oppose them, their houses were searched, and everything of value packed up. When, at breakfast, the captains had a long consultation whether to keep the town or not, some were for keeping it, but the majority were of a contrary opinion, and said it would be madness to do so, as the place was too far from their own castle. They, therefore, had the men busily employed until near nightfall in packing up their plunder, and at the point of six o'clock they set out on foot, except about sixty on horseback, and conducted down the streets more than 400 horses laden with cloths, linens, furs, and other plunder. Having bound all the inhabitants two and two, they had the gates opened after nightfall and departed; the baggage and prisoners went before with those on foot, and the captains followed close after on horseback. The night was dark, and as the country did not suspect that their stay would have been so short, they were not pursued, and reached Donzac about midnight, when they unpacked and examined their plunder. It was well for the companions that they left Montferrant as they did, for, had they stayed two days longer, they could not have attempted it without great danger to their lives, for the whole surrounding country was collecting, and large bodies of men were advancing to lay siege to them at the instigation of the Count-dauphin of Auvergne, and his daughter the Duchess of Bourbon.*

I have before mentioned the challenge which had been sent by the Duke of Gueldres to the King of France, which challenge was much talked of everywhere, from the rude and uncourteous language it contained. It was evident that the King of France was much provoked at it, and determined to have reparation; indeed the King's council had resolved that the matter should not remain quiet. The King was young, but of good courage, and if he suffered such insults with patience, the nobility of France considered that foreign countries would hold them very cheap, as they were the King's advisers, and had sworn to guard his honor; especially the Lord de Coucy showed clearly that he personally felt the insult. The Council of France, however, were unwilling to decide upon any bold measures in respect of the Duke of Gueldres until the affairs of Brittany were in a more satisfactory state, for the Duke of Brittany showed clearly a preference of war with France to peace, and was making many preparations of a warlike character; the Duke of Berry, therefore, resolved to send the Count d'Estampes to the duke to endeavor to win him over to the French party; but the attempt was perfectly unavailing; for though the duke entertained the count very handsomely, and on parting presented him with a beautiful white palfrey, saddled and equipped as if for a king, and a ring with a rich stone which cost at least 1,000 francs, he, nevertheless, was quite resolved to take his own course, whatever it might be, and showed no desire to side with the French. The Duke of Berry, therefore, on the return of Count d'Estampes, seeing nothing could be done, made light of the matter, and affairs remained in this state.

On the failure of the Duke of Lancaster's expedition, as has been already related, the whole country of Galicia returned to its allegiance to the King of Castille; for the Castillians and Galicians a good deal resemble the Lombards and

---

* Froissart here introduces the marriages of Lord Lewis of Blois with the Lady Mary of Berry, and the Lord John of Berry with the Princess Mary of France; both which marriages took place in the year 1386. Denis Savage in a marginal note says that Froissart, having omitted to notice these marriages at the proper time, prefers mentioning them here rather than omit them entirely.

Italians, who are always on the side of the strongest, and shout out, " The Conqueror forever." The Duke of Lancaster, while at Oporto, heard of all this without being able to provide a remedy, and it gave him great uneasiness. The King of Portugal gave him all the comfort he was able, saying, " Sir, you will keep your state in this country while you write to your brother and friends in England the melancholy event of your expedition, though they be now fully informed of all, and press them to send you, early in March next, 500 or 600 spears and 2,000 archers. I will then reassemble my forces, and make an effectual war upon the Castillians. A kingdom may be won and lost in one campaign." The duke thanked the King for his kindness; however, he too well knew that the English would not grant him any supplies, and therefore retired to Bayonne without troubling himself further about the matter.

Those who returned to England from this expedition abused Castille to all they met. France, they said, was a rich country, and has a temperate climate, with fine rivers; but Castille had nothing but rocks and high mountains, a sharp air, muddy rivers, bad meat, and wines so hot and harsh there was no drinking them. The inhabitants are poor and filthy, badly clothed and lodged, and quite different to us in their manners, so that it would be folly to go thither. Such were the reports of the English who returned from Castille, so that the ministers who ruled the country saw that any expedition would be very unpopular; moreover, the country was not as yet recovered from the troubles into which the execution of Sir Robert Tresilian and others, and the flight of the Duke of Ireland, had thrown it. The situation of England, with respect to its internal divisions, the desperate state of the affairs of the Duke of Lancaster, and all that related to the Duke of Ireland and his partisans, were known to the King of France and his council; and to gain more information on these subjects, the King, by the advice of his uncles, resolved to invite the Duke of Ireland into France; a knight and a clerk, who was one of the King's notaries, were sent to seek him. The duke was at Utrecht, and was much astonished when he first heard that the King of France wished to see him; however, he resolved to comply, and set out on his journey to Paris, for the King then resided at the castle of the Louvre. The duke was well received by the King and his uncles, who were desirous that he should fix his residence in France, and had a hotel prepared for him. There was now great disagreement in the French council as to the King's going into Germany to revenge himself for the outrageous challenge which the Duke of Gueldres had sent him. The wisest of the council thought that it would be too dangerous for him at such a moment to leave the realm; for they now saw clearly that the Duke of Brittany would listen to no terms of accommodation, and they felt his late conduct in arresting, confining, and ransoming the constable for 100,000 francs, three castles, and a town, highly offensive to the honor of France. Moreover, they heard that the duke had entered into a strong alliance with the King of England, and was laying up stores of all kinds in his different towns and castles. This, indeed, was quite true, for on April 7th, in the year of grace 1388, it was determined in the English council that Richard, Earl of Arundel, should be appointed commander-in-chief of a naval expedition; he was to have under him 1,000 men-at-arms, and 3,000 archers, who were to assemble at Southampton.

The King of England kept a grand feast this year on St. George's Day at Windsor, which was attended by a number of the lords who were to accompany the Earl of Arundel, and who then took leave of the King and Queen. On the day appointed the whole of the armament assembled at Southampton and in those parts, and embarked on board the fleet the twentieth day of May, when the weather was fine and clear. With the Earl of Arundel were the earls of Nottingham and Devonshire, the Lords Thomas Percy and Clifford, Sir John de Warwick, Sir John d'Ambreticourt, Sir Thomas Cook, Sir William Paulet, and several more; in the whole there were 1,000 good men-at-arms, and above 3,000 archers. They took no horses with them, for they hoped, if successful, to find horses in plenty in Brittany. On weighing anchor they made for the shores of Brittany or Normandy, with a determination to land nowhere else unless other intelligence should be brought to them; in the fleet they had some light vessels which drew but little water, and these they sent in advance to seek for adventure; in the same manner as knights and squires, mounted on the fleetest horses, are ordered to scour the country in front of an army, to see if there lie any ambuscades. We must, however, leave this army for the present, as other matters require attention.

The Duke of Gueldres, finding he could in no way succeed in recovering his three castles on the Meuse, of which we have already spoken, resolved to secure himself the possession of Grave from the Brabanters, who, this year, in the month of May, came with a powerful force to lay siege to it. The town of Grave is situated on the Brabant side of the Meuse, over which there is a bridge which connects it with Gueldres. The siege of it was a bold undertaking. The Duke of Gueldres was regularly informed of everything that passed at the siege, for he had fixed his residence only four leagues off at Nimeguen; he wrote frequently to England for assistance, and was in hope that the armament at sea under the Earl of Arundel would come to raise the siege. He knew the town was so strong that it could not be taken by storm, and he had too much confidence in the fidelity of the inhabitants to think that they would ever capitulate; the siege, consequently, lasted a considerable time.

It was not surprising that the Duke of Lancaster, considering his hopes were totally destroyed, should be sometimes melancholy; for the Count de Foix, one of the wisest of princes, in conversation with his knights, declared that the duke's expectations in regard to the crown of Castille were completely at an end; however, he was of a high spirit, and sought consolation in the prospect of the elevation of his children. He had with him a handsome daughter by the Lady Constance, daughter of Don Pedro, in whose right he had made war in Castille; musing, therefore, upon this subject, he said, "If fortune be now unfavorable to me, it may be otherwise to my daughter, who is young and handsome, and by her grandfather and mother the true heiress of Castille. Some gallant prince of France may seek her in marriage, either on account of her right or from her high birth." The duke would gladly have had some overtures made him from France on this head, for he knew that the King had a younger brother, the Duke of Touraine, and by his means he considered the crown of Castille might be gained: with such expectations did the Duke of Lancaster flatter himself; and his imaginations were in a way to be realized—not, indeed, by the brother of the King of France, but by one who was well qualified to change the face of affairs in Castille, and who completely governed France, I mean the Duke of Berry. He and his son were made widowers nearly at the same time. Now what I am about to relate I know of my own knowledge; for I, the author of this book, was at the time in the country of Blois, with my very dear and honored lord, Count Guy de Blois, by whose desire and encouragement this history was undertaken.

The Duke of Berry, among his other thoughts and plans, had a design to marry again. He frequently said to those about him, that a lord was nothing without a lady, nor a man without a wife. "Well, then," they replied, "let your son John marry." "He is too young," said the duke. "That is nothing, my lord," they would say; "do you not see that the Count de Blois has married his son, who is of the same age, with your daughter, Mary?" "True," answered the duke; "well, then, name a lady for him." "We name the daughter of the Duke of Lancaster." The duke mused awhile, and then said, "You propose marrying my son John with the daughter of the Duke of Lancaster, do you? well, by St. Denis, you have made me imagine that she will be an excellent match for myself, and I will shortly write to the duke on the subject. My son John shall marry elsewhere." Those to whom he spoke then began to laugh. "What are you laughing at?" said the duke. "We laugh, my lord, because it seems that you prefer to have a good thing yourself, rather than give it to your son." "By my faith, I am in the right, for my fair cousin of Lancaster will not so readily give his daughter to my son as he will to me." Negotiations were immediately set on foot respecting the marriage, which was highly agreeable to the Duke of Lancaster; indeed, he was so pleased with the Duke of Berry's proposal, that he was not willing it should be kept secret; on the contrary, he published it everywhere, that his enemies might be alarmed, and the matter known in the court of his adversary of Castille. Moreover, he wrote several long letters, detailing the whole business, with copies of the Duke of Berry's proposals, and his own answer of consent to the Count de Foix, because he knew that there was a continual intercourse of knights and squires from all countries at Orthes, going or returning to Castille, and on pilgrimages to and from St. Jago. He did the same also to the King of Navarre, who had married a sister of the King of Castille, in order that the intelligence of this marriage might be more readily believed in Castille than if told by common report. The subject was mentioned also to the King of Portugal; but the duke was silent respecting it in his letters to the King and his brothers in England, for he well knew that the English would not be pleased at it; indeed, as you will presently hear, they gave proof of their dislike to it as soon as they heard it; but, as the matter presses, I must now return to the Duke of Brittany.

Many councils were held in France, as well on the affairs of Gueldres, whither the King was still desirous of going, as of Brittany, for the duke would accept of no advances toward a reconciliation with France. The French council were much troubled on the account, for it was reported that the duke had been busily employed during the winter in victualling and reënforcing all his towns and castles, which plainly indicated his desire for war; and it was well known also that the English had a large fleet on his coast. After much consideration, therefore, it was determined that the Lord de Coucy and two other barons should go to the Duke of Brittany and make another attempt to bring matters to an amicable settlement. Before these noblemen left France the duke heard of their mission, though he was ignorant of the particulars with which they were charged; he was confident, however, that it related to matters of the greatest importance, by the Lord de Coucy's appointment; and at the advice of his council, who forcibly represented to him the exact situation of his affairs in reference both to France and England, he was induced, though reluctantly, to alter his plans. I believe everything went on well afterward, at least such were the appearances; for the duke, who had hitherto kept possession of the constable's castles, now gave them up to the officers of Sir Oliver. This was the first act of moderation on his part; however, it did not satisfy the King nor the Council of France, who insisted on the restitution of the money that had been paid as part of the ransom, and that the duke should come to Paris, and personally make excuses for his conduct to the King in the presence of the French peers, and also submit to such punishment as the King and his peers might after just deliberation adjudge to him.

The three envoys to Brittany were well pleased when they heard of the restitution of the castles, and the Lord de Coucy said, " Now, gentlemen, we have one obstacle less to surmount; I suppose the duke will listen to what we have to say to him." On reaching the castle de la Motte, near to Vannes where the duke resided, they dismounted, and were received with much joy, the duke telling them that they were welcome, and that he was very happy to see them. He took the Lord de Coucy by the hand and said, " Fair brother, I rejoice to see you in Brittany; before you leave me I will give you some fine sport with hunting stags, and in hawking. " Dear brother and lord," replied de Coucy, " I thank you, and I and my companions will gladly partake of it." The duke showed them every attention, and conducted them to his apartment laughing and joking. All four knew how to keep up a brilliant conversation, as well as, if not better than, any lords I ever saw, not excepting the Duke of Brabant, the Count de Foix, nor the Count de Savoy; in particular the Lord de Coucy shone above the others, as was acknowledged by all lords and ladies, in whatever country he visited, for he had seen much of the world, and had travelled to various parts.

While they were in conversation, spices were brought in handsome silver comfit-boxes, and fine wines in gold and silver cans; of these the lords partook, and then retired to their lodgings. Thus passed the first day without one word being said as to the cause of their coming.

While these things were going on in Brittany, the news of the intended marriage of the Duke of Berry with the daughter of the Duke of Lancaster was spreading far and wide; of course, it was heard of at the Court of King John of Castille. " Sire," said those about him to the King, " Have you heard the rumors that are abroad; the dangers from the Duke of Lancaster are thicker than ever, and the blast comes from France?" " What do you mean?" replied the King. " The report, sire, is everywhere current, that the Duke of Berry is to marry the Duke of Lancaster's daughter, and you may suppose that this will not be done without great alliances being made between them; so that you may in future suffer as much from the French as you have lately gained by them." He knew that what they said was quite true, and he requested them to advise him how he ought to act. It will be remembered that King Henry of Castille had made his peace with the King of Arragon by marrying his son John (the present King of Castille) to his daughter. By this lady King John had one son, and she herself died shortly after his birth. By the advice of his council, the King married again with the Lady Beatrice, daughter of the King of Portugal. This son by the Princess of Arragon, though very young, was a promising youth, and the Council of Castille, in reply to the King's demand of advice, said, " Sire, we can only see one remedy to avert the evil which may arise from this marriage of the Duke of Berry." "What is it?" said the King. "It is the infant Don Henry, your son, who alone is capable of preventing this match; for we are persuaded, that if the Duke and Duchess of Lancaster were informed that you were willing to unite him with the Lady Catherine, they would prefer him to the Duke of Berry." "You say well," answered the King, "and I will set about the matter at once."

Accordingly, ambassadors were chosen with the least possible delay and sent to the duke and duchess, who cordially listened to their proposal; for their hearts were wrapped up in the hopes of regaining the crown for themselves or their child. Thus there were proposals of marriage made from France and Castille to the Duke of Lancaster, for the marriage of his daughter; both were well received, and refusals made to neither; however, the marriage with Castille was, for obvious reasons, the more agreeable. I have just said that the Duke of Brittany received the French knights with much kindness, particularly the Lord de Coucy. Indeed, after some difficulty, the duke was prevailed upon to meet the dukes of Berry and Burgundy at Blois. A day was fixed for the meeting; and shortly after the arrival of the other two dukes came the Duke of Brittany; but with no grand array, attended only by those of his household, in number about 300 horse; for it was his intention to return to his own country as soon as the conferences should be over. Such, however, were not the intentions of the dukes of Berry and Burgundy; for they said that, whether he would or not, they would force him to come to Paris. The Duke of Brittany was lodged at the house of a canon of St. Sauveur, within the castle; but his attendants, with those of the other lords, were quartered in the town. The castle where these princes kept their state is very large, and one of the handsomest in the kingdom of France.

Conferences were held by the three dukes, and those from France showed much affection toward the Duke of Burgundy, and repeatedly thanked him for coming to Blois. The duke dissembled as much as he could, and said, " that it was indeed his love for them that had induced him to undertake such a journey, for that he was very unwell." In the course of these conversations they told the Duke of Brittany, " That since he had come so far he should continue his journey to Paris, as the King was very desirous to see him." The duke made every excuse he could think of, saying, " That his health was not good, and that he had not come prepared for a longer journey." However, they answered, " That it would not be decorous for him to visit his lord paramount with a larger company than he then had with him; that if he was too ill to ride, they were provided with litters and cars which were quite at his service; and that he was bound to pay his homage to the King, which he had never yet done." To this the duke replied, " That when the King should be of age, and take the reins of government into his own hands, he would come to Paris, or to any other place whither he might order him, and perform his homage as he was bound to do." The dukes of Berry and Burgundy made answer, " That he was now of sufficient age [g] and understanding to receive homage, and that every lord in France, and all who held fiefs under the Crown, excepting himself, had done homage to him." The duke, finding his excuses of no avail, said, " Should I go to Paris, it will be much against my inclination, and very prejudicial to my interests, for when there I shall meet Sir Oliver de Clisson, whom I hate, and we can never cordially love each other after what has passed; he will bitterly and injuriously reproach me, and then consider what may be the consequences."

[g] The King of France was now in his twenty-first year.

"Oh no," they said, "have no fear from that quarter; we solemnly swear that neither the constable nor John of Brittany, unless you wish it, shall see or speak to you. You shall see the King, and other barons and knights of France, who will make you good cheer; and when you have completed the object of your journey, you shall return home uninjured."

The duke was so courteously entreated, that he consented to go to Paris, having taken a pledge of the two dukes that he should neither see the constable of France nor John of Brittany. They remained five or six days in the castle of Blois, and then set out for Paris. The duke, on his approach, stopped one night at Bourg la Reine, previous to his entry into the city, which he made on the morrow.

The coming of the Duke of Brittany was great news for the Parisians, on account of the late events of the arrest and imprisonment of the constable, and the fruitless embassies that had been sent to summon him. It was on a Sunday, the vigil of St. John the Baptist, in the year 1388, at ten in the morning, that he entered Paris by the Gate de l'Enfer,[h] and passing the whole length of the Rue de la Harpe, crossed the Pont de St. Michael, and so came in front of the palace. As the duke passed through Paris he was much stared at by the common people, and when he entered the Louvre there was a great crowd in the apartment into which he was introduced, which was not only small, but had in it a table spread for the King's dinner, before which he himself was standing, with his three uncles. The moment the duke entered the room, a way was made for him by the lords falling back on both sides, and when in the royal presence he dropped on one knee, but speedily rose and advanced about ten or twelve paces, when he kneeled again. On rising he came close to the King, kneeled the third time, and saluted him, bareheaded, saying, "My lord, I am come to see you. May God preserve you." "Many thanks," replied the King; "I was anxious for your coming here, to see and converse with you at our leisure." On saying which, he took him by the hand and raised him up. A signal was then made to the master of the household to bring water, when the King washed, while the Duke of Brittany held the basin

[h] This is now called the gate of St. Michael. See Sauval, "Antiquités de Paris."

and towel. As soon as the King was seated the duke took leave of him and his uncles. The Lord de Coucy, the Lord de St. Pol, and other great barons, then conducted him to the court where his horses waited, and having mounted, he returned with his attendants the way he came, and entered his hotel. The duke had frequent conferences with the King of France and his uncles, to their mutual satisfaction; and when affairs were in so good a train that they had no reason to be suspicious of the duke, they thought it time to prepare for the expedition to Gueldres, for which the King was so impatient.

The Lord de Coucy was therefore ordered into the country, to mark out the line of march for the King and his army, and to excite the knights and squires of Bar and Lorraine to join him. He was in no way to introduce the King's name, but to engage them for himself, as if preparing for an expedition into Austria.

I have for some time been silent respecting the armament which was at sea under command of the Earl of Arundel. This fleet had remained the whole season on the coasts of Brittany and Normandy, except when driven off by storms; but it always returned to its station. When the Earl of Arundel heard of the proceedings of the Duke of Brittany, he was much affected by them, and called a council of his principal officers to consider how they were to employ their force during the remainder of the season. In this council it was resolved that they should sail for La Rochelle, and make war on that country; for, though they had no castles in those parts, they were yet in sufficient numbers to withstand any force which Saintonge or Poitou could send against them. They likewise intended to have their situation known to their friends in Limousin and Auvergne by some person in the fleet who was acquainted with the country, and whom they could land on the coast of Brittany. It fell out just as the earl and the English barons wished, for they found a man from Lower Brittany then on board, who came from near Vannes, and understood four languages, viz., that of Lower Brittany, English, Spanish, and French. Before they landed him they gave him the following instructions: "You will go by the large roads of this country, until you come to Chaluçet, where you will find Perrot le Béarnois; salute him for us, and tell him that we desire he will make war on France under our commission, with as many other garrisons of our party as he can. You will not carry any letters for fear of being stopped and searched. Tell Perrot to give instant alarm to Berry, Auvergne, and Limousin, by taking the field; for we will disembark near La Rochelle, and make such a war that he shall soon hear of us." The Breton did as he was directed, and arrived at Chaluçet; and on being introduced to Perrot he punctually delivered his message, and found him very eager to take the field. Indeed Perrot le Béarnois instantly got together as many captains and men-at-arms as he could, who were all as eager for war as himself; for such men could only enrich themselves by the losses of others. When all together, they amounted to full 400 lances, who thought themselves sufficiently strong for any gallant enterprise, and that there was not a lord in the country who would be able to withstand them.

While these things were going forward, the Earl of Arundel's fleet weighed anchor and left the coast of Brittany. It was a magnificent sight to see this fleet of six score vessels, whose streamers, emblazoned with the arms of their different lords, were glittering in the sun and fluttering with the wind. They floated, as it were, on a sea that seemed proud to bear them, and might be compared to a vigorous courser, which, after having been long confined in the stable, gains its liberty to bound over the plains. After coasting Saintonge and Poitou, the fleet cast anchor off Marans, near La Rochelle, when some of the more adventurous, observing the tide was flowing, entered their barges, and sailed up the river to the town. The watch on the castle had noticed the English fleet anchoring and the barges ascending with the tide, and had sounded his horn frequently, to alarm the townsmen, in order that they might save all they could of their property by placing it in the castle. The English, on entering the town with a view of plundering it, found only empty coffers, though they met with abundance of corn, wine, and salted provisions, which came very opportunely to them. They remained the night in the place, having arrived there about vespers, and sent to inform their companions of their situation, and the reason why they did not return. On the morrow, when the tide began to flow, the smaller vessels weighed anchor, and in them were embarked the armor and other necessaries from the large ships, that from their size could not enter the river. The alarm was soon spread over the country that the English had landed at Marans to the number of 400 combatants, including archers: the towns and castles in the Low Countries were much frightened, and the villagers fled to the neighboring forests for protection. If the English had had horses they would have much harassed the country round La Rochelle, for there were no men-at-arms to oppose them. True it is that the lords de Partenay, de Pons, and many other knights and squires of Poitou and Saintonge were in the country; but each was in his own castle; for they had not any suspicion that the English were coming to invade them. Had they been so fortunate as to have obtained notice of their intentions, they would have been prepared to receive them; but this was not the case, and they were so taken by surprise that all were frightened and impatient to save what they could.

The country, indeed, had two causes for alarm; they had the English army and fleet on one side, and rumor had already informed them that Perrot le Béarnois was on his march with more than 1,500 combatants, and had already entered Berry.

At the time the English landed at Marans there were two gallant knights from Beauce in the town of La Rochelle, Sir Peter de Jouy, and the Lord Taillepié, whom Sir Helion de Lignac had placed there for its defence. On hearing that the English had landed at Marans, these two knights told the mayor and principal citizens of the place that it would be right to beat up the English quarters. A body of 1,200 crossbows and varlets, including all sorts, was instantly assembled; and, at the first dawn of day, all set out for La Rochelle. When the cross-bow men arrived at the English quarters they began at once to shoot their bolts and arrows, which passed through the huts, made of boughs and leaves, to the great surprise of the English, who were asleep withinside on straw. Many were wounded before they discovered they were attacked by the French. After about six shots the bowmen retreated, according to their orders, and the men-at-arms advanced on horseback into the midst of the huts. Knights and squires speedily left their lodgings and drew up together; and the French captains, seeing that they were preparing themselves to take the field in earnest, made off after their crossbows and infantry, who were hastening homeward; but they were so hard pressed by the English, who immediately began to pursue, that many of them were killed, especially at the gate of La Rochelle. As it was near noon the Earl of Arundel sounded a retreat, when all his men returned in handsome array to their quarters, where they disarmed and refreshed themselves. The English remained near La Rochelle fifteen days, during which time they severely plundered the neighboring country; and then, the wind being fair, embarked a great quantity of wine, and other provisions, and put to sea.

We will now, for variety, return to the affairs of Brabant and Gueldres. You have before heard how anxious the Duchess of Brabant was to make war on the Duke of Gueldres, and to besiege Grave. There was a great force of knights and squires from the principal places before it, who declared their intention not to depart until they had compelled it to surrender. And the duchess, to show how interested she was in the matter, had fixed her residence at Bois-le-Duc, four leagues distance from it. The besieging army was plentifully supplied with all things that came thither by sea, or down the Meuse from the rich country of Brabant; so that the siege was long continued, and the Brabanters had many large machines which threw into the town stones of such weight as to do much damage wherever they fell. In addition to this, they flung into the town all the dead carrion of the army, to empoison the inhabitants by the stink. At times many of the knights and squires of Brabant came to skirmish with the garrison at the barriers, for the Duke of Gueldres had placed within the town some gallant companions, who were not shy of showing their courage when occasion called for it. The Duke of Gueldres had fixed his quarters at Nimeguen, but he could neither raise the siege nor offer combat to the Brabanters for want of sufficient force. He had sent to England, and quite expected to have a reënforcement from thence; but he was disappointed, for England at the time was in a very unsettled state, and new ministers had been forced upon the King by his uncles and the Archbishop of Canterbury.

During the siege of Grave the Brabanters resolved to throw

a wooden bridge over the Meuse, in order that they might have an entrance into Guelderland, overrun that country, and by investing the town of Grave on all sides, prevent any provisions from entering into it. As they finished the different parts of this bridge they joined them together, and placed them in their proper situations, and had made such advances that it was within the length of a lance of the opposite shore. You may suppose that the duke was no way ignorant of what they were about, but he made no interruption to the building of the bridge until it was nearly completed, when they advanced with cannon and other artillery, and attacked it so roughly, that it was set on fire and destroyed. Upon this the Brabanters called a council to determine how to act.

Three short leagues from Grave was the town of Ravenstein,[i] belonging to the Lord de Bourne, who is a vassal to Brabant, and who, at the solicitation of the Duchess of Brabant and her council, agreed to open the town, in order to enable them to gain an entrance into Guelderland. The Duke of Gueldres, somehow or other, gained information as to the intention of the Brabanters, and formed various plans how to act; at last, however, he determined that if the Brabanters entered his country by the bridge of Ravenstein, he would retaliate by that of Grave; for he was resolved not to be shut up in any town. Accordingly, after he had paid his devotion in the church, and made his offering at the altar of the Virgin, he set out from Nimeguen, attended by not more than 300 spears. The same day the seneschal of Brabant, with a large army, upward of 10,000 men, crossed the bridge of Ravenstein. Many resolved that day to ride as far as Nimeguen, and burn its mills, suburbs, and the villages round about. The duke was soon informed of this, and halted awhile to consider the best mode of proceeding; for some of his companions were alarmed at the smallness of their number in comparison with the enemy. Several assembled round the duke and advised him to return to Grave; but he replied, "That he would never do so: he preferred dying with honor to living in disgrace."

---

[i] Ravenstein is a town of the Netherlands, in Dutch Brabant, and capital of a country of the same name, with an ancient and strong castle. It belongs to the Elector Palatine, but the Dutch have a right to put a garrison there. It is situated on the Meuse, on the confines of Guelderland, ten miles southwest of Nimeguen.

Then, after a short pause, he added, in a loud voice, "Forward, forward; those who love me will follow me." This speech of the duke so much encouraged his men that they showed great eagerness to combat their enemies; they tightened their armors, lowered the visors of their helmets, regirthed their saddles, some new knights were made, and were marched in order toward the enemy.

The Brabanters had already crossed the river, when news was brought to the seneschal and his knights that the Duke of Gueldres had taken the field, and was so near that they must speedily see him. This intelligence much surprised them, for they concluded that the duke must have had with him at least six times more than he had. They instantly halted; but had not time to draw themselves up in array, for the Duke of Gueldres appeared with his company full gallop, with spears in their rests, and shouting out "Our Lady for Gueldres!" At the first charge more than six score Brabanters were unhorsed. Great confusion and dismay, with but a poor defence, reigned among them. They were so suddenly attacked that although they were so numerous and had so many great lords among them, they were completely dispersed. When the flight became general, many rushed into the river, whether on horseback or on foot, without sounding the bottom or knowing if it were fordable. In this way upward of 1,200 perished. This unfortunate event to the chivalry of Brabant happened between Grave and Ravenstein. Those who fled to Grave gave the alarm to the besieging army, begging them to retire as fast as they could, since nothing could now save them. At which report they were all seized with such fear that they would not stay to pack anything up, but leaped upon their horses and fled for safety to Bois-le-Duc and other places as fast as they could. Thus was the siege of Grave broken up, to the great loss of the Brabanters, whose disgraceful defeat I can scarcely, for shame, perpetuate; but since, at the commencement of this history, I promised to insert nothing but what was strictly true, I must detail the unfortunate consequences of this battle.

The young Duke of Gueldres gained this renowned victory about Madalen-tide in the month of July, 1388. When the defeat and pursuit were over, which took up about two hours' time, the heralds were ordered to examine the dead and report who had been slain. A council was then held in the field as to whether they should retire to Grave and take their prisoners there; but the duke opposed this, saying, " I made a vow to Our Lady of Nimeguen, when I left that town, and which I again renewed when we began the combat; in obedience to which I order that we gayly return to Nimeguen and offer our thanksgivings to the holy Virgin, who has assisted us in our victory. This command was obeyed, and all set out at once to Nimeguen, which is two leagues distant from the field of battle. On this fortunate news being told in the town, great rejoicing was made by both sexes; the clergy went out in procession to meet the duke as he entered, and the duke, on reaching Nimeguen, rode straight to the church where the image of Our Lady was, in which image he had great faith. When he entered the chapel he disarmed himself to his doublet, and offered up his armor on the altar, in honor of Our Lady, returning thanks for the victory he had gained; in this chapel the banners and pennons of the enemy were hung up. After this the duke retired to his hotel and his knights to their respective homes.

As you may suppose, the Duchess of Brabant was much vexed at this unfortunate turn in her affairs; she wrote frequently to the Duke of Burgundy, and eagerly pressed him to assist her in her recovery of her losses: at the French Court the news of this victory on the part of the Duke of Gueldres produced but little surprise, for it was imagined that when the King marched thither, he would soon make ample amends; indeed, the King's ardor for the invasion of Guelderland was no way abated—he was anxious to undertake it at all events, for the challenge had so mightily enraged him, that he declared that cost what it would he would have ample reparation. It was resolved, therefore, as Guelderland was a dependence on the empire, to make the Emperor fully acquainted with the Duke of Gueldres's rash conduct, and lay before him the insolent challenge he had sent to the King of France, who, to make him sensible of his folly, was preparing to march an army into Germany, not with any hostile intentions to the Emperor or to his territories, but solely against the Duke of Gueldres, and to attack him wherever he should be found. Accordingly ambassadors were appointed, who, having received their instructions, took leave of the King and his uncles, and immediately set out to have an interview with the Emperor.

The time was now come for the Duke of Brittany to be dismissed; he had surrendered the castles and town of Jugon to the officers of the constable, but still made great difficulty about paying back the 100,000 francs; he was, however, so fairly spoken to, that he promised the King and the Duke of Burgundy to repay the sum in the course of five years, by yearly payments of 20,000 francs. The duke after this took leave of the King, who made him very handsome presents of jewels, and having arranged his affairs, he set out on his journey, taking the road to Estampes: but I will now leave the Duke of Brittany, who strictly kept the engagements he had entered into with the King of France; he has never since done anything worthy of being remembered in this history, but if he should, I will relate it according to the manner in which it shall be told me.

The King of France was busily employed in making his preparations for invading Guelderland, and heard with great pleasure that the chivalry of Bar, Lorraine, and Burgundy were ready and willing to attend him. The ambassadors who had been sent to the Emperor, found him at Convalence, and after dismounting at their hotels, made themselves ready to wait upon him. Their interview with the Emperor was very satisfactory, and he dismissed them by saying, " I am by no means dissatisfied with what is doing in France. Thank my cousin for the information he sends me; let him come in God's name, for I do not intend to move in the business." The ambassadors forthwith departed; and even before their return the King of France left Montereau-sur-Yonne, and took the road to Châlons and Champagne. The Duke of Berry was still in his own country awaiting the answer of the Duke of Lancaster, respecting his marriage with his daughter; none, however, came to him; the Duke of Lancaster kept dissembling, for he as well as his duchess showed a decided preference to a union with Castille, provided the ambassadors would agree to his terms, which were the payment of 600,000 francs within three years, 12,000 annually for his life and that of the duchess, and 2,000 more for the duchess's household. As soon as it was known that the King had left Montereau for Châlons, all his nobles hastened to join him; thither, among others, came the Duke of Berry, the Duke of Bourbon, the counts de Sancerre, de St. Pol, and de Tonnerre. Moreover, the ambassadors from the Emperor found the King at Châlons, and as soon as the satisfactory intelligence was reported, the King gave orders for the army to proceed on its march.

# CHAPTER II

Scots Invade England During Its Internal Troubles—Sir Alexander Ramsay and Others—Earl Douglas Takes the Pennon of Sir Henry Percy—The Famous Battle of Otterbourne.

I HAVE before related in this history the troubles which King Richard of England had suffered from his quarrel with his uncles. By advice of the Archbishop of Canterbury, and the King's new council, the Lord Neville, who had commanded the defence of the frontiers of Northumberland for five years against the Scots, was dismissed, and Sir Henry Percy appointed in his stead, which circumstance created much animosity and hatred between the Percys and the Nevilles. The barons and knights of Scotland, considering this a favorable opportunity, now that the English were quarrelling among themselves, determined upon an inroad into the country, in order to make some return for the many insults that had been offered to them. That their intention might not be known, they appointed a feast to be held at Aberdeen, on the borders of the Highlands; this feast the greater part of the barons attended, and it was then resolved that in the middle of August, in the year 1388, they should assemble all their forces at a castle called Jedworth, situated amidst deep forests on the borders of Cumberland. When all things were arranged the barons separated, but never mentioned one word of their intentions to the King; for they said among themselves that he knew nothing about war. On the day appointed James, Earl of Douglas, first arrived at Jedworth, then came John, Earl of Moray; the Earl of March and Dunbar; William, Earl of Fife; John, Earl of Sutherland; Stephen, Earl of Menteith; William, Earl of Mar; Sir Archibald Douglas, Sir Robert Erskine, and very many other knights and squires of Scotland. There had not been for sixty years so numerous an assembly—they amounted to 1,200 spears, and 40,000 other men and archers.

With the use of the bow the Scots are but little acquainted, but they sling their axes over their shoulders, and when in battle give very deadly blows with them. The lords were well pleased at meeting, and declared they would never return home without having made an inroad into England; and the more completely to combine their plans, they fixed another meeting, to be held at a church in the forest of Jedworth called Zedon.*a*

Intelligence was carried to the Earl of Northumberland, to the seneschal of York, and to Sir Matthew Redman, governor of Berwick, of the great feast which was to be kept at Aberdeen, and in order to learn what was done at it, these lords sent thither heralds and minstrels, at the same time making every preparation in case of an inroad; for they said, " If the Scots enter the country through Cumberland, by Carlisle, we will ride into Scotland, and do them more damage than they can do to us, for theirs is an open country, which can be entered anywhere; but ours, on the contrary, contains well-fortified towns and castles." In order to be more sure of the intentions of the Scots, they resolved to send an English gentleman, well acquainted with the country, to the meeting in the forest of Jedworth, of which the minstrels told them. The English squire journeyed without interruption until he came to the church of Yetholm, where the Scottish barons were assembled; he entered it as a servant following his master, and heard the greater part of their plans. When the meeting was near breaking up, he left the church on his return, and went to a tree thinking to find his horse, which he had tied there by the bridle, but it was gone, for a Scotsman (they are all thieves) had stolen him, and being fearful of making a noise about it, he set off on foot, though booted and spurred. He had not, however, gone more than two bow-shots from the church before he was noticed by two Scottish knights, who were conversing together.

The first who saw him said, " I have witnessed many wonderful things, but what I now see is equal to any; that man yonder has, I believe, lost his horse, and yet he makes no inquiry about it. On my troth, I doubt much if he belongs to us; let us go after him and ascertain." The two knights soon over-

---

*a* The monastery of Zedon, at which the Scottish leaders are said to have held their meeting previous to entering England, is supposed by some to be the modern Kirk-Yetholm, exactly upon the borders and near the foot of Cheviot: the name is pronounced Yetto'm, which comes very near to Yedon.

took him, when they asked him where he was going, whence he came, and what he had done with his horse. As he contradicted himself in his answers, they laid hands on him, saying, that he must come before their captains. Upon which, they brought him back to the church of Yetholm, to the Earl of Douglas and the other lords, who examined him closely, for they knew him to be an Englishman, and assured him that if he did not truly answer all their questions, his head should be struck off, but if he did, no harm should happen to him. He obeyed, though very unwillingly, for the love of life prevailed; and the Scots barons learned that he had been sent by the Earl of Northumberland to discover the number of their forces, and whither they were to march. He was then asked where the barons of Northumberland were. If they had any intention of making an excursion? Also what road they would take to Scotland, along the sea from Berwick to Dunbar, or by the mountains through the country of Menteith to Stirling. He replied, "Since you will force me to tell the truth, when I left Newcastle there were not any signs of an excursion being made; but the barons are all ready to set out at a minute's warning, as soon as they shall hear that you have entered England. They will not oppose you, for they are not in number sufficient to meet so large a body as you are reported to be." "And at what do they estimate our numbers," said Lord Moray. "They say, my lord," replied the squire, "that you have fully 40,000 men and 1,200 spears, and by way of counteracting your career, should you march to Cumberland, they will take the road through Berwick to Dunbar, Dalkeith, and Edinburgh; if you follow the other road they will then march to Carlisle, and enter your country by these mountains."

The Scottish lords, on hearing this, were silent, but looked at each other. The English squire was delivered to the governor of the castle of Jedworth, with orders to guard him carefully. The barons were in high spirits at the intelligence they had received, and considered their success as certain, now they knew the disposition of the enemy. They held a council as to their mode of proceeding, at which the wisest and most accustomed to arms, such as Sir Archibald Douglas, the Earl of Fife, Sir Alexander Ramsay, and others, said, "That to avoid any chance of failing in their attempt, they would advise the army to be divided, and two expeditions to be made, so that the enemy might be puzzled whither to march their forces. The largest division with the baggage should go to Carlisle in Cumberland, and the others, consisting of three or four hundred spears and 2,000 stout infantry and archers, all well mounted, should make for Newcastle-on-Tyne, cross the river, and enter Durham, spoiling and burning the country. They will have committed great waste in England," they continued, "before our enemy can have any information of their being there; if we find they come in pursuit of us, which they certainly will, we will then unite, and fix on a proper place to offer them battle, as we all seem to have that desire, and to be anxious to gain honor; for it is time to repay them some of the mischief they have done to us." This plan was adopted, and Sir Archibald Douglas, the Earl of Fife, the Earl of Sutherland, the Earl of Menteith, the Earl of Mar, the Earl of Strathearn, Sir Stephen Frazer, Sir George Dunbar, with sixteen other great barons of Scotland, were ordered to the command of the largest division that was to march to Carlisle. The Earl of Douglas, the Earl of March and Dunbar, and the Earl of Moray were appointed leaders of the 300 picked lances and 2,000 infantry, who were to advance to Newcastle-on-Tyne and invade Northumberland. When those two divisions separated, the lords took a very affectionate leave of each other, promising that if the English took the field against them, they would not fight till all were united. They then left the forest of Jedworth, one party marching to the right and the other to the left. The barons of Northumberland not finding the squire return, nor hearing anything of the Scots, began to suspect the accident which had happened; they therefore ordered everyone to prepare and march at a moment's notice.

We will now follow the expedition under the Earl of Douglas and his companions, for they had more to do than the division that went to Carlisle. As soon as the earls of Douglas, Moray and March were separated from the main body, they determined to cross the Tyne, and enter the bishopric of Durham, and after they had despoiled and burned that country as far as the city of Durham, to return by Newcastle, and quarter themselves there in spite of the English. This they executed, and riding at a good pace through by-roads, without attacking town, castle or house, arrived on the lands of the Lord Percy, and crossed the Tyne without any opposition at the place they had fixed on, three leagues above Newcastle, near to Brancepeth, [b] where they entered the rich country of Durham, and instantly began their war by burning towns, and slaying the inhabitants. Neither the Earl of Northumberland, nor the barons and knights of the country, had heard anything of the invasion; but when intelligence came to Durham and Newcastle that the Scots were abroad, which was now visible enough, from the smoke that was everywhere seen, the earl sent his two sons, Sir Henry and Sir Ralph Percy, to Newcastle, while he himself remained at Alnwick and issued his orders.

In the meantime the Scots continued burning and destroying all before them. At the gates of Durham they skirmished, but made no long stay, setting out on their return as they had planned at the beginning of the expedition, and carrying away all the booty they could. Between Durham and Newcastle, which is about twelve English miles, the country is very rich, and there was not a town in all this district, unless well enclosed, that was not burned.

All the knights and squires of the country collected at Newcastle; thither came the seneschal of York, Sir Ralph Langley, Sir Matthew Redman,[c] Sir Robert Ogle, Sir John Felton, Sir William Walsingham, and so many others, that the town could not lodge them all. These three Scottish lords, having completed the object of their first expedition in Durham, lay three days before Newcastle, where there was an almost continual skirmish. The sons of the Earl of Northumberland, from their great courage, were always first at the barriers. The Earl of Douglas had a long conflict with Sir Henry Percy, and in it, by gallantry of arms, won his pennon, to the great vexation of Sir Henry and the other English. The earl, as he bore away his prize, said, "I will carry this token of your prowess with me to Scotland, and place it on the tower of my castle at Dalkeith, that it may be seen from far." "By God," replied Sir Henry, "you shall not even bear it out of Northumberland; be assured you shall never have this pennon to brag of." "You must come this night and seek it, then," answered Earl

---

[b] Brancepeth is about four miles from Durham. The ruin of a fine old castle still remains.     [c] Governor of Berwick.

Douglas; "I will fix your pennon before my tent, and shall see if you will venture to take it away." As it was now late, the skirmish ended, and each party retired to their quarters. They had plenty of everything, particularly fresh meat. The Scots kept up a very strict watch, concluding from the words of Sir Henry Percy that their quarters would be beaten up in the night time; however, they were disappointed, for Sir Henry was advised to defer his attack.

On the morrow the Scots dislodged from Newcastle, and taking the road to their own country came to a town and castle called Pontland,[d] of which Sir Raymond de Laval was lord: here they halted about four o'clock in the morning, and made preparations for an assault, which was carried on with such courage that the place was easily won, and Sir Raymond made prisoner. They then marched away for Otterbourne,[e] which is eight English leagues from Newcastle, and there encamped. This day they made no attack, but very early on the morrow the trumpet sounded, when all advanced toward the castle, which was tolerably strong, and situated among marshes. After a long and unsuccessful attack, they were forced to retire, and the chiefs held a council how they should act. The greater part were for decamping on the morrow, joining their countrymen in the neighborhood of Carlisle. This, however, the Earl of Douglas overruled by saying, "In despite of Sir Henry Percy, who, the day before yesterday, declared he would take from me his pennon, I will not depart hence for two or three days. We will renew our attack on the castle, for it is to be taken, and we shall see if he will come for his pennon." Everyone agreed to what Earl Douglas said. They made huts of trees and branches, and fortified themselves as well as they could, placing their baggage and servants at the entrance of the marsh, on the road to Newcastle, and driving the cattle into the marsh lands.

I will now return to Sir Henry and Sir Ralph Percy, who were both greatly mortified that this Earl of Douglas should have conquered their pennon, and who felt the disgrace the more because Sir Henry had not kept his word. The English imagined the army under the Earl of Douglas to be only the

---

[d] A village on the Blythe five miles from Newcastle.

[e] Otterbourne is in the parish of Elsdon, Northumberland.

van of the Scots, and that the main body was behind, for which reason those knights who had the most experience in arms strongly opposed the proposal of Sir Henry Percy to pursue them. They said, " Many losses happen in war; if the Earl of Douglas has won your pennon he has bought it dear enough, and another time you will gain from him as much, if not more. The whole power of Scotland have taken the field. We are not strong enough to offer them battle; perhaps this skirmish may have been only a trick to draw us out of the town. It is much better to lose a pennon than 200 or 300 knights and squires, and leave our country in a defenceless state." This speech checked the eagerness of the two Percys, when other news was brought them by some knights and squires, who had followed and observed the Scots, their number and disposition. " Sir Henry and Ralph Percy," they said, " we are come to tell you that we have followed the Scottish army, and observed all the country where they now are. They halted first at Pontland, and took Sir Raymond de Laval in his castle. Thence they went to Otterbourne, and took up their quarters for the night. We are ignorant of what they did on the morrow; but they seemed to have taken measures for a long stay. We know for certain that the army does not consist of more than 3,000 men, including all sorts." Sir Henry Percy, on hearing this, was greatly rejoiced, and cried out, " To horse, To horse! For by the faith I owe to God, and to my lord and father, I will seek to recover my pennon, and beat up the Scots' quarters this night." Such knights and squires in Newcastle as learned this, and were willing to be of the party, made themselves ready. The Bishop of Durham was daily expected at that town, for he had heard that the Scots lay before it, and that the sons of the Earl of Northumberland were preparing to offer them battle. The bishop had collected a number of men, and was hastening to their assistance; but Sir Henry Percy would not wait, for he had with him 600 spears of knights and squires, and upward of 8,000 infantry, which he said would be more than enough to fight the Scots, who were but 300 lances and 2,000 others. When all were assembled, they left Newcastle after dinner, and took the field in good array, following the road the Scots had taken toward Otterbourne, which was only eight short leagues distant.

The Scots were supping, and some indeed asleep, when the English arrived, and mistook, at the entrance, the huts of the servants for those of their masters; they forced their way into the camp, which was tolerably strong, shouting out, "Percy, Percy!" In such cases, you may suppose, an alarm is soon given, and it was fortunate for the Scots the English had made the first attack upon the servants' quarters, which checked them some little. The Scots, expecting the English, had prepared accordingly; for, while the lords were arming themselves, they ordered a body of the infantry to join their servants and keep up the skirmish. As their men were armed, they formed themselves under the pennons of the three principal barons, who each had his particular appointment.

In the meantime the night advanced; but it was sufficiently light for them to see what they were doing, for the moon shone, and it was the month of August, when the weather is temperate and serene. When the Scots were properly arrayed, they left the camp in silence, but did not march to meet the English. During the preceding day they had well examined the country, and settled their plans beforehand, which, indeed, was the saving of them. The English had soon overpowered the servants; but as they advanced into the camp they found fresh bodies of men ready to oppose them and to continue the fight. The Scots, in the meantime, marched along the mountainside, and fell on the enemy's flank quite unexpectedly, shouting their war-cries. This was a great surprise to the English, who, however, formed themselves in better order and reënforced that part of the army.

The cries of Percy and Douglas resounded on each side. The battle now raged. Great was the pushing of lances, and at the first onset very many of each party were struck down. The English, being more numerous than their opponents, kept in a compact body and forced the Scots to retire. But the Earl of Douglas, being young and eager to gain renown in arms, ordered his banner to advance, shouting, "Douglas, Douglas!" Sir Henry and Sir Ralph Percy, indignant at the affront the Earl of Douglas had put on them by conquering their pennon, and desirous of meeting him, hastened to the place from which the sounds came, calling out, "Percy, Percy!" The two banners met, and many gallant deeds of arms ensued. The English were in superior strength, and fought so lustily that they drove the Scots back. Sir Patrick Hepburne and his son did honor to their knighthood and country under the banner of Douglas, which would have been conquered but for the vigorous defence they made; and this circumstance not only contributed to their personal credit, but the memory of it is continued with honor to their descendants. I learned the particulars of the battle from knights and squires who had been engaged in it on both sides.

There were also with the English two valiant knights † from the country of Foix, whom I had the good fortune to meet at Orthes, the year after the battle had been fought. On my return from Foix, I met likewise, at Avignon, a knight and two squires of Scotland, of the party of Douglas. They knew me again, from the recollections I brought to their minds of their own country; for in my youth I, the author of this history, travelled through Scotland, and was full fifteen days resident with William, Earl of Douglas, father of Earl James, of whom we are now speaking, at his castle of Dalkeith, five miles from Edinburgh. At that time Earl James was very young, though a promising youth; he had also a sister named Blanche. I had, therefore, my information from both parties, and they agree that it was the hardest and most obstinate battle that was ever fought. This I readily believe, for the English and Scots are excellent men-at-arms, and never spare each other when they meet in battle, nor is there any check to their courage as long as their weapons last. When they have well beaten each other, and one party is victorious, they are so proud of the conquest that they ransom their prisoners instantly, and act in such a courteous manner to those who have been taken that on their departure they return them thanks. However, when engaged in war, there is no child's play between them, nor do they shrink from combat; and in the further details of this battle you will see as excellent deeds as were ever performed. The knights and squires of either party were most anxious to continue the combat with vigor, as long as their spears might be capable of holding. Cowardice was unknown among them, and the most splendid courage everywhere exhibited by the gallant youths of England and Scotland; they

† Sir John de Châteauneuf and John de Cautiron.

were so densely intermixed that the archers' bows were useless, and they fought hand to hand, without either battalion giving way. The Scots behaved most valiantly, for the English were three to one. I do not mean to say that the English did not acquit themselves well; for they would sooner be slain or made prisoners in battle than reproached with flight.

As I before mentioned, the two banners of Douglas and Percy met, and the men-at-arms under each exerted themselves by every means to gain the victory; but the English, at the attack, were so much the stronger that the Scots were driven back. The Earl of Douglas, seeing his men repulsed, seized a battle-axe with both his hands; and, in order to rally his forces, dashed into the midst of his enemies, and gave such blows to all around him, that no one could withstand them, but all made way for him on every side. Thus he advanced like another Hector, thinking to conquer the field by his own prowess, until he was met by three spears that were pointed at him. One struck him on the shoulder, another on the stomach, near the belly, and the third entered his thigh. As he could not disengage himself from these spears, he was borne to the ground, still fighting desperately. From that moment, he never rose again. Some of his knights and squires had followed him, but not all; for, though the moon shone, it was rather dark. The three English lances knew they had struck down some person of considerable rank, but never supposed it was Earl Douglas; for, had they known it, they would have redoubled their courage, and the fortune of the day would have been determined to their side. The Scots also were ignorant of their loss until the battle was over; and it was fortunate for them, for otherwise they would certainly from despair have been discomfited. As soon as the earl fell his head was cleaved with a battle-axe, a spear thrust through his thigh, and the main body of the English marched over him without once supposing him to be their principal enemy.

In another part of the field the Earl of March and Dunbar fought valiantly, and the English gave full employment to the Scots who had followed the Earl of Douglas, and had engaged with the two Percys. The Earl of Moray behaved so gallantly in pursuing the English that they knew not how to resist him. Of all the battles, great or small, that have been described in this history, this of which I am now speaking was the best fought and the most severe: for there was not a man, knight or squire who did not acquit himself gallantly hand to hand with the enemy. The sons of the Earl of Northumberland, Sir Henry and Sir Ralph Percy, who were the leaders of the expedition, behaved themselves like good knights. An accident befell Sir Ralph Percy, almost similar to that which happened to the Earl of Douglas; having advanced too far, he was surrounded by the enemy and severely wounded, and being out of breath surrendered himself to a Scottish knight, called Sir John Maxwell, who was of the household of the Earl of Moray. As soon as he was made prisoner, the knight asked him who he was. Sir Ralph was so weakened by loss of blood that he had scarcely power to avow himself to be Sir Ralph Percy. "Well," replied the knight, "Sir Ralph, rescued or not, you are my prisoner: my name is Maxwell." "I agree," said Sir Ralph; "but pay me some attention, for I am so desperately wounded that my drawers and greaves are full of blood." Upon this the Scottish knight took care of him, and suddenly hearing the cry of Moray hard by, and perceiving the earl's banner advancing, Sir John addressed himself to him, and said, "My lord, I present you with Sir Ralph Percy as a prisoner; but let him be well attended to, for he is very badly wounded." The earl was much pleased, and said, "Maxwell, thou hast well earned thy spurs this day." He then ordered his men to take care of Sir Ralph, and bind up his wounds.

The battle still continued to rage, and no one, at that moment, could say which side would be the conquerors. There were many captures and rescues which never came to my knowledge. The young Earl of Douglas had performed wonders during the day. When he was struck down there was a great crowd round him, and he was unable to raise himself, for the blow on his head was mortal. His men had followed him as closely as they were able, and there came to him his cousins, Sir James Lindsay, Sir John and Sir Walter Sinclair, with other knights and squires. They found by his side a gallant knight who had constantly attended him, who was his chaplain, but who at this time had exchanged his profession for that of a valiant man-at-arms. The whole night he had followed the earl, with his battle-axe in hand, and by his exertion had more than once repulsed the English. His name was Sir William of North Berwick. To say the truth, he was well formed in all his limbs to shine in battle, and in this combat was himself severely wounded. When these knights came to the Earl of Douglas they found him in a melancholy state, as well as one of his knights, Sir Robert Hart, who had fought by his side the whole of the night, and now lay beside him covered with fifteen wounds from lances and other weapons. Sir John Sinclair asked the earl, "Cousin, how fares it with you?" "But so so," he replied; "thanks to God, there are but few of my ancestors who have died in chambers or in their beds. I bid you, therefore, revenge my death, for I have but little hope of living, as my heart becomes every minute more faint. Do you, Walter and Sir John, raise up my banner, for it is on the ground, owing to the death of Sir David Campbell, that valiant squire who bore it, and who this day refused knighthood from my hands, though he was equal to the most eminent knight for courage and loyalty. Also, continue to shout 'Douglas!' but do not tell friend or foe whether I am in your company or not; for should the enemy know the truth they will greatly rejoice." The two Sinclairs and Sir James Lindsay obeyed his orders.

The banner was raised, and "Douglas!" shouted. Those men who had remained behind, hearing the shout of Douglas so often repeated, ascended a small eminence, and pushed their lances with such courage that the English were repulsed and many killed. The Scots, by thus valiantly driving the enemy beyond the spot where Earl Douglas lay dead, for he had expired on giving his last orders, arrived at his banner, which was borne by Sir John Sinclair. Numbers were continually increasing, from the repeated shouts of "Douglas," and the greater part of the Scottish knights and squires were now there. Among them were the earls of Moray and March, with their banners and men. When all the Scots were thus collected, they renewed the battle with greater vigor than before. To say the truth, the English had harder work than the Scots, for they had come by a forced march that evening from Newcastle-on-Tyne, which was eight English leagues distant, to meet the Scots; by which means the greater part were exceedingly fatigued before the combat began. The Scots, on the contrary, had rested themselves, which was of the greatest advantage, as was apparent from the event of the battle. In this last attack they so completely repulsed the English, that the latter could never rally again, and the former drove them beyond where the Earl of Douglas lay on the ground.

During the attack, Sir Henry Percy had the misfortune to fall into the hands of the Lord Montgomery. They had fought hand to hand with much valor, and without hinderance from any one; for there was neither knight nor squire of either party who did not find there his equal to fight with, and all were fully engaged. The battle was severely fought on both sides; but such is the fickleness of fortune, that though the English were a more numerous body, and at the first onset had repulsed the Scots, they, in the end, lost the field, and very many knights were made prisoners. Just as the defeat took place, and while the combat was continued in different parts, an English squire, whose name was Thomas Felton, and who was attached to the household of Lord Percy, was surrounded by a body of Scots. He was a handsome man, and, as he showed, valiant in arms. That and the preceding night he had been employed in collecting the best arms, and would neither surrender nor deign to fly. It was told me that he had made a vow to that purpose, and had declared at some feast in Northumberland, that at the very first meeting of the Scots and English he would acquit himself so loyally, that, for having stood his ground, he should be renowned as the best combatant of both parties. I also heard, for I believe I never saw him, that his body and limbs were of strength befitting a valiant combatant; and that he performed such deeds, when engaged with the banner of the Earl of Moray, as astonished the Scots: however, he was slain while thus bravely fighting. Through admiration of his great courage they would willingly have made him a prisoner, and several knights proposed it to him; but in vain, for he thought he should be assisted by his friends. Thus died Thomas Felton, much lamented by his own party. When he fell he was engaged with a cousin of the King of Scotland, called Simon Glendinning.

According to what I heard, the battle was very bloody from its commencement to the defeat; but when the Scots saw the English were discomfited and surrendering on all sides, they behaved courteously to them. The pursuit lasted a long time, and was extended to five English miles. Had the Scots been in sufficient numbers, none of the English would have escaped death or captivity; and if Sir Archibald Douglas, the Earl of Fife, the Earl of Sutherland, with the division that had marched for Carlisle, had been there, they would have taken the Bishop of Durham and the town of Newcastle, as I shall explain to you.

The same evening that Sir Henry and Sir Ralph Percy had left Newcastle, the Bishop of Durham, with the remainder of the forces of that district, had arrived there and supped. While seated at table, he considered that he should not act very honorably if he remained in the town while his countrymen had taken the field. In consequence he rose up, ordered his horses to be saddled, and his trumpets to sound for his men to prepare: they amounted in all to 7,000: that is, 2,000 on horseback and 5,000 on foot. Although it was now night, they took the road toward Otterbourne, and they had not advanced a league from Newcastle when intelligence was brought that the English were engaged with the Scots. On this the bishop halted his men, and several more joined them, out of breath from the combat. On being asked how the affair went on, they replied, "Badly and unfortunately. We are defeated, and the Scots are close at our heels." The second intelligence being worse than the first, gave alarm to several, who broke from their ranks; and when, shortly after, crowds came to them flying, they were panic-struck, and so frightened with the bad news, that the Bishop of Durham could not keep 500 of his men together. Now, supposing a large body had come upon them, and followed them to the town, would not much mischief have ensued? Those acquainted with arms imagine the alarm would have been so great that the Scots would have forced their way into the place with them.

When the bishop saw his own men thus join the runaways in their flight, he demanded of Sir William de Lussy, Sir Thomas Clifford, and other knights of his company, what they were now to do? These knights either could not or would not advise him; so at length the bishop said, "Gentlemen, everything considered, there is no honor in foolhardiness, nor is it requisite that to one misfortune we should add another. Our men are defeated, and we cannot remedy it. We must, therefore, return this night to Newcastle, and to-morrow we will march and find our enemies." Upon this, they all marched back to Newcastle.

I must say something of Sir Matthew Redman, who had mounted his horse to escape from the battle, as he alone could not recover the day. On his departure, he was noticed by Sir James Lindsay, a valiant Scottish knight, who, with his battle-axe hung at his neck and his spear in hand, through courage and the hope of gain, mounted his horse to pursue him. When so close that he might have struck him with his lance, he cried out, "Sir knight, turn about, it is disgraceful thus to fly; I am James Lindsay, and if you do not turn, I will drive my spear into your back." Sir Matthew made no reply, but spurred his horse harder than before. In this state did the chase last for three miles, when Sir Matthew's horse stumbling under him, he leaped off, drew his sword, and put himself in a posture of defence. The Scottish knight made a thrust at his breast with his lance; but Sir Matthew escaped the blow by writhing his body, the point of the lance was buried in the ground, and Sir Matthew cut it in two with his sword. Sir James upon this dismounted, grasped his battle-axe, which was slung across his shoulder, and handled it after the Scottish manner, with one hand, most dexterously, attacking the knight with renewed courage. They fought for a long time, one with his battle-axe and the other with his sword, for there was no one to prevent them. At last, however, Sir James laid about him such heavy blows, that Sir Matthew was quite out of breath, and, desiring to surrender, said, "Lindsay, I yield myself to you." "Indeed," replied the Scottish knight, "rescued or not?" "I consent," said Sir Matthew. "You will take good care of me?" "That I will," replied Sir James; and, upon this, Sir Matthew put his sword into the scabbard and said, "Now, what do you require, for I am your prisoner by fair conquest?" "What is it you wish me to do?" replied Sir James. "I should like," said Sir Matthew, "to return to Newcastle, and within fifteen days I will come to you in any part of Scotland you shall appoint." "I agree," said Sir James, "on your pledging yourself to be in Edinburgh within three weeks." And when this condition had been sworn to, each sought his horse, which was pasturing hard by, and rode away; Sir James to join his companions, and Sir Matthew to Newcastle.

Sir James, from the darkness of the night, mistook his road, and fell in with the Bishop of Durham, and about 500 English, whom he mistook for his own friends in pursuit of the enemy. When in the midst of them, those nearest asked who he was, and he replied, "I am Sir James Lindsay;" upon which the bishop, who was within hearing, pushed forward and said, "Lindsay, you are a prisoner." "And who are you?" said Lindsay. "I am the Bishop of Durham." Sir James then told the bishop that he had just captured Sir Matthew Redman, and ransomed him, and that he had returned to Newcastle under a promise to come to him in three weeks' time. Before day dawned after the battle the field was clear of combatants; the Scots had retired within the camp, and had sent scouts and parties of light horse toward Newcastle, and on the adjacent roads, to observe whether the English were collecting in any large bodies, that they might not be surprised a second time. This was wisely done—for when the Bishop of Durham was returned to Newcastle and had disarmed himself, he was very melancholy at the unfortunate news he had heard that his cousins, the sons of the Earl of Northumberland, and all the knights who had followed them, were either taken or slain; he sent for all knights and squires at the time in Newcastle, and requested to know if they would suffer things to remain in their present state, since it was very disgraceful that they should return without ever seeing their enemies. They therefore held a council, and determined to arm themselves by sunrise, march horse and foot after the Scots to Otterbourne, and offer them battle. This resolution was published throughout the town, and the trumpet sounded at the hour appointed; upon which the whole army made themselves ready, and were drawn up before the bridge.

About sunrise they left Newcastle, through the gate leading to Berwick, and followed the road to Otterbourne; including horse and foot, they amounted to 10,000 men. They had not advanced two leagues when it was signified to the Scots that the Bishop of Durham had rallied his troop, and was on his march to give them battle. Sir Matthew, on his return to Newcastle, told the event of the battle, and of his being made prisoner by Sir James Lindsay, and to his surprise he learned from the bishop or some of his people that Sir James had in his turn been taken prisoner by the bishop. As soon, therefore, as the bishop had quitted Newcastle, Sir Matthew went to seek for Sir James, whom he found at his lodgings very sorrowful, and who said on seeing him, " I believe, Sir Matthew, there will be no need of your coming to Edinburgh to obtain your ransom, for as I am now a prisoner, we may finish the matter here, if my master consent to it." To this Redman replied by inviting Sir James to dine with him, at the same time stating that they should soon agree about the ransom.

As soon as the barons and knights of Scotland heard of the Bishop of Durham's approach, they held a council, and resolved to abide the event where they were. Accordingly they made the best arrangements they could, and then ordered their minstrels to play merrily. The bishop and his men on approaching heard the noise, and were much frightened. The concert, after lasting a considerable time, ceased; and after a pause, when the Scots thought the English were within half a league, they recommenced it,g continuing it as long as before, when it again ceased. The bishop, however, kept advancing with his men in battle array, until within two bow-shots of the enemy, when the Scots began to play louder than before, and for a much longer time, during which the bishop examined with surprise how well the Scots had chosen their encampment; and as it was deemed advisable not to risk an attack, he and his army returned to Newcastle. The Scots, perceiving that the English did not intend to offer them battle, made preparations for their own departure.

I was told that at the battle of Otterbourne, which was fought on the nineteenth day of August, 1388, there were taken or left dead on the field, on the side of the English, 1,040 men of all descriptions; in the pursuit 840, and more than 1,000 wounded. Of the Scots there were only about 100 slain, and 200 made prisoners. When everything had been arranged, and the dead bodies of the Earl of Douglas and Sir Simon Glendinning were

---

g The Scottish custom was, when assembled in arms, for those on foot to be well dressed, and each to have a large horn slung round his neck, after the manner of hunters; at times these blew all together, and the horns being of different sizes, the noise was then so great that it could be heard many miles off, to the great dismay of their enemies, and to their own delight and encouragement.

enclosed within coffins and placed in cars, the Scots began their march, carrying with them Sir Henry Percy and upward of forty English knights. They took the road to Melrose on the Tweed, and on their departure set fire to the huts. At Melrose, which is an abbey of black monks, situated on the borders of the two kingdoms, they halted, and gave directions to the friars for the burial of the Earl of Douglas, whose obsequies were very reverently performed on the second day after their arrival. His body was placed in a tomb of stone with the banner of Douglas suspended over it. Of the Earl of Douglas, God save his soul, there was no issue, nor do I know who succeeded to the estates; for when I was in Scotland, at his castle of Dalkeith, during the lifetime of Earl William, there were only two children, a boy and a girl. As soon as the Scots had finished the business which brought them to Melrose they departed each to his own country, and those who had prisoners carried them with them, or ransomed them before they left Melrose. It was told me, and I believe it, that the Scots gained 200,000 francs by the ransoms; and that never since the battle of Bannockburn,*h* when the Bruce, Sir William Douglas, Sir Robert de Versy, and Sir Simon Frazer, pursued the English for three days, have they had so complete or so gainful a victory. When the news of it was brought to Sir Archibald Douglas, the earls of Fife and Sutherland, before Carlisle, where they were with the larger division of the army, they were greatly rejoiced, though at the same time vexed that they had not been present. They held a council, and determined to retreat into Scotland, since their companions had already marched thither. We will now leave the English and Scots, and speak of other matters.

We left the King of France on his march to Gueldres; his army was very numerous, and well appointed, and Duke Juliers and his subjects much dreaded their approach, for they knew they should be first attacked; the duke, therefore, sent

---

*h* This ever-memorable battle was fought on the banks of the brook called Bannockburn, in the month of June, 1314, between King Edward II of England, and Robert Bruce, King of Scotland. Both parties had made great preparations for it; and it is generally reported that the English never, before or afterward, whether in France or Scotland, lost so dreadful a battle; nor did the Scots ever gain one of like importance. The loss on the part of the English was immense; very many of the best and bravest of the nobility were left dead upon the field, and very many made prisoners; indeed the whole of King Edward's large army was either dispersed or destroyed.

ambassadors to the King, and at last came himself to him, endeavoring to make excuses for his son's conduct. The King of France on his coming received him graciously, and the duke had restored to him the territory of Vierson, for which he paid homage to the King, who quartered his army on a friendly footing in the duchy of Juliers, while the duke went in company with the Archbishop of Cologne to his son, and, by remonstrances and negotiations, concluded a peace with him.

We must now return to the Duke of Lancaster, and speak of his negotiations with the King of Castille and the Duke of Berry respecting the marriage of his daughter. The King of Castille was desirous of having her for his son, as the means of peace with England; and the Duke of Berry wished her for himself, being very impatient to marry her. The Duke of Lancaster was wise and prudent; he saw that the most advantageous alliance for himself and his countess was Castille, for by it he should recover the inheritance of that country for his daughter; if he gave her to the Duke of Berry, and he should die before her, she would be poor in comparison with other ladies, for the duke had children by his first marriage, who would be entitled to all his landed property. The duchess likewise was more inclined to the connection with Castille, and so the marriage was agreed upon. Proper contracts were drawn up, and sealed with covenants to prevent any danger of breaking off the match; and the duchess consented, when the whole should be concluded, to conduct her daughter to Castille.

The King of France, being now twenty-one years of age, had taken upon himself the government of his kingdom, and on hearing of the intended marriage he sent to the King of Castille, remonstrating with him not to enter into any alliance which might be prejudicial to him or to his kingdom. The Duke of Berry, having been disappointed of marrying the daughter of the Duke of Lancaster, was told that the Count de Boulogne had a beautiful daughter named Jane, who was not residing with her father and mother, but in the country of Béarn with his good friend and cousin the Count de Foix, at whose castle she had been for the space of nine years, and who had the wardship of all her property. The duke, therefore, sent to the count demanding this lady in marriage; however, though the count gave a handsome reception to the duke's messengers, he did not at once settle the business, for he was not a person to act hastily, and prudently thought that many questions would arise before the business could be concluded.

About this time the fleet under command of the Earl of Arundel, which had been cruising on the coasts of Normandy, returned to England, and shortly after the Duchess of Lancaster made preparations for her journey into Castille, whither she was to carry her daughter to solemnize her marriage with the son of the King of that country. It was her intention when in Castille to visit the field of the battle of Monteil, where her father, Don Pedro, had lost his life, and make strict inquiries where his body had been buried, which when found was to be taken up, conveyed to the city of Seville, and magnificently interred there, in a manner beoming a king.

The party having set out from Bordeaux, and traversed the kingdom of Navarre, met King John of Castille at Burgos. And when the marriage had been duly solemnized, and all contracts signed, the duchess left her daughter with the King and her young husband, who was then but eight years old, and went to Monteil; on arriving at which place such search was made that she discovered where her father had been buried, and had his bones taken up, washed and embalmed, and carried in a coffin to Seville. The bones were then reverently buried in the cathedral with very solemn obsequies, which were attended by King John, his son, the young Prince of Galicia, and the greater part of the prelates and barons of the realm.

The marriage of the daughter of the Duke of Lancaster with the Infant of Castille was no sooner concluded, than the Duke of Berry became more urgent in his negotiations with the Count de Foix, who at length acceded to his proposals, and sent to him his cousin of Boulogne, whom the duke married with the least possible delay. The marriage was very magnificent; the feastings and tournaments lasted for four days, and I, the writer of this book, was a partaker of them all.

After this a truce for three years was negotiated between the French and the English and all their allies; and notwithstanding it was objected to on the part of the Scots, in consequence of their recent success against the English at the battle of Otterbourne, it was finally settled, through the means of commissioners of high rank on both sides, who held their conference at a place called Leulinghem, between Boulogne and Calais.

# CHAPTER III

Grand Doings on the Entrance of Queen Isabella Into Paris—The King of France Visits the Pope at Avignon—Three Knights of France Undertake to Hold a Field of Arms at Calais Against All Foreign Knights and Squires for Thirty Days—Death of Pope Urban—The Tournament—Expedition Against the Town of Africa—Disturbances with the Free Companies—Amerigot Marcel and Perrot le Béarnois—Siege of La Roche de Vendais—Death of Amerigot Marcel—The Christian Army Lands on the Shore of Africa—The Dog of Our Lady—A Challenge from the Saracens—The Siege.

YOU who delight in this history must know, that on my leaving the castle of the noble Count Gaston de Foix, I returned through Auvergne and France in company with the gallant Lord de la Riviere, and Sir William de la Tremouille, who had conducted the Lady Jane of Boulogne to the Duke of Berry, in the town of Riom, where he married her. I then went to Paris, and met there the noble Lord de Coucy, one of my patrons, who had lately married a daughter of the Duke of Lorraine. From Paris I went to Valenciennes, and after staying there a fortnight set out to Holland to visit my gallant patron and lord the Count de Blois, whom I found at Schoenhoven. I then returned to France to learn the particulars of the conference which was being held at Leulinghem, between the English and French, and likewise to be present at the magnificent feasts which were to be given on the occasion of Queen Isabella's public entry into Paris, where as yet she had never been.[a] It was on Sunday, the twentieth day of June, in the year of our Lord 1399, that the Queen entered Paris. In the afternoon of that day the noble ladies of France who were to accompany the Queen assembled at St. Denis,

[a] Froissart seems to intimate that this was the first visit which the Queen had paid to Paris. Such, however, does not appear to be the fact, as she was there in the year 1386, when Charles wrote to her on the twenty-eighth of April from Montdidier, to send the taxes to Amiens, and to hasten from Paris all the men-at-arms and foreigners who were intended for the invasion of England.

with such of the nobility as were appointed to lead the litters of the Queen and her attendants. The citizens of Paris, to the number of 1,200, were mounted on horseback, dressed in uniforms of green and crimson, and lined each side of the road. Queen Joan and her daughter the Duchess of Orleans entered the city first about an hour after noon, in a covered litter, and passing through the great street of St. Denis, went to the palace, where the King was waiting for them.

The Queen of France, attended by the Duchess of Berry and many other noble ladies, began the procession in an open litter most richly ornamented. A crowd of nobles attended, and sergeants and others of the King's officers had full employment in making way for the procession, for there were such numbers assembled that it seemed as if all the world had come thither. At the gate of St. Denis was the representation of a starry firmament, and within it were children dressed as angels, whose singing and chanting was melodiously sweet. There was also an image of the Virgin holding in her arms a child, who at times amused himself with a windmill made of a large walnut. The upper part of this firmament was richly adorned with the arms of France and Bavaria, with a brilliant sun[b] dispersing his rays through the heavens; and this sun was the King's device at the ensuing tournaments. The Queen, after passing them, advanced slowly to the fountain in the street of St. Denis, which was decorated with fine blue cloth besprinkled over with golden fleurs-de-lys; and, instead of water, the fountain ran in great streams of clairé,[c] an excellent piement. Around the fountain were young girls handsomely dressed, who sang most sweetly, and held in their hands cups of gold, offering drink to all who chose it. Below the monastery of the Trinity a scaffold had been erected in the streets, and on it a castle, with a representation of the battle with King Saladin performed by living actors, the Christians on one side and the Saracens on the other. The procession then passed on to the second gate of St. Denis, which was adorned as the first; and as the Queen was going through the gate two angels descended and gently placed on her head a

---

[b] Louis XIV took the same device, with the motto, "Nec pluribus impar."

[c] Clairé is no doubt intended for clairet or claret, a clear red wine; and piement, according to Du Cange, is a drink made of honey, wine, and different spices.

rich golden crown, ornamented with precious stones, at the same time singing sweetly the following verse:

> Dame enclose entre fleurs de Lys,
> Reine êtes vous de Paris.
> De France, et de tout le païs,
> Nous en r' allons en paradis.

Opposite the chapel of St. James a scaffold had been erected, richly decorated with tapestry, and surrounded with curtains, within which were men who played finely on organs. The whole street of St. Denis was covered with a canopy of rich camlet and silk cloths. The Queen and her ladies, conducted by the great lords, arrived at length at the gate of the Châtelet, where they stopped to see other splendid pageants that had been prepared. The Queen and her attendants thence passed on to the bridge of Notre Dame, which was covered with a starry canopy of green and crimson, and the streets were all hung with tapestry as far as the church. It was now late in the evening, for the procession, ever since it had set out from St. Denis, had advanced but at a foot's pace. As the Queen was passing down the street of Notre Dame, a man descended by means of a rope from the highest tower of Notre Dame church, having two lighted torches in his hands, and playing many tricks as he came down. The Bishop of Paris and his numerous clergy met the Queen at the entrance of the church, and conducted her through the nave and choir to the great altar, where, on her knees, she made her prayers, and presented as her offering four cloths of gold, and the handsome crown which the angels had put on her head at the gate of Paris. The Lord John de la Riviere and Sir John le Mercier instantly brought one more rich, with which they crowned her. When this was done she and her ladies left the church, and as it was late, upward of 500 lighted tapers attended the procession. In such array were they conducted to the palace, where the King, Queen Joan, and the Duchess of Orleans were waiting for them.

On the morrow, which was Monday, the King gave a grand dinner to a numerous company of ladies, and at the hour of high mass the Queen of France was conducted to the holy chapel, where she was anointed and sanctified in the usual manner. Sir William de Viare, Archbishop of Rouen, said mass. Shortly after mass the King, Queen, and all the ladies entered the hall: and you must know that the great marble table[d] which is in this hall was covered with oaken planks four inches thick, and the royal dinner placed thereon. Near the table, and against one of the pillars, was the King's buffet, magnificently decked out with gold and silver plate; and in the hall were plenty of attendants, sergeants-at-arms, ushers, archers, and minstrels, who played away to the best of their ability. The kings,[e] prelates, and ladies, having washed, seated themselves at the tables, which were three in number: at the first, sat the King and Queen of France, and some few of the higher nobility; and at the other two, there were upward of 500 ladies and damsels; but the crowd was so great that it was with difficulty they could be served with dinner, which indeed was plentiful and sumptous. There were in the hall many curiously arranged devices: a castle to represent the city of Troy, with the palace of Ilion, from which were displayed the banners of the Trojans; also a pavilion on which were placed the banners of the Grecian kings, and which was moved, as it were, by invisible beings to the attack of Troy, assisted by a large ship capable of containing 100 men-at-arms; but the crowd was so great that this amusement could not last long. There were so many people on all sides that several were stifled by the heat, and the Queen herself almost fainted. The Queen left the palace about five o'clock, and, followed by her ladies, in litters or on horseback, proceeded to the residence of the King at the hotel de St. Pol. The King took boat at the palace, and was rowed to his hotel, where, in a large hall, he entertained the ladies at a banquet; the Queen, however, remained in her chamber, where she supped, and did not again appear that night.

On Tuesday, many superb presents were made by the Parisians to the King and Queen of France, and the Duchess of Touraine. This day the King and Queen dined in private,

[d] This table is reported to have been of such immense size that it was generally supposed to be the greatest slab of marble existing. We learn from the "Antiquités de Paris," that this table served for two or three hundred years very different purposes. At one time it was used for a theatre on which the attorney's clerks acted their mummeries; at another, for the royal feasts, when only emperors, kings, and princes of the blood were admitted with their ladies. It was consumed by fire in 1618.

[e] The King of Armenia was present at the banquet with the King of France.

at their different hotels, for at three o'clock the tournament was to take place in the square of St. Catherine, where scaffolds had been erected for the accommodation of the Queen and the ladies. The knights who took part in this tournament were thirty in number, including the King; and when the jousts began they were carried on with great vigor, everyone performing his part in honor of the ladies. The Duke of Ireland, who was then a resident at Paris, and invited by the King to the tournament, tilted well; also a German knight from beyond the Rhine, by name Sir Gervais di Mirande, gained great commendation. The number of knights made it difficult to give a full stroke, and the dust was so troublesome that it increased the diffculty. The Lord de Coucy shone with brilliancy. The tilts were continued without relaxation until night, when the ladies were conducted to their hotels. At the hotel de St. Pol was the most magnificent banquet ever heard of. Feasting and dancing lasted till sunrise, and the prize of the tournament was given, with the assent of the ladies and heralds, to the King as being the best tilter on the opponent side; while the prize for the holders of the lists was given to the Halze de Flandres, bastard brother to the Duchess of Burgundy. On Wednesday the tilting was continued, and the banquet this evening was as grand as the preceding one. The prize was adjudged by the ladies and heralds to a squire from Hainault, as the most deserving of the opponents, and to a squire belonging to the Duke of Burgundy, as the best tenant of the field. On Thursday also the tournament was continued; and, this day, knights and squires tilted most promiscuously, and many gallant jousts were done, for everyone took pains to excel. When night put an end to the combat there was a grand entertainment again for the ladies at the hotel de St. Pol. On Friday the King feasted the ladies and damsels at dinner, and afterward very many returned to their homes, the King and Queen thanking them very graciously for having come to the feast.

After this grand festival was over, the King of France, seeing that his kingdom was now at peace, and that there was a truce with England, had a great desire to visit the more distant parts of his government, particularly Languedoc. At the advice of his ministry, he also prepared to visit the Pope and cardinals at Avignon. Before he set out upon his journey he yielded to the request of the Lord de Coucy, and gave orders that the Duke of Ireland should quit France about Michaelmas, 1399. The King of France set out from the Castle of Beauté, near Paris, where he left the Queen, and took the road to Troyes, in Champagne, on his way to Burgundy. He was accompanied by his uncles, the Duke of Bourbon, the Duke of Touraine, the Lord de Coucy, and many other knights, and continued his journey until he arrived at Dijon, where he was received with every respect and affection by the Duchess of Burgundy, and all who had come hither to do him honor. Grand entertainments were given on the occasion, and the King remained eight days at Dijon, and then went to Villeneuve, near Avignon, where his palace had been prepared. From Villeneuve he proceeded to the palace of Pope Clement, who was waiting for him in full consistory,[f] seated in his robes, on his papal chair. When the King came into his presence he bowed, and, when near to him, the Pope rose up and the King kissed him. The Pope then seated himself, and made the King sit by him. When dinner was ready, the Pope took his place at a table alone in much state, and the King was placed at another table below that of the Pope, and alone also. The cardinals and dukes seated themselves according to their rank. The dinner was splendid, plentiful, and long continued: when over, the King retired to an apartment prepared for him in the palace. The Pope and cardinals were much rejoiced at the visit of the King of France, as indeed they had good reason to be; for without his support they would have been in but small estimation. There were no kings in Christendom who paid the Pope obedience but such as were allied to France. The Pope, on the joyful occasion of the King's visit, gave pardons to the clergy who were in his court, and plenary indulgences to all for one month to come. He likewise presented the King with the nominations to all his cathedrals and other churches, and in each church to reversions of two prebends, deferring all his former promises, that those now made to the King might have the precedency. He gave also reversions to the dukes of Touraine, Berry, and

---

[f] A consistory is a court Christian, or court spiritual. Every bishop has his consistory court held before his chancellor or commissary.

Burgundy, and the Lord de Coucy; and was so courteous and liberal on this occasion that none left him discontented. The King remained with the Pope about eight days; and, on leaving, he dismissed to their homes the dukes of Berry and Burgundy, to their great dissatisfaction; and then continued his journey to Languedoc. At Montpellier he resided upward of twelve days; indeed he appeared to enjoy himself much at this place, and danced and carolled with the frisky ladies of Montpellier all night.

You know, or must have heard it mentioned, that the intercourse of young gentlemen with the fair sex encourages sentiments of honor and love of fame. I mention this because there were with the King of France three gentlemen of great valor and enterprise, which they were probably induced by that intercourse to display in the manner I shall relate. The names of the three were Sir Boucicaut the younger, Sir Reginald de Roye, and the Lord de Saimpi. These knights were chamberlains to the King, and much esteemed by him; and being desirous of advancing themselves in the estimation of all present, and especially the ladies, they offered to hold a field of arms on the frontier of Calais in the course of the ensuing summer, against all foreign knights and squires, for the space of thirty days, and to tilt with blunt lances or others. The King of France was well pleased with the courageous challenge of his three knights, and declared his consent to it; moreover, he called them into his closet, and said, " Boucicaut, Reginald, and Saimpi, be attentive in this enterprise to guard your honor well, and that of our kingdom; let nothing be spared in the state you keep, for I will not fail to assist you as far as 10,000 francs." The King after this left Montpellier, following the road to Alipian, where he dined, and lay that night at St. Thibery.

On the morrow, after his morning draught, he set off and came to Beziers, where he was received most joyfully. He did not, however, remain long in this place, but made the best of his way to Toulouse, when, at the advice of his council, he summoned to him the Count de Foix, who had left Béarn, and fixed his residence in a town of Foix, called Mazeres, fourteen leagues from Toulouse. The marshal of France and the Lord de la Riviere were appointed to acquaint the count with the King's request; and he at once consented to comply. "Tell the King," said he to the messengers, "that I will be with him in Toulouse in four days." The count accordingly made his preparations, and set forward to meet the King, attended by 200 knights and squires from Béarn; his two brothers, Sir Peter and Sir Arnold de Béarn, and his two bastard sons, whom he affectionately loved, also accompanied him. The count made his entry into Toulouse rather late in the evening, and remained all that night at the convent of the Friar Preachers, where he and his household were lodged. On the morrow he and his retinue passed through the streets of Toulouse to the castle where the King resided. The count entered the hall, whither the King had gone from his chamber to await his arrival, bareheaded, for indeed he never wore a cap; on seeing the King he bent his knee very low; he afterward rose up and knelt a second time close to the King, who raised him with his hand, and embracing him, said, "Fair cousin of Foix, you are welcome, for your visit gives us great joy." "My lord," replied the count, "I thank you much for what you are pleased to say." A magnificent and sumptuous dinner was then provided; and after dinner, when the tables were removed and grace said, the company amused themselves in various ways. Wine and spices were afterward brought, and the comfit-box was presented solely to the King by the Count de Harcourt. Sir Gerard de la Pierre did the same to the Duke of Bourbon, and Sir Menaut de Noailles to the Count de Foix.g When this was done it was about four o'clock in the afternoon; the count then took his leave and returned to his lodgings, much pleased with the reception and entertainment which the King of France had given him. Not many days after this, the Count de Foix, attended by his barons and knights, waited on the King at the castle, and paid him homage for his country of Foix.

About this period Pope Urban VI died, at Rome, to the sorrow of the Romans, who loved him much. He was buried with great solemnity in the church of St. Peter; and when the

g This custom of the comfit-box, or "drageoir," as it was called, appears to have prevailed only at the tables of the King and great barons. Spices and wine formed the ordinary desserts of the times; but on occasions, and especially when honor was to be paid to any particular guest, the comfit-box was used. The box itself was generally of gold or silver, and contained spices of the greatest variety. It was the office of a squire, or some person of distinction, to present it.

ceremony was ended, the cardinals formed a conclave to elect another pope, and hastened the matter, that it might be done before any intelligence of the death of Urban could be carried to Avignon. Pope Clement and his cardinals did not hear of the death of Urban until the tenth day after it had happened; however, they immediately assembled at the palace, when many proposals were discussed, for they had great hope that the schism of the Church would be concluded, and a union formed of the two parties. This subject was canvassed far and wide, and at the University of Paris it became the occasion of great disputes among the students, who neglected their usual studies, and employed themselves in disputing how the cardinals would act, whether they would elect a pope in the room of Urban, or acknowledge the Pope of Avignon. It was very soon reported, however, that the Roman cardinals had assembled in conclave, and elected to the papacy the Cardinal of Naples, a prudent and courageous clerk, who took the name of Boniface.*h* The King of France and his lords were much annoyed at this, for it seemed as if the schism in the Church would now continue for a long time.

The time was now come for the three French knights, who had undertaken to maintain the lists against all comers at St. Inglevere, near Calais, to make good their engagement. This tournament had been proclaimed in many countries, especially in England, where it caused much surprise, and several valiant knights and squires undertook to attend. Sir John Holland, half-brother to the King of England, was the first to cross the sea; and with him were more than sixty knights and squires, who took up their quarters in Calais. On the twenty-first of May, as it had been proclaimed, the three knights were properly armed, and their horses ready saddled, according to the laws of the tournament; and on the same day, all those knights who were in Calais sallied forth, as spectators or tilters, and being arrived at the spot, drew up on one side. The place of the tournament was smooth and green with grass. Sir John Holland, Earl of Huntingdon, was the first who sent his squire to touch the war target of Sir Boucicaut, who instantly issued from his pavilion, completely armed, and having mounted his horse and grasped his spear, the two combatants took their

*h* Boniface IX; his name was Pietro, or Perrin de Tomacelli.

distances. They eyed each other for some time, and then spurred their horses and met full gallop, with such force indeed that Sir Boucicaut pierced the shield of the Earl of Huntingdon, and the point of his lance slipped along his arm, but without wounding him. The two knights having passed, continued their gallop to the end of the list. This course was much praised.

At the second course they hit each other slightly, but no harm was done; and their horses refused to complete the third. The Earl of Huntingdon, who was heated, and wished to continue the tilt, returned to his place, expecting that Sir Boucicaut would call for his lance; but he did not, and showed plainly that he did not wish to tilt more with the earl that day. Sir John, seeing this, sent his squire to touch the war target of the Lord de Saimpi. This knight, who was waiting for the combat, sallied out from his pavilion, and took his lance and shield. When the earl saw he was ready, he violently spurred his horse, as did the Lord de Saimpi. They couched their lances, and pointed them at each other. At the onset their horses crossed, notwitstanding which they met, but by their crossing, which was blamed, the earl was unhelmed. He returned to his people, who soon rehelmed him; and, having resumed their lances, they met full gallop, and hit each other with such force in the middle of their shields that they would have been unhorsed had they not kept tight seats, by the pressure of their legs against the horses' sides. They went to their proper places, when they refreshed themselves and took breath. Sir John, who had a great desire to shine in the tournament, had his helmet braced, and grasped his spear again, when the Lord de Saimpi, seeing him advance in a gallop, did not decline meeting; but, spurring his horse on instantly, they gave blows on their helmets, that were luckily of well-tempered steel, which made sparks of fire fly from them. At this course the Lord de Saimpi lost his helmet; but the knights continued their career, and returned to their places.

The tilt was much praised, and both French and English said that the Earl of Huntingdon, Sir Boucicaut, and the Lord de Saimpi had excellently well jousted. The earl wished to break another lance in honor of his lady, but it was refused him. He then quitted the lists to make room for others, for he had run his six lances with such ability and courage as gained him praise from all sides. After this, various other combatants entered the lists, and the tilting was continued till evening, when the English returned to Calais, and the French to St. Inglevere.

On Tuesday after mass, and drinking a cup, all those who intended to tilt, and those who wished to see them, left Calais, and rode to the same place where the lists had been held the preceding day. That day and the next the tilting continued, until the tornament was at an end, by reason of no more tilters appearing on the part of the English. The English and French knights separated in a most friendly manner on the plain of St. Inglevere; the former took the road to Calais, where, however, they made no long stay, for on Saturday morning they went on board passage boats, and landed at Dover about mid-day.

From the time the English knights left Calais, I never heard that any others came from England to St. Inglevere to try their skill in arms. The three knights, however, remained there until the thirty days were fully accomplished, and then leisurely returned each to his own home. When they waited on the King of France, the Duke of Touraine, and the other lords at Paris, they were most handsomely received; indeed, they were entitled to such a reception, for they had behaved themselves gallantly, and well supported the honor of the King, and of the realm of France.

I must not forget, nor indeed defer any longer to mention a grand and noble enterprise that was undertaken by some knights of France, England, and other countries, against the kingdom of Barbary, at the solicitation of the Genoese. The cause of this expedition was that the Africans had attacked the country of Genoa, plundered the islands belonging to it, and carried off many prisoners. Moreover, the Genoese, who were rich merchants, bore great hatred to the town of Africa,[i] situated on the sea-shore of Barbary, because its corsairs frequently watched them by sea, and fell upon and plundered their ships. Reports of the intended invasion of Barbary soon

---

[i] Africa was a very strong place, surrounded with high walls and ditches, about seventy miles distant from Tunis. It was razed to the ground by Andrew Doria, by command of the Emperor, Charles V, and has never been rebuilt.

spread far and wide, and many gallant men-at-arms prepared to take part in it; on being mustered by the marshal, these amounted in all to 1,400 knights and squires, who, on St. John Baptist day, in the year of grace 1390, embarked from Genoa on board ships and galleys, which had been properly equipped for the voyage. It was a beautiful sight to see the fleet with the emblazoned banners of the different lords glittering in the sun, and fluttering with the wind; to hear also the minstrels and other musicians sounding their pipes, clarions, and trumpets. When all were embarked, they cast anchor and remained that night at the mouth of the harbor; but the servants and horses were left behind on the shore. A horse worth fifty francs was on the embarkation sold for ten, as many of the knights and squires were uncertain when they should return, if ever. They, therefore, on departing, made of their horses what money they could, which was little enough. At daybreak they weighed anchor, and rowed coastwise that and the succeeding night. The third day they made Porto-fino, where they lay that night, and at sunrise rowed to Porto-Venere, and again cast anchor. The ensuing morning they took to the deep, putting themselves under the protection of God and St. George.

When they had passed the island of Elba they encountered a violent tempest, which drove them back into the gulf of Lyons, a position always dangerous; they waited, therefore, the will of God: the storm lasted a day and a night, and dispersed the fleet. When the weather became calm and the sea tranquil, the pilots steered as directly as they could for the island of Commeres, which is but thirty miles from the town of Africa, whither they were bent. But we must leave the Genoese expedition in Commeres for a while, to speak of events that happened in France, more particularly in Auvergne.

During the time of the assembling of this body of men-at-arms in France, for an expedition to extend the Christian faith, and gain renown, there were other men-at-arms wholly given up to plunder in Limousin, Auvergne, and Rouergue, who, in spite of the truce, were continually doing mischief to the countries which thought themselves in security. The King of France had caused the truce to be publicly notified to the captains of the freebooters, particularly to Perrot le Béarnois, governor of Chaluçet, Amerigot Marcel, and others, who were publicly named in the act, and were assured that if the truce were in the smallest degree infringed, those guilty of it should be corporally punished, without hope of mercy. Some of the captains, fearful of a disgraceful death, or of incurring the King's indignation, kept the peace very well; others did not, for which they paid severely, as you will hear in the continuation of this history.

You have before heard it related in these chronicles, indited and arranged by me, Sir John Froissart, treasurer and canon of Chimay, how peace had been agreed upon with many of the captains of castles in Auvergne and other places, by the mediation of John, Count d'Armagnac, and the Dauphin of Auvergne, to whom they had surrendered their castles for different sums of money; and that they had undertaken to accompany the count to Lombardy, or whithersoever he might lead them. Count d'Armagnac and the dauphin had labored hard to gain over these captains, and the country had submitted to be heavily taxed in order to get rid of them: however, Amerigot Marcel and his garrison still continued to do much mischief, and could not be induced to join the count. Fond of plundering, he resolved to continue it, and having a desire to gain possession of a strong fort called La Roche de Vendais, he and his companions set out thither, and when they had gained the place fortified it, and made it as strong as they could. This done, they began to overrun the neighboring country—to make prisoners and ransom them. They laid in stores of flesh, meal, wax, wine, salt, iron, steel, and other necessaries; for nothing came amiss to them that was not too hot or too heavy.

The inhabitants of the country were much astonished at this, for they thought themselves in perfect security on account of the truce; but these robbers seized whatever they pleased in their houses, or in the fields, calling themselves the Adventurers. Amerigot and his men became the terror of the whole neighborhood. The countries of Auvergne and Limousin were in a continual state of alarm because of him, and the knights and squires, with the townsmen of Clermont, Montferrant, and Riom, and the towns on the Allier, resolved to send notice of their situation to the King of France. When it was known to those companies who had been disbanded, and were now out of pay, that Amerigot Marcel was continuing the war, many of them came to offer him their services, and he had very soon more than he wished; none of them asked for pay, but solely to be retained by him, for they well knew that those under him would gain a sufficiency from the overplus of the plunder which he gave up to his men. Sometimes he made excursions in the upper parts of the district, and sometimes in an opposite direction; nothing was talked of in Auvergne and Limousin but the robbers of La Roche de Vendais, and greatly was the country frightened by them. The garrison of Chaluçet, under command of Perrot le Béarnois, steadily adhered to the truce, and were much angered when they learned that Amerigot was thus harassing the country. The King of France and his council, on hearing the harm that Amerigot and his companions were doing, immediately turned their attention to the matter, and sent the Viscount de Meaux with a large body of men to oppose them. Amerigot was preparing to ravage the country between Clermont and Montferrant, when it was told him that the viscount was advancing, and this intelligence made him defer his intended excursion, for he foresaw that his fortress would be attacked. Tolerably near to La Roche de Vendais was another fort, called St. Soupery, under the government of Amerigot, where his wife resided, and whither he had sent the greater part of his wealth; he gave orders for the servants and horses to be received into the fort until better times. La Roche de Vendais was naturally strong, and the present garrison had fortified it by every means in their power; it was separated from the high mountains that surround it, and seated on an insulated rock, one side of which the garrison had so strongly fortified that it could only be approached in front, and attacked by skirmishes. The force under command of the Viscount de Meaux advanced and laid siege to the place; it was about the middle of August, the weather was warm and pleasant, and all the knights were comfortably lodged under huts made of green boughs.

The siege of La Roche de Vendais lasted nine weeks, and during it there were constant skirmishes between the two parties, in which many were wounded. The garrison had much the advantage of the besiegers, and I will tell you how;

they could sally out whenever they pleased, for it would have required at least 6,000 men to have completely surrounded this castle. When the siege first took place Amerigot felt that he was acting wrong; but to turn the matter as much to his advantage as he could, and if possible to preserve La Roche de Vendais, he determined to send one of his men to England with credential letters to the King and the Duke of Lancaster. Accordingly, with the advice of his uncle, Guyot du Sel, who was with him in the fort, he instructed a well-educated varlet, and sent him off with three letters, one to the King, another to the Duke of Lancaster, and the third to the King's council. The man performed his journey satisfactorily, and was fortunate enough to find the King, his two uncles of Lancaster and York, with the council, at the palace of Westminster, considering the affairs of Northumberland, and what force they should send thither, for the Scots no way observed the truce. The messenger of Amerigot soon obtained a hearing, and having been well tutored, and not afraid of speaking, after delivering the letters, he explained so eloquently the reason of his coming, and the wishes of his master, that he was attentively listened to, and was at length told that the King would write to the Viscount de Meaux, and the Duke of Berry, in the manner Amerigot had desired. The Duke of Lancaster promised to do the same, and that the letter should be delivered by an English squire attached to him; that Derby the herald should cross the sea, and accompany them when they gave their letters, in order to aid their success, for he was well known to many lords in Auvergne, particularly to the Duke of Berry.

Amerigot was delighted on his messenger's return, and told him that he had done justice to his commission, for which he would reward him handsomely. The English squire and Derby set out at once for La Roche de Vendais, and, when arrived at the place where the besiegers lay, inquired for the quarters of the Viscount de Meaux, to whom they presented their letters. The viscount, after examining the seals, read the contents of the letters several times over, and then said to the squire and the herald, " My fair sirs, the intelligence you have brought demands full consideration; I will advise upon it, and you shall soon have my answer." The squire and the herald then withdrew, and a council was moved, before which the viscount laid the letters he had received; the knights were much surprised how intelligence of the siege could have been carried to England for such letters to come from them, as the siege had not lasted one month. "I will tell you what I imagine," said the viscount: "this Amerigot is a cunning fellow, and the moment he perceived we intended to besiege him, he sent a person to England to request such letters might be written as these now before you, which I shall obey or not as I please." Upon this the messengers were introduced again, and the viscount told them to take back word that he was a subject of the King of France, and had been ordered thither by him: "In consequence, my fair sirs," he continued, "I shall strictly obey the commands I have received, and loyally acquit myself of my duty; of course, then, I shall not move hence until I have possession of the fort and garrison, which now holds out against me and my companions."

The squire and the herald then took their leave, by no means contented with the message they had received. "We have had ill-success," said the squire,[j] "we must wait on the Duke of Berry." "Yes, he is lord of the whole country," said Derby, "and if he will order the viscount to decamp he must do so, for he dare not disobey him." They went accordingly to the duke, who when he received the letters read them twice over, and then gave such courteous answers that both were satisfied; for he said, from his affection to his cousins, he would do all in his power to comply with their request; he therefore exerted himself to have the siege of La Roche de Vendais raised, and wrote to the viscount to this effect, engaging that if Amerigot Marcel were left in quiet possession of his fort, he should not hereafter molest the country, and that he should make reparation to the King of France for having offended him. The viscount, on receiving this intimation, said to his companions, "Gentlemen, we shall never have peace, since the Duke of Berry supports Amerigot; the duke commands me to raise the siege the instant I have read this letter; but, by my faith, I will do no such thing."

I must now relate what happened to Amerigot, and to his

[j] This squire's name was Thomas Cherburg; he was attached to the household of the Duke of Lancaster.

fort. Amerigot had a quick imagination, and concluding from the continuance of the siege that the letters from the King of England and the Duke of Lancaster had failed, he thought of another expedient, which was to leave his castle, and ride night and day to the garrisons of Perigord, and other places, to seek succor from other pillagers, and entice them by fair speeches to enter Auvergne for the sake of plunder, and then to advance some morning or evening to La Roche de Vendais, and capture the knights and squires before it, which would bring them more than 100,000 francs for their ransoms, without counting smaller articles of pillage. He explained his whole plan to his uncle, Guyot du Sel, and asked his opinion. Guyot replied that he very much approved of it. "Well, uncle," said Amerigot, "since you approve I will undertake it, only I must beg that during my absence you never sally out of the castle, nor open the barriers." "It shall be so," answered Guyot: "we will remain shut up here until we hear from you." Within three days after Amerigot left the castle attended only by a page, and without the besiegers being aware of his absence. The castle continued to be assaulted as usual, and on one occasion Guyot du Sel, forgetful of his promise to Amerigot, was induced to sally forth, when he was surprised by an ambuscade, and obliged to surrender the place. News of the loss of La Roche de Vendais was carried to Amerigot Marcel as he was raising troops to break up the siege, and on learning that it was occasioned by an imprudent sally of Guyot du Sel, he exclaimed, "Ah, the old traitor! By St. Marcel, if I had him here I would slay him; he has disgraced me and all my companions; this misfortune can never be recovered."

Amerigot Marcel was indeed sadly cast down; he knew not from whom to ask advice, nor whether to return to Auvergne or to go to Bordeaux, send for his wife, and have his fortune brought thither by little at a time. If he had followed this plan, he would have done well; but he acted otherwise, and, as the event will show, suffered for it. It is thus Fortune treats her favorites; when she has raised them to the highest pitch of her wheel, she suddenly plunges them in the dirt—witness Amerigot Marcel. The foolish fellow was worth, as was believed in Auvergne, more than 100,000 francs in money, which he lost in one day, together with his life. I therefore say that Dame Fortune played him one of her tricks, which she has played to several before, and she will do the same to many after him. In his tribulation, Amerigot bethought himself of a cousin he had in Auvergne, a squire, by name Tournemine, to whom he resolved to apply and ask for advice. This he did, and attended only by one page entered the castle of his cousin, with whom he thought to meet with a good reception, but he was disappointed; for his cousin immediately arrested him, and shortly after he was conveyed to Paris, where his head was cut off, and his four quarters affixed over four different gates. Such was the sad end of Amerigot Marcel; I know not what became of his wife, or of his wealth. I have dwelt very long on his actions, that I might illustrate his life and death; for, in such a history as this, both good and bad actions must be spoken of, that they may serve as an excitement or warning in times to come. Had Amerigot turned his mind to virtue he would have done much good, for he was an able man-at-arms, and of great courage; but having acted in a different manner, he came to a disgraceful death.

We will now return to the noble enterprise which the knights of France and other countries had undertaken against Africa, and continue our narrative from the place where we left off.

It was at the island of Comino[k] that the knights assembled after encountering the great storm in the Gulf of Lyons, to wait for those who had separated from the fleet, as that island was but thirty miles from Africa. They remained there nine days, and then reëmbarked on board their galleys with a good will to meet their enemies, the Saracens. The sea was now calm and the weather fine; it was a pleasure to see the rowers force their vessels through its smooth surface, which seemed to delight in bearing these Christians to the shores of the infidels. Late in the evening the Christians saw the town of Africa; everyone was rejoiced at the sight, and not without cause, as they had in part accomplished the object of their voyage. The Saracens, who observed them from the town, were astonished at the number of vessels which were coming to be-

---

[k] In a former passage this is called Commeres, and in some printed and MS. editions it is called Conimbres and Cominieres. In all probability it answers to Cuminum, formerly called Hephestia, a small island in the Mediterranean, between Gozo and Malta, belonging to the Knights of Malta.

siege them; however, they were not cast down, for they knew the place was strong, well fortified, and plentifully stored with artillery and provisions. On first noticing the fleet, the Saracens, according to custom, sounded a number of bells in the towers to alarm the country. There were encamped, near the town, a large body of barbarians and infidels, whom the kings of Tunis and Bugia had sent thither to defend the coast.

As I, John Froissart, the author of these chronicles, never was in Africa, I sought all the information I could from those knights and squires who had been on this expedition, and made several journeys to Calais to learn the truth of all that had passed. The town of Africa was reported to me to be in the form of a bow, like Calais, extending its arms toward the sea; wonderfully strong, and surrounded with high walls at proper distances. The entrance of the harbor was defended by a tower larger than the rest, on which was placed a bricolle.[1] When the Christians approached the harbor, the walls of the town seemed hung with cloths or tapestry similar in appearance to the coverlets of beds. They cast anchor about one league from the port, rejoicing that, through God's pleasure, they had so far succeeded as to have the town of Africa now before them. The Saracens this night held a council as to their future proceedings; when, by advice of an ancient lord, named Bellius, of great influence among them, it was determined to avoid all general engagements with the Christians, and remain quietly in their quarters while they landed and encamped.

The next morning the Christians entered the port of Africa, and took up their quarters. The Duke of Bourbon, as commander-in-chief, lodged in the centre of his army. The device of his banner, powdered over with fleurs-de-lys, was a figure of the Virgin Mary in white, seated in the centre, and an escutcheon of Bourbon at her feet; and all the great lords who accompanied him were quartered on the right and left. When the Christians were encamped, it was necessary for them to be careful of the provisions they had brought, for they could not venture to forage in the country, nor even collect wood or boughs for huts; they, therefore, kept their provisions on board the vessels, and there were boats continually employed

[1] A bricolle, according to Du Cange, was a machine to throw stones—a sort of sling.

in bringing different articles for them as they were needed. Moreover, the inhabitants of the neighboring islands, such as Sicily and others, exerted themselves to supply them with all they wanted.

You must know, that these infidels, the Saracens, had for a long time been menaced by the Genoese, and had made preparation accordingly. The better to resist them they assembled on the present occasion the most experienced warriors from the kingdoms of Bugia, Morocco, and Tunis. They took advantage of a large and thick wood in their rear, to avoid danger from ambuscades or skirmishes on that side. According to estimate, they amounted to about 30,000 archers, and 10,000 horse, and they received continually supplies of fresh provisions which were brought on the backs of camels.

The second day after the Christians had landed, the Saracens about dawn came to attack the camp; indeed, during the whole of this siege the Christians were never quiet: for every night and morning the camp was attacked by the enemy.

Among the Saracens was a young knight, by name Agadinquor Oliferne, excellently mounted on a beautiful courser, which he managed as he willed, and which, when he galloped, seemed to fly with him. From his gallantry, he showed he was a good man-at-arms; and when he rode abroad he had with him three javelins well feathered and pointed, which he dexterously flung according to the custom of his country. He was completely armed in black, and had a kind of white napkin wrapped round his head. His seat on horseback was graceful, and from the vigor and gallantry of his actions the Christians judged he was excited thereto by his affection to a young lady of the country. True it is, he most sincerely loved the daughter of the King of Tunis, who, according to the report of some Genoese merchants who had seen her, was very handsome. During the siege this knight performed some handsome feats of arms to testify his love.

The Saracens within the town of Africa were anxious to know on what pretence the Christians had come with so large an army to make war upon them; and they resolved to send a person who could speak Genoese to ascertain. The Christians told the messenger, that they were come to revenge the injuries which the Saracens had done to their God and faith;

and that to effect this, they would exert themselves to the utmost of their power. Shortly after this message, the Saracens determined in council to remain quiet for seven or eight days, and when the Christians should think themselves in perfect security to fall upon their camp like a deluge. This plan was adopted; and the ninth evening, a little before midnight, they secretly armed their men and marched silently in a compact body toward the Christian camp. They had proposed making a severe attack on the opposite quarter to the main guard; and they would no doubt have succeeded in this mischievous endeavor, if God had not watched over and preserved them by miracles.

As the Saracens were approaching they saw before them a company of ladies dressed in white, one of whom, their leader, was incomparably more beautiful than the rest, and bore in front a white flag, having a vermilion cross in the centre; and at this vision they were so greatly terrified that they lost all strength and inclination to proceed.

The Genoese cross-bows, as I heard, had brought with them a dog from beyond sea, but whence no one could tell, nor did he belong to any person in particular. This dog had been very useful to them, for the Saracens never came to skirmish, but by his noise he awakened the army; in consequence of which they called him "the dog of our Lady." This night the dog was not idle, but made a louder noise than usual; so that when the Saracens were approaching, the Christians were prepared to receive them.

By an exact account, the siege lasted sixty-one days, during which many were the skirmishes before the town and at the barriers. The Saracens, however, were well defended, for the flower of the infidel chivalry was in the town. Night and day the two parties studied how they could most effectually annoy each other. At length the Saracens resolved to send a challenge to the Christians, offering a combat, ten of their men against ten Christians. Most persons in the Christian army were loud in praise of this offer, except the Lord de Coucy, who said, "Hold your tongues, you youngsters; I see no advantage in this combat for many reasons: one is, that ten noble and distinguished gentlemen are about to fight with ten Saracens. How do we know whether the opponents are gentlemen; they may, if they choose, bring to the combat ten varlets or knaves, and if they are defeated, what is the gain?" But, notwithstanding this speech, the Lord de Coucy armed himself with the rest, and went in good array to meet the Saracens. The challenge was accepted, and at the time the whole army was ordered to be drawn up in proper order; so that if the Saracens had formed any bad designs, they might be prepared to meet them. The ten knights and squires appointed to engage were advanced on the plain waiting for their opponents, but they came not; for, when they saw the Christians so handsomely drawn out, they were afraid to approach, though they were thrice their numbers. This was the hottest day they felt; it was so entirely oppressive, that the most active among them were almost stifled in their armor, and yet they remained, expecting the ten Saracens; but in vain, for they never heard one word from them. The army was then ordered forward to attack the town; which it did, and gained by storm the first enclosure; but no one inhabited that part, and the Christians paid dear for an inconsiderable advantage: for the heat of the sun and its reflection on the sands, added to the fatigue of fighting which lasted until evening, caused the death of several valiant knights and squires. Thus was the siege of Africa continued. To say the truth, this was a very great enterprise, and those who engaged in it showed much courage and perseverance in continuing the siege in so unhealthy a climate, after the great losses they had suffered, without assistance from anyone. But we must now leave the affairs of Africa to speak of the handsome feasts which at this time were given in London.

## CHAPTER IV

Tournament at Smithfield—Return of the French from the Siege of Africa—Death of Count d'Armagnac, also of Count Gaston of Foix—The Viscount de Chatelbon Declared Heir of Foix—Meeting of the Lords of France and England at Amiens to Negotiate a Peace—The King of England Waits the Determination at Dover—Sir Peter de Craon Attempts to Murder the Constable of France—His Wonderful Escape—Sir Peter de Craon Pursued in All Directions—Secretly Protected by the Duke of Brittany—The King of France Declares War Upon the Duke—A Strange Encounter in the Forest of Mans—The King Becomes Deranged in Intellect—Is Cured by Master William de Harseley.

THE King of England and his three uncles had received the fullest information of the splendid feasts and entertainments made for Queen Isabella's public entry into Paris; and in imitation of it, they ordered grand tournaments and feasts to be held in the city of London, where sixty knights should be accompanied by sixty noble ladies richly ornamented and dressed. The sixty knights were to tilt for two days; that is to say, on the Sunday after Michaelmas Day, and the Monday following, in the year of grace 1390. They were to set out at two o'clock in the afternoon from the Tower of London with their ladies, and parade through the streets, down Cheapside, to a large square called Smithfield. There they were to wait on the Sunday the arrival of any foreign knights who might be desirous of tilting; and this feast of the Sunday was called the challengers'.

The same ceremonies were to take place on the Monday, and the sixty knights to be prepared for tilting courteously, with blunted lances, against all comers. The prize for the best knight of the opponents was a rich crown of gold, that for the tenants of the lists a very rich golden clasp. They were to be given to the most gallant tilter, according to the judgment of the ladies who should be present with the Queen of England, and the great barons, as spectators. On Tuesday the tournaments were to be continued by squires against others of the same rank who wished to oppose them. The prize for the opponents was a courser saddled and bridled, and for the tenants of the lists a falcon. Accordingly when Sunday came, about three o'clock, there paraded from the Tower of London, which is situated in the square of St. Catherine, on the banks of the Thames, sixty barbed coursers ornamented for the tournament, and on each was mounted a squire of honor. Then came sixty ladies of rank mounted on palfreys most elegantly and richly dressed, following each other, everyone leading a knight with a silver chain, completely armed for tilting; and in this procession they moved on through the streets of London, attended by numbers of minstrels and trumpets, to Smithfield. The Queen of England and her ladies and damsels had already arrived, also the King. When the ladies who led the knights reached the square, the servants were ready to assist them to dismount from the palfreys, and conduct them to the apartments prepared for them. The knights remained until the squires of honor had dismounted and brought them their coursers, which having mounted, they had their helmets laced on, and prepared themselves in all points for the tilt. When the tournament began everyone exerted himself to the utmost, many were unhorsed, and many more lost their helmets. The jousting continued, with great courage and perseverance, until night put an end to it. The company then retired, and when supper time was come the lords and ladies attended. The prize for the opponents at the tournament was adjudged, by the ladies, lords, and heralds, to the Count d'Ostrevant, who far eclipsed all who had tilted that day; that for the tenants was given to a gallant knight of England called Sir Hugh Spencer.

On the morrow, Tuesday, the tournament was renewed by the squires, who tilted until night in the presence of the King, Queen, and all the nobles. The supper was as before at the bishop's palace, and the dancing lasted until daybreak. On Wednesday the tournament was continued by all knights and squires indiscriminately. The remainder of the week was spent in feasting, and the King conferred the Order of the Garter on Count d'Ostrevant—a circumstance at which the King of France and many of his people were much annoyed.

To return to the siege of Africa. You have before heard what pains the Christians took to conquer the town of Africa. The siege still continued, although after the before-mentioned loss on the part of the Christians little advantage was gained, and the men-at-arms were greatly discouraged, in consequence of which many began to murmur. Moreover, there was a rumor current in the Christian camp that the Genoese were treating with the Saracens to betray and deliver up to them the remainder of the army. So that, after remaining sixty days before the town of Africa, they broke up the siege and set sail from that country in sight of the Saracens. When the Christian fleet sailed from Africa all crossed the sea, but did not disembark at the same port. Part met with heavy tempests, which put them in great danger. Most, however, returned to Genoa. In France religious processions were being made for their safety, for they knew not what was become of them, having had no intelligence since their departure. The ladies of Coucy, Sully, and the Dauphiness of Auvergne were in the greatest anxiety for their lords, and much rejoiced at seeing them. The King also was well pleased at their return, and after asking them many questions said, "If we manage to restore union to the Church, and establish a firm peace between us and England, we should very much like to lead a great army to Barbary to exalt the Christian faith, confound the infidels, and acquit the souls of our predecessors, King Philip of happy memory, and King John our grandfather; for both of them put on the vermilion cross to pass the sea for the Holy Land; and they would have done so if violent wars had not nearly overturned their kingdom. Now, if we can restore peace to the Church, and lengthen our truce with England, we are resolved to undertake this expedition."

About two years after the marriage of the daughter of the Duke of Lancaster to Don Henry, Prince of Galicia, King John of Castille departed this life and was buried in the city of Burgos.*a* On this event the great barons and prelates of the realm assembled and declared their intention of having

---

*a* King John of Castille died August 24, 1390, aged thirty-two. His death is generally reported to have occurred from the injuries he sustained in a fall from his horse.

for their King the young Prince of Galicia. This was done, and the prince was crowned in the ninth year of his age; his queen being six years older. Thus the daughter of the Duke of Lancaster, by the Lady Constance, became Queen of Castille, and of all the possessions of Don Pedro, Don Henry, and Don John, excepting those parts which had been assigned to the Duke and Duchess of Lancaster for their joint lives.

About this time the Count d'Armagnac, who had gone on his expedition into Lombardy, died; his body was embalmed, put into a coffin, and afterward buried in the cathedral church of Rodez; and not very long after him died likewise the noble and gallant Count de Foix. I will tell you how it happened. Of all the pleasures of the world the count took most delight in the chase, and was always well provided with hounds of all sorts, having never less than 1,600. At this season he was hunting in the forest of Sauveterre, on the road to Pampeluna, in Navarre, not far distant from Orthes. The day he died he had, in the forenoon, been hunting a bear, and it was late in the evening when he was taken and cut up. His attendants asked where he would dine. "At the inn in Rion," he said, "and in the cool of the evening we will ride to Orthes." His orders were obeyed. The count and his companions rode at a foot's pace to the village of Rion, and dismounted at the inn. The count went to his chamber, which he found ready strewed with rushes and green leaves; the walls were hung with boughs newly cut, for perfume and coolness, as the weather was marvellously hot. When seated, the count conversed with Sir Espaign du Lyon on the dogs that had hunted best; during which conversation his bastard son, Sir Evan, and Sir Peter Cabestan, entered the apartment, as the table had been there spread. He called for water to wash, and two squires advanced, Raymonet de Lasne and Raymonet de Copane. Ernaudon d'Espaign took the silver basin, and another knight, called Sir Thibaut, the napkin. The count rose from his seat, and stretched out his hands to wash; but no sooner had his fingers touched the cold water, than he changed color from an oppression at his heart, and his legs failing him, fell back on his seat, exclaiming, "I am a dead man! Lord God have mercy on me!" He never spoke after this, though he did not die immediately. The knights present and his son were much terrified; they carried him gently in their arms to another chamber, and laid him on a bed, covering him well, for they thought he was only chilled. The two squires who had brought the water in the basin, to free themselves of the charge of having poisoned him, said, " There is the water. We have already drunk of it, and will now in your presence;" which they did to the satisfaction of all. They then put into his mouth bread, water, and spices, with other comforting things, but to no purpose, for in less than half an hour he was dead. God out of his grace was merciful to him.

The knights seeing Evan lamenting and wringing his hands, said to him, " Evan, the business is over. You have lost your lord and father. We know that he loved you in preference to all others. Take care of yourself. Mount your horse; ride and gain possession of Orthes, and the treasures within it, before anyone knows of our lord's death." Sir Evan made them a low reverence, and replied, " Gentlemen, I return you many thanks for the friendship you now show me, and I trust I shall not forget it; but tell me what are my lord's tokens, or I shall not gain admittance into the castle." " You say true," said the knights; "take them." The tokens were a small golden ring the count wore on his finger, and a little knife with which he sometimes cut his meat at table. These were the tokens the porter of the castle at Orthes was acquainted with, and had he not seen them he would never have opened the gate. Sir Evan left the inn at Rion with only two servants, and rode in haste to Orthes, where nothing was known of the count's death. He spoke to no one as he passed through the streets, and in coming to the castle the porter asked, " Where is my lord?" " At Rion," answered the knight, " and he has sent me to seek for some things that are in his chamber. Look, here are his tokens, his ring and his knife." The porter knew them well, and at once admitted Evan, who having passed the gate said to the porter, " Thou art a dead man if thou obey me not." The porter, in alarm, asked the cause. " My lord and father is dead," said the knight, " and I wish to gain possession of his treasure before anyone knows of it." Sir Evan knew well where his treasure was deposited; but he had three pairs of strong doors to open, and with separate keys, before he could gain admittance, and these keys he could not find.

Now it happened, after he left Rion, that the chaplain of the count, Sir Nicholas de l'Escalle, found a little steel key hanging to a piece of silk, which the count wore over his shirt, and recognized it to be the key of a small steel casket, in which the other keys were kept; and as it was in vain for Sir Evan to try to enter the treasury without this key, the chaplain hastened with it to the castle, where he found Sir Evan very melancholy, and not knowing what to do. While he was in this distress, and Sir Nicholas on the road to assist him, it was known at Orthes that the Count de Foix was dead. This was very afflicting news, for he was greatly beloved by all ranks. The whole town was in motion: some said, " We saw Sir Evan ride up the town toward the castle, he seemed much distressed; without doubt, what we have heard is true." As the men of Orthes were thus conversing, Sir Nicholas came up, to whom they said, "Sir Nicholas, how fares my lord? they tell us he is dead; is it true?" "No," replied the chaplain, " he is not dead, but most dangerously ill, and I am come to seek for something that may do him good." On saying which he passed on to the castle. The townsmen, however, began to suspect that the count was dead, and resolved to keep watch at the castle, and send privately to Rion to ascertain the truth of the case. Sir Evan de Foix soon found what the townsmen were about, and that the death of the count was known; he said, therefore, to the chaplain, " Sir Nicholas, I have failed in my attempt; I must humble myself to these men, for force will be of no avail." Sir Evan then went to a tower near the gate, which had a window looking over the bridge to a square where the townsmen were assembled, and having opened the window, he said, " Good people of Orthes, I know well why you are thus assembled and sorrowful. You have good cause for it, and I entreat you most earnestly not to be displeased if I have hastened to take possession of this castle, for I mean nothing but what is just. I shall open the gates for your free admittance; I never thought of closing them against you." The chief among the townsmen answered Sir Evan, " You have well spoken, and we are satisfied. It is our intention that you keep this castle, and all that is within it. Should the Viscount de Chatelbon, your cousin, who is heir to the territory of Béarn, and the nearest relation to our late lord, claim anything belonging to this castle we will strenuously defend you and your brother Sir Gracien in your rights."

This same day the body of the count was put into a coffin and brought to Orthes. It was borne with its face uncovered to the Church of the Cordeliers, when it was openly embalmed and put into a leaden coffin, in which it was left until the day of its interment. It was handsomely watched, for there were burning continually around it, night and day, twenty-four large wax tapers, which were held by as many varlets.

The death of the count was now public in various places, and more were sorry than rejoiced at it. The King of France sent at once the Bishop of Noyon, and the Lord de la Riviere, into the country of Foix, to make arrangements for taking possession of that inheritance; and the Viscount de Chatelbon, on hearing the intelligence, instantly set out for Béarn, and arrived at Orthes.

Great were the numbers who attended the funeral of Gaston Count de Foix, the last of the name, on Monday, October 12th, in the year of our Lord 1391. In addition to barons and knights there were three bishops present. The church was splendidly illuminated, and during mass four knights displayed in front of the altar the emblazoned banners of Foix and Béarn. Every part of the obsequies was most honorably and magnificently performed according to the custom of the country; and when this was over, the body of the count was taken from the leaden coffin, enwrapped with a new and handsome waxed cloth, and buried in front of the grand altar in the choir of the church. Of him there is an end: God pardon his sins.

As soon as the funeral was over, the Viscount de Chatelbon sent commissioners to the French, to demand possession of the succession which had fallen to him by the death of the Count de Foix, and afterward to the same purport to the King of France, his commissioners in both cases being Sir Roger d'Espaign and Sir Espaign du Lyon. But we must just say a word respecting the King of France and the Duke of Brittany.

The great hatred which subsisted between the Duke of Brittany and Sir Oliver de Clisson, constable of France, has been repeatedly mentioned in this history. The duke on account of this hatred was very backward in his duties to the Crown of France, and when he could, absolutely refused to pay them. He knew he was acting wrong; but still he persisted in this conduct, sending secretly to England for men-at-arms and archers, whom he placed in forts, giving out that he was expecting war to be made upon him, but his subjects could not guess from what quarter. The Duchess of Burgundy alone knew the real state of his affairs, and his intentions. These hatreds and jealousies kept daily increasing; and although the Duke of Brittany went to Paris, and paid his homage to the King, I will not pretend to say that it was done from the heart; for, on his return to Brittany, very little change was observed in his conduct. At length, however, it was resolved on the part of the French, that the Duke of Brittany should be invited to come to Tours, where the King of France should give him a meeting, attended only by the dukes of Berry and Burgundy and one or two members of his council. A day was fixed for the meeting; and the duke, after keeping them waiting a fortnight, at last arrived, when negotiations began on both sides. Ambassadors also came from England, with a view to promote peace.

To return to the commissioners of Béarn and Foix. Sir Roger d'Espaign and Sir Espaign du Lyon acquitted themselves handsomely and satisfactorily, in regard to the business of the Viscount de Chatelbon, and practised so successfully with the Court of France, that he was declared heir and successor to the Count de Foix, by letters patent from the King; the substance of these letters, as I learned from creditable persons, being as follows: "We, Charles by the grace of God, King of France, order and command our reverend Father in God, the Bishop of Noyon, and our Knight and Chamberlain the Lord de la Riviere, to allow the Viscount de Chatelbon, heir of Foix and Béarn, to have peaceable possession and enjoyment of the same, and of all dependencies thereto belonging, on condition that he first pay into your hands the sum of 60,000 francs. In addition, we expect payment of 20,000 francs for the expenses of your journey to and from the country of Foix on this occasion; saving and reserving that Sir Evan and Sir Gracien de Foix, bastard sons of the late Gaston Count de Foix, of happy memory, have a reasonable share of the movable property and inheritances of their deceased father, according to the discretion and advice of Sir

Roger d'Espaign, the Viscount de Bruniquel, Sir Raymond de Châteauneuf, and the Lord de Corasse. And, should any demur arise, either on the part of the four knights to whom we have entrusted this business, or from obstinacy and rebellion on the part of the Viscount de Chatelbon, we annul and declare all treaties we have entered into void and of no effect. In testimony whereof, we have given these letters under our seal, in the city of Tours, this fifteenth day of December, in the twelfth year of our reign."

We will now return to the Duke of Brittany.

The negotiations at Tours still continued; but the duke gave the King and his council a great deal of trouble, for he would not abate any of his pretensions, and things remained in this state upward of three months, without any progress being made in the treaties. At length it was proposed, as a means of reconciliation, that a marriage should take place between the son of the Duke of Brittany and a daughter of the King of France; and, as John of Brittany had a son, a similar connection should be formed with the daughter of the Duke of Brittany. These articles being agreed upon, this business was thus brought to a conclusion, and the duke restored to the friendship of the King of France and his uncles. However, the hatred between him and Sir Oliver de Clisson still continued.

We will now speak of Sir Roger d'Espaign and Sir Espaign du Lyon, and say how they prospered on their departure from Tours to Toulouse, where the Bishop of Noyon and the Lord de la Riviere were waiting for them. Their arrival at Toulouse gave great pleasure, for they had been long expected. They instantly waited on the French commissioners to show the papers which they had received from the King, and which fully explained the successful issue of their journey. The Bishop of Noyon and the Lord de la Riviere entertained them well, and showed they were much rejoiced that the succession, with all its dependencies, of the Count de Foix devolved on the Viscount de Chatelbon, according to the tenure and form whereby the Count Gaston had held them, and in the manner detailed in the written documents. After considering the business they thought it advisable that Sir Roger d'Espaign and Sir Espaign du Lyon, who had taken so much pains about it, should wait on the viscount and the councils of Foix and Béarn, to inform them what had been agreed upon, that all things might be regularly managed to bring the whole to a happy conclusion. The knights consented to the proposal, and having refreshed themselves two days in Toulouse, set out for St. Gaudens. It happened that the viscount was just then at a beautiful castle at the entrance of Béarn called Pau, where they found him. He was happy to see them, and much more so when he learned that the King of France desisted from taking possession of the country of Foix.

I believe my readers as well as myself will think I have said enough respecting the affairs of Foix and Béarn. I will therefore leave them and enter on other matters, for it would take up too much time to pursue in detail everything that passed there, on the return of the two knights from France. To conclude, the Viscount de Chatelbon[b] was acknowledged Count de Foix and Béarn, on the same terms on which Count Gaston de Foix, of happy memory, had held them; and he received the homage of all his vassals. He satisfied his two cousins, Sir Evan and Sir Gracien, by the handsome allotment he gave them of the inheritances and movables of their father, and paid at once to the commissioners from France the mortgage that was on Foix. Before all these things were accomplished summer was far advanced, and the Bishop of Noyon remained at Toulouse with the Lord de la Riviere; for they would not depart till everything was completely settled to the honor and profit of the Crown, according to the instructions they had received.

We will now speak of a grand assembly of the lords of France and England which was held in the city of Amiens, to treat for a final peace between the two countries at mid-lent, in the year of grace 1391. Great preparations were made for the arrival of the lords; and in particular those made for the King, his three uncles, and many of the great barons and prelates, were very sumptuous. Other lords were desirous to make a figure, for it was currently reported and believed that

[b] The heir to the estates of Foix and Béarn is, in some places in the Chronicles, styled the Viscount de Chatelbon, and in others, the Viscount de Chateaubon. He was acknowledged as sovereign of Béarn at Orthes, July 5, 1393. His wife was the only daughter of Don John, King of Arragon. Sir Gracien de Foix married Isabella de la Cerda, a daughter of the King of Castille.

King Richard of England intended being there in person; however, he did not come. That he had the intention of being there was certain, for he came as far as Dover with his three uncles of Lancaster, York, and Gloucester, meaning to cross the sea with them. Many councils were held at Dover to debate whether the King should proceed further or not, and all things having been considered, it was decided that he should remain in the castle at Dover, and the Duke of Gloucester with him; the dukes of Lancaster and York, the earls of Huntingdon and Derby, Sir Thomas Percy, the bishops of London and Durham, and others of the King's council prepared to cross the Channel; and when the day approached for the meeting at Amiens, these lords set out from Calais together, more than 200 in number. The King of France had given orders that during the time the conference should last all the expenses of the English in coming to and returning from Amiens to Calais, should be defrayed by his treasury. In company with the dukes of York and Lancaster was their niece, daughter of their sister and the Lord de Coucy; she was styled Duchess of Ireland, having been married to the duke so called.

It had been ordered by the King and council of France that the English lords who were coming to Amiens to arrange a solid peace should be received with the greatest honors, and that the four dukes then at Amiens, viz., the dukes of Touraine, Berry, Burgundy, and Bourbon, should ride out of the town to meet and bid them welcome, which they accordingly did. At the entrance of the city the honors paid to the English were increased, for the Duke of Lancaster rode between the dukes of Berry and Burgundy, and when their horses moved it was but a foot's pace; in this manner they continued to the palace of the bishop, where the King and the Duke of Touraine were. Having dismounted they ascended the steps, and the dukes of Berry and Burgundy, taking the English dukes by the hands, led them toward the King, the other lords following. When in the King's presence the three dukes who supported the uncles of the King of England, and the other French lords, cast themselves on their knees; but the two English dukes remained as they were, only gently inclining their heads in honor of the King, who instantly advanced, took them by the hand, and entered into a friendly conversation with them. It had been strictly forbidden by the King and council that any outrages whatever should be committed during the holding of these conferences, under pain of death, or any quarrelling or riot with the English during their stay in the city of Amiens.

All knights and squires were commanded by the King, under pain of incurring his indignation, not to talk of or propose any deeds of arms to any knight or squire from England, but to treat them with the utmost civility and attention when they should meet in the fields, the palace, or in church—that no pages nor varlets of any French lord should cause riot or quarrels in the inns under pain of losing their heads, and that whatever the English knights or squires might ask for should immediately be given them—that no innkeeper should demand payment for meat or drink, or other common necessaries; it was also forbidden any knight or squire of France to be out at night without a torch, but the English might do so if they pleased; and if any Englishman was found on the roads, or in any other place, having lost his way, he should be courteously conducted to where he lodged. Four guards of 1,000 men each were stationed at the four squares of Amiens, and should there be a fire during the night, these guards were not to move on any account from their posts; but when the fire-bell rang, those appointed to that duty were to hasten to extinguish the flames.

It was likewise ordered that no knight or squire should advance from his place to speak with the King unless called, or spoken to by his Majesty; and that during the time the English barons were in the King's presence no knights or squires should converse together, nor address the English. It was commanded under heavy penalties that no innkeeper or others steal or put aside out of avarice any of the bows or arrows of the English; but if, out of courtesy, the English thought proper to give any to them, they might accept such presents.

You must know that these orders and regulations were formed with great deliberation, to do the more honor to the English who were come to negotiate a peace, and proclaimed several times that they might be strictly attended to. Every, day conferences were held with the English lords, with scarcely any intermission during a fortnight. They stayed at Amiens however without coming to any conclusion, for the difference in their demands was so great. The French would have Calais razed to the ground, so that it never again should be habitable; but the English would not listen to this, for the commons of England loved Calais more than any town in the world; saying that as long as they are masters of Calais, they carry the keys of France at their girdle. Still, however great were the differences of the lords of France and England on those matters, they nevertheless separated in good humor on both sides. The King of France entertained the English lords three times most magnificently at dinner in the episcopal palace; and the dukes of Touraine, Berry, Burgundy, and Bourbon, the Lord de Coucy, and the Count de St. Pol, gave each a dinner to the English commissioners. Indeed, whatever the English wanted was delivered to them free of cost by clerks who were appointed to take account of all things they had, and refer to the King's exchequer for payment. The conferences respecting a peace continued to be held at Amiens with great perseverance and attention on both sides; and it was indeed wonderful why the matter failed, for the dukes of Burgundy and Lancaster were much in earnest to bring it to a happy conclusion, reserving always what was contained in their private instructions, which they dare not go beyond.

The French perceiving the English were obstinate in their terms, in order to soften them, offered, if they would consent to raze Calais, the peaceable possession of what they held in Aquitaine, with nine bishoprics independent of all other jurisdictions, and payment of 1,400,000 francs within three years. To this the Duke of Lancaster and his council replied, " Be assured that my brother York and myself will use every diligence to bring this matter to a conclusion, according to your wishes, but we dare not mention to the English what you demand concerning Calais." The King of France, as well as his uncles, was tolerably well satisfied with this answer, and said that if when returned to England they could exert themselves to obtain peace, a trifle on their part should not prevent it, for the war had lasted too long, and caused numberless misfortunes to both countries. During the assembly the commissioners bethought themselves that as the truce between England and France would expire upon St. John Baptist's Day, they might prolong it, for themselves and their allies, for one year without blame. With regard to the determination which might be given by Parliament to their proposals, they desired to send two knights[c] to England to bring back the final answer. I was told, and really believe it, from the appearance I observed, that the King of France was very desirous of peace; for there were reports current throughout France that Amurat had invaded with a powerful army of Turks the kingdom of Hungary. This intelligence had been brought to the elder Lord Boucicaut, marshal of France, and Sir John de Carouge, who were lately returned from Greece, and parts of Turkey. The King of France, when younger, had an anxious wish to undertake an expedition against Amurat, and recover Armenia, which the Turks had seized from King Leon, who was then present at the conferences at Amiens; he had stated his grievances to the dukes of Lancaster and York, who knew him well, for he had been to England to offer his mediation for peace between the two countries, when the King of France was encamped near Sluys.

The King of France, weighing the invasion of the Turks in his mind, and his former promises of support to the King of Armenia, spoke thus to the Duke of Lancaster when he took his leave: "Fair cousin, if peace shall be established between us and the King of England, we may undertake an expedition to Turkey, to assist the King of Armenia and the Emperor of Constantinople, whom Amurat presses very hard, and recover Armenia from the hands of the Turks. They tell us that Amurat is a man of great valor and enterprise, but of a sect contrary to our faith, which he daily oppresses; we ought, therefore, to unite against him, and I entreat, fair cousin, that you will consider of it, and do everything you can to promote this expedition when returned to England." The Duke of Lancaster promised to comply with this request, and to exert himself so strongly in the matter, that the effects would soon be apparent. The conferences at Amiens lasted fifteen days, and the lords of England were the first to separate, carry-

[c] The names of these two knights were the Lord de Châteaumorant, and Sir Taubin de Cantemerle.

ing with them the outlines of a treaty to lay before the King of England and his council. The Duchess of Ireland bade adieu to her father, the Lord de Coucy, and accompanied her uncles on their return. All the English on their road to and from Calais, and while at Amiens, needed not to have expended a farthing unless they chose it, for the King had ordered their whole expenses to be defrayed by his officers. In company with the dukes of York and Lancaster were the two French knights who were sent to England by orders from the King of France. They all crossed the Channel to Dover, where they found the King and the Duke of Gloucester waiting for them. A grand council was held by the King and his lords on all that had passed at Amiens; the King was well pleased with what his uncles had done there, but the Duke of Gloucester, who was always against any treaty with France, declared that not any propositions for peace could be determined on till they were laid before the Parliament, which ought instantly to be summoned, and whatever measure the three estates of the realm should resolve on, that ought to be adopted, and none other.

This proposal of the Duke of Gloucester was agreed to; indeed they dared not oppose him, for he was too much in favor with the commons of England. The French knights were therefore told that they must continue their journey to London, otherwise they could not obtain any answer; to this they willingly consented, and set out with the King and his lords, the greater part of whom went straight to London, but the King turned off at Dartford, and took the road to Eltham, where he had a handsome palace; he stayed there some little time with the Queen, and then they came to Shene together, and thence to Windsor, where the knights received an answer; but before I say what that answer was, I must speak of the King of France.

After the conferences at Amiens, the King of France, unfortunately, but through his own imprudence, was seized with a burning fever, for which he was advised to change the air; he was, therefore, put into a litter, and carried to Beauvais, where he remained in the bishop's palace until cured. When perfectly recovered and able to ride, he went to Gisors, at the entrance of Normandy, for the pleasure of hunting; while there he received homage of Sir Bernard d'Armagnac, brother to the count, who lately died in Italy; and about Ascension Day returned to Paris in perfect health, and fixed his residence at the hotel de St. Pol, which had been prepared for him, the Queen and the Duchess of Touraine having arrived there first. The French knights were all the time waiting for an answer in England; they had attended the Feast of St. George at Windsor, where was a brilliant company of barons and the King's uncles. The lords who had been at Amiens consulted together on the promises they had made the King of France, as well as in respect to an answer for the two knights, who were very pressing to have one; but after considering the matter they could come to no conclusion, and so the two knights were obliged to return home, having letters given to them fully explanatory of the delay, and being informed that if they or any others would return to England during the sitting of Parliament, they should receive such answer as the three estates of the kingdom should think proper to give. The King ordered all their expenses to be paid, and had them conducted to Dover, where the bailiff provided a vessel for them and their horses. By short journeys they reached Paris, delivered their letters, which were read, but I believe no great reliance was placed upon them, and in a short time there were other affairs of greater consequence at home to attend to.

About this period Sir Peter de Craon, who some while ago had fallen under the displeasure of the King of France, held frequent conversations with the Duke of Brittany on what means they could employ to put to death Sir Oliver de Clisson, whom they both hated; indeed, the duke often expressed his regret that he had not taken away his life when in his castle of Ermine, adding, he would willingly give 100,000 francs if he could once more have him in his possession. When meditating alone on this subject, Sir Peter de Craon thought of an extraordinary expedient: he resolved, whatever might be the consequence, that he would himself assassinate the constable, or have it done under his own eyes, and not attend to anything until the deed was performed. He was by no means afraid of what John de Blois or the Viscount de Rohan, who had married the constable's two daughters, could do against him, for the house of Blois was much weakened at the time. Sir

Peter, therefore, persevered in his design, urged on by that enemy who never sleeps, and who delights in the heart of the wicked man that is inclined toward him.

It is truly said, however, that a too great desire to accomplish an object clouds the understanding, and that vicious inclinations overrule virtue. Thus it happened to Sir Peter de Craon, whose eagerness to destroy the constable made him listen to the counsels of folly and madness. He had secured a safe retreat with the Duke of Brittany after the deed should be done, and the constable dead, without fear of any search being there made for him, for the duke had promised him an asylum; and should the King of France follow him with a powerful army to Brittany, in one night he might embark and sail for Bayonne, Bordeaux, or England, where he could not come after him. The English mortally hated Clisson from his great severity toward them from the time he had turned to the French. Sir Peter long brooded in silence over his intended deed. I do not know if he told it even to the Duke of Brittany. Some think he must, and others think not. I will not dwell upon surmises, but relate the facts; for I, the author of this history, was at Paris when this misfortune happened to Sir Oliver de Clisson, and ought, therefore, to be well informed from the inquiries I made respecting it. You must know that Sir Peter de Craon had a very handsome house near the churchyard of St. John, at Paris.[d] This hotel was, in his absence from the city, placed under the care of a house-steward; and, during the last Lent season, he had sent thither varlets with orders to lay in a large store of wines, and all sorts of provisions. He had likewise written to the steward to purchase armor, such as coats of mail, gauntlets, steel helmets, and other things, sufficient for forty men; and to let him know when they were ready, that he might send for them, observing the greatest secrecy possible. The steward, thinking no harm,

---

[d] Sauval, in his "Antiquités de Paris," has the following observations on the house of Sir Peter de Craon: "The street of the Mauvais-garçons, in the rue des Boucheries, took its name from a sign. With regard to the other rue des Mauvais-garçons, which leads from the rue de la Verrerie to that of la Tixeranderie, it was formerly called rue de Chartron: but when the lords de Craon built a house there, which is now a churchyard, it was called rue de Craon, to the time when Peter de Craon hid himself and his accomplices within it to assassinate Sir Oliver de Clisson. The street then changed its name and was called la rue des Mauvais-garçons. The hotel, by orders from the King, was razed to the ground, and the spot given to the churchwardens of St. John's, to enlarge their churchyard."

obeyed the orders; and Sir Peter, who resided in a handsome castle in Anjou, called Sablé, sent off there, at different times, four or more determined fellows in the most secret manner possible to his hotel at Paris. At length those bravos amounted to forty; among them were several who, had they known the business they were engaged in, would not have come; but Sir Peter took good care not to betray his secret.

About the Feast of Whitsuntide he himself came to his hotel —not in state, but as privately as his men. On his arrival he commanded the porter to admit neither man nor woman into the hotel without his special orders; and all his people were confined within the walls of the hotel until the Feast of the Holy Sacrament. You may suppose that Sir Peter had his spies fully employed in bringing him intelligence; but it was not until the eve of the feast that he found a fit opportunity to execute his scheme, which vexed him much. On the Feast of the Holy Sacrament the King of France kept an open court at the hotel de St. Pol, where he entertained all barons and lords who were in Paris. He was in high enjoyment, as was also the Queen, and the Duchess of Touraine. To add to the amusement, after dinner lists were prepared within the courts of the hotel, and young knights and squires, ready armed and mounted, came thither and jousted very gallantly. The prize for the best tilter was adjudged, by the Queen and her ladies, to Sir William de Flandres, Count de Namur. The King entertained at supper all who wished to partake of it; and afterward, dancing continued until one o'clock in the morning. When this was over, everyone returned home without guard and without suspicion. Sir Oliver de Clisson was the last, and, after bidding adieu to the King and the Duke of Touraine, he left the hotel, and found his servants and horses waiting for him in the square. There were not more than eight or ten torches, which were borne before him as he rode down the broad street of St. Catherine. Sir Peter de Craon's spies had so exerted themselves this day that he knew every particular respecting the constable—of his staying behind the rest of the company—the exact number of his horse and attendants. He had, in consequence, quitted his hotel with his men all mounted, and secretly armed; but there were not six among them who knew what his real intentions were. On advancing to the causeway, near the place of St. Catherine, he and his people lay hid there, waiting for the constable to pass.

The constable having left the street of St. Pol, turned into the great square, advancing at a foot's pace, with a torch on each side to light him, and engaged in the following conversation with one of his squires: "I am to have at dinner tomorrow my Lord of Touraine, the Lord de Coucy, and several more. Be sure and take care they have all things comfortable, and let nothing be spared." As he said these words, Sir Peter de Craon and his company advanced, and, without saying a word, fell on the constable's attendants and extinguished their torches. The constable thought at first that it was the Duke of Touraine who was playing him a trick, and cried out, "My lord, by my faith this is too bad; but I excuse it, you are so young, you make a joke of everything." At these words, Sir Peter de Craon, drawing his sword, said, "Death! death! Clisson, you must die!" "Who art thou?" said Clisson. "I am Peter de Craon, thine enemy, whom thou hast so often angered, and now thou shalt pay for it." Then calling to his people, he said, "Advance, advance!" He and his men then fell upon Sir Oliver, who was quite unarmed, except only a short cutlass, not two feet long, which, however, he drew, and with it defended himself as long as he could. His servants being quite defenceless were soon dispersed. Some of Sir Peter's men asked if they were to murder all. "Yes," he replied, "all who put themselves in a posture of defence." Sir Peter's men fully intended to murder the constable, and their master wished nothing more than to see it done; but, as I heard from some of those who had been in this attack, the moment they learned that the person they were assassinating was the constable of France, their arms became nerveless through surprise, and fear made their blows weak.

The constable defended himself tolerably well with his short cutlass; but his defence would have been of no avail if God's providence had not protected him. After some time, he was villanously struck on the back part of his head, which knocked him off his horse, and in his fall he hit against the hatch of a baker's door, who was already up attending to his business. Having heard the noise, and high words on the causeway, the baker had, fortunately for the constable, half-opened the hatch, and Sir Oliver, falling, burst it quite open, and rolled into the shop. Those on horseback could not, of course, follow him, as the entrance was neither wide enough nor high enough for them. It must be owned, for truth, that God showed great favor to the constable; for if he had not fallen exactly against the hatch, or if it had been closed, he would infallibly have lost his life, and have been trampled to death by the horses. Several imagined that the blow on his head, which unhorsed him, must have caused his death; and Sir Peter said, "Come, let us away, we have done enough; if he be not dead he can never recover from the last blow." Upon this they collected, and leaving the place at a good trot, passed the gate of St. Anthony and gained the field.

Thus was Sir Oliver left for dead at the baker's, who was much frightened when he learned that it was the constable. Sir Oliver's attendants, who, as Sir Peter de Craon's men were only bent on killing their master, were little hurt, collected together as well as they could, and, dismounting before the baker's door, entered the shop, where they found their lord severely wounded on the head, and his face covered with blood. News of this was carried to the King, at the hotel de St. Pol, just as he was getting into bed. In much alarm they said, "Ah, sire! we dare not conceal from you a shocking event that has just happened in Paris." "What event?" asked the King. "Your constable, Sir Oliver de Clisson, is murdered." "Murdered!" repeated the King. "How, and who has done it?" "Sire, that we know not; but this misfortune has befallen him hard by, in the great street of St. Catherine." "Come, light torches quickly, and I will go and see him," replied the King. The torches were soon ready and carried by varlets. The King threw only a cloak over him, and the men-at-arms and the ushers of the guard of the palace escorted him. Those who were gone to bed, on hearing what had passed, got up and followed the King, who on arriving at the baker's shop entered, but the chamberlains with the torches stayed without. The King found his constable nearly in the state he was represented to be, except that he was not dead, for his servants had stripped him to see if he had received many wounds. The first words the King said were, "Constable, how fares it with you?" "Dear sire," he replied, "but so so, and very weak."

"And who has put you in this state?" "Peter de Craon and his accomplices have traitorously, and without the smallest suspicion, attacked me." "Constable," said the King, "nothing shall ever be more severely punished than this crime. Run quickly for doctors and surgeons." These had before been sent for, and they arrived from all quarters, particularly those attached to the King's person. The King, on seeing them, requested that they would attend Sir Oliver well; and then, addressing himself to the constable, he added, "Take care of yourself, and do not think of them or any other business. They shall pay for it as if it were done to myself." On this, the King took leave and returned to his palace, when he sent at once for the provost of Paris; and as soon as he came, said to him, "Take with you a body of armed men and pursue that traitor, Peter de Craon, who has nearly murdered our constable." The provost replied, "Sire, I will do everything in my power; but what road do you suppose he has taken?"

At that time, the four principal gates of Paris were always open, night and day—a regulation which had been observed from the time the King returned from Flanders, after defeating the Flemings at the battle of Rosebecque; and when the Parisians, showing symptoms of rebellion, had their mallets taken from them. In order the more easily to chastise the Parisians, Sir Oliver de Clisson had advised the chains to be taken from across the streets, and the gates off their hinges, which had been done; and the gates had been, for the last ten years, lying against the walls, so that anyone might enter or go out of Paris at all hours.

Now, observe how the seasons repay. Sir Oliver de Clisson reaped what he had sown. Had the gates and chains remained, Sir Peter de Craon would not have dared to commit this outrage, for he could never have got out of Paris; but knowing he could set off at any hour, he was encouraged thus to disgrace himself. When he left the constable he concluded he would never recover; but it was not so, as you have heard, to his great mortification. Sir Peter quitted Paris by St. Anthony's gate about one o'clock in the morning, and, as some say, crossed the Seine at the bridge of Charenton, and continued his road to Chartres; but, according to others, after going out of Paris, he returned by the gate of St. Honoré, under Montmartre, and crossed the Seine at Ponçon. Whichever way he passed the river, he arrived at Chartres at eight o'clock in the morning, with some of the best mounted of his accomplices. On his way to Paris, he had ordered twenty horses to be in waiting for him at the house of a canon, who was a friend of his; but it had been better for him never to have known him, although the canon was ignorant of the crime he had committed. Sir Peter de Craon, on his arrival at Chartres, drank some wine, and changed horses, and then instantly departed, taking the road for Maine. He continued his journey until he came to his strong castle called Sablé, where he stopped and refreshed himself, and said he would go no further, but wait until he heard some intelligence of the constable.

On Friday, the day following the assassination, it was all the news of Paris, and everyone blamed Sir Peter de Craon. The Lord de Coucy, as soon as he heard of it, mounted his horse and rode to the constable's hotel, and the Duke of Touraine accompanied the King on his next visit. The Duke of Berry, who was at Paris at the time, seemed to make light of what had passed. I, the author of this history, was informed that if he had pleased the accident would not have happened, for it was in his power to have prevented it. The provost of Paris, with upward of sixty horse, issued out of the gate of St. Honoré, on the traces of Sir Peter de Craon. On arriving at Ponçon, to cross the Seine, he asked the bridge-keeper if anyone had passed that morning, and the answer was, "Yes, my lord, a company of about twelve horsemen; but I did not see among them any knight or person whom I knew." "And what road did they take?" demanded the provost. "That leading to Vannes," said the bridge-master. "Ah," replied the provost, "it may be they who are making for Cherbourg." Upon this they quitted the road to Chartres, following that to Cherbourg, and thus lost all traces of them.

When they had proceeded along the road to Vannes till it was dinner time, they met a knight of that country, hare-hunting; and making inquiry of him, he said that he had seen in the morning about fifteen horsemen riding over the fields, and he thought they were going to Chartres. The provost again changed his road, and arriving in the evening at Chartres, learned that Sir Peter de Craon had been at the canon's house about eight o'clock in the morning, where he had disarmed himself and changed horses. He now found that any further pursuit would be vain, as Sir Peter had got so much before him; and he, therefore, returned to Paris on Saturday.

Sir John le Barrois, also, with sixty horse, had followed after Sir Peter de Craon, at the instigation of the King and the Duke of Touraine; but they were as unsuccessful as the provost.

On Saturday morning the officers of justice, who had been searching all the villages round Paris, discovered in a hamlet about seven leagues off two men-at-arms, squires to Sir Peter de Craon, and his page, who had stopped at this village from inability or unwillingness to proceed further. They were arrested, brought back to Paris, and executed on the following Monday; before execution, however, they were led to the place where the crime had been committed, and each had his hand cut off at the wrist. They were then beheaded in the market-place, and their bodies hung on a gibbet. On the Wednesday following, Sir Peter's house-steward was executed. The canon of Chartres, at whose house Sir Peter had stopped to refresh himself and change horses, was arrested and confined in the bishop's prison. Everything he possessed was confiscated, and himself condemned to perpetual imprisonment on bread and water. No excuses he could plead for his innocence in this matter were of the smallest avail, though he bore in Chartres the character of an honest and prudent man.

Sir Peter de Craon was sadly vexed when he heard for certain that the constable was not dead, and that he had not received any wound that in six weeks' time would prevent him from mounting his horse. He, therefore, considered that it would not be safe for him to remain where he was; so, giving the charge of his castle to some of his own people, he took the road to Brittany, where he arrived without stopping, and found the duke at Susmet. The duke, on receiving Sir Peter, said to him, "You are a poor creature, who cannot slay a man when you have him in your power." "My lord," replied Sir Peter, "it was a damnable business. I believe all the devils in hell defended him, and preserved him from our blows. Upward of sixty thrusts and cuts were made at him with swords and cutlasses, and when he was knocked off his horse he had the good fortune to fall against the hatch of a baker's shop, which was half open, and roll in." "Well," said the duke, "it cannot be otherwise at present. Keep quiet near me; I am convinced that things cannot remain long as they now are. The King and the constable will wage a serious war against me; however, since I promised you protection, I will keep my word."

Some days after this, intelligence was brought to the King of France that the Duke of Brittany had received Sir Peter de Craon; and immediately, at the advice of his counsellors, he summoned the duke to deliver him up. The duke, however, sent back word, excusing himself from knowing anything of Sir Peter, and requesting to be considered to have nothing to do with the quarrel. This answer was deemed by no means satisfactory, and war was immediately declared against the Duke of Brittany. The handsome hotel which Sir Peter had near the churchyard of St. John was ordered to be razed to the ground, and the spot was given as an addition to the churchyard.

Preparations for the war with Brittany were made with great vigor, and as soon as the constable was sufficiently recovered, the King and all who attended on the expedition advanced to Mans, where they remained three weeks; for, in consequence of the difference of opinion which was entertained upon this expedition, the King fell into a very feverish state, and was unfit to ride. His physicians told the Duke of Orleans and his uncles, that he was oppressed with too much business, and was not able to go through it—that rest and quiet were absolutely necessary; for that ever since he had left Amiens his health had not been so good as it was formerly.

The King would not pay any attention to what the physicians said; he was so impatient to carry the war into Brittany, that he told his uncles he was always better when on horseback, and added, "whoever advises me to the contrary will highly displease me, and show that he has not any love for me." Out of affection for his uncles, however, the King was prevailed upon to send four knights into Brittany, who remonstrated strongly with the duke upon the subject of Sir Peter de Craon's conduct; but the duke answered, prudently, that he would be most happy to arrest him, and give him up to the King, if he knew where he was; and added, "I do not feel that I am any way so blamable in this matter, that war should be declared against me; if it please God, I will never infringe the alliances that have been entered into between my lord the King of France and myself, as well in regard to the marriage of our children as respecting other matters." The King, upon the return of the French knights, expressed himself by no means satisfied, and declared, that since he had come so far, he would never return until he had humbled the Duke of Brittany.

There was at this time a report in Mans, and many other places in France, that the Lady Jolande de Bar, Queen of Arragon, had thrown into prison at Barcelona a knight who was unknown to her and her people, and who, from his refusal to tell his name, was thought to be Sir Peter de Craon; and the Queen wrote to the King of France an account of the arrest of this person. The King, however, was not inclined to put any credit in this intelligence, for nothing would alter his opinion that Sir Peter de Craon was in Brittany; and without further delay he set out on his expedition.

You must know, in order perhaps to account truly for what follows, that the King during his stay at Mans labored hard and assiduously in the council, where he had but little assistance, and was besides not perfectly recovered in health. He had been the whole summer feeble in mind and body, scarcely eating or drinking anything, and almost daily attacked with fever, to which he was naturally inclined, and which was increased by any contradiction or fatigue. The insult offered to his constable affected him much, and his physicians and uncles noticed that at times his intellect was deranged; but they could not do anything with him, nor would he consent on any account to defer the expedition.

As the King was passing through the forest of Mans, a strange accident happened to him: a man, bare-headed, with naked feet, clothed in a jerkin of white-russet, rushed out from the trees, and boldly seized the reins of his horse, saying, "King, ride no further, but return; for thou art betrayed." The men-at-arms beat the man off, and he escaped; but his speech made such an impression on the King's mind, that his understanding was shaken. He and his army passed on; it might be about twelve o'clock when they were clear of the forest. The heat and dust were most oppressive. The King rode by himself, and the dukes of Berry and Burgundy kept on his left at no great distance; two of his pages also followed him. As they were riding, the pages, who were but children, grew negligent of themselves and their horses; and the one who bore the King's lance fell asleep, and let it fall on the casque of the page before him, which made both the lance and the casque ring loudly. The King was startled and alarmed, for he had in his mind the words of the man whom he met in the forest of Mans, and fancied a host of enemies were come to slay him. In this distraction of mind he drew his sword, for his senses were quite gone, and advancing on the pages, he gave blows, indifferent on whom they fell, bawling out, "Advance, advance on these traitors." He then made up to the Duke of Orleans, who was not far off, and the duke seeing him approach, and the state he was in, spurred his horse and made off, but the King followed him. All were in the greatest amazement, and knew not what to do; at last, when quite wearied out from fatigue, a Norman knight, called Sir William Martel, came behind the King and caught him in his arms, by which means he prevented further mischief.[e] The other lords then came up and took his sword from him, and having undressed and cooled him as gently as they could, they laid him on a litter and carried him slowly to Mans. The whole army was then informed that there was an end to the expedition.

The evening the King was brought back to Mans his physicians were much occupied with him, and the princes of the blood were in the utmost trouble. The whole French nation was dismayed and greatly concerned when it was publicly known that he labored under a frenzy. Much was said against those who had advised this expedition into Brittany, and people declared that he had been betrayed by those who urged him on against the duke and Sir Peter de Craon. The King was carried to Creil, and put under the care of four knights and his physicians. The men-at-arms were disbanded and sent home, and it was strictly forbidden the Queen's household and all

---

[e] It would appear from Froissart's account, that no one was mortally injured by this fit of madness. "Les Grandes Chroniques de France," however, says that the King killed four men.

others, under pain of being severely punished, to mention this misfortune to the Queen, who was far gone with child.

At this time there was a learned physician in France, a friend of the Lord de Coucy, who had not his equal anywhere. His name was Master William de Harseley, and he had fixed his residence in the city of Laon. On first hearing of the King's disorder, and the cause of it, knowing as he thought the King's constitution, he said, "This disorder of the King proceeds from the alarm in the forest, and by inheriting too much of his mother's weak nerves."

The whole of the council and the principal barons and prelates of the realm assembled at Paris, to consult on the government of the kingdom during the King's illness; and whether the Duke of Orleans or his uncles, or all three, should have the regency. They were upward of fifteen days before they could agree: at last it was thought advisable, from the youth of the Duke of Orleans, which made him unfit to bear so great a weight, that the two uncles of the King should govern the kingdom; but that the Duke of Burgundy should be the principal, and that the Duchess of Burgundy should remain with the Queen, and be respected as second to her in rank. The Lord de Coucy was not unmindful of what Master William de Harseley had said; but spoke of him to the King's uncles, who had him sent for in order that he should try his skill to recover the King. Master William came as directed, and on arriving at Creil, where the King was, took lead over the other physicians, undertaking to make a cure. News of the King of France's illness was carried far and near, producing various sensations. The Duke of Brittany and Sir Peter de Craon were of course not much affected at it. Pope Boniface, also, and the cardinals at Rome, found reason to rejoice that such a calamity had befallen one who had so strenuously supported the anti-pope of Avignon.

In a church at Haspres, in Hainault, dependent on the abbey of St. Vast at Arras, lies the canonized body of St. Aquaire, in a rich silver shrine. This saint is celebrated for the cures he has performed on those afflicted with madness, and on that account is much visited from all parts. To pay due respect to the saint, there was made a figure of wax, resembling the King, which was sent thither with a large wax taper, and offered with much devotion at the shrine of the saint, that he might pray to God to alleviate this cruel affliction of the King. A similar offering was made to Saint Hermier, in Rouais, who has the reputation of curing madness; and wherever there were saints supposed to have efficacy by their prayers to God in such disorders, thither were sent offerings from the King with much ceremony and devotion.

The dukes of Berry and Burgundy continued at Paris; they had not as yet made any changes in the government, but they shortly intended doing so, in regard to many who were not in their good graces. Among others, Sir Oliver de Clisson got very rudely treated. He had come, one afternoon, to the hotel d'Artois to remonstrate with the Duke of Burgundy, respecting the pay due to the knights and squires who had been engaged in the late expedition. On entering the duke's apartment, the constable took off his hood, and bowing said, "I am come, my lord, to know how to act respecting the payment of the knights and squires who were of the late expedition, for my office is perpetually besieged by them; and as you and my lord of Berry at present govern the kingdom, have the goodness to inform me?" The Duke of Burgundy replied, angrily, "Clisson, Clisson, you need not trouble yourself about the state of France, for without your office it will be perfectly well governed; in an evil hour you have interfered with it. Quit my presence and leave my house—let me never see you again; if it were not from regard to my own honor, I would have your other eye put out." At these words the duke went away, leaving the Lord de Clisson astonished. He quitted the apartment very melancholy, taking a private way to his own hotel, without saying a word, and when there formed various plans for his future conduct. He foresaw that very shortly public affairs would be badly managed. Suspecting, after what had passed, that the Duke of Burgundy would arrest him, he determined not to wait the event, but ordered his most confidential servants to pack up all he should want, and in the evening set off from Paris, attended by only two persons, and continued his journey to his castle of Montlhery, seven leagues from the city, where he remained till he heard that he was pursued, when he retreated into Brittany, and entered another of his castles called Château-Josselin, which was well provided with all things.

When the regents found that the constable had escaped, they resolved to proceed in a different manner. It was ordered, that he should be summoned by the court of Parliament of Paris, to appear before it, and answer such charges as should be made against him, under pain of being dishonored and banished from France. Commissioners were sent after him into Brittany to summon and arrest him. They went from town to town, demanding him, but without success; at length, being tired of the pursuit, they were obliged to return to Paris. Sir Oliver de Clisson was then publicly summoned in all legal form, allowing the usual interval between each summons, to prevent those attached to him saying, that hatred or malice had outstripped justice. After every adjournment was completed without any intelligence received from him, and after he had been summoned, first at the door of the chamber of Parliament, then publicly at the gates and on the steps of the palace, with every usual solemnity, without any answer being returned, the most cruel sentence was passed by the court. He was banished the kingdom of France, for a false and wicked traitor to the Crown, condemned to pay a fine of 100,000 marks of silver, and be deprived for ever of the office of constable of France. The Duke of Orleans was invited to be present when this sentence was passed, but he excused himself.

The dukes of Berry and Burgundy were there with a great many of the barons of France. This sentence made a great noise in France and elsewhere: some pitied him, and said, in secret, that he had been unjustly treated; others said, it was fortunate he had not been laid hold of and hanged, for he richly deserved it. In such a manner was Sir Oliver de Clisson accused, and the proverb says truly, "That those whom necessity forces to sell, have never a fair offer."

The King continued to reside at Creil, under the charge of Master William de Harseley, who was very attentive to him, and by little and little restored him to health. He first got rid of the fever and great heat he complained of, and then brought back to him his appetite, sleep, and recollections of things about him. Until he was strong enough to bear the removal for change of air, he allowed him to ride, hunt, and amuse himself with hawking.

On the news of the King's recovery, the whole kingdom of

France was rejoiced, and most heartily and sincerely were thanksgivings offered up to God for having restored the King to his senses and memory. Master William de Harseley was in high spirits, and not without reason, for he had performed an astonishing cure. It was thought desirable to retain him in the King's service, but he excused himself, and so was permitted to depart, being presented with 1,000 crowns of gold, and an order for four horses on the post-master whenever he should please to come to court. I believe he never returned; but continued in the city of Laon, where he died very rich, being possessed of 30,000 francs.

## CHAPTER V

Negotiations for Peace Continued—Marriage of a Young Squire and Damsel of the Royal Household of France—Disastrous Result of the Masque at the Hotel de St. Pol on the Occasion—Dukes of Berry and Burgundy Govern France—The Treatment of the Constable—The Appointment of Lord Philip d'Artois to That Office—War Between Sir Oliver de Clisson and the Duke of Brittany—The Duke of Lancaster Advocates Peace with France—Commissioners Appointed, and Conferences Held on the Subject—The French Desire the Restoration of Calais, Which is Most Decidedly Objected to by the English—In the Opinion of Froissart No Peace Was Concluded, Only the Truces Prolonged for Four Years—Death of the Pope of Avignon—Schism Continued—Expedition Against Ireland—Duke of Lancaster Appointed Lord of Aquitaine—Death of the Lady Anne, Queen of England—Sir John Froissart Visits England—Presents a Handsome "Book of Poesy" to King Richard—St. Patrick's Hole—Henry Castide, an English Squire, Relates the Account to the Irish Expedition—Marriage Set on Foot Between King Richard and the Daughter of the King of France.

TO continue this noble and pleasant history, undertaken at the request of that very liberal and potent prince, my very dear lord and patron, Guy de Chastillon, Count de Blois, Lord of Avesnes, Chimay, Beaumont, Schoenhoven, and Turgow; I, John Froissart, priest and chaplain to my very dear lord before named, and at this time treasurer and canon of Chimay and Lille in Flanders, set myself to work at my forge to produce new and notable matter relative to the wars between France and England and their allies, as clearly appears from the various treaties which are of this date, and which excellent materials, through the grace of God, I shall work upon as long as I live; for the more I labor at it, the more it delights me; just as a gallant knight or squire-at-arms, who loves his profession, the longer he continues in it so much the more delectable it appears.

You have had it before related that a truce had been agreed upon at Leulinghen between France and England for three years, and that ambassadors from France had accompanied the dukes of York and Lancaster to London, to learn the intention of the King and Parliament of England in regard to the advances which had been made at Amiens toward a solid peace between the two nations. These ambassadors had returned to France, for they were told nothing could be done in the matter till the meeting of the Parliament, which was appointed to be held at Westminster at Michaelmas. When it was known in England how grievously the King of France was afflicted, the business was much retarded; nevertheless the King and the Duke of Lancaster were desirous of peace, and if it had depended on them, the matter would have been at once concluded; as it was, after considerable discussion, it was determined that a truce should take place between the two countries, and their respective allies, by sea and land, to last from Michaelmas to St. John the Baptist's Day, and one year longer.

Not long after this a marriage took place between a young squire of Vermandois and a damsel of the Queen, both of the royal household; the court was much pleased at it, and the King resolved that the wedding feast should be kept at his expense. It was held at the hotel of St. Pol, and great crowds of nobility attended, among whom were the dukes of Orleans, Berry, and Burgundy, with their duchesses. The wedding day was passed in dancing and rejoicing; the King entertained the Queen at supper in great state, and everyone exerted himself to add to the gayety; seeing how much delighted the King appeared. There was in the King's household a Norman squire, a near relative to the bridegroom, who thought of the following piece of pleasantry to amuse the King and the ladies. In the evening he provided six coats of linen covered with fine flax the color of hair; in one of them he dressed the King, and the Count de Joigny, a young and gallant knight, in another; Sir Charles de Poitiers had the third, Sir Evan de Foix the fourth; the son of the Lord de Nantouillet, a young knight, had the fifth, and Hugonin[a] dressed himself in the sixth. When thus dressed they appeared like savages, for they were covered with hair from head to foot. This masquer-

---

[a] His name was Hugonin de Gensay. The marriage took place on January 29, 1392.

ade pleased the King greatly, and he expressed his pleasure to his squire; it was so secretly contrived that no one knew anything of the matter but the servants who attended them. Word was sent to the room where the ladies were, commanding in the King's name that all the torches should be placed on one side, and that no person come near six savage men who were about to enter; the torch-bearers, therefore, withdrew on one side, and no one approached the dancers so long as the savages stayed in the room.

The apartment was now clear of all but ladies, damsels, and knights and squires, who were dancing with them. Soon after the Duke of Orleans entered, attended by four knights and six torches, ignorant of the orders that had been given, and of the entrance of the savages; he first looked at the dancing, and then took part himself, just as the King of France made his appearance with five others dressed like savages, and covered from head to foot with flax to represent hair; not one person in the company knew them, and they were all fastened together, while the King led them dancing. Everyone was so occupied in examining them, that the orders about the torches were forgotten; the King, who was their leader, fortunately for him, advanced to show himself to the ladies, and passing by the Queen, placed himself near the Duchess of Berry, who, though his aunt, was the youngest of the company. The duchess amused herself in talking with him, and as the King rose up, not wishing to discover himself, the duchess said, "You shall not escape thus; I will know your name." At this moment a most unfortunate accident befell the others, through the youthful gayety of the Duke of Orleans, who, could he have foreseen the mischief he was about to cause, would not on any consideration have acted so. Being very inquisitive to find out who they were, while the five were dancing he took one of the torches from his servants, and holding it too near, set their dresses on fire. Flax, you know, is instantly in a blaze, and the pitch with which the cloth had been covered to fasten the flax added to the impossibility of extinguishing it. They were likewise chained together, and their cries were dreadful; some knights did their utmost to disengage them, but the fire was so strong that they burned their hands very severely. One of the five, Nantouillet, broke the chain, and rushing into the buttery, flung himself into a large tub of water, which was there for washing dishes and plates; this saved him, or he would have been burned to death like the rest, but he was, withal, very ill for some time.

The Queen was so much alarmed that she fainted, for she knew that the King was one of the six; the Duchess of Berry, however, saved the King by throwing the train of her robe over him. This terrible accident happened about twelve o'clock at night, in the ball-room of the hotel de St. Pol, and it was a most melancholy spectacle—of the four that were on fire, two died on the spot; the other two, the bastard of Foix and the Count de Joigny, were carried to their hotels, and died two days afterward in great agonies. This sad affair made a great disturbance in Paris, and the next morning the King and his attendants mounted their horses, and rode through Paris, from the hotel de St. Pol to the Church of Notre Dame, to appease the people. The accident by degrees was forgotten, and obsequies, prayers, and alms were made for the dead. Ah! Count Gaston de Foix, hadst thou been alive and heard the cruel death of this thy favorite son, I know not how thou wouldst have been consoled.

We will now return to the affairs of France. Notwithstanding the King's recovery, the dukes of Berry and Burgundy still continued to govern as they pleased; the Lord de la Riviere and Sir John le Mercier were kept confined in the bastile of St. Anthony, and it was current through Paris that they would be put to death; indeed, had the Duchess of Burgundy been listened to, they would have suffered a most disgraceful and public death, without hopes of mercy, for she hated them, because with Sir Oliver de Clisson they had advised the King of France to make the expedition into Brittany, to destroy her cousin the duke.

You heard just now that the constable was publicly summoned by the Parliament of Paris, and that commissioners had been sent into Brittany after him, but to no purpose; the office, therefore, was declared vacant, and the dukes of Berry and Burgundy, with their councils, who all hated him, and wished his ruin, determined to offer the appointment to the Lord de Coucy, who, however, excused himself, and positively refused to accept it, though he should be forced to leave

France. Seeing him so determined, they were obliged to look elsewhere, and at length they invested the Lord Philip d'Artois, Count d'Eu, with the high distinction, in consideration of his marriage with the Lady Mary of Berry, widow of the Lord Lewis de Blois. Sir Oliver de Clisson was soon informed that the Count d'Eu was nominated constable of France, and was to do the duty and receive the profits from the day of his appointment. To all this he was perfectly indifferent; he felt that his loyalty and honor were as firm as ever, and that he had never done anything against the King or Crown of France, but that all these proceedings originated in the hatred and malice of the dukes of Berry and Burgundy. This determined him to prosecute the war with prudence and vigor against the Duke of Brittany, and a severe and bloody struggle it was, for neither party, when they met, made a sham of fighting, but killed each other without mercy. The Lord de Clisson rode frequently from one of his castles to another, and being superior in numbers, had more ambuscades than the duke. None of the Breton chivalry would interfere by bearing arms on either side; but when the duke sent for them, they came to know what he wanted. He demanded from them aid and advice to correct his vassal Sir Oliver de Clisson, who had greatly misbehaved himself toward him. The barons of Brittany, such as the Viscount de Rohan, the Lord de Dinant, Sir Hermen de Lyon, and many more, excused themselves by saying, that they were uninterested in the quarrel, and therefore would not bear arms against the Lord de Clisson, but that they would heartily labor to mediate between him and the duke, if they knew how, or saw any probability of establishing peace between them. The duke, seeing he could not prevail on them to join him, and that in this warfare he was losing more men than the Lord de Clisson, consented to send the above-named barons to treat with him, and bring him under safe passports to Vannes, that they might confer together.

For the sake of doing good the knights willingly undertook the mission, and set out in search of Sir Oliver, whom, I believe, they found at Château-Josselin. They told him the message they were charged with, and urged him strongly to accept of peace. "Sir Oliver," they said, "we are thus pressing, in the hope that you will be pleased to wait upon our lord, and for your safety and secure return we pledge ourselves to remain in your castle of Josselin, without ever stirring beyond the gates." To this Sir Oliver replied, " My good sirs, what advantage can my death be to you? Do you think I know not the Duke of Brittany? The moment I shall be in his presence he will have me put to death in spite of his promises to you; and if I am killed your fate of course will be the same, as my people will of course retaliate on you." " Fair cousin," replied Sir Charles de Dinant, " you may say as you please; but the duke has the strongest desire to accommodate all matters of dispute; we therefore beg of you to consent." Sir Oliver answered, " I believe firmly that you wish me every good, but not on these terms; I will accept no other pledge for my safety than his only son, who is betrothed to a princess of France; let him send him hither, to remain under the guard of my men in Château-Josselin until I return, and I will set out at once to wait on him." When the barons saw he was determined, they took their leave, and returned to Vannes to relate to the duke what Sir Oliver had said. In regard to sending his son, the duke absolutely refused, and the war continued on the same footing as before, so that no merchants or others dared travel the country. All commerce was at a stand in Brittany, which was severely felt in the cities and large towns; even the laborers and all husbandry were in a state of idleness.

You have before heard of the conferences that were held at Amiens, respecting a peace between France and England, and on what terms the Duke of Lancaster had gone back. The English, notwithstanding all that was urged in its favor, were unwilling to consent to a peace; because the majority of the commons were desirous of war, and two-thirds of the young knights and squires knew not how to employ themselves, and looked to war as their means of support. However, they were forced to submit to the opinions of the King, his uncles, and the more intelligent part of the nation. The Duke of Lancaster, considering the matter as well in regard to the welfare of his two daughters, the Queens of Castille and Portugal, as in respect to his nephew the King of England, who was greatly inclined to peace, took much pains to bring it about; because he thought it would, likewise, be for the honor and advantage of England.

On the part of France, the Duke of Burgundy greatly exerted himself, for he found the whole weight of the government rested on him, since his nephews, the King and the Duke of Orleans, were weak in body and mind. The duke was a long-sighted politician, as I was told by those who ought to know; and he and the Duke of Lancaster effected that the conferences should be renewed at Leulinghen, and that the commissioners should have full power to conclude a peace. The conferences were to be held in the ensuing month of May, 1393. It had been thus agreed to by both parties, and commissioners[b] were appointed by each King. On the part of the King of England, were his two uncles the dukes of Lancaster and Gloucester; the last of whom was very popular with the Commons of England, and all others who preferred war to peace. From among the prelates were selected the Archbishop of York, the Bishop of London, and other clerks learned in the law, to expound the Latin letters. Soon after St. George's Day these lords repaired to Calais. The dukes of Berry and Burgundy came to Boulogne, and the King of France to Abbeville, that they might be near at hand to the place of conference. It was told me, (for I, John Froissart, the writer of this history, was at Abbeville, that I might learn the truth of what was passing,) that after the procurations from the two Kings had been verified as to the commissioners' powers of concluding a peace, the French proposed that Calais should be demolished, so that it could never again be made habitable. The dukes of Lancaster and Gloucester instantly answered, that they need not have made this proposition; for that Calais would be the very last town the Crown of England would part from; and, if they intended this as a basis for treating, there was an end to the business, for they would hear nothing more.

The dukes of Berry and Bergundy, perceiving the commissioners of England so determined, dropped the matter, for they found it would be in vain to press it. The English for a time demanded restitution of everything that had been yielded

---

[b] According to the fœdera, the commissioners were, the Duke of Lancaster, the Duke of Gloucester; Walter, Bishop of Durham; Thomas, Earl Marshal, Governor of Calais; Sir Thomas Percy, Sir Lewis Clifford, Richard Rouhall, Doctor of Laws.

to the late King Edward; and, in addition to these territories, the balance of the ransom that had been due when the war was renewed between France and England. This was resisted strenuously by the French dukes, who argued, with regard to the first demand, that it was impossible that the whole territory which had been yielded to King Edward should be restored; for the inhabitants of the towns, castles, and lands, which had been assigned to England by the treaty of Bretigny, and afterward confirmed at Calais in the year 1360, were too adverse to such restoration; and the King of France, to whom they had voluntarily surrendered themselves, had in consequence accepted their homage, granted them protection, and such other privileges, on his royal word, as could not be broken. It was then resolved between the four dukes, on whom it solely depended whether there should be peace or war, that each party should reduce to writing their different grounds of treating, and mutually deliver them to each other, to consider of them at their leisure, with their clerks learned in the law, to determine on what parts they could agree to and what would not be accepted. This was assented to by all; for the dukes were before much fatigued in hearing the various papers read and discussed; more especially the English commissioners: for, as the conference was carried on in French, they were not so well used to the finesse and double meanings of that language as the natives, who turned and twisted it to their own advantage at pleasure. Indeed, there were so many difficulties of this sort that the conferences were greatly lengthened. The English held themselves obliged to demand restitution of all the lands dependent on Aquitaine and the profits since the commencement of the war, as they had been charged to do by the Parliament of England.

To this the French would not agree; they were willing to yield the countries of Tarbes, Bigorre, Agen, and the Agenois, with Perigord, but declared they would never restore Cahors, Rouergue, Quercy, and Limousin, nor give up any part of Ponthieu, or Guines, more than the English possessed at the present moment. On these grounds things remained as they were. They stood out for fifteen days, and only came to the conclusion that the matter should be laid before the two kings, which was done respectively by the dukes of Berry and

Burgundy to the King of France, and the dukes of Lancaster and Gloucester to the King of England. The two kings, but more especially the King of France, were desirous of peace, and the four dukes received full power from their respective monarchs to conclude it: they, therefore, continued the conferences, and with such success that there was a report current in Abbeville of a peace having been made between France and England with their allies. But I, the author of this history, who at the time resided in Abbeville, to learn news, could never understand that a peace had been concluded; only the truces prolonged for four years, on sea and land, between all parties.

In the month of September of this year, Robert de Geneve, who in this history we have called pope, died at his palace in Avignon.c It happened to him just as he had wished, that he might die pope. He died, indeed, with the honor and state I have mentioned; but whether he enjoyed these wrongfully or not, I shall not pretend to determine, for such matters do not belong to me. Immediately upon his death, the cardinals at Avignon resolved to form a conclave,d and elect one from among themselves as his successor.

The health of the King of France, which had for some time been much impaired, was again beginning to return, to the great joy of all who loved him, and of his good Queen, who had been in great affliction. The college of cardinals at Avignon elected the Cardinal Legate de Luna, pope; to say the truth, he was a devout man, and of a contemplative life, and he was chosen, subject to the approbation of the King of France and his council, otherwise the election would not have been maintained.

Consider now how much the Church must have been degraded by this schism, when those who were, or ought to have been, free, thus subjected themselves to the will of others whom they should have commanded. All the solemnities required at the coronation of a pope were paid to the Cardinal de Luna, who took the name of Benedict. He offered a general pardon to all clergy who should come to Avignon; and,

---

c Robert de Geneve died on September 16, 1394.

d A conclave is an assembly or meeting of the cardinals, for the purpose of electing a pope; it also signifies the place at which the meeting is held. The conclave in the Vatican is a range of small cells, ten feet square, made of wainscot, which are numbered and drawn by lot.

by the advice of his cardinals, wrote letters to the King of France to announce his elevation to the papacy. I heard that the King paid but little attention to his letters, for he was not yet determined whether to acknowledge him as pope or not; and to have the best advice on the occasion, he summoned before him the most learned and prudent clerks of the university of Paris, Master John Gigencourt and Master Peter Playons, who told the King, as did others, that the schism in the Church corrupted the Christian faith; that the Church ought not longer to be kept in this state; for, that all Christendom suffered from it; and that it was unbecoming the university to send to Pope Benedict at Avignon lists of those priests who had need of briefs. The King, on hearing their opinions, thought them reasonable, and consented that there should be a cessation of such lists as were usually sent to the pope, until the disputes between the two popes were at an end.

Things therefore remained in this state. The Duke of Berry strenuously supported the new pope. The Duke and Duchess of Burgundy, the Duke of Orleans, with many other great lords of France, dissembled their real opinions on the subject. The Duke of Brittany readily followed the opinion of the King of France; for he had been in former times so scandalized by the information given him of the rebellion in the Church, that he would never allow of Clement being a true pope, although the clergy paid him obedience. When any of the churches in France became vacant, the King disposed of them to clergymen without ever speaking of it to Pope Benedict, who as well as his cardinals was greatly surprised at such conduct, and began to fear the King would deprive them of the benefices they held in his realm. They resolved, therefore, to send a well-instructed legate to France, to remonstrate with the King and council on the state of the Church, and to learn their intentions; likewise to assure them that the pope they had elected was only conditionally chosen in case of his proving agreeable to the King; but, that otherwise they would dethrone him, and exalt another more to his pleasure.

It happened about this period that a legate came from Pope Boniface to the King of France, who listened to his arguments and sermons with great pleasure. The legate from Avignon, a subtle and learned clerk, was also heard by the King and his court, and those attached to the pope at Avignon took good care to push him forward, and contrived that he should often have audiences. It was the opinion of the council, but it was not without great difficulty the university of Paris subscribed to this opinion, that means should be found to make the rival popes resign their dignities, as well as all the cardinals, and then select the most learned and prudent among the clergy from Germany, France, and other countries, who should form a general council; and, without favor or affection to any party, restore the Church to its former unity, discipline, and stability. This idea, which was proposed in the presence of the King, and the dukes of Orleans and Burgundy, in council, was approved of; and the King having agreed to it, said he would cheerfully write on the subject to the kings of Germany, Bohemia, Hungary, and England; and that he thought he could depend on the kings of Castille, Navarre, Arragon, Sicily, Naples, and Scotland, obeying whatever pope he should acknowledge. Letters were accordingly sent off to the kings above mentioned; but answers were not returned by them so soon as was expected.

It is time, however, that we now quit this subject, and speak of other matters. The truces that had been agreed upon between the Kings of France and England, and their allies, were well observed on sea and land. There were, however, some pillagers still in Languedoc, who came from foreign countries; and you may suppose that the captains of such forts as Lourdes in Bigorre, Bouteville, and Mortaign, were sorely vexed that they could no longer overrun the country, and make their accustomed pillages; as they had been particularly forbidden to infringe the articles of the truce under pain of being severely punished.

At this period an expedition against Ireland was proposed in the English council; for, in the truces which King Richard had agreed to with France and her allies, young as he was, he had reserved Ireland from being included, as his predecessors had always claimed it as their right; and his grandfather, King Edward of happy memory, had signed himself King and Lord of Ireland, and had continued his wars against the natives, notwithstanding his pressure from other quarters. The young knights and squires of England, eager to signalize themselves in arms, were rejoiced to learn that King Richard intended leading a large power, of men-at-arms and archers, into Ireland; and that he had declared he would not return thence until he should have settled everything to his satisfaction. It was at the same council ordered that the Duke of Lancaster, who in his time had labored hard on sea and land for the augmentation of the honor of England, should make a journey to Aquitaine with 500 men-at-arms and 1,000 archers. He was to embark at Plymouth or Southampton, as he pleased. It was the intention of King Richard and his council, that the Duke of Lancaster should hold in perpetuity for himself and heirs the whole territory of Aquitaine, with all its seneschalships and domains, in such manner as King Edward of England, his father, and the former dukes of Aquitaine, had held them, and which King Richard held at this moment, with the reserve of homage to the kings of England. The Duke of Lancaster was to enjoy all other rights, lordships, and rents, which stipulation was confirmed by the King wholly and fully under his seal.

The Duke of Lancaster was very thankful for this magnificent gift, as he had reason to be, for, in truth, the duchy of Aquitaine has wherewithal to enable its lord to keep a grand estate. He accordingly thanked, in the first place, the King his nephew, then his brothers, and the barons and prelates of the council; after which he began to make most sumptuous preparations for crossing the sea, and taking possession of his duchy. Purveyors were likewise busy in preparing on a large scale for the King's expedition to Ireland. Both these expeditions were delayed about two months, by an event which I will now relate.

The Lady Anne, Queen of England, to the great distress of the King and her household, fell sick, and her disorder increased so rapidly that she departed this life on the Feast of Whitsuntide, in the year of grace 1394.*e* The King and all who loved her were greatly afflicted at her death. She was buried in the cathedral church of London; but her obsequies

---

*e* According to Stowe, Queen Anne died at Shene in Surrey, and was buried at Westminster. "The King took her death so heavily, that, besides cursing the place where she died, he did also, for anger, throw down buildings unto which former kings, being weary of the city, were wont, from pleasure, to resort."—Stowe's "Chronicles." See The Life and Character of this Queen, in Agnes Strickland's "Queens of England."

were performed at leisure, for the King would have them magnificently done. Abundance of wax was sent for from Flanders, to make flambeaux and torches, and the illumination was so great on the day of the ceremony that nothing like to it was ever before seen. The Queen left no issue, for she had never borne children.

Although the expeditions to Ireland and Aquitaine were delayed by the Queen's death, those lords who were named to go to Ireland did not fail to continue their preparations; and as their purveyances were ready, they sent them across the sea to Ireland from Brisco,*f* and Lolighet in Wales; and the conductors were ordered to carry them to a city in Ireland, called Dimelin, which had always been steadily attached to England, and was an archbishopric.

Soon after St. John Baptist's Day, King Richard left London, and took the road to Wales. Those ordered to attend him began their journey, such as his two uncles of York and Gloucester; the Earl of Kent, half-brother to the King; Sir Thomas Holland, his son; the Earl of Rutland, son of the Duke of York; the earl marshal; the earls of Salisbury and Arundel; Sir William Arundel, the Earl of Northumberland; Sir Thomas Percy, his brother, high steward of England; the earls of Devonshire and Nottingham, with numbers of knights and squires. A considerable body remained at home to guard the borders of Scotland; for the Scots are a wicked race, and pay no regard to truces or respites, but as it suits their own convenience. At the time the King of England undertook this expedition, he had not the company of his other half-brother, Sir John Holland, Earl of Huntingdon, for he was on a journey to Jerusalem and Saint Catherine of Mount Sinai, and was to return through Hungary. Having heard at Paris, as he passed through France, where he had been handsomely treated by the King and his court, that the King of Hungary and Amurat *g* were to have a battle, he declared he would not fail to be present.

The King of England had with him, in his Irish expedition, full 4,000 men-at-arms, and 30,000 archers. The army, on

---

*f* No doubt, Brisco is meant for Bristol; and by Lolighet, perhaps, Holyhead is intended; and by Dimelin, Dublin.

*g* The person thus called, according to Mr. Johnes, was the Sultan Bajazet I, who began his reign in 1391.

landing, quartered themselves in the country round Dublin; and the King, his uncles, and the prelates were accommodated in the city. I was told, that during the campaign they were well supplied with all sorts of provisions; for the English are expert in war, and know well how to forage, and take proper care of themselves and horses.

I, Sir John Froissart, treasurer and canon of Chimay, had, during my stay at Abbeville, a great desire to see the kingdom of England; more especially since it was a time of truce. Several reasons urged me to make this journey, but principally because in my youth I had been educated at the Court of King Edward, and that good Lady Philippa, his Queen, with their children. I had taken care to form a collection of all the poetry on love and morality that I had composed during the last twenty-four years, which I had caused to be fairly written and illuminated. I was also minded to go to England from a desire to see King Richard, whom I had not seen since the time of his christening in the cathedral of Bordeaux; and my book of poesy, finely ornamented, bound in velvet, and decorated with silver-gilt clasps and studs, I took as a present for him. Having provided myself with horses, I crossed from Calais to Dover, on the twelfth day of July, and on Wednesday by nine o'clock arrived at Canterbury, to visit the shrine of St. Thomas and the tomb of the late Prince of Wales, who had been buried there. I heard high mass, made my offerings at the shrine, and returned to my inn to dinner; when I heard that the King was to come on a pilgrimage to St. Thomas. I thought, therefore, that it would be well to await his arrival, which I did; and on the morrow he came in great state, accompanied by lords and ladies, with whom I mixed; but they were all new faces to me. I did not remember one of them; times and persons had greatly changed since I was last in England, eight-and-twenty years past. I addressed myself to Sir Thomas Percy, high steward of England, whom I found gracious and of agreeable manners; and who offered to present me to the King. He went to the King's apartment for that purpose, to see if it were proper time, but finding that he had retired to rest, he bade me return to my inn.

When I thought the King might be risen, I went again to the palace of the archbishop, where he lodged; but Sir Thomas

Percy and his people were preparing to set out for Ospringe, whence he had come that morning. I asked Sir Thomas's advice how to act. "For the present," he said, "do not make further attempts to announce your arrival, but follow the King, and I will take care, when he comes to his palace in the country, which he will do in two days, that you shall be well lodged as long as the court tarries there." The King was going to a beautiful palace in the county of Kent, called Leeds Castle, and I followed Sir Thomas Percy's advice, by taking the road to Ospringe. I lodged at an inn where I found a gallant knight of the King's chamber, who had that morning stayed behind on account of a slight pain in his head with which he had been seized on the preceding night. This knight, Sir William de Lisle, seeing I was a foreigner and a Frenchman, made acquaintance with me, and I with him, for the English are courteous to strangers. He asked my situation and business in England, which I related to him at length, as well as what Sir Thomas Percy had advised me to do. He replied, that I could not have better advice, for that the King would, on Friday, be at Leeds Castle, and would there find his uncle the Duke of York. I was well pleased to hear this, for I had letters to the duke, and when young was known to him.

As a means of gaining greater intimacy with the King's household, I courted the acquaintance of Sir William de Lisle. On the Friday we rode together, and by the way I asked if he had accompanied the King on his expedition to Ireland. He said he had. I then asked if there were any foundation in truth for what was said of St. Patrick's hole. He replied, there was; and that he and another knight, during the King's stay at Dublin, had been there. They entered it at sunset, remained there the whole night, and came out at sunrise the next morning. I requested he would tell me whether he saw all the marvellous things which are said to be seen there. He made me the following answer: "When I and my companion had passed the entrance of the cave, called the Purgatory of St. Patrick, we descended three or four steps, (for you go down into it like a cellar,) when we found our heads so much affected by the heat, that we seated ourselves on the steps, which are of stone, and such a drowsiness came over us that we slept the whole night." I asked if, when asleep, they knew where they were, and what visions they had. He said they had many strange dreams, and they seemed, as they imagined, to see more than they would have done if they had been in their beds. This they were both assured of. " When morning came, and we were awake, the door of the cave was opened, for so we had ordered it, and we came out, but instantly lost all recollection of everything we had seen, and looked upon the whole as a phantom." I did not push the conversation further, although I should have much liked to have heard what he would say of Ireland; but other knights joined us, and so we rode to Leeds Castle, where the King and his court arrived shortly after. The Duke of York was there already, and I made myself known to him by presenting letters from his cousins, the Count of Hainault and the Count d'Ostrevant. On being introduced to the King, I was graciously and kindly received. He took all the letters I presented to him; and, having read them attentively, said I was welcome, and that since I had belonged to the household of the late King and Queen, I must consider myself still as of the royal household of England. This day I did not offer him the book I had brought; for Sir Thomas Percy told me it was not a fit opportunity, as he was much occupied with serious business.

The council was deeply engaged on two subjects: first, in respect to a negotiation with France to treat of a marriage between the King and the Lady Isabella, eldest daughter of the King of France, who at that time was about eight years old; and, secondly, in respect to the chief magistrates of Bordeaux, who had come to England and greatly persecuted the King since his return from Ireland, for an answer to their petitions and remonstrances on the gift the King had made his uncle, the Duke of Lancaster, of all Aquitaine with its lordships, baronies, and dependencies. In order that these matters might more fully be considered, the King summoned the principal barons and prelates of the realm to meet him on Magdalene Day, at his palace of Eltham, seven miles from London, and the same distance from Dartford. And when the King and his council quitted Leeds Castle on his way thither, I set out with them. The King arrived at Eltham on a Tuesday, and the next day the lords came from all parts.

The Parliament was held in the King's apartment; and the

knights from Gascony, and the deputies from the cities and towns, as well as those sent by the Duke of Lancaster, were present. I cannot say what passed at this Parliament; for I was not admitted, nor were any present but the members of it. It sat for upward of four hours. When it was over, I renewed my acquaintance after dinner with an ancient knight whom I well knew in my youth. His name was Sir Richard Sturry, and he was one of the principal advisers of the King. He immediately recollected me, though it was twenty-four years since we had seen each other, and from him I learned many particulars respecting the dispute with Gascony and Aquitaine. On the Sunday the whole council went to London except the Duke of York, who remained with the King, and Sir Richard Sturry. These two, in conjunction with Sir Thomas Percy, mentioned me again to the King, who desired to see the book I had brought for him. I presented it to him in his chamber, and laid it upon his bed. He opened it and looked into it with much pleasure. He ought to have been pleased, for it was handsomely written and illuminated, and bound in crimson velvet, with ten silver-gilt studs, and roses of the same in the middle, with two large clasps of silver-gilt, richly worked with roses in the centre. The King asked me what the book treated of. I replied, "Of love." He was pleased with the answer, and dipped into several places, reading parts aloud; for he read and spoke French perfectly well; and then gave it to one of his knights to carry to his oratory, and made me many acknowledgments for it.

It happened the same Sunday after the King had received my book so handsomely, that an English squire called Henry Castide[h] made acquaintance with me, and having been informed that I was an historian, he addressed me thus: "Sir John, have you as yet found anyone to give you an account of the late expedition to Ireland, and how four kings of that country submitted themselves to King Richard?" I replied, I had not. "I will tell it you then," said the squire, who might be about fifty years old, "in order that, when you return home, you may at your leisure insert it in your history, to be had in perpetual remembrance." He began as follows:

[h] The name of this squire is variously written, some MSS. have Christed. Stowe calls him Henry Cristale.

"It is not in the memory of man that any king of England ever led so large an armament of men-at-arms and archers to make war on the Irish as the present King. He remained upward of nine months in Ireland at a great expense, which, however, was cheerfully defrayed by his kingdom. Only gentlemen and archers had been employed on the expedition, and there were with the King 4,000 knights and squires, and 30,000 archers, all regularly paid every week. To tell you the truth, Ireland is one of the worst countries to make war in or to conquer, for there are such impenetrable and extensive forests, lakes, and bogs, that there is no knowing how to pass them and carry on the war advantageously; it is so thinly inhabited, that whenever the Irish please they desert the towns and take refuge in the forests, living in huts made of boughs like wild beasts. Moreover, whenever they perceive any parties advancing with hostile intentions, and about to enter their country, they fly to such narrow passes, that it is impossible to follow them. When they find a favorable opportunity to attack the enemies to advantage, which from their knowledge of the country frequently happens, they fail not to seize it; and no man-at-arms, be he ever so well mounted, can overtake them, so light of foot are they. Sometimes they leap from the ground behind a horseman and embrace the rider so tightly that he can in no way get rid of them.

"The Irish have pointed knives with broad blades, sharp on both sides, like a dart head, with which they kill their enemies; but they never consider them as dead until they have cut their throats like sheep, opened their bellies, and taken out their hearts, which they carry off with them; and some, who are well acquainted with their manners, say, that they devour them as delicious morsels. They never accept of ransom for their prisoners; and when in any skirmishes they find they have not the advantage, they instantly separate and hide themselves in hedges, bushes, or holes under ground, so that they seem to disappear, no one knows whither. Sir William Windsor, who had made war in Ireland longer than any other English knight, has never been able during his residence among them to learn correctly their manners, nor the condition of the people. They are a very hardy race, of great subtlety, and of various tempers, paying no attention to cleanliness, nor to any gentleman, although the country is governed by kings, of whom there were several; but seem desirous to remain in the savage state in which they have been brought up. True it is, that four of the most potent kings of Ireland have submitted to the King of England, but more through love and good humor than by battle or force. The Earl of Ormond, whose lands join their kingdoms, took great pains to induce them to go to Dublin, where the King our lord resided, and to submit themselves to him and to the Crown of England. This was considered by everyone as a great acquisition, and the object of the armament accomplished; for, during the whole of King Edward's reign, he had never such success as King Richard. The honor is great, but the advantage little; for with such savages nothing can be done.

"I will tell you an instance of their savageness; you may depend upon its truth, for I was an eye-witness of what I shall relate, as they were about a month under my care and governance at Dublin, to learn the usages of England, by orders of the King and council, because I knew their language as well as I did English and French; for in my youth I was educated among them, and Earl Thomas, father of the present Earl of Ormond, kept me with him out of affection for my good horsemanship.

"It happened that the earl above mentioned was sent with 300 lances and 1,000 archers, to make war on the Irish. The Earl of Ormond, whose lands bordered on his opponent's, had that day mounted me on one of his best horses, and I rode by his side. The Irish having formed an ambuscade, advanced from it, but were so sharply attacked by the English archers that they soon retreated. The earl pursued them and I kept close by him; it chanced in their pursuit, that my horse took fright and ran away with me into the midst of the enemy. My friends could never overtake me; and in passing through the Irish, one of them, by a great feat of agility, leaped on the back of my horse and held me tight with both his arms, but did me no harm; for more than two hours he pressed my horse forward, and conducted him to a large bush in a very retired spot, where he found his companions, who had run thither to escape the English. He seemed much rejoiced at having made me his prisoner, and carried me to his house, which was strong and in a town surrounded with wood, palisades, and stagnant water. His name was Bryan Costeret, and a very handsome man he was. I have frequently made inquiries after him, and hear that he is still alive, but very old. This Bryan kept me with him seven years, and gave me his daughter in marriage, by whom I have two girls.

"I will tell you how I obtained my liberty. It happened in the seventh year of my captivity, that one of the kings, Arthur Macquemaire, King of Leinster, raised an army against Lionel, Duke of Clarence, son of Edward, King of England, and both armies met very near the city of Leinster. In the battle that followed many were slain and taken on both sides; but the English gaining the day, the Irish were forced to fly, and the King of Leinster escaped. The father of my wife was made prisoner, under the banner of the Duke of Clarence; and, as Bryan Costeret was mounted on my horse, which was remembered to have belonged to the Earl of Ormond, it was then first known that I was alive, that he had honorably entertained me at his house in Herpelin, and given me his daughter in marriage. The Duke of Clarence, Sir William Windsor, and all of our party, were well pleased to hear this news; and Bryan was offered his liberty, on condition that he gave me mine, and sent me to the English army, with my wife and children. He at first refused the terms, for his love to me, his daughter, and our children; but when he found none other would be accepted, he agreed, provided my eldest daughter remained with him. I returned to England and fixed my residence at Bristol; my two children are married—the one in Ireland has three boys and two girls, and her sister four boys and two daughters.

"Because the Irish language is as familiar to me as English, for I have always spoken it in my family, I was chosen by our lord and King to teach and accustom to the manners of the English these four Irish kings, who have sworn obedience forever to England. I must say, that these kings were of coarse manners and understanding; and, in spite of all that I could do to soften their language and nature, very little progress has been made, for they would frequently return to their former coarse behavior.

"I will more particularly relate the charge that was given

me over them, and how I managed it. The King of England intended that these four kings should adopt the manners, appearance, and dress of the English; for he wanted to create them knights. He gave them, first, a very handsome house in the city of Dublin, for themselves and attendants, where I was ordered to reside with them, and never to leave the house without absolute necessity. I had been with them for three or four days without anyway interfering, that we might become accustomed to each other. I observed that, as they sat at table, they made grimaces, and I resolved in my own mind to make them drop that custom. When these kings were seated at table, and the first dish was served, they would make their minstrels and principal servants sit beside them, eat from their plates, and drink from their cups. They told me this was a praiseworthy custom in their country, where everything was in common but their bed. I permitted this to be done for three days; but on the fourth I ordered the tables to be laid out and covered properly, placing the four kings at an upper table, the minstrels at another below, and the servants lower still. They looked at each other and refused to eat, saying, I had deprived them of the old custom in which they had been brought up. In order to appease them, I replied, with a smile, that their custom was not decent nor suitable to their rank, nor would it be honorable for them to continue it: for, that now they should conform to the manners of the English; and to instruct them in these particulars was the motive of my residence with them.

" When they heard this, they made no further opposition to whatever I proposed. They had another custom which I knew to be common in that country, which was the not wearing breeches. I had, in consequence, plenty of breeches made of linen and cloth, which I gave to the kings and their attendants, and accustomed them to wear them. I took away many rude articles as well in their dress as in other things, and had great difficulty at first to induce them to wear robes of silken cloth, trimmed with squirrel-skin or miniver;[i] for the kings

---

[i] Miniver appears to have been the name given to ermine. Among the entries in the housekeeper's book of the Earl of Lancaster, quoted by Stowe, is the following:
"Item, for 7 furs of variable miniver (or powdered ermin), 7 whoods of purple, 395 furs of budge, for the liveries of barons, knights, and clearks, 123 furs of lambe for esquiers, bought at Christmas, 147li. 17s. 8d."—See Stowe's " Survey."

only wrapped themselves up in an Irish cloak. In riding, they neither used saddles nor stirrups; and I had some trouble to make them conform in this respect to the English manners. I once made inquiry concerning their faith; but they seemed so much displeased, that I was forced to silence; they said they believed in God, and the Trinity, without any difference from our creed. I asked what pope they were inclined to; they replied, without hesitation, 'to that of Rome.' I inquired if they would like to receive the order of knighthood, for the King would willingly create them such after the usual mode of France and England, and other countries. They said, they were knights already, which ought to satisfy them. I asked when they were so made. They answered, at seven years old: that, in Ireland, a king makes his son a knight, and should the child have lost his father, then the nearest relation; and a young knight begins to learn to tilt with a light lance, against a shield fixed to a post in a field, and the more lances he breaks, the more honor he acquires. 'By this method,' added they, 'are our young knights trained, more especially kings' sons.' Although I asked this, I was before well acquainted with the manner of educating their children to arms. I made no further reply than by saying, that this kind of childish knighthood would not satisfy the King of England, and that he would create them in another mode. They asked in what manner. I answered, 'In church, with most solemn ceremonies.' And I believe they paid attention to what I said.

"About two days after this, the King was desirous to create these kings*j* knights; and the Earl of Ormond, who spoke Irish well, was sent to wait on them, that they might have more confidence in the message from the King and council. On his arrival they showed him every respect, which he returned, and they seemed happy at his coming. The result of the interview was, that the four kings were made knights in the cathedral of Dublin, by the hand of the King of England on the Feast of Our Lady, in March, which that year fell on a Thursday. The four kings watched all the Wednesday night in the cathedral; and on the morrow, after mass, they were

---

*j* The names of the four kings were, Aneel the Great, King of Mecte; Brun de Thomond, King of Thomond and Aire; Arthur Macquemaire, King of Leinster; and Contruo, King of Chenour and Erpe.

created knights with much solemnity. They were very richly dressed, and that day dined at the table of King Richard. It was certainly, Sir John, a great novelty to see four Irish kings."

"I readily believe you," I said, "and would have given a great deal to have been there. Last year I had made arrangements for coming to England, and should have done so had I not heard of the death of Queen Anne. But I wish to ask you one thing which has much surprised me; I should like to know how these four Irish kings have so readily submitted to King Richard, when his valiant grandfather, who was so much redoubted everywhere, could never reduce them to obedience, and was always at war with them? You have said, it was brought about by a treaty, and the grace of God: the grace of God is good, and of infinite value to those who can obtain it; but we see few lords nowadays augment their territories otherwise than by force."

To this, Henry Castide answered, "In truth, Sir John, I cannot fully explain how it was brought about; but it is generally believed by most of our party that the Irish were exceedingly frightened at the great force the King landed in Ireland, where it remained nine months. The coasts were so surrounded that neither provisions nor merchandise could be landed. The inland natives, however, were indifferent to this, as they are unacquainted with commerce, and live like wild beasts. Those who reside on the coast opposite to England are better informed, and accustomed to traffic. King Edward of happy memory had in his reign so many wars to provide for, in France, Brittany, Gascony, and Scotland, that his forces were dispersed in different quarters, and he was unable to send any great armament to Ireland. Formerly, when Saint Edward, who had been canonized, and was worshipped with much solemnity by the English, was their King, they defeated the Danes on sea and land. This Saint Edward, King of England, Lord of Ireland and of Aquitaine,[k] the Irish loved and feared more than any other king of England, before or since. It was for this reason that, when our King went thither last

---

[k] Mr. Johnes remarks, very justly, that this must be a mistake; for Aquitaine was brought to the Crown of England by the marriage of Eleanora, the divorced Queen of Louis le Jeune, King of France, with Henry II.

year, he laid aside the leopards and flowers-de-luce, and bore the arms of St. Edward, emblazoned on all his banners: these were a cross patencé or, on a field gules, with four doves argent on the shield or banner as you please.

"This we heard was very pleasing to the Irish, and inclined them more to submission; for, in truth, the ancestors of these four kings had done homage and service to St. Edward: they also considered King Richard to be a prudent and conscientious man. Thus have I related to you how our King accomplished the object of his expedition to Ireland. Keep it in your memory, and when you return home insert it in your chronicles." "Henry," said I, "you have well spoken, and it shall be done."

Upon this, we separated; and meeting soon after the herald March, I said, "March, tell me what are the arms of Henry Castide, for I have found him very agreeable, and he has kindly related to me the history of the King's expedition to Ireland?" "He bears for arms," replied March, "a chevron gules on a field argent, with three besants gules, two above the chevron and one below." I remained in the household of the King of England as long as I pleased; but I was not always in the same place, for the King frequently changed his abode. He went to Eltham, Leeds Castle, Kingston, Shene, Chertsey, and Windsor. I was told, for truth, that the King and his council had written to the Duke of Lancaster to return to England, for those from Aquitaine had lately declared they would not submit to any other lord than the King of England.

I will now say something of the Earl of Rutland, the earl marshal, and other English ambassadors, who had been sent to France to treat of a marriage between King Richard and the young daughter of the King of France. These ambassadors, during their stay at Paris, were frequently with the King, who, together with his brother and uncles, showed them every attention, out of respect to the King of England. They were, however, some time before they could obtain an answer to their proposals; for it was a matter of great surprise to everyone that the English should be so forward to offer such an alliance, after the bitter wars that had been carried on between the two nations for such a length of time. Some in the council said, "We think, that before such a measure can take place, there ought to be a solid peace established between France, England, and their allies."

The chancellor of France, at this period Sir Arnaud de Corbie, was a very wise man, who saw far into events likely to happen, and knew well the different interests that swayed the kingdom; at his advice principally it was determined that the ambassadors from England should receive kind answers, and have hopes given them, before their departure, that their proposal would be complied with. The Queen of France resided at the hotel of St. Pol, on the banks of the Seine; and the better to please the English lords, their request to visit the Queen and the children was granted. They had been at first refused, for the council excused themselves by saying, that the princess was but a child; and that, at her age of eight years, nothing could be judged as to what she might turn out. She had, however, been well educated, and this she showed the English lords when they waited on her; for when the lord marshal had dropped on his knees, saying, "Madam, if it please God, you shall be our lady and Queen;" she instantly replied, without anyone advising her, "Sir, if it please God, and my lord and father, that I shall be Queen of England, I shall be well pleased thereat: for I have been told that I shall then be a great lady." She made the earl marshal rise, and taking him by the hand led him to the Queen, who was much pleased at her answer. The appearance and manners of the young princess were very agreeable to the English ambassadors, and they thought among themselves that she would be a lady of high honor and great worth.

When they had stayed at Paris more than twenty days, having had their expenses defrayed by the King of France, they received favorable answers to their demands from the King and council, with great hopes that the object of their misssion would be accomplished, but not immediately; for the princess was very young, and had likewise been betrothed to the son of the Duke of Brittany. This obstacle, they were told, must first be got over before anything could be done in the matter; it must, therefore, remain in this state the ensuing winter; and during Lent the King of France would send to England information of what had been done. The ambassadors then took leave of the Queen, her daughter, the Lady Isabella, and the rest of the court, and left Paris for England. The King was much rejoiced at their return, and at the answer which they brought. About this time the Lord de la Riviere and Sir John le Mercier obtained their liberty, to the great joy of all who were attached to them.

## CHAPTER VI

Differences Between Sir Oliver de Clisson and the Duke of Brittany Reconciled—Their Interview—Threats of Bajazet—The King of Hungary Makes War Against Turkey, Assisted by John, Son of the Duke of Burgundy—Tax Levied by the Duke to Pay His Son's Expenses—The Queen of Naples and Sir Peter de Craon—The Duke of Lancaster Marries His Third Wife—Nicopoli in Turkey Besieged by the Christian Army—15,000 Turks Overthrown by the Lord de Coucy—The Duke of Gloucester Desires to Prevent the Alliance Between France and England—The Counts of Hainault and Ostrevant Prepare to Invade Friesland—Fierabras de Vertain Collects Men-at-arms in England—King Richard Goes to Calais—The Great Frieslander—Defeat of the Frieslanders.

YOU have heard much of the feuds between the Duke of Brittany and Sir Oliver de Clisson, and that whenever the two parties met a deadly engagement ensued. In this warfare, however, Sir Oliver had the advantage, for two-thirds of the country were in his favor. Now, the end of the quarrel was as follows: the Duke of Brittany, as great a prince as he was, saw plainly he could no way bend the Lord de Clisson to his will, for he had too many friends in Brittany, and he was well aware that he himself was not beloved by his subjects; he was afraid, therefore, should he die during the subsisting hatred of Sir Oliver, his children would have many enemies. He perceived, also, that the English, who had certainly raised him to the honors he now possessed, were becoming indifferent to his welfare, and would probably increase in coldness, if the information he had received of the approaching connection between the kings of France and England were true. All these things, but especially the last-mentioned, alarmed him much, and he resolved to throw aside all dissembling, and openly and honestly to make peace with Sir Oliver, and also with John of Brittany, leaving them to say what amends, if any, he should make for the damages done them during the war. Having maturely weighed all circumstances without asking advice from anyone of his council, he called a secretary, to whom, on entering his chamber, he gave a large sheet of paper, and said, " Write down as I shall dictate."

The letter was indited in the most friendly terms to Sir Oliver de Clisson, desiring him to devise some means for them to have an interview, when everything should be settled in the most agreeable manner. This letter, when folded and sealed, was given to a trusty varlet, who was told thus: " Hasten to Château-Josselin, and say boldly, that I have sent thee to speak with my cousin, Sir Oliver de Clisson. Salute him for me; if he return the salute, give him this letter, and bring me back his answer; but on thy life tell no man, woman, or child whither thou art going, or who has sent thee."

The varlet having promised obedience, set out, and on his arrival at Château-Josselin the guards were greatly surprised when they heard that the Duke of Brittany had sent him to speak with their lord. Nevertheless, they informed Sir Oliver of his coming, who ordered him into his presence and immediately received the letter. De Clisson, having examined the private signet of the duke, opened the letter and read it two or three times over, being much surprised at the affectionate terms in which it was written. The varlet was ordered to retire. The attendants of the Lord de Clisson were confounded at what they saw and heard, for never before had anyone come from the Duke of Brittany, who had not been instantly put to death or confined in the deepest dungeon. When Sir Oliver was alone, his thoughts were occupied with the contents of the letter, and his hatred to the duke was extinguished from the submissive and affectionate manner in which it was written. He determined, however, to prove him and see if he was really in earnest before he went; and he wrote in the most friendly way possible to the duke, stating, that if he wished to see him, he must send his son as an hostage, who should be taken the greatest care of until his return. The duke acceded to the request, and the heir of Brittany,[a] accompanied by three knights, was sent off to Château-Josselin.

Sir Oliver, on seeing the boy, and this proof of the duke's confidence, was much affected, and at once made preparation

[a] He was about seven years old.

for his departure, taking with him the three knights and the heir of Brittany; for he said that he would give him back to his father, as henceforward he should never distrust the duke after the trial he had made of him. Indeed, such generosity was shown on both sides, that it was no wonder a firm peace was the consequence. Sir Oliver and his party continued their journey to Vannes, where, according to the duke's orders, they dismounted at a convent of Dominicans,[b] situated without the town, for the duke had fixed the meeting to take place there. When he heard that Sir Oliver had brought back his son he was highly delighted, and set out from his castle of La Motte for the convent, where he and Sir Oliver shut themselves up in a chamber: having continued there in conversation for some time, they went privately into the garden, thence to the banks of a river, where they entered a small boat that conveyed them to a large vessel which lay at anchor at the river's mouth; this vessel they boarded, and, when at a distance from the people, continued in conference for a long time.

I cannot pretend to say what passed between them, but I will relate the consequences. They were upward of two hours together on shipboard, and entered into a firm peace, which they mutually swore to observe most religiously. When about to return, they called the boatman, who rowed them back to the place he had brought them from, and they entered the church by a private door, through the garden and cloisters of the convent, whence they soon departed for the castle of La Motte; the duke holding Sir Oliver by the hand. All who thus saw them were well pleased; indeed, the whole of Brittany was very happy when the news of this reconciliation was made public, and greatly surprised on hearing how it had been brought about. In order to confirm and strengthen this peace, a marriage was concluded between the son of John of Blois and a daughter of the Duke of Brittany, so that those who looked for a continuance of war were disappointed. In France and England the intelligence of this peace caused very great surprise. You have before heard how Sir Peter de Craon incurred the indignation of the King of France and the Duke

---

[b] The Dominicans were a religious order, called in some places Jacobins and in others Predicants or Preaching Friars. They take the name from Dominic de Guzman, their founder. Not long before his death, Dominic sent Gilbert de Tresney with twelve of his brethren into England, who founded a monastery at Oxford in the year 1221, and soon after another at London.

of Touraine from his attempt to murder Sir Oliver as he was returning in the night-time from the King's palace to his hotel, and that the King had declared war upon the Duke of Brittany, for having supported and given him an asylum; which war was put an end to by the sudden illness of the King. Sir Peter continued to make the strongest entreaties that he might be restored to favor, and allowed to return to the Court of France. His negotiators were the Duke of Burgundy and Sir Guy de la Tremouille, who would easily have succeeded had not the Duke of Orleans opposed them. He prevented any treaty being made in favor of Sir Peter de Craon, as long as hostilities continued between the Duke of Brittany and the Lord de Clisson; but when they were reconciled, his hatred against Sir Peter was much softened.

It happened at this period, that the Queen[c] of Naples and Jerusalem was prosecuting Sir Peter in the courts of justice at Paris for the restitution of 100,000 francs which she claimed from him as due to her late lord; and the better to attend to her affairs, she resided privately in Paris. Sir Peter found himself in a very disagreeable situation; he was fearful of the decision of the Parliament, for the lady was of great personal weight, and besides, he knew he had incurred the displeasure of the King and the Duke of Orleans. The Duke and Duchess of Burgundy gave him all the consolation they could, and he was allowed to come to Paris privately, where he remained chiefly at the hotel d'Artois, under the protection of the duchess.

About this time, Sigismond, King of Hungary, wrote very affectionate letters to the King of France, which he sent by a bishop and two of his knights. These letters related to the threats of Bajazet, and his boastings to the King of Hungary of carrying war into the midst of his realm, and thence to Rome, where his horse should eat his oats on the altar of St. Peter. He said he would establish that place for the seat of his imperial government, and be attended by the Emperor of Constantinople and all the principal barons of Greece; each of whom should follow his own laws, for he would only reserve to himself his authority as the lord paramount.

The King of Hungary entreated the King of France to

[c] Widow of the late Duke of Anjou.

listen to his distress, and make it as public as he could, in order that all knights and squires might be moved to provide themselves with every necessary for a journey to Hungary, to oppose the Sultan Bajazet, prevent holy Christendom from being violated by him, and his vain boasting from being accomplished. Those who brought the letters were men of rank and understanding, and acquitted themselves so well, that King Charles was much inclined to their request; and the proposition from King Richard for the marriage of his daughter was sooner agreed to on account of the intelligence from Hungary; for, as King of France, and eldest son of the Church, he was very desirous of providing a remedy for the evils that threatened it. The subject of these letters was soon made public, both at home and abroad, to move the hearts of gentlemen knights and squires, who were desirous to travel in search of glory.

At the time this news came to Paris, there were with the King the Duke and Duchess of Burgundy, their eldest son, John of Burgundy; Count de Nevers, who was not then a knight; Sir Guy and Sir William de la Tremouille, with other great barons. It was proposed therefore, at the hotel of the Duke of Burgundy, who was eager to send assistance to Hungary, that his son, the Count de Nevers, should undertake an expedition thither, as commander-in-chief of the French and other chivalry. John of Burgundy was a courteous and amiable youth of twenty-two years old, greatly beloved by the knights and squires of Burgundy, and, indeed, by all who were acquainted with him. He had married a devout and prudent lady, the daughter of Duke Albert of Bavaria, who had borne him two children.

It was soon published in Paris and elsewhere, that John of Burgundy was to lead a large body of men-at-arms into Hungary, to oppose Bajazet; that, when this was done, he was to advance to Constantinople, cross the Hellespont, enter Syria, gain the Holy Land, and deliver Jerusalem and the Holy Sepulchre from the hands of the infidels, and the bondage of the Sultan. Knights, squires, and others desirous of renown, began to collect together. The King of Hungary was greatly rejoiced at the return of his ambassadors, and gave orders that large stores of provisions should be provided against the arrival of the French; he also sent messengers to his brother the King of Germany, and his cousin, the Duke of Austria, for all the passes in their territories to be thrown open, as it would be necessary for them to march that way. Moreover he sent information of the expected assistance from France to the grand master of the Teutonic order, and to the Knights of Rhodes, that they might be ready to meet John of Burgundy.

While the news of this expedition was the matter of conversation everywhere, the Lord de Coucy returned from the frontiers of Genoa, where he had been upward of a year negotiating with the Genoese; for some of the leading men of Genoa had informed the Duke of Orleans that persons composing the government of that city were desirous of having for their duke one of the blood-royal of France: and as he had married the daughter of the Duke of Milan, it would be very suitable for him. In consequence of this, the Lord de Coucy had come into these parts, when some of those lords, who had sent the information to the Duke of Orleans, waited on him, and with many friendly expressions welcomed him to their country, and offered him their castles. The Lord de Coucy, however, was as prudent as he was valiant, and being well acquainted with the character of the Lombards and Genoese, was unwilling to trust too much to their offers and promises. The issue of his negotiations was unsuccessful, and when it was found he could not do anything, he was remanded to Paris, at the time when the expedition to Hungary was in agitation.

The Duke and Duchess of Burgundy were happy at his return, and sending for him to the hotel d'Artois, addressed him thus: "Lord de Coucy, we have the highest opinion of your understanding, valor, and prudence; and as John, our son and heir, will undertake the command of an expedition which we hope will turn out to the honor of God and Christendom, knowing that you of all the knights of France are the best informed in warlike affairs, we beg and entreat most earnestly, that you will be his counsellor and companion." The Lord de Coucy replied, "My lord, and you, madam, what you request is to me an order. I will surely be of this expedition, if it please God, for two reasons: first, from devotion, and to defend the faith of Jesus Christ; secondly, from the honor you do me, by giving me the charge of advising my lord John, your son. I shall, therefore, obey and acquit myself in all respects to the best of my abilities; but, my dear lord, and you, my dear lady, you may readily excuse me from this weight, and lay it on the Lord Philip d'Artois, constable of France, and on the Count de la Marche; for they are nearly related to him, and intend to form part of the expedition." The duke answered, " Lord de Coucy, you know more of war than either of our cousins, and we entreat you to comply with our request." " My lord," said the Lord de Coucy, " your words are commands; I will do as you require." The lords of France made vast preparations for the expedition to Hungary, and solicited the company and services of different barons, knights, and squires.

Nothing was spared in the preparations for the young John of Burgundy with regard to horses, armor, emblazonments, dressing, silver and gold plate. Large sums of florins were given to his servants, who paid them to the different workmen as they finished and brought home their works. The barons, knights, and squires, to do him honor, exerted themselves to make their equipment as handsome as possible. The Duke of Burgundy, considering that this expedition would cost him very large sums, and that the state of his wife, himself, and his son Anthony, ought not to be any way diminished, bethought himself of a tax he had in reserve in order to find a supply of money for these expenses. He had received from cities and towns in Burgundy, as the usual tax on his eldest son receiving the order of knighthood, six score thousand golden crowns; but this additional tax was laid on all knights who held fiefs from him, to attend his son into Hungary or compound in money. Some were taxed at 1,000 livres, others at 2,000; some at 500; each according to his wealth or the value of his lands. Ladies and ancient knights, who were unfit or disabled to undertake such an expedition, paid compositions at the duke's pleasure. The young knights and squires were told, " My lord does not want your money: you must accompany the Lord John at your own costs and charges." Of the last tax the Duke of Burgundy received from the gentlemen of his duchy, 60,000 crowns.

News of this expedition to Hungary was spread far and near; on its being announced in Hainault, many knights and squires, eager for renown, resolved to attend, and the Count d'Ostrevant, brother-in-law to John of Burgundy, expressed a desire to march to Hungary; he was, however, advised by his father to attempt in preference the reconquest of Friesland, which belonged to them. Knights and squires were all alive at the wars which seemed likely to take place in opposite quarters. Some made themselves ready for the expedition to Hungary; others for that to Friesland. The Count de Nevers was prepared; and all those knights had been enrolled who were to be under his charge and to accompany him. In all there were 1,000 knights, and as many squires, all men of tried courage and enterprise. They left their homes about the middle of March, and advanced in good array by companies. All the roads were open to them, for the King of Germany had commanded that his country and Bohemia should afford them every friendly assistance to supply their wants, and that the price of provisions should be on no account raised. The Duke of Austria gave the French lords a handsome reception, but he was particularly attentive to John of Burgundy, for the Lord Otho, eldest son to the duke, had espoused Mary of Burgundy, his sister.

You have before heard that the King of England had sent ambassadors to the King of France, to conclude a marriage between him and his eldest daughter Isabella. These succeeded so well in the business, that they returned to England in high spirits, and gave the King great hopes that his wishes would be gratified. To conclude the business, however, the ambassadors were sent again to Paris. During the time they were at Paris negotiating the marriage of the King of England, the dowager Queen of Naples was busily employed in her own concerns, and in prosecuting her charge against Sir Peter de Craon. The suit continued for a long time; at last, however, the following decision was given by the president, who, on rising, said that the Parliament had determined that Sir Peter de Craon was indebted to the Queen of Naples in the sum of 100,000 francs, which he must pay to her, or be committed to prison until it was done completely to her satisfaction. The ambassadors of England remained for twenty-two days in Paris; their negotiations were successful, and the marriage between the King of England and the Princess Isabella was agreed upon. She was betrothed and espoused by the earl marshal, as proxy for the King of England, and the lady was ever after styled Queen of England. I was told at the time, it was quite pleasant to see that, young as she was, she knew well how to act the queen.

When this business was completed and the different treaties signed and sealed, the ambassadors took their leave of the King and his court, and departed from Paris to Calais on their return to England, where they were joyfully received by the King, the Duke of Lancaster, and the lords attached to the King's person. However much others might be pleased, it was not so with the Duke of Gloucester; he saw plainly that by this marriage peace would be established between the two kingdoms, which sorely displeased him, unless it should be such a peace as would redound to the honor of England, and everything was placed on the same footing as when the war broke out in Gascony. He frequently conversed on the subject with his brother the Duke of York, and endeavored to draw him over to his way of thinking: he dared not, however, speak so freely to his elder brother the Duke of Lancaster, who was of the King's party, and well satisfied with this marriage on account of his two daughters, the Queens of Castille and Portugal.

At this period the Duke of Lancaster married his third wife, the daughter of a knight of Hainault, called Sir Paon de Ruet, who had formerly been one of the knights to the good and noble Queen Philippa of Hainault. Before the Lady Blanche's death, and even when married to his second wife Constance, the daughter of Don Pedro, the duke cohabited with the Lady Catherine,[d] who was then married to an English knight, now dead. The duke had three children by her previous to his marriage, two sons and a daughter. The eldest son was John, Lord Beaufort of Lancaster, and the younger, Thomas, whom the duke kept at the schools in Oxford, and made a great churchman and civilian. He was afterward Bishop of Lincoln, which is the richest bishopric in the kingdom: from affection to these children, the duke married their mother, to the great astonishment of France and England, for she was of base extraction in comparison of his two former duchesses.

[d] The Lady Catherine de Ruet was married to Sir Hugh Swynford.

The English ladies of high rank, such as the Duchess of Gloucester, the Countess of Derby, the Countess of Arundel, and others, were greatly shocked at the announcement of this marriage, and thought the duke much to blame. Indeed, many looked upon him as a doting fool for thus marrying his concubine, and declared they would never honor his lady by calling her sister. Catherine Ruet, however, remained Duchess of Lancaster, and the second lady in England, as long as she lived; indeed, she was a lady accustomed to honors, for during her youth she had been brought up at court; and the duke fondly loved the children he had by her.

I must mention that, when the sentence of the court of Parliament of Paris had been pronounced against Sir Peter de Craon, he was confined. At the advice of the Duke and Duchess of Burgundy, however, he made application to the Queen of England to intercede with the Queen of Naples to grant him liberty for fifteen days, in order that he might seek out his friends in Paris to pay this money, or to become his sureties until he had procured it in Brittany or elsewhere. The request was complied with, on condition that he should every night sleep in his prison at the Louvre; but Sir Peter sought in vain for aid among his relatives, for the sum was too great for them to advance, and he was forced to return to his prison, where he was strictly guarded day and night, and at his own proper costs.

On the arrival of the Count de Nevers with his army at Buda, in Hungary, the King gave them a most hearty reception, as, indeed, he ought, for they came to serve him. It was his intention, before he took the field, to obtain some certain intelligence of the movements of Bajazet, who, since February last, had given him notice to increase his forces, as he would, in the course of the month of May, lead an immense army across the Danube, and offer combat to the Hungarians. When the month of May arrived, however, and nothing was heard of Bajazet, the King of Hungary sent scouts across the Danube to gain intelligence, and, at the same time, issued his summons for his powers to assemble. The Knights of Rhodes came thither in numbers during the month of May, looking for the arrival of the Saracens, but there was no news of them. The King again sent out some Hungarians, who were used to arms, and well acquainted with the country; but they were as unsuccessful as his former scouts in not meeting with Bajazet: they heard, however, that he was still in Asia—at Damascus, Antioch, or Alexandria.

On receiving this information, the King called a council of his lords, and those who were come from France, to consider how they should act. He told them that he had sent some expert men-at-arms to seek Bajazet, and that there was no appearance that he would put his threat into execution this summer. Upon this the Lord de Coucy, having consulted with the other barons, made answer, that if Bajazet should have deceived them by not keeping his word, they ought not for that to remain idle, but should attempt some deeds of arms, since they had come thither to that effect; that all the French, Germans, and other foreigners were willing to meet the Turks, and if under command of Bajazet, so much the better. Orders were, in consequence, issued by the King and marshals that everyone should be prepared by a certain day, the octave of St. John the Baptist, to march for Turkey. The orders were punctually obeyed. The lords of France being desirous of making a handsome figure, examined well their armor and equipages, sparing no money in order to have them as complete as possible. When they took the field from Buda, their appearance was grandly magnificent. The constable of Hungary, who well knew the country, and led with him a large body of Hungarians and Germans, had command of the van division; and next to him marched the French lords. With the King of Hungary rode the greatest barons of his realm, and by his side John of Burgundy. They were full 60,000 horse: the infantry, however, were very few, indeed there were none but the followers of the army.

This army crossed the Danube in barges, boats, and pontoons, prepared some time since for this purpose. It was more than eight days before all had passed. The Danube divides the kingdoms of Hungary and Turkey; and when the whole army had crossed, they were delighted to find themselves on Turkish ground, for they were impatient to try the courage of the Turks. After a council, they resolved to besiege a town in Turkey called Comecte, and made preparation to invest it on all sides, which could easily be done, for it is situated in an open plain, upon a river deep enough to bear vessels. The King of Hungary encamped his army before this place without opposition, for no one made any attempt to prevent the siege. Many attacks were made upon the town; but they were valiantly opposed by the inhabitants, in the daily expectation of receiving reinforcements from Bajazet. None, however, came, and the city was taken by storm, with great slaughter of men, women and children; for the Christians on entering it, spared none. After this the King of Hungary advanced further into Turkey, toward the large city of Nicopoli. On his way thither he took the town of Laquaire, and came before another town and castle, called Brehappe, governed by a Turkish knight, the lord of the place, who had with him a strong garrison. The Count de Nevers had been created a knight by the King of Hungary on his entering Turkey; and the day he displayed his banner, upward of 300 were knighted. Those who had advanced to the town won it, within four days, by assault; but the castle resisted all their attacks.

The Lord of Brehappe, whose name was, I believe, Corbadas, a very valiant man, saved many of his people within the castle. He had three brothers—Maladius, Balachius, and Ruffin. After the capture of the town, the Christians were seven days before the castle, and attacked it many times; but finding they lost more than they gained they decamped, and advanced to the siege of Nicopoli. Corbadas was well pleased to observe the Christians marching away, and after expressing to his brothers his surprise that Bajazet had not come, he said, "I propose the following plan: I and my brother Maladius will go to Nicopoli to assist in its defence; Balachius shall remain here to guard Brehappe; and Ruffin shall cross the sea, and haste to find Bajazet, to inform him of everything that has happened, that he may take instant measures to prevent the dishonorable loss of his possessions."

The three Turks approved what the brother had said, and promised obedience. Nicopoli was besieged by the Christian army, amounting to nearly 100,000 men. Corbadas and his brother gained admittance into the town, to the great joy of the inhabitants; Balachius remained in the castle of Brehappe; and Ruffin took the first opportunity of crossing the Hellespont, to learn intelligence of Bajazet. In truth Bajazet was at Cairo, with the Sultan of Babylon, to solicit his aid, and there the Turk found him. When Bajazet saw him he was much surprised, and imagined something extraordinary had happened. He called to him, asked how things were going on in Turkey. "My lord," he replied, "they are very anxious to see you there: the King of Hungary, with an immense force, has crossed the Danube, and invaded the country; and you must know, that in his army there is a body of Frenchmen, the most gallant and best appointed that can be seen. It behooves you, therefore, to summon your friends and vassals, and hasten to Turkey, with an army powerful enough to drive these Christians back again."

"How many are they?" asked Bajazet.

"Upward of 100,000," said the Turk, "and all on horseback, armed in the best possible manner."

Bajazet made no reply, but entered the chamber of the Sultan of Babylon, leaving the Turk, who had brought the intelligence, among his own people. He related what you have just heard to the Sultan, who answered, "You must provide yourself accordingly, and shall have men enough to oppose them, for we must by all means defend our religion and possessions."

"That is true," replied Bajazet. "My wishes are now accomplished, for I was desirous that the King of Hungary should cross the Danube. At present I shall let him have full scope; but in the end he shall repay me fully for what he has done. It is now four months since I heard of the expedition from my good friend the Duke of Milan, who advised me to draw up my men with prudence. They have, as the duke writes, undertaken the expedition solely through valor to do some deeds of arms, that may gain them renown. For this I feel thankful; and within three months from this time the desire shall be gratified."

Bajazet made no long stay at Cairo with the Sultan of Babylon, who promised to send a great army to his aid, under command of his best men-at-arms. Messengers were despatched on all sides, entreating assistance; for should the French conquer Turkey, all the surrounding kingdoms would tremble, their religion be destroyed, and themselves reduced to slavery under the Christians. Many Saracen kings obeyed the summons, which Bajazet and the Sultan of Babylon sent as far as Persia, India, and Tartary; and to the north, to the kingdom of Lecto,*e* beyond the frontiers of Prussia. Having heard that the army of the Christians was composed of the flower of their chivalry, the Saracen monarchs selected from their own sect those of the greatest ability, and who had most experience in arms. But we will now leave Bajazet, and return to the Christians, who were besieging the strong city of Nicopoli.

The garrison was very numerous and defended the place valiantly. During the siege the Lord de Coucy and some other French knights took a fancy to make an expedition further into Turkey, leaving the King of Hungary to continue his approaches to the town: they took with them 500 lances and as many cross-bows on horseback, and selected as guides some of the best mounted Hungarian scouts well acquainted with the country. This same week the Turks likewise, to the number of 20,000 men, took the field, and advanced to a pass through which it was necessary the Christians should march, in order to enter the open country. After waiting two days, the Hungarian scouts came galloping up to the place where they lay in ambush. The Christians advanced near enough to see that the Turks were very numerous, and then returned to inform the Lord de Coucy and the other lords what they had seen. The Christians were rejoiced at hearing it, and the Lord de Coucy said, " We must advance and see what kind of people they are." As many as heard him approved what he said; and all tightened their armor, regirthed their horses, and advanced at a greater pace to the place where the Turks lay. There was a small wood between the two parties; on coming to which the French knights halted, and the Lord de Coucy said to Sir Reginald de Roye and the Lord de Saint Py, " I would advise, in order to draw the Turks out of their ambush, that you two advance with 100 of our men, while we post the remainder in this wood. When the Turks quit the ambush, do you suffer yourselves to be pursued, and as soon as you have passed this wood wheel round on them. We will instantly sally forth, and thus enclose and conquer them at our pleasure."

This plan was adopted: the two knights set off with about

*e* In all probability Lithuania is intended.

100 of the best mounted, and the main body, about 800 men of tried courage, entered the wood. The Turks were much pleased as they saw them approach, and thinking that they were the whole force of the enemy, they quitted their ambuscade, and advanced on the plain. The Christians observing this, turned about, and suffered themselves to be pursued; but, as they were so well mounted, the Turks could not come up with them. Both parties passed the wood without the ambush being noticed, when the Lord de Coucy sallied forth with his men, shouting out " Our Lady, for the Lord de Coucy!" and falling on the rear of the Turks, struck many down. On finding themselves thus surrounded the Turks halted and made the best defence they could, but it was of little avail; for, not suspecting any forces behind, they were thunderstruck when they were attacked on all sides. The French displayed great valor, they slew heaps upon the field, and all they overtook in the flight. In the evening they returned to the camp before Nicopoli. News was soon spread throughout the army that the Lord de Coucy had, by his valor, overthrown more than 15,000 Turks; very many were loud in his praise for this action. Not so the Count d'Eu, who said the expedition had been undertaken through vanity, and that he saw nothing praiseworthy in it. Indeed, during the whole expedition, the Count d'Eu never had any friendship for de Coucy, notwithstanding he saw that he was beloved and respected by all the French and foreign knights. Such was the beginning of that hatred between them, which at last broke out and caused the destruction of the Christian army, as will shortly be related. It is time, however, that we leave this subject and return to what was passing between the kings of France and England.

The marriage of the King of England with the Princess of France was approaching, and the two kings showed great affection for each other, as did their relatives on either side, except the Duke of Gloucester, who had no joy in it, for he knew that by this connection peace would be established between the two kingdoms, which he was unwilling to see; and, therefore, excited all whom he thought so inclined to throw every obstacle in the way. At that time, there was a knight in the duke's service by name Sir John Lackingay, who knew all the secrets of the duke, and who, by encouraging his warlike disposition, followed the natural bent of his own inclinations. At this period the Duke of Gueldres came to England to visit the King and his uncles, and to offer his loyal services, for he was so bounden by faith and homage. He had many conversations with the Duke of Lancaster respecting the intended expedition of the counts of Hainault and Ostrevant against Friesland; for at this moment Fierabras de Vertain, the Count Ostrevant's principal adviser, was in England seeking men-at-arms and archers. The Earl of Derby had been requested to accompany his cousins of Hainault and Ostrevant, to which he was well inclined, if it met the approbation of the King and his father. The Duke of Lancaster spoke to the Duke of Gueldres on this subject, and desired him to say what he thought of it. He replied, that the expedition would be attended with much danger; that Friesland was not a country to be easily conquered; that the inhabitants are a people void of honor and understanding, and show mercy to none who fall in their way; that the country was very strong, surrounded by the sea, and full of bogs, islands, and marshes. " I have been much pressed," he continued, " to join this expedition, but I will never enter such a country; and I would not advise that my cousin of Derby go thither. I am satisfied that my brother-in-law d'Ostrevant will undertake the expedition, for he is very eager to do so, and that he will lead many Hainaulters with him, but there is a chance if any of them come home again."

This speech of the Duke of Gueldres had such an effect on the Duke of Lancaster, that he made up his mind the Earl of Derby should not go to Friesland, and signified to him his intentions secretly—for his son did not live with him; telling him, that, notwithstanding the engagements he had entered into, he must break them off, for neither the King nor himself would consent that he should go on this expedition. Thus did the Duke of Gueldres prevent the Count of Hainault and his son from having the company of the Earl of Derby, in which respect he was not well advised, nor was he thanked by either. Notwithstanding this disappointment Fierabras was not the less diligent in collecting forces, and engaged many knights and squires, with more than 200 archers; and the King of England, to do honor to his cousin of Hainault, ordered vessels to be prepared on the Thames, at his cost, to carry such knights as went on the expedition to Encuse,[f] a seaport belonging to the Earl of Hainault, at the extremity of Holland, and twelve leagues by water from Friesland.

About this time the King of France sent Waleran Count de Saint Pol to England, to press forward the treaty for peace, and secretly to urge the King of England to conclude it. Robert the Hermit, who had before been in England on this subject, accompanied the Count de Saint Pol. The King was at Eltham with his brothers, the earls of Kent and Huntingdon, and his uncle, the Duke of Lancaster, when the count arrived; and after hearing what he had to say, the King took him aside and said, "Fair brother of Saint Pol, with regard to the treaty of peace with my father-in-law the King of France, I am heartily inclined to it; but I cannot accomplish it alone. My uncle of Gloucester is violently against it, and he leads the Londoners as he will, and may attempt to stir up a rebellion in the country, and set the people against me; consider then the danger I shall run in the event of a second rebellion, headed by the Duke of Gloucester and other great barons and knights who are, as I know, of his way of thinking." "My lord," answered the Count de Saint Pol, "you must gain him over by fair and kind speeches. Make him handsome presents, and should he demand anything, however unreasonable, grant it him instantly. Continue this till your marriage be completed, your Queen brought hither, and all affairs concluded; you may then follow a different method; for, as the King of France will be at all times ready to assist you, you will be powerful enough to crush all your enemies or rebellious subjects." "In God's name," said the King, "you speak to the purpose; it shall be done as you advise."

During his stay in England the Count de Saint Pol was lodged in London; he had, however, frequent conferences with the King and Duke of Lancaster at Eltham on the subject of the marriage. It had been ordered at Paris, as the count told the King, that the King of France and his uncles should come to St. Omer, and bring the young princess with them: it was their wish, therefore, that the King of England should come

[f] Perhaps Enchuysen is intended. D. Sauvage, in a marginal note, calls it Neuse.

to Calais, and that between the towns of St. Omer and Calais an interview should take place between the two kings, who from personal knowledge would have their affection for each other much strengthened, and then some secret treaties respecting a peace might be made, without employing too many persons in the business, before the King carried his Queen to England. If a peace could not be concluded, the truce was then to be prolonged for the term of thirty or forty years between England, France, and the allies.

This proposal seemed so fair and honorable that orders were instantly issued for purveyances of every kind to be made ready for the King's voyage and residence at Calais. The Duke and Duchess of Gloucester were invited by the King to be of the party, as were also the dukes and duchesses of York and Lancaster. The King of England and his train of lords and ladies soon arrived at Calais; the Duke of Burgundy came to St. Omer to press forward the treaties, which were carried on through the mediation of the Count de St. Pol, and Robert the Hermit. On the eve of Our Lady, in the middle of August, the duke was conducted by the count to Calais, to wait on the King of England and his uncles, from whom he met with a cordial reception, and they conferred together for some time on the articles for a peace. When the Duke of Burgundy had stayed two days at Calais, the King told him that on his return to England he would lay all the articles before the Parliament; for that neither himself nor his lords could agree to anything conclusive without the assent of the people of England; he added that he would himself go over and return, so making one journey for the conclusion of all things. The determination was approved; the King of England and his lords returned to London; but the ladies remained until they should come back again, which was speedily done. During this period the expedition from Hainault against the Frieslanders took place, and it is time that we relate the arrangement of it.

You have heard that King Richard out of affection to his cousin had sent him some men-at-arms, and 200 archers; these were under command of three English lords, one named Cornewall, another Colleville, but the third, who was a squire, I have forgotten. Duke Albert of Bavaria set out from the Hague in company with his son, the Count d'Ostrevant, for Hainault, and convened the States of that country at Mons. He laid before them his wishes to invade Friesland, and remonstrated on the lawful claim he had upon it; in proof of which he read to them certain letters patent, apostolical and imperial, authoritatively sealed with lead and gold, which showed evidently his right over that country. The duke addressed the meeting: "My lords and valiant men our subjects; you know that everyone ought to guard and defend his inheritance, and that in defence of himself or his country man has a right to make war. You know also that the Frieslanders ought to acknowledge themselves our subjects; but they rebel against us, and against our rights, like men without law or religion; in this necessity, therefore, we entreat your assistance, both personal and pecuniary, that we may subject these disobedient Frieslanders to our will."

To this remonstrance the three estates unanimously assented, and presented the duke with 30,000 francs ready money, without including the town of Valenciennes, which town performed its duty equally well. Duke Albert and his son were very joyful at seeing their subjects so forward to assist the war, as it assured them that they were well beloved by them; and since they had not sufficient money, they resolved to inform the King of France of the intended expedition, and to request aid from him. The matter was variously received at the French Court, and after much discussion it was determined to send to the duke's assistance 500 lances. Upon hearing this intelligence Duke Albert assembled all his barons and vassals of Hainault in his hall of Mons, and addressed them, saying that he hoped they would all arm and provide themselves with followers and every necessary, each according to his power, to assist him in his intended expedition; and that out of affection to him, and regard to their own honor and renown, they would embark with him for Upper Friesland. All the knights, squires, and lords instantly promised him their services like loyal vassals. Duke Albert and the Count d'Ostrevant found them punctual in the performance of their promises.

About the beginning of August, in the year 1396, they assembled and marched off in companies handsomely arrayed toward Antwerp, whence they embarked for Enchuysen, the general rendezvous. You may suppose that when all these preparations were making for the departure of so many knights and squires, the ladies and damsels were not in high spirits; we must allow they were very much cast down, for they saw their fathers, brothers, uncles, husbands, and lovers going on a dangerous expedition, not having forgotten how in former times the Hainaulters with Count William had remained on the field of battle in Friesland; they were therefore fearful that what had happened to their predecessors might befall them, and loudly praised the Duchess of Brabant for having forbidden any gentleman or others of her country to take part in this expedition. The ladies frequently pressed their lovers and friends to decline going, and many meetings were held, but to little purpose. The Duke of Bavaria and his son, having been so successful in Hainault and Zealand, made the same request of assistance to the Hollanders.

To say the truth, the Hollanders were much pleased to hear war was about to be made on the Frieslanders, for they hated them, particularly the knights and squires, and they mutually plundered each other on the frontiers of the two countries: very many, therefore, were inclined to join in the expedition, and it was not long before they assembled at Enchuysen, where vessels had been provided to carry them to Friesland. Everyone was now ordered to embark, which being done they hoisted sail, recommended themselves to God, and put to sea. The water was smooth, and seemed to take pleasure in bearing them: the Frieslanders had long been informed of Duke Albert's intention of marching against them with a powerful army, and they determined to combat their enemies at the very moment of their landing; they also resolved not to accept ransom for any person, however high his rank, but to put their prisoners to death, or keep them in banishment from their own countries.

Among the Frieslanders was a man of high birth and renown, of great strength and stature, for he was a head taller than the rest of his countrymen; his name was Yves Jouvere, but the Hollanders, Zealanders, and Hainaulters called him "the great Frieslander." This valiant man had gained much reputation in Prussia, Hungary, Turkey, and elsewhere; and when he heard his countrymen thus really resolved on battle, he said, "O ye noble men and free Frieslanders, know that there is no fortune stable: if in former times you have by your prowess conquered the Hainaulters, Hollanders, and Zealanders, those now about to invade us are men expert in war, and be assured they will act otherwise than their predecessors; I would therefore advise that we suffer them to land, and make what progress they can into the country: let us guard our towns and fortresses, and give them the plains—our country will not long support them: it is besides cut up with ditches and dikes, so that they cannot advance far into the interior, and will be forced to retire after having burned ten or twelve villages; the damage they can do will be very trifling, and we can soon repair it; but if we offer them battle, I very much fear we shall be overpowered, for I have been informed they are 100,000 men under arms." He said truly, for they were at least as many. The valiant Friesland knights seconded the proposal; the people, however, would not listen to it, and they opposed what the great Frieslander offered, with such success as to occasion it to be determined that as soon as they should hear of the enemy landing they were to march and offer them battle. This having been resolved on, the assembly broke up, that each one might make his preparations. To say the truth, they were in general badly armed; many had no other defensive covering than their waistcoats made of coarse, thick cloth, scarcely better than horse cloths; some were armed in leather, others with rusty jackets of mail, which seemed unfit for service; some, however, were perfectly well armed.

When the Frieslanders were ready to march they took from their churches the crosses and banners, and divided themselves into three battalions, each consisting of about 10,000 men; they halted on arriving at a pass defended by a ditch, very near to where the Hainault army was to land, and plainly saw the Hainaulters, Hollanders, and Zealanders, for they were close to the shore, and preparing to disembark. It was on St. Bartholomew's Day, which this year fell on a Sunday, that Duke Albert and his army landed in Friesland. The Frieslanders noticing the movements of their enemies, sallied forth, in number about 6,000, and mounted the dike to see if they could in any way prevent their landing. The disembarkation was strongly contested, and numbers were killed and wounded; but from the advantages of their bows and cross-bows, and by their superior mode of fighting, the Hainaulters gained the dike, and remained victors of the field at this first attack. The Frieslanders on the loss of the dike retreated to another pass where they had cast up the earth in the front, and the ditch was very deep; they amounted to about 30,000. On Sunday and Monday they pitched their tents, and some few skirmishes took place.

On Tuesday morning both armies were ready prepared for battle, and several new knights were made of the Hainaulters, Hollanders, and Zealanders. All drew up in handsome array, placing the archers in front, intermixed with the ranks. The Frieslanders guarded themselves from the arrows by means of the mound of earth, which was as high as their heads; but the Hainaulters leaped into the ditch, and made bridges of their pikes and lances. The new knights acquitted themselves honorably, and the enemy displayed great courage; they are a lusty race, though very badly armed, and some of them without even shoes or stockings: nevertheless, they made an obstinate defence. During the skirmish the Lord de Ligne with other Hainault knights, following the course of the ditch, found a passage for their horses, and fell upon the rear of the Frieslanders, to their utter dismay; to upset this attack they quitted the defence of the ditch, but the Hainaulters charged them so vigorously that they were dispersed, and the Hollanders and Zealanders crossed the ditch and joined in the fray. The battle was now very murderous, and Yves Jouvere, the great Frieslander, was killed; not long after which the Frieslanders yielded the field, and took to flight as fast as they could; the carnage in the pursuit was horrible, for none were spared, the Hollanders in particular killed all they could overtake. To conclude, the Frieslanders were completely defeated, and the greater part killed.

The Lord of Kuynder, who was lord of the town where they landed, had surrendered himself on the Monday, and himself and his two sons were in the battle against the Frieslanders; after the victory the Hainaulters and their companions quartered themselves about Kuynder, and took several towns and castles; the captures, however, were inconsiderable, for the Frieslanders did them much harm by ambuscades and skirmishes. If they made any prisoners, they had no ransom to offer, and it was seldom they would surrender, but fought until they were slain. When the Hainault army had been in the country about five weeks, and had burned and destroyed many towns and villages, the weather began to be very cold, and it rained almost daily; Duke Albert and his son, in consequence, marched their army into Holland, the more comfortably to pass the winter, which had set in very hard. On arriving at Enchuysen the lords dismissed their men, particularly the strangers, with whom they were well contented, and paid them their full pay, at the same time thanking them for the service they had rendered. Thus was this great army disbanded without having made any conquest.

## CHAPTER VII

**Negotiations for Peace Continue—Kings of England and France Have an Interview—Marriage of the Young Princess of France with King Richard—Their Return to England—Siege of Nicopoli Continued—Bajazet and His Immense Army—Defeat of the Christian Army Through the Imprudence of the French—John of Burgundy and Many Noble Lords Taken Prisoners—Great Cruelty of Bajazet—The Lord Boucicaut Spared—Sir James de Helly Carries the News of the Defeat to France—Presents to Bajazet—Ransom and Preparation for the Return of the Prisoners—The Duke of Gloucester Excites Rebellion in England—His Arrest by Means of an Ambuscade at Stratford.**

IT has been mentioned that the King of England had returned from Calais to London, to wait the meeting of his Parliament at Michaelmas. Meanwhile great purveyances were made for him and his barons, and sent to Calais and Guines: the larger part was forwarded down the Thames, but a good deal was collected in Flanders at Damme, Bruges, and Sluys, and sent by sea to Calais. In like manner great preparations were made on the part of the French, indeed no expense was spared on either side, and the lords of each country were emulous to outshine one another. The session of Parliament, which usually lasts forty days, and is held in the King's palace at Westminster, was now abridged, for the King attended it only five days; when the business was settled the King and his two uncles of Lancaster and Gloucester, and the members of his council, set out from London, and crossed the sea to Calais. The Duke of York and the Earl of Derby did not accompany the King, but remained behind to guard England in his absence. Information was immediately sent to the French Court of the King of England's return to Calais, and the Duke and Duchess of Burgundy came to St. Omer, and fixed their residence in the abbey of St. Bertin. The King of France sent the Comte de Saint Pol to Richard as soon as he heard of his arrival, to compliment him in his name, and to lay before him the orders that had been given for the ceremony of his marriage.

The King of England eagerly listened to this, for he took much pleasure in the business; and the Count de Saint Pol on his return to St. Omer was accompanied by the dukes of Lancaster and Gloucester, and many other barons and knights, who were handsomely received by the Duke and Duchess of Burgundy. The Duke of Brittany came thither also, having left the King of France and the young Queen of England at Aire. You must know that every honor and respect that could be imagined was paid to the English lords; the Duchess of Burgundy entertained them splendidly at dinner; there were an immense variety of dishes and decorations on the tables, and very rich presents made of gold and silver plate; nothing in short was spared, so that the English were astonished where such riches could come from. When the entertainment was over the company took leave of each other, and the two dukes with their duchesses and children returned with the other knights and barons to Calais, and related to King Richard how grandly they had been received, and the rich presents that had been made them.

Their praises pleased the King much, for he was delighted whenever he heard the King of France or the French well spoken of, so much was he already enamored with them on account of the King's daughter, whom he was to marry.

Shortly after this the King of France, accompanied by the Duke of Brittany, came to St. Omer, and took up his lodgings in the abbey of St. Bertin. The dukes of Berry, Burgundy, and Bourbon went forward to confer with the King at Calais, where they were splendidly entertained, and concluded certain treaties with the King and his uncles. Many both in France and England thought that a peace had been concluded, for by this time the Duke of Gloucester was well inclined to it, in consideration of the kind promises of the King, who had engaged, if a peace were made, to create his son Humphrey, Earl of Rochester, and make the annual revenue of it equal to £2,000 sterling; also to present the Duke of Gloucester with 50,000 nobles on his return to England. When the French lords had concluded the business they took leave of the King, and returned to the King of France and the Duke of Orleans at St. Omer.

The King of France now left St. Omer, and resided in the fort of Ardres; the plain was covered with tents and pavilions full of French and English; the King of England and the Duke of Lancaster were lodged at Guines. On the vigil of the Feast of St. Simon and St. Jude, which fell on a Friday, in the year of grace 1396, the two kings left their lodgings on the point of ten o'clock, and, accompanied by their attendants, went to the tents which had been prepared for them; thence they advanced on foot to a certain spot which had been fixed on for their meeting, which was surrounded by 400 French, and as many English knights, brilliantly armed with swords in hand. These 800 knights were so drawn up that the two kings passed between their ranks, conducted in the following order: the Dukes of Lancaster and Gloucester supported the King of France, and the dukes of Berry and Burgundy the King of England, and when the two kings were on the point of meeting, the 800 knights fell on their knees and wept for joy. The two kings met bareheaded, and having saluted, took each other by the hand, when the King of France led the King of England to his tent; the four dukes took each other by the hand and followed them. The French and English knights remained at their posts, looking at their opponents with good-humor, and never moving until the whole ceremony was over. The spot where the two kings met was marked, and a chapel in honor of the Virgin Mary was proposed to be erected on it, but I know not if it were ever put into execution.

At the entrance of the two kings into the tent, the dukes of Orleans and Bourbon came forward and cast themselves on their knees; the kings stopped and made them rise; the six dukes then assembled in front, and conversed together; the kings passed on, and had some conversation, while wines and spices were preparing. The Duke of Berry served the King of France with the comfit-box, and the Duke of Burgundy with the cup of wine; in like manner the King of England was served by the dukes of Lancaster and Gloucester. After the kings had been served, the knights of France and England took the wine and spices, and served the prelates, dukes, princes, and counts; and after them squires and other officers of the household did the same to all within the tent, until everyone had partaken. Shortly after the two monarchs took leave of each other, as did the different lords. When their horses were ready the King of England and his uncles mounted and rode toward Calais—the King to Guines, the dukes of Lancaster and Gloucester to Hamme, and the others to their lodgings. The King of France also returned to Ardres, accompanied by the Duke of Orleans, for nothing more was done that day, although the tents and pavilions were left standing.

At eleven o'clock on Saturday morning another meeting took place in the tent of the French King. Dining tables were laid out; that for the kings was long and handsome, and the sideboard covered with most magnificent plate. The two kings sat by themselves; the King of France at the top of the table, and the King of England below him at a good distance from each other; they were served by the dukes of Berry, Burgundy, and Bourbon, the last of whom entertained the two monarchs with many gay remarks: addressing the King of England, he said, "My lord, King of England, you ought to make good cheer, for you have all your wishes gratified: you have a wife, or shall have one, for she will speedily be delivered to you." "Bourbonnois," replied the King of France, "we wish our daughter were as old as our cousin of St. Pol, for then she would love our son of England much more." The King of England on hearing these words bowed to the King of France, and replied, "Good father-in-law, the age of our wife pleases us right well; we pay not so much attention to her age, as we value your love, and that of our subjects; for we shall now be so strongly united that no king in Christendom shall any way hurt us."

When dinner was over, the cloth was removed, the tables carried away,[a] and wine and spices brought. After this the Queen of England entered the tent, attended by a great number of ladies and damsels; the King led her by the hand and gave her to the King of England, who instantly after took his leave; the Queen was placed in a rich litter which had been prepared for her, but of all the French ladies who were there, only the Lady de Coucy went with her. Many of the principal

---

[a] One among many passages in the old Chronicles which prove that in baronial times the tables were taken away after dinner, and the hall left clear; indeed, for this very purpose the tables were generally on trestles.

ladies of England received Queen Isabella with great joy; when the ladies were ready the King of England and his lords departed, and riding at a good pace, arrived at Calais. The King of France and his court returned to St. Omer, where he had left the Queen and Duchess of Burgundy, and stayed there the Sunday and Monday following. On the Tuesday, which was All Saints' Day, the King of England and the Lady Isabella of France were married by the Archbishop of Canterbury, in the Church of St. Nicholas, at Calais. Great was the feasting on the occasion, and the heralds and minstrels were most liberally paid. On Thursday the King and Queen of England, having heard an early mass, embarked for Dover, which they reached in less than three hours. The King dined at the castle, and lay that night at Rochester; passing through Dartford, he arrived at his palace of Eltham, where the lords and ladies took leave of the King and Queen, and went home. Fifteen days after this the Queen made her entry into London, grandly attended by lords, ladies, and damsels; she lay one night in the Tower and the next day was conducted in great pomp through the streets to Westminster, where the King was waiting to receive her.

During the time the court was at Westminster, a tournament was ordered to be held at Candlemas, in Smithfield, between forty knights and as many squires, notices of which were given to the heralds that they might publish it beyond sea, and as far as Scotland.

When the Duke of Brittany took leave of the King of France and his lords, after the marriage of King Richard, he carried with him his cousin, Sir Peter de Craon, having made interest with the Duke of Burgundy to gain his liberty, and I imagine he engaged to pay the Queen of Jerusalem her 100,000 marks by instalments. But I will for the present leave speaking of these matters, and return to what was passing in Turkey.

The Christians were besieging Nicopoli, and as yet nothing had been heard of any assistance from Bajazet. During the whole summer he had been busily employed in raising a large army of Saracens and infidels, and had even sent to Persia for succor. These, to the amount of 200,000, crossed the Hellespont, and advanced so secretly, that they were close to Nicopoli before the Christians knew that they had begun their march.

Bajazet was as well acquainted as most persons with the stratagems of war, and marched to raise the siege in the following order. His army was drawn up in the form of a harrow, and occupied about a league of ground; in front of the main body were 8,000 Turks, to mask the body of the army, which was divided into two wings, and Bajazet was in the midst of the main body.

It happened on the Monday preceding Michaelmas Day in the year 1396, about ten o'clock, as the King of Hungary and his lords were seated at dinner, news was brought that the Turks were at hand. This was agreeable information to many who were desirous of arms; they instantly arose, pushed the tables aside, and demanded their horses and armor. Being somewhat heated with wine, they hastened to the field, and banners and pennons were displayed. The banner of the Virgin Mary was unfurled, and the guard of it given to that valiant knight, Sir John de Vienne, admiral of France. The French were the first in the field, and seemingly fearless of the Turks, for they were ignorant of their immense numbers, and that Bajazet commanded them in person. The King of Hungary sent to entreat them not to begin the battle before they heard from him again; but the Count d'Eu, the constable of France, was impetuous, and determined to fight the enemy.

The infidels were now fast approaching, and in such numbers that the Christians became completely surrounded, and found it impossible to retreat. Many knights and squires, who were used to arms, knew that the day must be lost; nevertheless they advanced. The French lords were so richly dressed out in their emblazoned surcoats, that they looked like little kings; but, as I was told, when they met the Turks they were not more than 700 in number. Had they waited for the Hungarian army, they might, perhaps, have gained the victory; to their pride and presumption was the whole loss owing—a loss which was so great, that never, since the defeat of Roncesvalles, when twelve peers of France were slain, did the French suffer so considerably. However, before they were overcome they made a great slaughter of the Turks; indeed, they defeated the van battalion, and put it to flight, pursuing it into a valley where Bajazet was posted with the main army. The French would have returned, but could not, for they were now enclosed on all sides. The battle raged with fury, and lasted a considerable time.

The King of Hungary, when informed of the engagement, was very angry that his orders had not been obeyed: "We shall lose the day from the vanity of the French," he said to the Grand Master of Rhodes, who was beside him. "If they had waited for us to join them, we should have had sufficient strength to cope with the enemy." As he thus spoke, he looked back, and saw his men flying panic-struck, and the Turks pursuing them. It was a most unfortunate day for the Hungarians and French. As they fled, in the greatest confusion, the Turks followed, killing them, or making prisoners at pleasure. God assisted the King of Hungary and the Grand Master of Rhodes, for, on arriving at the banks of the Danube, they fortunately found a small vessel, into which they entered, and, by means of it, crossed to the opposite shore.

Sir William de la Tremouille and his son displayed great feats of valor before they were slain. Sir John de Vienne, also, who bore the banner of our Lady, in spite of his deeds of arms, was killed, grasping the banner in his hands, and was thus found after the battle. Very many of the French were saved from the extreme richness of their armor—they were dressed like kings: and the Saracens and Turks, who are very avaricious, thought, by saving their lives, that they should gain large ransoms; for they believed them to be much greater lords from their appearances than they really were. The Count de Nevers was made prisoner, as were also the counts d'Eu and de la Marche, the lords de Coucy, Boucicaut, and others. The battle lasted three hours; more were killed in the pursuit than in the battle, and numbers were drowned. Happy indeed was he who could escape from such danger by any means. When the business was over, the Turks, Persians, and others retired to the tents and pavilions, which they had conquered from the Christians, and enjoyed themselves.

Bajazet dismounted at the sound of many minstrels, at the principal tent that had belonged to the King of Hungary, which was very large and richly adorned. When he was disarmed, to cool and refresh himself, he sat on a silken carpet in the middle of the tent, and sent for his principal friends to chat and joke with them. He began the conversation by saying that he would now conquer Hungary, and all the rest of Christendom; and that, as he was descended from his blood, he would reign like Alexander *b* of Macedon, who for twelve years governed the whole world. He then gave three orders: first, that everyone who had made prisoners should produce them before him next day; secondly, that the dead should be carefully examined, and the nobles and great lords set apart and left untouched until he had seen them; thirdly, that exact inquiries should be made after the King of Hungary, that he might know whether he was dead or alive.

When Bajazet had refreshed himself he resolved to visit the dead on the field of battle, where, to his great surprise and anger, he found that the victory had cost him dear; for where one Christian lay dead, there were thirty of their enemies around them. The next morning, before Bajazet was risen, great numbers came to his tent to learn his will respecting the prisoners. It had been rumored that he intended having them all put to death without mercy; this, however, was not the case: his orders were, "Let those alone be spared who are nearly related to the King and willing to pay for their liberty a great sum of money, and all others be put to death."

Shortly after, the Sultan made his appearance to his people before the tent; who, bowing down, made him obeisance. The army was drawn up in two wings. The Sultan with his nobles, the Count de Nevers, and all those prisoners who were to be spared, were in the centre; for he would they should witness the execution of their companions, which the Saracens were eager to perform. Many excellent knights and squires of France and other nations were now brought forth in their shirts one after another before Bajazet, who eyed them a little as they were led on, and as he made a signal they were instantly cut to pieces by men waiting for them with drawn swords. Such was the cruelty of Bajazet this day, when upward of 300 gentlemen were piteously murdered. It was a cruel case for them to suffer for the love of our Saviour, Jesus Christ, and may he receive their souls!

Among the murdered of that day was the gallant knight, Sir

---

*b* Alexander, surnamed the Great, was the son of Philip, King of Macedon, and born at Pella, B.C. 356. He succeeded his father at the age of twenty; and after a period of singular and wonderful success in a political point of view, he closed his career of conquest through excess of drinking, at the early age of thirty-one.

Henry d'Antoing. May God show mercy to his soul! The Lord Boucicaut, marshal of France, was led naked like the others before Bajazet, and would have suffered the same cruel death, had not the Count de Nevers left his companions and flung himself on his knees before the Sultan, entreating him to spare the Lord Boucicaut, who was much beloved by the King of France, and well able to pay a considerable ransom. Bajazet consented, and thus the Lord Boucicaut was put aside with those who were not to be killed. Others were brought forward, until the number I have mentioned was completed; such was the cruel revenge the infidels had on the Christians.

Three knights, of whom Sir James de Helly was one, were brought before Bajazet and the Count de Nevers, who was asked which of the three he wished should go to the King of France, and his father the Duke of Burgundy, to acquaint them with their condition. Sir James de Helly had the good fortune to be made choice of, and he set out forthwith, it being the Sultan's intention that Sir James should publish wherever he passed the great victory which he had gained over the Christians. It was about noon on Christmas Day that Sir James Helly arrived in Paris, and the moment he dismounted at his inn he inquired where the King was. On being told that he was at the hotel de St. Pol, on the banks of the Seine, he went thither in the same dress he had rode in, booted and spurred. On approaching the King he fell upon his knees, and told all that he had been charged with as well by Bajazet as by the Count de Nevers and the French lords, his fellow-prisoners. The King and his lords listened attentively to all he said. Many questions were asked, in order to hear a more detailed account, to all of which Sir James answered pertinently, and to the satisfaction of the King, who was greatly affected at the loss the King of Hungary and his chivalry had suffered. When the intelligence which Sir James de Helly had brought was made public, all who had lost any relations were in the utmost consternation, as may easily be supposed.

The high nobility of France, such as the Duchess of Burgundy, and the Lady Margaret of Hainault, were greatly afflicted on account of their son and husband, the Count de Nevers; the Countess d'Eu lamented her lord the constable, as did the Countess de la Marche; the ladies of Coucy, of Bars, and Sully, in like manner, bewailed the melancholy situation of their lords. The Duke of Burgundy treated Sir James most kindly for having brought him intelligence of his son; he made him many rich gifts, and retained him for one of his knights, with a pension of 200 livres a year during his life. The King of France also, and the lords of the court, gave him handsome presents.

Sir James remained in Paris about twelve days, and then, having received his despatches, set out on his way to Turkey, following the same road by which he had come.

After his departure, the Duke of Burgundy was constantly employed in preparing presents for the Sultan, which were entrusted to Sir John de Châteaumorant to convey to him. They consisted of pieces of the best worked tapestry, from Arras, representing the history of Alexander the Great, and his conquests, the finest linens from Rheims, and scarlet and crimson cloths, which were packed on six sumpter horses. All these things were easily to be had for money; but there was great difficulty in procuring white gerfalcons,[c] and when they were got Sir John began his journey, fifteen days after Sir James de Helly.

Immediately after the battle, Bajazet disbanded his army and marched to the city of Bursa, carrying his prisoners with him, who were placed under strict confinement, and had very few comforts allowed them. Sir James de Helly found him at Poly, another town of Turkey, to which he had retired. On entering his presence he humbled himself much before him, and said, " Most dear and redoubted lord, here is your prisoner, who has delivered to the best of his abilities the message with which you have charged him." Bajazet replied, " Thou art welcome, and in consideration of thy service, I give thee thy liberty." Sir James thanked him, and then said, that the King of France and the Duke of Burgundy had sent him an honorable knight

---

[c] The gerfalcon was the proper bird to be used by a king. The books of Hawking assign different sorts of hawks to different ranks of persons:

The earl, the vulture, and the merloun were for an emperor.
The gerfaulcon, and the tercel of the gerfaulcon, for a king.
The faulcon gentle, and the tercel gentle, a prince.
The faulcon of the rock, for a duke.
The faulcon peregrine, for an earl.
The bastard, for a baron.
The sacre, and the sacret, for a knight.
The lanere, and the laneret, for an esquire.
The marlyon, for a lady.
The hobby, for a young man.
The goshawk, for a yeoman.
The tercel, for a poor man.
The sparrow-hawk, for a priest.
The musket, for a holy-water clerk.
The kesteret, for a knave or servant.
—See Strutt's " Sports."

with credential letters, as ambassador, and likewise with very grand presents, and that he was now at Buda waiting for passports. "We are willing he should have them," replied Bajazet; "let them be made out in any form you please." About an hour after, Sir James requested the Sultan's permission to visit and converse with the French prisoners. To this Bajazet, after some silence, said, "Thou shalt see one of them, but no more." He then made a sign to his attendants, and the Count de Nevers was brought to converse with Sir James for a short space of time, and then was carried back to prison. As soon as the passports were ready Sir James set out with them to Buda, to Sir John de Châteaumorant; but on mentioning to the King of Hungary the object of their journey into Turkey, he would not consent that Bajazet should have the presents. "In respect of the gerfalcons," he said, "I am indifferent whether he have them or not, for birds fly anywhere, and are as soon lost as given; but with respect to the fine tapestry, which would remain as a proof of his boastings being true, I will not consent that he enjoy the pleasure of possessing it. Therefore, Châteaumorant, if you wish to journey into Turkey to see Bajazet to present him with the falcons you may do so, but you shall carry nothing else to him."

Sir John made a respectful reply; and, being in doubt how to act, sent off to the King of France and the Duke of Burgundy requesting their advice. The matter was discussed in the French council, where the conduct of the King of Hungary was greatly condemned, and the King of France at last wrote courteous letters to him, requesting that he would no longer prevent his ambassadors from proceeding on their journey to take presents to the Court of Turkey.

The King of France had every year relapses of his frenzy, without any physician or surgeon being able to prevent them. Some, indeed, boasted that they could restore him; but his disorder never ceased until it had run its course, in spite of prayers and medicines. A strong suspicion was about this time excited that the King had been poisoned or enchanted by some pernicious herbs, and that the Duchess of Orleans, daughter to the Duke of Milan, was the cause of the mischief, that she might succeed to the crown of France. The Duke of Orleans was very melancholy on hearing such injurious reports against his duchess; and Galias, Duke of Milan, her father, felt the disgrace so deeply that he twice or thrice sent ambassadors to France to exculpate his daughter to the King and his council, at the same time offering a knight or knights, who should engage in mortal combat any person who should dare to accuse his daughter of such iniquitous and treasonable practices. Moreover, on account of this accusation, he himself threatened to make war on France.

The Duke and Duchess of Burgundy did everything in their power to find means to pay the ransom of their son, the Count de Nevers, and the other prisoners. They reduced as much as possible their own expenses, and by means of a rich Lombard, who lived at Paris, by name Dinde Desponde, gained the interest of the Genoese merchants, and others who were likely to aid them in the matter. Through the intervention of the Grand Master of Rhodes, the King of Hungary, before the arrival of the letter of the King of France, permitted the ambassadors to continue their journey to Turkey. The Sultan was much pleased at seeing them, and seemed very proud of the presents which had been sent to him. The knights were only permitted to have one interview with the Count de Nevers, and after that returned to the King of France at Paris.

I must now say something of the Duke of Gloucester, whose heart was by no means inclined to the French, and who was more pleased than hurt at the melancholy loss which they had sustained in Turkey. The duke's most confidential adviser was a knight, by name Sir John Lackingay, with whom he held such conversations as the following: "These rare boasting Frenchmen have been nearly annihilated in Turkey. Such knights and squires as join company with them are very ill-advised; they are too vain and presumptuous ever to bring anything they undertake to a successful issue. This has often been apparent during the wars of my lord and father, and our brother the Prince of Wales, for they never could obtain a victory over our men. I know not why we have truces with them. If the King of England had a good head, and were as desirous as I am of war, and would take some pains to recover the inheritance the French have so shamefully stolen from him, he would find 100,000 archers and 6,000 men-at-arms ready to cross the sea and serve him with their lives and fortunes.

"There never was so favorable an opportunity to carry the war into France as the present, for the flower of the French chivalry is slain or in captivity. If peace continue, we shall languish and become more enervated than ever since my nephew came to the throne. Things cannot long remain in this state; the people will perceive and redress them. The King raises heavy taxes on the merchants, who are greatly discontented; he squanders the money no one knows how, and thus is the kingdom impoverished. True it is he gives largely to those about him, and in whom he confides; but the people pay for this, and it will shortly cause a rebellion. As soon as the truces between France and England are signed, he gives out that he will make a voyage to Ireland; he has been there already and gained but little, for Ireland is not worth conquering. The Irish are a poor and wicked people, with an impoverished country; and he who should conquer it one year, would lose it the next. Lackingay, Lackingay! all you have just heard me say, consider as truth."

The duke had conceived a great hatred to his nephew the King of England, and could no way speak well of him. When the King sent for him, if it was his pleasure he would come; but more frequently he stayed at home; and when he obeyed, he was always the last to come and the first to depart. He had a handsome castle in Essex, thirty miles from London, called Pleshy: indeed, the Lord Thomas was a great lord, and could afford to spend annually 60,000 crowns. He was Duke of Gloucester, Earl of Sussex and Buckingham, and constable of England, and, from his rough manner, was more dreaded by the King than any other of his uncles; through his influence many severe and hasty executions had taken place in England —that gallant and prudent knight, Sir Simon Burley, was beheaded—the Archbishop of York and the Duke of Ireland banished. The Duke of Gloucester's two brothers of Lancaster and York resided generally with the King. He was jealous of them, and said to several who went to visit him at his castle of Pleshy, that his brothers were so expensive to the King, and that it would be more decent for them to live at their own houses. The duke gained by every possible means the love of the Londoners, for he thought that, if he acquired popularity with them, the rest of England would follow their example. He had a nephew, son to his brother Lionel, Duke of Clarence, and who was called John, Earl of March; this nephew he would gladly have seen on the throne of England, and King Richard deposed from it; and he made no secret of this opinion to those who were in his confidence. He invited this Earl of March to come and see him, and when at Pleshy unbosomed himself to him of all the secrets of his heart, telling him that he had been selected for King of England—that King Richard and his Queen were to be confined, but with ample provision for their maintenance—that he should certainly make a point of putting his plans into execution, and that he was already joined by the Earl of Arundel, Sir John Arundel, the Earl of Warwick, and many prelates and barons of England. The Earl of March was thunderstruck at this proposal, and prudently replied that he never thought of such things. The duke desired him to keep secret what he had told him; this he promised, and taking his leave, instantly went to his estates in Ireland, and would never listen nor send any answers to all the proposals his uncle made him. The Duke of Gloucester employed all possible means to stir up troubles in England.

The year that a truce had been signed between England and France to last for thirty years, King Richard and his Queen came to London on their return from France, and the Duke of Gloucester whispered the citizens to petition the King to abolish all taxes and subsidies, since a truce for so long a term had been signed, and they had been levied solely as war taxes. This advice was soon acted upon by the Londoners, and many of the principal towns; they collected together, and went in a body to the King at Eltham, where they made their demand; only two of the King's uncles were present, viz., the dukes of Lancaster and York, when the citizens presented their petition, and at the King's request the former answered them: "My fair sirs, you will now each of you return to your homes, and within a month from this day come to the palace of Westminster, when the King, his nobles, and prelates of the council shall be assembled, and your petition shall be taken into consideration." This answer contented some, but not all, and at the month's end they went again to the King at Westminster. The Duke of Gloucester was present, and leaned much to the petitioners, though he dissembled somewhat his real thoughts.

The Duke of Lancaster replied for the King, and said, "Ye citizens of London, in obedience to the King's command, I declare to you what the King and council have determined. Ye know that to provide against dangers to the kingdom, ye as well as the other citizens and towns within the realm, about six years ago agreed that a tax of thirteen per cent. should be laid on all merchandise that was sold, for which the King granted to you many privileges. If, then, ye now turn rebellious, he will recall his former favors. Consider, therefore, the matter calmly; the state of the King demands great expense—the war has involved greater costs than were provided for—the expenses of the ambassadors for peace and the King's marriage have called for large sums. The garrisons in Gascony, the Bourdelois, Bayonnois, and Bigorre must be supported—the fleet must be maintained to guard our coasts and harbors—the frontiers of Scotland, and our possessions in Ireland, must not be left defenceless—all these matters annually absorb large sums. Give thanks to God that ye have peace, and consider that ye are much better off than those of France, Lombardy, and other countries where your merchandise is carried; for they are taxed and taxed over again three or four times a year, while ye have only a moderate duty imposed upon your wares."

The duke addressed the people so mildly and calmly, that, although they came thither with the worst intentions from the machinations of others, they were satisfied, and the assembly broke up. The Duke of Gloucester, however, was not contented; he returned to his castle at Pleshy, and was constantly engaged in devising means for exciting disturbances in England, and causing a rupture with France. About this time the Count de St. Pol arrived in England, whither he had been sent by the King of France to see his daughter, and to cultivate affection between the two countries. I was informed that about a month after the departure of the Count de St. Pol the King became exceedingly unpopular, for it was rumored that the count had come to treat with the King for the restoration of Calais to the French. Nothing could agitate the English more than such reports; and the people were so uneasy, that the Londoners went to Pleshy to consult the Duke of Gloucester on the occasion. The duke, instead of calming them, only excited them more by saying, he could do nothing in the business, for he was sure the French would give all the daughters of the King if they could secure Calais. This answer made the Londoners very melancholy; they said they would see the King and remonstrate with him on the agitation the whole country was in. "Do so," replied the duke; "remonstrate firmly and make him fear you. Tell me what answer he makes you, and then I will give you my advice how to act."

The Londoners did as they were instructed; they went to Eltham, told the King the cause of their visit, not in a haughty or harsh manner, but with courteous speech, and repeated to him reports which were current throughout England. The King assured them that there was not one word of truth in all the rumors that were so industriously circulated; and when he had done speaking, the Earl of Salisbury addressed the citizens: "My good people of London, withdraw to your homes, and be satisfied that the King and his council wish for nothing more than the honor and profit of England. Those who have busily said the contrary have been ill-advised, and show plainly that they wish to see the country in trouble. Depend upon it that, when the people are wicked, neither justice nor truth will be attended to."

The citizens were appeased, and, having taken leave of the King, departed on their return to London. The King remained at Eltham, very melancholy at what he had heard. He had received positive information that the Duke of Gloucester and the Earl of Arundel had plotted to seize his person, and that of the Queen, and carry them to a strong castle, where they should be confined under proper guards, but allowed sufficient for the table, and other necessary expenses; that four regents were to be appointed over the kingdom; and that some means were to be discovered for rekindling the war with France. These were the plans that had been concerted by many of the English, particularly the Londoners, for they hated the King; and several now repented that they had checked the mobs from the different counties of England which attacked London.

It is not to be wondered if the King were considerably alarmed at the discovery of so much hatred and malice lurking against him. He paid greater court than ever to the Duke of Gloucester and the citizens when they came to see him; but all in vain. At times he mentioned the matter privately to the dukes of Lancaster and York: " My good uncles, for the love of God, advise me how to act! I am duly informed that your brother, the Duke of Gloucester, the Earl of Arundel, and others are determined to seize and confine me in one of their castles, to separate my Queen from me, and send her to some other place of confinement. My dear uncles, it is now twenty years since you paid me homage, and swore obedience to me as your sovereign. I entreat you, therefore, for the love you bear me, and on the oaths you have taken, that you assist me on this occasion; for everything assures me the Duke of Gloucester only desires that war be renewed with France, in spite of the truces which you, with us and all England, have sworn to observe. Give me, then, the best advice you are able, since I require it from you."

The dukes of York and Lancaster, seeing their nephew's great anguish of heart, and knowing, at the same time, that the greater part of what he said was strictly true, replied, " My lord, have a little patience. We know that our brother of Gloucester has the most passionate and wrong-headed temper of any man in England; but you need not fear him, if you follow our advice. He talks frequently of things he cannot execute, and neither he nor his abettors can break the truce which has been signed, or confine you in any castle. We therefore humbly beg you will be appeased; for, please God, everything will end well! "

By such means the dukes calmed the King's mind; as, however, they foresaw that from the bad management of public affairs trouble was at hand, and that the hatred between their nephew and brother was daily increasing, to avoid being called upon by either party they took leave of the King, and retired to their different castles. This measure they had afterward great reason to repent, for such things shortly happened as troubled the whole kingdom, which would not have been the case had they remained with the King, for they would have advised him more prudently than such counsellors as he listened to. There was not one of the King's servants who did not fear the Duke of Gloucester, and wish his death, no matter by what means. That gallant and loyal knight, Sir

Thomas Percy, had been for a long time steward of the household, and all the accounts passed through his hands. He noticed with grief the hatred that subsisted between the King and the Duke of Gloucester, and, like a man of understanding, foresaw that public affairs would end badly; in consequence of which he resigned his office, and went to reside on his own estate. The King had about him many young counsellors who too much dreaded the Duke of Gloucester, and frequently said to him, "Very dear sir, it is a dangerous office to serve you, for we have seen our predecessors, in whom you had great confidence, meet but a poor reward."

King Richard continually pondered upon this, and shortly after the departure of his two uncles of Lancaster and York, he summoned up more courage than usual, saying to himself that it would be better he should destroy than be destroyed, and that within a short time he would hold his uncle of Gloucester so securely that he should be incapable of injuring him: this intention he discovered to the earl marshal*d* his cousin, and also gave him most minutely his orders how to act. The earl marshal, from the favors he had received, loved the King above the Duke of Gloucester, and kept the secret which he had entrusted to him from all but such as he was forced to employ, as he could not do the whole himself. What I am about to say will explain the matter.

The King, under pretence of deer-hunting, went to a palace which he had at Havering-at-the-Bower, in Essex; it is about twenty miles from London, and as many from Pleshy. One afternoon he set out for Havering without many attendants, for he had left them behind with the Queen at Eltham, and arrived at Pleshy about five o'clock; the weather was very hot, and he came so suddenly to the castle, that no one knew it until the porter cried out, "Here is the King!" The Duke of Gloucester had already supped, for he was very temperate in his diet, and never sat long at dinner or supper; he immediately went out to meet the King, and paid him all the respect due to a sovereign, as did his duchess and her children. When the King entered the hall the table was again laid out for him, and he ate some little; but he had before said to the duke, "Good uncle, have five or six horses saddled, for you must

*d* The Earl of Nottingham.

accompany me to London, as I am to have a meeting to-morrow with the citizens: we shall surely see my uncles of Lancaster and York, but I shall advise with you what answer to make to the Londoners' demands. Tell your house steward to follow us with your servants to London, where they will find you." The duke, suspecting nothing wrong, too easily consented; everything being ready, the King took leave of the duchess and her children, mounted his horse, and the duke did the same, attended by only three squires and four varlets. They took their way to Bondelay, to avoid the high road to London and Brentwood, with the other towns through which it passes. They rode hard, for the King pretended impatience to get to London, and conversed all the way with the Duke of Gloucester. On their arrival at Stratford, near the Thames, where an ambuscade had been laid, the King galloped forward, leaving his uncle behind; on which the earl marshal went to the rear of the duke with a large body of men, and said, " I arrest you in the King's name." The duke was panic-struck, for he saw he had been betrayed, and cried aloud after the King; but he galloped on faster than before, followed by his attendants. We will now leave this matter for the present.

## CHAPTER VIII

Death of the Lord de Coucy—Also of the Lord Philip of Artois—Magnificence of the Sultan Bajazet—His Address to John of Burgundy—The Knights of Rhodes—The Women of Cephalonia—Means of Raising the Ransom—The Plague—The King of Hungary and the Venetians—Lord Boucicaut Appointed Constable of France—The Count de Nevers Tells the King of France and His Lords About Bajazet—Attempts Made to Heal the Schism in the Church—Death of Guy de Chatillon, Count de Blois—King Richard and the Duke of Gloucester—The Duke Carried Off to Calais—His Miserable Death—The Earl of Arundel Publicly Beheaded in Cheapside—Dissensions Between the King and His Uncles—Richard Seizes Upon the Duke of Gloucester's Estate at Pleshy—An Assembly at Rheims Upon the State of the Church—The Emperor of Germany and the King of France.

ON the return of Sir John de Châteaumorant and Sir James de Helly from Turkey, the King of France and the Duke and Duchess of Burgundy were encouraged to exert themselves in procuring the ransom of the prisoners. About the time I am now speaking of, that gallant knight and excellent man, the Lord Enguerrand de Coucy, Count de Soissons, and a potent lord in France, died at Bursa, in Turkey. Sir Robert d'Esne, who had been sent to him by the Lady de Coucy to make inquiries respecting him, had not advanced further than Vienna, when he was informed of his death. He returned with this news to France, and told it to the family of the Lord de Coucy, before whom he did not appear till the governor of the castle of St. Gobin was sent to seek the body, have it embalmed, and brought to France. It was conveyed to the abbey of Nogent, near to Coucy, and received by the Duchess of Bar, the Bishop of Laon, and many abbots. There the gentle knight was buried, and thus ended the year of grace 1397.

Shortly after, while negotiations were going on respecting the ransom of the prisoners, Lord Philip of Artois, Count d'Eu, and constable of France, died also; when dead, he was opened and embalmed, and in this state put into a coffin, and carried to France, where he was buried in the Church of St. Lawrence at Eu. By means of Sir Dinde de Desponde and the Genoese merchants, a ransom was at last agreed to, which was fixed at 200,000 ducats for the twenty-five prisoners; security was given for the amount to the satisfaction of Bajazet, and the French ambassadors, Sir Guissebreth de Linrenghen and Sir James de Helly, who had attended the negotiation, returned to carry the joyful news of their success to the King, and the other lords, who were so greatly interested in it. On quitting harbor the sea was calm, and the weather temperate; but they had not advanced far before it changed, and became so tempestuous, that Sir Guissebreth, sorely tormented by sea-sickness, died before they could reach Mathelin. Sir James was much grieved at his loss, and engaging a vessel sailed to Rhodes; he published everywhere the deliverance and speedy arrival of the Count de Nevers and his companions, to the great joy of the Knights of Rhodes. On his arrival in France he made the King, the Duke and Duchess of Burgundy, and the whole nation happy, by the good news he brought.

The Sultan Bajazet, having had everything respecting the ransom of the French prisoners settled to his satisfaction, resolved to allow them more liberty, for indeed they were no longer prisoners; and before the departure of the ambassadors, he invited them to his presence to show them the magnificence of his establishments, which were said to be very grand. The Sultan conversed daily with the Count de Nevers, by means of an interpreter, and paid him much respect, for he knew that he was a high lord in France, by the great exertions that were made, and the large sums of money paid for his ransom. The count and the other French lords were greatly astonished at the power and state of Bajazet; he was attended by such numbers that they were always encamped, for no town could lodge them, and the expense must have been great to supply so many with food. It was surprising where such quantities came from; notwithstanding the natives of warm climates are very temperate in their diet, eating but little meat, living on spices and sugar, of which they have abundance, as well as goats' milk, the common beverage of the Turks and Saracens, and they **have plenty of bread made of millet.**

The Sultan had at this time 7,000 falconers, and as many huntsmen; one day, in the presence of the Count de Nevers, he flew a falcon at some eagles; the flight did not please him, and he was so wroth, that he was on the point of beheading 2,000 of his falconers, scolding them exceedingly for want of diligence in the care of his hawks, when the one he was fond of had behaved so ill. Another time when the Count de Nevers and the French barons were with the Sultan, a poor woman came in tears to demand justice against one of his servants, saying, that he had that morning entered her house and seized by force the goat's milk which she had provided for herself and children. The Sultan was very rigidly determined that all crimes committed within his dominions should be severely punished; he therefore gave the woman an attentive hearing, and ordered the varlet to be brought and confronted with her. The varlet, who dreaded Bajazet, began to make excuses, saying that it was false; the woman, however, told a plain tale, and persisted in its truth. "Woman," said the Sultan, "consider well thy accusation, for if I find thou hast told me a lie, thou shalt suffer death." "Sir," replied the woman, "I consent to it, for were it not true, I could have no reason to come before you, and I only ask for justice." "You shall have it," said the Sultan. He then ordered the varlet to be seized and to have his belly opened to see whether he had drunk the milk. It was there found, for it had not had time to be digested, and the Sultan on seeing it said to the woman, "Thou hadst just cause of complaint; go thy way, for the injury done thee has been punished."

The time was now come for the French lords to depart, and the count and his companions waited on the Sultan to thank him for his kindness and courtesy. On taking his leave, the Sultan said to the count, "John, I am well informed that in thy country thou art a great lord. Thou art young, and hast many years to look forward; and perchance, to shake off the blame of the ill-success of thy first attempt in arms, thou mayst collect a powerful army, and again offer me battle. If I feared thee, I would make thee and thy companions also swear never to bear arms against me. But no, I will demand no such oath, for thou wilt always find me prepared and ready to meet thee in the field of battle." These high words the count and his companions well understood, and never forgot. When all things were ready for their departure, they were conducted by Ali bashaw and Soli bashaw, with a large escort, to the lords de Mathelin and d'Amine, and others who were interested in their liberty. News was soon carried to the island of Rhodes that the Sultan had accepted a ransom for the French lords, and that they were now at Mathelin. The intelligence gave much pleasure to the Grand Master and all his knights, who equipped and armed two galleys, and sent them to Mathelin to convey the count and his companions to Rhodes.

These Knights of Rhodes, who wear a white cross in memory of the cross of our Lord Jesus Christ, who suffered to deliver others from the pains of hell, are valiant men, and make daily assaults by sea and land on the infidels, to support and defend the Christian faith. When the count and the lords of France landed, they were received by the grand prior of Rhodes, and the grand prior of Aquitaine, in their robes of ceremony, who offered to lend them any sum of money to enable them to discharge their daily expenses. The offer was thankfully accepted, for in truth they were in want of money, and the grand prior of Aquitaine lent the Count de Nevers 30,000 francs. The French lords remained some time in Rhodes to recover themselves, and during the time they were in the island Sir Guy de la Tremouille was seized with a dangerous illness and died. At his own order, his body was buried in the Church of St. John, in the island of Rhodes, and his funeral was honorably attended by the French lords, who shortly after took their departure, having embarked on board some Venetian galleys, the captains of which resolved to touch at the different islands, that their passengers might sail more at their ease, and refresh themselves by landing occasionally. They first steered for Modon,[a] thence to Colefo, and next to Cephalonia, where, having anchored, they landed and were met by a large party of ladies and damsels who have the government of the island. The Count de Nevers and his friends were very happy with the dames of Cephalonia, for they entertained them gayly, telling them their arrival had been a matter of joy to them from their being knights of honor and renown, for in general they had no other visitors but merchants.

[a] A town and port in the Morea.

I may be asked if the island were solely inhabited by women. I answer, No; but women have the sovereignty of it: they employ themselves in needlework and other occupations, and make such fine cloths of silk that none others can be compared to them. The men of the island are employed in carrying these works abroad wherever they think to gain the greatest profit, but the women remain at home. The men honor the fair sex for their work, and because they have a sufficiency of wealth. The state of the island is such that no one dare approach it to commit any injury, for which cause these ladies live in peace without fear of anyone; they are amiable, good-tempered, and without pride, and certainly, when they please, converse with fairies and keep them company.

After the Count de Nevers and his companions had amused themselves in this island for five days, they took leave of the ladies, and the count made them such handsome presents for their courteous treatment of them, that they thanked him gratefully on his departure. Favorable winds soon carried these lords to a territory called Ragusa, and thence to Clarence, which is 100 miles from Venice: from Clarence they made sail for Pareuse, into which port all large vessels and galleys are forced to put, which cannot from want of water land their cargoes at Venice. Here, however, the French knights made no long stay before they embarked in smaller vessels and arrived at Venice, where they were received with great joy. On landing they also returned thanks to God for their happy deliverance from the hands of the infidels, of which at one time they had despaired. The count and his companions went to hotels which had been prepared for them; for, as their coming was known and expected for some time, their friends had sent servants and equipages to await their arrival. The count found part of his attendants whom the duke and duchess had sent thither ready to receive him. Sir Dinde de Desponde had also been at Venice some time waiting for them with the amount of their ransoms, for without his assistance nothing could be done.

The French lords, immediately on their arrival at Venice, employed clerks and messengers to write and carry letters to France and elsewhere, to inform their friends of their happy deliverance. The Duke and Duchess of Burgundy lost no time in preparing everything suitable to the rank of their son; such as silver plate, linen, tapestry, and clothes of all sorts, which were packed up on sumpter horses, and sent to Venice under the care of the Lord de Hangiers and Sir James de Helly. In like manner did all the friends and relations of the other lords send them every necessary suitable to their ranks.

You may suppose all this was done at a great expense, for nothing was spared; their residence at Venice cost much, for it is one of the dearest towns in the world for strangers, and it was proper these lords should keep up a state becoming their rank. The different negotiations and embassies also called for a large sum of money; for, though the ransom was but 200,000 florins to Bajazet, yet the other costs and expenses amounted to as much more, as was declared by those through whose hands the money passed. It was a matter of much consideration how this immense sum of money was to be raised; at length it was resolved by the duke's council to lay a tax upon all towns under his obedience, more especially those of Flanders; for they abounded in wealth, from their commerce. When the subject was mentioned to the men of Ghent, they readily declared their willingness to present their young lord with 50,000 florins to aid him in his ransom. Bruges, Mechlin, Antwerp, and the other towns in Flanders, also expressed their readiness to assist.

While the Duke and Duchess of Burgundy, the King of France, and others, were diligently despatching the business of the ransom, the lords spent their time most joyously at Venice; it happened, however, before the ransom was settled, that an infectious disorder afflicted that town and neighborhood: it began in the month of August, and never ceased till St. Andrew's Day. Great numbers fell victims to it, and among the rest the Lord Henry de Bar, eldest son of the Duke of Bar, and, in right of his wife, heir to all the estates of the late Lord de Coucy, excepting the dower of his widow. Thus were the two ladies de Coucy made widows in one year. The body of Lord Henry was embalmed and brought to France, and I believe buried at Paris; for his obsequies were there performed with much solemnity. On account of this epidemical distemper, and to avoid its danger, the Count de Nevers left Venice, and fixed his residence at Treviso, where he and the other French lords remained with their households for upward of four months.

During their stay at Treviso, the King of Hungary was informed by the Knights of Rhodes, that the French lords had made peace with Bajazet, and obtained their liberty, by payment of 200,000 francs; and he, in consequence, sent letters by a bishop, and some of his knights, to the Count de Nevers, to mark his affection to him. The bishop and knights were ordered to address the count as follows: "My lord, we are sent hither by our redoubted lord and your cousin, the King of Hungary, who salutes you by us. He is sincerely rejoiced at the escape of yourself and your companions, for without the means you have pursued, it would never have been effected. Dear sir, our lord is well assured that your treating with the Sultan must have cost you immense sums of money, and that the losses you all suffered at the disastrous battle of Nicopoli will have made it difficult for you to procure a sufficiency for your ransom. Our sovereign, therefore, orders us to make you his excuses for not offering you his assistance on the present occasion; if it were in his power, he would most cheerfully do so; but he and his subjects have had such losses by the late defeat, that you, who are a person of great understanding, will readily believe and know the impossibility of his giving any aid at this time. The revenues of Hungary are ruined for this and the ensuing year, but whenever they are recovered, and the usual payments made, he will assuredly come forward to your service. That you may believe our most redoubted sovereign and your cousin is in earnest, we must acquaint you, that he has ordered us to offer for sale, to the rulers of Venice, the rents he receives from this town, whch amount to 7,000 ducats yearly; and that whatever these may produce you are to dispose of as if it were your own; for which we will sign receipts to the Venetians, having full authority so to do."

This speech was very agreeable to the French lords, who answered it by the Lord de Rochefort, saying, that they were very sensible of this mark of kindness from the King of Hungary, who, to oblige his cousin the Count de Nevers, offered to sell his inheritance to aid them; that this was not an offer to be refused, nor the friendship and courtesy of it forgotten; and that the count desired to have a little time to consider of his answer to the King. This was agreed to, and within a few days the ambassadors were told by the Count de Nevers, that it would be very unbecoming him to pledge or sell the inheritance of another; but that, if it were agreeable to them, who had such powers, to prevail on the Venetians to advance on the security of these rents a sufficient sum for the count's daily expenses, and to enable him to acquit himself of the 30,000 florins which the grand prior of Aquitaine had lent him, he should consider it as a great favor, and most kindly thank the King of Hungary and his council for so doing. The ambassadors cheerfully promised to make the proposals to the Venetians, who, when they heard of it, coldly replied that they would consider the matter, and demanded fifteen days to weigh their determination. When these were expired, they answered, as I was told by one who heard it, that if the King of Hungary was disposed to sell his whole kingdom, the Venetians would willingly make the purchase, and pay the money down; but as for such a trifle as 7,000 ducats of yearly revenue which he possessed in the city of Venice, it was of so little value, that they could not set a price on it either to buy or sell, and that they would not trouble themselves about so small an object.

Such was the answer made by the Venetians to the ambassadors of the King of Hungary. Some said, the reply was mere dissimulation. Things, therefore, remained in the state they were before, and the ambassadors took their leave.

You have heard that the Count d'Eu, constable of France, died in his bed at Bursa in Turkey, to the great regret of all who knew him: by his death the constableship became vacant, and that office is of such weight, that it must not long remain so. Councils were therefore held to appoint his successor, and the Lord Louis de Sancerre was nominated to the vacant office. He had for a long time been marshal of France, and resided in Languedoc. Being sent for by the King to Paris, he was invested with the office of constable, and by this vacated the charge of marshal; on which the King said, that he had already thought of a successor, for no one should have the office but his knight, the Lord Boucicaut; and in this choice all the lords agreed. Boucicaut was at Venice at the time of his appointment; he returned, however, shortly after, for the ransoms were paid, and all those who had been prisoners in

Turkey came back to France, to the great joy of their friends and countrymen.

The Count de Nevers waited on the Duke and Duchess of Burgundy, and was well feasted by them and others. After he had remained some time with them, he visited the King of France and the Duke of Orleans; both of whom gave him a most kind reception. He was made welcome also by all the lords and ladies of the court. The King and the duke made many inquiries of him respecting the battle of Nicopoli, the adventures he had met with, how he was made prisoner, and the state of Bajazet. He was well spoken, and satisfied them with his answers; he made no complaint of the Sultan, but said that he found him courteous and affable, and that he himself was very well treated by him. He did not forget to tell the lords to whom he was speaking that Bajazet, on his taking leave, had said that he was born to arms, and that he would with pleasure meet with them in battle whenever they might choose; that it was his intention to march to Rome, and feed his horse on the altar of St. Peter. The count added, that the Sultan thought our faith erroneous, and corrupted by those who ought to have kept its purity; that many Saracens declare that Christianity will be destroyed, and that Bajazet was born to accomplish its ruin, and be king over all the world. "Such," he continued, "was the language the interpreter translated to me; and, from what I saw and heard, I believe they are perfectly well acquainted in Turkey, Tartary, and Persia, and throughout the whole of the infidel countries, with our schisms in the Church, and how the Christians are at variance one with another respecting the two popes of France and Italy."

This speech of the Count de Nevers gave the King and lords of France enough to think about. Some said the Saracens were in the right, and that it was time to lower the pomp of the priests.

It was secretly told the King of France, by those who loved him and were desirous he should regain his health, that it was the common opinion throughout France that he would never be perfectly recovered until the Church was properly regulated. They added, that his father, King Charles of happy memory, had on his death-bed charged his council with this matter;

that he suspected he had been deceived by these popes, and had made his determination too soon, for which he felt his conscience was loaded. He excused himself, saying, "When our lord and father died we were very young. We have followed the counsel of those who have hitherto governed, and if we have acted wrong or foolishly, it has been their fault and not ours; but, since we have had fuller information, we will now soon attend to this business."

The King of France immediately gave his attention to the matter, and spoke of it to his brother, the Duke of Orleans, who instantly inclined to his opinion, as did the Duke of Burgundy; for, notwithstanding he had acknowledged the pope who styled himself Clement, he had no great faith in him.

A private council was held on this subject, when it was determined, that if a union of the Church was sought for, it was necessary to have the assent of Germany; and, accordingly, learned men were sent to the King of Bohemia and Germany, with instructions to prevail upon him to meet the King of France in the city of Rheims.

About this time died the Lord Guy de Chatillon, Count de Blois, in his hotel at Avesnes in Hainault. He was carried to Valenciennes, and buried in the Church of the Franciscans, in a chapel called the Chapel of Artois. True it is, that he had made a large enclosure from the Franciscans, and intended erecting a tomb within it; but he died so much in debt, that his countess, the Lady Mary of Namur, was obliged to renounce all claim to his movables; she dared not act under his will, but retired to her dowry of the lands of Chimay and Beaumont, and the estates went to their right heirs.

You have seen in the course of this history that King Richard of England could not longer conceal the great hatred he bore his uncle of Gloucester, but determined to have him cut off. You have heard likewise, how the King rode to the castle of Pleshy, thirty miles from London, and with fair words cajoled the duke out of his castle, and was accompanied by him to a lane that led to the Thames, where they arrived between ten and eleven at night; and how the earl marshal, who lay there in ambush, had arrested him in the King's name, and forced him toward the Thames, in spite of his cries to the King to deliver him. From the moment of his arrest he was conscious that his end was resolved on, and this suspicion was confirmed to him by the King turning a deaf ear to his complaint, and riding in full gallop to London, where he lodged in the Tower. The duke had other lodgings; for, whether he would or not, he was forced into a boat that carried him to a vessel at anchor on the Thames, into which he was obliged to enter. The earl marshal with his men embarked also, and having a favorable wind and tide, they fell down the river, and arrived late the next evening at Calais[b] without anyone knowing it.

You may suppose that when news was brought to Pleshy of the Duke of Gloucester's arrest, the duchess and her children were greatly dismayed; and since the measure taken was so bold, were greatly afraid of the consequences. Suspecting the duke's life was in great danger, they consulted Sir John Lackingay what would be best for them to do. He advised them to send instantly to the dukes of Lancaster and York, the duke's brothers; for, by their mediation, perhaps, the King's choler would be appeased. The duchess followed this advice, and instantly despatched messengers to both, for they lived at some distance from each other. At hearing that their brother had been arrested, they were much enraged, and bade the duchess not be much distressed at what had happened, for the King would not dare to treat her husband otherwise than by fair and legal measures.

The morning after the arrest of the Duke of Gloucester, the King left the Tower at a very early hour, and rode to Eltham, where he remained. The same day, toward evening, the earls of Arundel and Warwick were brought to the Tower by the King's officers, and there confined, to the great surprise of the citizens. Their imprisonment caused many to murmur, but they were afraid to act or do anything against the King's pleasure lest they might suffer for it.

When the Duke of Gloucester saw himself confined in the castle of Calais, abandoned by his brothers, and deprived of his attendants, he began to be much alarmed. He addressed himself to the earl marshal, saying, "For what reason am I thus carried from England, and confined here? It seems that you

---

[b] The earl marshal was Governor of Calais, and could enter at all hours without any notice being taken of it. He carried the duke with him to the castle, and there confined him.

mean to imprison me. Let me go and view the castle, its garrison, and the people of the town."

"My lord," replied the earl, "I dare not comply with your demands, for you are consigned to my guard, under pain of death. The King, our lord, is at this moment somewhat wroth with you, and it is his orders that you abide here awhile in banishment, which you must have patience to do until we have other news: and God grant it may be soon, for, as the Lord may help me, I am truly concerned for your disgrace, and would cheerfully aid you if I could; but you know I am bound to obey the oath I have taken to the King."

The duke could not obtain any other answer; and, as he judged from appearances that he was in danger of his life, he asked a priest who said mass, if he would confess him. This he did, with great calmness and resignation; and with a devout and contrite heart, cried before the altar of God, the Creator of all things, for mercy. He was right thus to exonerate his conscience, for his end was nearer than he imagined: I was informed that, on the point of his sitting down to dinner, when the tables were laid, and he was about to wash his hands, four men rushed out from an adjoining chamber, and throwing a towel round his neck, strangled him by two drawing one end and two the other.[c] When he was quite dead they carried him to his chamber, undressed him, placed the body between two sheets, with his head on a pillow, and covered him with furred mantles. They then returned to the hall, properly instructed what to say and how to act, and declared that the duke had been seized with a fit of apoplexy, as he was washing his hands before dinner, and that they had great difficulty to carry him to bed. This was spoken of in the castle and town, when some believed it, though others did not. Within two days after it was published abroad that the Duke of Gloucester had died in his bed at the castle of Calais; and in consequence, the earl marshal put on mourning, for he was nearly related to him, as did all the knights and squires in Calais.

The event was sooner known in France and Flanders than in England. The French rejoiced at it much, for it was com-

[c] The correct account appears to be, that the Duke of Gloucester was smothered with pillows, and not strangled, in the manner related by Froissart. Hall, one of the accomplices in the murder, made a public confession of all the circumstances.

monly reported that there would never be any solid peace between France and England, as long as the Duke of Gloucester lived; and it was well remembered that in the negotiations for peace he was more obstinate in his opinions than either of his brothers: for this reason, then, his death was no loss to France. Many knights and squires in the household of the King of England, also, had reason to rejoice at his death. They recounted how he had driven the Duke of Ireland into banishment, and ignominiously beheaded that gallant knight, Sir Simon Burley, who had been so much beloved by the Prince of Wales, and done such essential services to his country. The deaths of Sir Robert Tresilian, Sir Nicholas Bramber, Sir John Standwich, and others, were not forgotten; so that the Duke of Gloucester was but little lamented in England, except by those of his own party. The duke's body was honorably embalmed at Calais, put into a leaden coffin, with an outer one of wood, and, in this state, transported by sea to England. The vessel which carried the body landed at Hadleigh Castle, on the Thames, and thence it was conveyed on a car, unattended, to his castle of Pleshy, and then placed in the church which the duke had founded.d The duchess, her son Humphrey, and her two daughters, were sorely grieved when the body of the duke arrived, the duchess, indeed, had double cause for affliction, for the Earl of Arundel, her uncle, had been publicly beheaded in Cheapside by order of the King. No baron or knight dared to interpose, for the King himself was present at this execution, which was performed by the earl's son-in-law, the earl marshal, who bandaged his eyes. The Earl of Warwick, also, ran great risk of suffering the same death. The Earl of Salisbury, however, and several others, interceded for him; and the King listened to their solicitations, on condition that he were sent to a place he could not leave; for he would never absolutely pardon him, as he was deserving of death for having joined the Duke of Gloucester and the Earl of Arundel in their attempts to annul the truce which had been signed and sealed by the kings of France and England. The Earl of Warwick was, therefore, banished to the Isle of Wight, which is a dependency on England, situated opposite to

---

d The church was dedicated to the Holy Trinity, and attached to it were twelve canons, for the devout performance of divine service.

the coast of Normandy, which had space enough for the residence of a great lord; but he must provide himself with all he may want from the adjacent countries, or he will be badly supplied with provisions, and other things.

Thus were affairs carried on in England, and daily going from bad to worse, as you will find related. The dukes of Lancaster and York, on hearing of their brother's death, instantly suspected that the King, their nephew, was guilty of it; and hastened to London, because they knew the citizens were very angry at the event. On their arrival they had several meetings, and declared that the putting to death of the Duke of Gloucester for a few foolish words was not to be endured; for, although he had warmly opposed the treaty with France, he had not acted upon it: and there was an essential difference between talking and acting. The King was at this time at Eltham, whither he had summoned all his vassals and dependants. He had collected round London, and the counties of Kent and Essex, upward of 10,000 archers, and had with him his brother, Sir John Holland, the earl marshal, the Earl of Salisbury, and many other great knights and barons. He sent orders to the citizens of London not to admit the Duke of Lancaster within the walls; to which, however, they were unwilling to comply.

The Londoners considered that great mischief might befall England from these dissensions between the King and his uncles; that, since the Duke of Gloucester was now dead, it could not be helped; they, therefore, prudently dissembled their thoughts; and, as what was done could not now be undone, they feared, should matters be pushed to extremities, they might suffer considerably in their commerce from the King of France. In this manner the resentment of the citizens began to cool; they offered to mediate between the King and the Duke of Lancaster, and the King obtained peace on promising that, from that day forward, he would be guided solely by the advice of the Duke of Lancaster: this promise, however, he paid no attention to, but followed the counsels of the rash and evil-minded, for which, as the event proved, he afterward severely suffered.

When peace was restored, the King of England governed more fiercely than before. He went, with his state, to Pleshy in Essex, which had belonged to his uncle of Gloucester, and should have descended to his son, Humphrey, as heir to his father; but the King took possession of it, for it is the rule in England for the King to have the wardship of all children who have lost their fathers, and are under twenty-one years of age, at which period their estates are restored to them. King Richard took his cousin, Humphrey of Gloucester, in ward, appropriating all his possessions to his own profit. The late Duke of Gloucester was, by inheritance, constable of England; but the King deprived his heir of it, and gave it to his cousin, the Earl of Rutland. The King now assumed greater state than ever kings of England had done before, nor had there been anyone who had expended such large sums of money, by one hundred nobles. He also took the wardship of the heir of Arundel, son of the late earl. At this period there was no one, however great, in England, who dared speak his sentiments of what the King did, or intended doing. He had formed a council of his own from the knights of his chamber, who encouraged him to act as they advised. The King had in his pay full 2,000 archers, who were on guard day and night, for he did not think himself perfectly safe from his uncles and the Arundel family.

At this period, there was a numerous assembly of great lords in the city of Rheims, as well from the empire of Germany as from France, whose object was to restore union to the Church. At the solicitation of the King of France, the Emperor had come thither in person, attended by his ministers; but, because they wished it not to be publicly known that this meeting was to take into consideration the rivalship of the two popes of Rome and Avignon, they had it rumored that the lords of the empire came to Rheims to treat of a marriage between a son of the Marquis of Brandenburg and a daughter of the Duke of Orleans. When the Emperor was about to make his entry into Rheims, all these lords and prelates, with Charles, King of Navarre, went to meet him; and, after receiving him in a most honorable manner, they conducted him first to the Church of Our Lady, and then to the abbey of St. Remy, where he was lodged, with all his lords. The King of France had ordered that all the expenses of the Emperor and the Germans, during their residence in Rheims, should be paid by his officers, in the most ample manner. In consequence, there were delivered to the Germans ten tons of herrings—for it was Lent—and 800 carp, without counting different sorts of fish, and other things, which cost the King immense sums. On the two monarchs meeting they paid many compliments to each other, as they well knew how to do, especially the King of France; for the Germans are a rude, unmannered race, except in what regards their personal advantage, and in that they are active and expert enough.

The King of France entertained the whole party at dinner, of which I will mention some particulars. At the top of the King's table was seated the Patriarch of Jerusalem; next to him the King of France and the King of Navarre: no more were at that table. The dinner was splendid, and abundantly well served; the Duke of Orleans supplied the company with such quantities of plates of gold and silver, as though they had been made of wood. I was told that the King made a present to the Emperor of all the gold and silver plate that was used, as well as what was on the sideboard, with all the tapestry and ornaments of the apartment whither the Emperor retired, after dinner, to partake of wine and spices: this gift was estimated at 200,000 florins. During the residence of these monarchs at Rheims, the ministers frequently met to consider the marriage of the Marquis of Brandenburg, and the reformation of the Church. The marriage was agreed on, and published in Rheims; but the consultation and resolutions concerning the Church were kept secret. I heard, however, afterward, that it was determined that Peter d'Ailly, Bishop of Cambray, should be sent as ambassador from the Emperor and King of France, to the person who styled himself Pope Boniface at Rome, and negotiate with him, in their names, with a view of inducing him to submit to a new election: and should the choice fall on him again, he should be acknowledged by them as pope; but if not, then he was to resign. The bishop was also to declare the same to the Pope of Avignon; adding, that if either of the popes refused to comply, he would be degraded, and every honor and profit of the Church taken from him. Thus ended the meeting; the two monarchs separately amicably, and each returned to his usual place of residence.

## CHAPTER IX

The Earl of Derby and the Earl Marshal—Palm Sunday at Eltham Palace—The Earl Marshal Challenges the Earl of Derby—Challenge Accepted: Preparations for the Contest—King Richard Interferes, and the Two Earls are Banished—The Schism in the Church—The Bishop of Cambray—The Pope and His Cardinals—The King of Hungary Resolves to March Against Bajazet—Death of John, Duke of Lancaster—Sad Troubles in England—The Earl of Derby and the Lary Mary of Berry—Tournament at Windsor—King Richard Prepares to Go to Ireland—The Earl of Derby Returns to England—Prepares to Besiege Richard at Bristol—Richard's Escape, and Capture at Flint Castle—Confinement in the Tower of London—Richard Resigns His Crown to Henry of Lancaster—Coronation of Henry—Death of King Richard.

YOU must know that the Earl of Derby and the late Duke of Gloucester had married two sisters, daughters of the Earl of Hereford and Northampton, constable of England. The children, therefore, of the Earl of Derby and Duke of Gloucester were cousins-german by their mother's side, and one degree removed by the father's. To say the truth, the death of the Duke of Gloucester had displeased many of the great barons of England, who frequently murmured at it when together.

About this time, a conversation passed between the Earl of Derby and the earl marshal, in which the state of the King and the counsellors whom he trusted became the subject of discussion. The earl marshal caught at the following words the other had made use of: "Holy Mary, fair cousin, what does the King intend to do next? will he drive all the nobles out of England? he plainly shows he is not desirous to add to the honor of his realm." The earl marshal made no reply at the time; but soon after this conversation, in order to flatter and gain favor with the King, he said, "My lord, all your enemies and ill-wishers are not dead nor out of the kingdom." "How do you know this, cousin?" said the King. "I know it well," answered the earl marshal; "for the moment I will say no more; but, that you may provide a remedy in time, have it proclaimed that you will hold a solemn feast on the ensuing Palm Sunday, and invite all the princes of the blood, particularly the Earl of Derby, when you shall hear something that will surprise you." The King begged the earl marshal to give him further information; I know not whether he did so, but if he did the King kept it to himself, and allowed the earl to act in the matter as he pleased.

The feast was proclaimed to take place at Eltham on Palm Sunday, and the dukes of Lancaster and York were invited. On the day of the feast, after dinner, when the lords had retired with the King to his council chamber, the earl marshal cast himself on his knees before the King, and said, " My dear and renowned lord, I am of your kindred, your liege man, and marshal of England, and I have besides sworn on my loyalty that I would never conceal anything from you on pain of being accounted a traitor." The King, fixing his eyes on him, asked what he meant. " My very dear lord, order the Earl of Derby to come into your presence and I will speak out." The Earl of Derby made his appearance, and the marshal spoke as follows: "Earl of Derby, I charge you with having thought and spoken disrespectfully against your natural lord, the King of England, when you said he was unworthy to hold his crown, and that without a shadow of reason he banished those valiant men from his kingdom who ought to be its defenders; for all of which I present my glove, and shall prove my body against yours, that you are a false and wicked traitor." At this address the Earl of Derby was confounded, and retired a few paces without demanding from the duke, his father, or any of his friends how he should act. Having mused awhile, he advanced with his hood in his hand toward the King, and said, " Earl marshal, I say that thou art a false and wicked traitor, which I will bodily prove on thee, and here is my glove." The earl marshal, seeing his challenge was accepted, showed a good desire for the combat by taking up the glove, and saying, " I refer your answer to the good pleasure of the King and the lords present. I will prove that what you have said is false, and that my words are true."

Each of the lords then withdrew, and the time for serving

wine and spices was passed by, for the King showed he was sore displeased, and retired to his chamber. Soon after he called to him his uncles, and demanded from them how he was to act on this occasion. "Sire," they said, "order your constable hither, and we will tell you." The Earl of Rutland, constable of England, came, and was told to go to the Earl of Derby and the earl marshal, and oblige them to promise not to quit the kingdom without the King's permission. The constable obeyed the order.

You may believe that the whole court was greatly troubled by this event, and many barons and knights were much displeased, and blamed the earl marshal for his conduct.

The Earl of Derby resided in London, for he had his house there; and the dukes of Lancaster and York, the Earl of Northumberland, and many others, were his securities to appear and answer the challenge. The earl marshal was sent to the Tower of London, where he lived with his household.

These two lords made ample provision of all things necessary for the combat, and the Earl of Derby sent off messengers to Lombardy, to procure armor from Sir Galeas, Duke of Milan. The duke readily complied with the request, and gave the knight who brought the message the choice of all his armor, and when he had selected all he wished for, in plated and mail armor, the Lord of Milan, out of his abundant love to the earl, ordered four of the best armorers in Milan to accompany the knight to England, that the Earl of Derby might be more completely armed. The earl marshal, on the other hand, sent into Germany, whence he thought he should be ably assisted by his friends. Each provided himself most magnificently to outshine the other; but the greater splendor was certainly shown by the Earl of Derby; for I must say, that when the earl marshal undertook this business, he expected to have been better supported by the King than he was.

The news of this combat made a great noise in foreign parts; for it was to be for life or death, and to take place before the King and the great barons of England. Most men of sense and prudence were sadly vexed that the King of England did not interfere to prevent this discord, especially the Duke of Lancaster, who considered the consequences that might ensue, and at times said to those in whom he most confided, "Our nephew will ruin everything before he has done. Should he live long he will lose by little and little all that it has cost his predecessors and ourselves so much to gain. He encourages discord between his nobles and great lords, by whom he ought to be honored and his country guarded. He has put my brother to death, likewise the Earl of Arundel, because they have told him the truth. He cannot sooner ruin the country than by the course he is pursuing. The French are a subtle race, and will be glad enough to find us disagreeing; every day there are examples of the miseries of kingdoms when divided. Such has been the unfortunate lot of France itself, of Castille, Naples, and the Roman state. The present schism is the ruin of the contending popes, as well as of the Church. Flanders is another example of this self-destruction. Friesland, again, is at this moment in a similar state; and unless God prevent it, such will be our condition. The King has consented that my son and heir, for I have none other by my first two marriages, should be challenged to mortal combat for a mere trifle; and I, his father, dare not say a word against it."

Such were the reflections of the Duke of Lancaster. Meanwhile the two earls made every preparation for the combat. The Duke of Lancaster never went near the King, and but seldom saw his son. He knew the Earl of Derby was very popular with all ranks of persons in England, particularly with the Londoners, who waited on him and made him an address full of much kindness.

I must tell you, that King Richard, notwithstanding he had suffered this challenge and appeal to arms to be made, was quite uncertain how to act, and whether to allow the combat to take place or not. Although he was King of England, and the most feared of any who had worn the crown, he was guarded day and night by 2,000 archers, who were regularly paid every week, and he could put confidence in none but his brother, the Earl of Huntingdon, and the earls of Salisbury and Rutland.

When the day for the combat drew near, and the two lords had made their preparations, and were waiting only for the King's commands, King Richard's secret advisers said to him, "Sire, what is your intention respecting this combat; will you permit?" "Yes," replied the King; "why not? I intend to be present myself, and see their prowess. But tell me, why do you ask this question?" "Sire," they replied, "we are bound to advise you to the best of our knowledge and ability; we sometimes hear what you do not." "What do you mean?" said the King, "speak out." "Sire," they continued, "the common report throughout England, and especially in London, is, that you are the cause of this combat, and that you have induced the earl marshal to challenge the Earl of Derby. The Londoners in general, and many of the prelates and nobles, say, that you are going the direct road to destroy all your kindred and kingdom, and that they will not suffer it to be done. Now, were the citizens to rise, and be joined by the nobility, who would oppose them? You have no power but from your vassals, and those, from your marriage with a princess of France, are more suspicious of you than ever. Three parts of England say, that when you heard the charge of the earl marshal you should have acted otherwise than you did, and checked the quarrel."

The King, on hearing these words, changed color, turned aside, and leaned on a window, where he mused a considerable time. He then turned to those who addressed him, who were the Archbishop of York, the earls of Huntingdon and Salisbury, and three other knights of his chamber, and said, "I have attentively heard your advice, and should be blameworthy if I followed it not. Consider, therefore, how you would have me act." "Sire," replied the spokesman of the counsellors, "what we have been talking of is a matter of great danger. It is believed throughout England that the earl marshal behaved very ill; he must therefore suffer for so doing, and the Earl of Derby be acquitted. We have considered the matter in every point of view, and our advice is, that before they arm, or make further preparations, you send them your commands to appear before you, and to abide by whatever you determine. You will then give judgment, that within fifteen days the earl marshal quit England without hope of ever returning, and the Earl of Derby be banished for the space of ten years. When the time of their departure arrives, you will, to please the people, abridge four years of the Earl of Derby's sentence, so that his banishment will be only for six years, but he must not expect further favor. Such is our advice; be very careful to prevent them meeting in arms, or the greatest mischief may arise."

The King was thoughtful and replied, "It shall be done." Not long after this King Richard assembled a large council of his nobles and prelates at Eltham. The Earl of Derby and the earl marshal were sent for, and put into separate chambers; for it had been ordered that they were not to meet. The King showed that he wished to mediate between them, and require that they would submit themselves to his decision. The two earls bound themselves to abide by whatever decision the King should give; and when this was reported King Richard said, "I order that the earl marshal, for having caused trouble in the kingdom, by uttering words which he could not prove otherwise than by common report, be banished the realm; he may seek any other land he pleases to dwell in; but he must give over all hope of returning hither, as I banish him for life. I also order that the Earl of Derby, our cousin, for having angered us, and because he has been in some measure the cause of the earl marshal's crime and punishment, prepare to leave the kingdom within fifteen days, and be banished hence for ten years, without daring to return unless recalled by us; but we shall reserve to ourself the power of abridging this term in part or altogether."

The sentence was satisfactory to the lords present, who said, "The Earl of Derby may readily amuse himself in foreign parts for two or three years. He is young enough; and although he has already travelled to Prussia, the Holy Sepulchre, Cairo, and St. Catherine's,[a] he will find other places to visit. He has two sisters, queens of Castille and Portugal, with whom he may cheerfully pass his time. The treatment of the earl marshal is somewhat hard; but, to say the truth, he deserves it, for all this mischief has been caused by his foolish talking." The two earls were much cast down at the sentence; however, it was necessary for them to make preparations for their departure, which they did with the least possible delay: the Earl of Derby went over to France, and the earl marshal went first to Flanders and thence into Lombardy.

It has already been mentioned, some time before this, that a

[a] The monastery of St. Catherine's, on Mount Sinai.

meeting had taken place at Rheims between the Emperor of Germany and the King of France, relative to the present schism in the Church. In consequence of the plans then formed, Peter d'Ailly, Bishop of Cambray, was sent as ambassador to Pope Boniface at Rome. The bishop met the Pope at Fondi; but the latter immediately left that place and went to reside at the Vatican at Rome, where he held a convocation of cardinals. At this consistory no one was present but the Pope and the cardinals, before whom the holy father laid the propositions of the Bishop of Cambray, and then demanded their advice, as to what answer he should make to them. Much discussion ensued, for the cardinals were averse to undo what they had done.

"Holy father," they said to the Pope, "considering our situation, we think you should conceal your real sentiments on this matter; but to encourage the hopes of the King of France and those of his creed, we will in your answer declare your willingness to comply with whatever the Emperor of Germany, the King of Hungary, and the King of England shall advise you; that the person who resides at Avignon, and who styles himself Pope Benedict, whom the King of France and his nation have acknowledged, must first resign all claims to the papacy, and that then you will cheerfully attend a general council, wherever the above-named kings shall appoint, and bring your cardinals with you." This advice was very agreeable to Boniface, and a reply in conformity to it was given to the Bishop of Cambray.

Great were the murmurings throughout Rome when the inhabitants heard that the Emperor and the King of France had written to the Pope to resign his dignity. They were fearful they should lose the holy see, which was of great consequence, and also profit to them, from the general pardons, which were personally sought for, and which obliged such multitudes to visit Rome. The jubilee, also, was soon to take place, for which great preparations had been made; and many were uneasy, lest they might have incurred expenses for nothing. The principal inhabitants of Rome, therefore, waited on the Pope, and showed him greater love than ever, saying, "Holy father, you are the true Pope; remain in the inheritance and patrimony of the Church, which belonged to St. Peter, and let no one advise you to do otherwise. Whoever may be against you, we will be your steadfast friends, and expend our lives and fortunes in defence of your rights." Boniface replied, " Be comforted, my children, I will never resign the popedom; whatever the Emperor or the King of France may do, I will not submit to their wiles." With this answer the Romans were satisfied, and returned to their homes.

The Bishop of Cambray, on his return from Pope Boniface found the Emperor at Constance, to whom he delivered the answer you have heard. The Emperor said, " Sir Bishop, you will carry the answer to the King of France, our brother and cousin, and, according as he shall act, so will I; but, from what I see, he must begin, and when he has deposed his Pope, we will depose ours." The bishop set out for Paris, when he delivered to the King and his lords the answer from the Pope, and also the message from the Emperor, which was kept secret until the King should assemble a great council of his nobles, to have their advice on the matter. Prior to this, some of the prelates of France such as the Archbishop of Rheims, Sir Guy de Roye, the archbishops of Rouen and of Sens, the bishops of Paris, Beauvais, and Autun, had strongly supported the Pope of Avignon, particularly Clement, who had promoted them to their benefices. These six prelates, therefore, by special orders, were not summoned to the council; but others were substituted for them. In this council it was determined, to the satisfaction of the King and all the nobles, that the King of France should send his marshal, the Lord Boucicaut, to Avignon, to prevail on Pope Benedict, by negotiation or by force, to resign the papacy, and submit himself to the determination of the King and his council: that the Church in France should remain neutral as to the true Pope, until union were restored, according to the decrees of a general council of prelates and churchmen which was to be called instantly. The Bishop of Cambray was ordered to attend the marshal; and these two lords left Paris, and travelled together as far as Lyons, where they separated. The marshal was to remain at Lyons until he heard from the bishop, who continued his journey to Avignon, to learn what answer the person who styled himself pope would make to the proposal of the King of France.

On his arrival at Avignon, the bishop fixed his lodgings in the great wood-market. Some of the cardinals suspected the cause of his coming; however, they dissembled their thoughts, until they heard what he had to say, and what Benedict would answer. After taking some refreshment the bishop changed his dress, and waited on the Pope in his palace. On entering his presence he made the proper obeisances; but not so reverently as if he and all the world acknowledged him for the true Pope. Being well versed in Latin and French, he made an elegant harangue, to explain the object of his mission. When, however, the Pope heard that it was the intention of the Emperor and the King of France that he, as well as Pope Boniface, should resign their dignities, he frequently changed color, and, raising his voice, said, " I have labored hard for the good of the Church, and have been duly elected Pope. I will never consent to resign; and I wish the King of France to know this." " Sire," answered the Bishop of Cambray, " I always thought your reverence more prudent than I find you to be. Fix a day for the meeting of your cardinals, to consult with them as to your answer." To this the Pope, at the intercession of two of the cardinals, agreed, and the bishop returned to his lodgings.

The next morning the consistory bell was rung, and a conclave of all the cardinals then at Avignon held at the Pope's palace. The Bishop of Cambray spoke in Latin as to the object of his visit; and, when he had finished speaking, he was requested to withdraw, and given to understand that he should receive his answer presently. Benedict and his cardinals were for a considerable time in council: many opinions were expressed. At length the Cardinal of Amiens said, " My fair sirs, whether we will or not, we must obey the Emperor of Germany and the King of France, since they are now united. We must submit, or we shall be excluded from all our benefices, and how then shall we live? In truth, holy father, we elected you Pope, on condition that you would exert yourself in the reform of abuses in the Church, and promote a union. Answer for yourself, therefore, in a temperate manner, for you must be better acquainted with your own mind and courage than we are." Many of the cardinals, speaking at once, said, " Holy father, the Cardinal of Amiens says what is right: let us know your intentions, we beg." Upon this Benedict replied, "I have always had an earnest desire for a union of the Church, and have taken great pains to promote it; but since, through the grace of God, you have raised me to the papacy, I will never resign it, nor submit myself to any king, duke, or count, nor agree to any treaty that shall include my resignation of the popedom." The cardinals all rose: there was much murmuring and difference of opinion, and the conclave broke up in discord; many of the cardinals departed to their hotels without even taking leave of the Pope; but those who favored his opinion remained with him.

The Bishop of Cambray, observing the manner in which the cardinals left the palace, was assured there had been some great disagreement, and, entering the hall of the conclave, he advanced to Benedict, who was still on his throne, saying, "Sire, give me your answer, I cannot wait longer. Your council is dismissed. Let me have your final determination, for I must now depart." Pope Benedict, still heated by anger at the speech of the Cardinal of Amiens, replied, "Bishop, I have consulted my brother cardinals, who have elected me to this dignity, and they all agree that every due solemnity has been used, such as is usual in such cases. Since, therefore, I am Pope, and acknowledged as such by all my subjects, I will preserve the dignity as long as I live, for I have never done anything to forfeit the divine protection. You will tell our son of France that hitherto we have considered him a good Catholic; but that from the bad advice which he has lately received, he is about to embrace errors of which he will have to repent. I entreat you to tell him from me not to follow any counsels the result of which may trouble his conscience." On saying this, Benedict rose from his throne, and retired to his chamber. The Bishop of Cambray went to his inn, dined, and then mounting his horse crossed the Rhone, passed through Villeneuve, and lay at Bagnols that night. While there he learned that the Lord Boucicaut was at St. Andrieu, within nine leagues of Avignon. Thither, therefore, he went on the following morning, and related to him all that had passed.

When the bishop had finished speaking, the Lord Boucicaut said, "Bishop, you may now return to France; for you have nothing more to do here, and I will execute my part." The bishop replied, "God's will be done!" On the morrow he set out for Paris.

The marshal instantly set clerks and messengers to work in summoning knights, squires, and men-at-arms, in the Viverais, Auvergne, and from the countries as far as Montpellier. The summons of the marshal was readily obeyed; and, soon after, he sent a message of defiance to the Pope in his palace, and to his cardinals at Avignon. This was a severe blow for the cardinals, as well as the inhabitants, who knew well that they could not withstand the power of the King of France. A council was called, and Benedict was remonstrated with; but he replied, like a madman, "Your city is strong, and well provided. I will send to Genoa, and elsewhere, for men-at-arms, and write to my son, the King of Arragon, who is the standard-bearer of the Church, to come to my assistance. Depart hence, and guard your town: I will defend my palace. Why be alarmed at trifles?" Pope Benedict was a bold and determined character, not easily dismayed, and his palace at the time was like a fortress, well stocked with wines, corn, salted meat, oil, and other necessaries.

The Marshal Boucicaut began his march, and fixed his head-quarters at St. Verain, near Avignon: his army kept daily increasing, and, in a short time, the city was so completely surrounded, that nothing could enter by land or water without leave. The seneschal of Beaucaire, who assisted the marshal with 500 combatants, fixed his quarters at Villeneuve. The marshal had with him 2,000 men-at-arms. When all were prepared, the marshal sent notice to the townsmen, that if they did not open their gates and submit, he would burn and destroy all the houses and vineyards, as far as the river Durance. This greatly dismayed the inhabitants, who thought it best at once to surrender. The cardinals also agreed to this, and the army was admitted into the town, with an understanding that it might besiege the palace; but that no harm should be done to the cardinals, their dependants, nor the towns-people.

Pope Benedict on hearing of this arrangement was much cast down; however, he declared he would never surrender as long as he had breath. Before the marshal entered Avignon the Pope had sent to the King of Arragon, humbly entreating him to succor him in his distress; adding, that if he would extricate him from his present situation, he would establish the holy see at Perpignan, or at Barcelona; the King, however, paid little attention to the request.

The palace at Avignon was so strictly invested that nothing could enter it; of food, indeed, it had sufficient for two or three years, but as there was a scarcity of fuel to dress the victuals, those within began to be alarmed. The King of France held a weekly correspondence with the Lord Boucicaut on the state of affairs, and ordered him not to depart till he had completed the business with the Pope. Boucicaut in consequence increased the guard round the palace, and the result was, that Benedict finding himself thus constrained—that there was no fuel, and the provisions daily decreasing—begged for mercy through the mediation of some of his cardinals. A treaty was concluded, the terms of which were that the Pope was not to leave the palace of Avignon until union should be restored to the Church; that he should be put under guard of proper persons, and that the cardinals and richest citizens of Avignon should be responsible for his appearance, dead or alive. This satisfied the marshal, and thus the business ended.

The Lord Boucicaut returned to Paris; however, he did not long remain unemployed, for it having been reported that Bajazet was assembling a large army of Turks, Arabians, Persians, Tartars, Syrians, and others, he made preparations to go to Hungary, to join the King of Hungary, who was collecting a numerous army, and very desirous of offering battle to Bajazet. The Earl of Derby, who resided at Paris, at the hotel de Clisson, near the Temple, much wished to join this expedition: for as he received every week from the French treasury 500 golden crowns for his expenses, he felt himself under great obligation to the King of France, and was unwilling to be a charge to him longer: however, before he undertook to do so, at the advice of his most confidential friends, he sent over to England to ask the opinion of his father, the Duke of Lancaster.

While these things were being done, the King of France sent ambassadors to Germany to inform the Emperor that he had Pope Benedict in his power. The Emperor on hearing it requested to know the determination of the King of England, for whom the King of France had taken upon himself to answer. The King of France in consequence of this sent a grand embassy to England, to remonstrate with the King on the present distracted state of the Church. The King himself would willingly have joined his father-in-law, but he had not his prelates nor his subjects as much under his command as he kept them in France. All this he told in confidence to the French ambassadors; at the same time promising them to do his utmost to comply with the request of the King of France.

However, to please his father-in-law, he summoned a meeting of the prelates and clergy of his realm at his palace of Westminster: when they met he eloquently harangued them on the miserable schism in the Church, and on the plan which the King of France had adopted of remaining neutral between the two rival popes. The kings of Scotland, Castille, Arragon, and Navarre had followed his example, and all Germany, Bohemia, and Italy intended doing the same; he therefore entreated that his kingdom would adopt like measures. The prelates, who were ignorant why they had been called together, on hearing this were greatly astonished. "Our King is quite a Frenchman," murmured some; "his only wish is to ruin us; what! does he mean to make us change our creed? We will have nothing to do with this matter." As no conclusion could be arrived at, the meeting broke up, and the clergy retired to their inns in the city of London. The citizens soon learned what the King had proposed, and their anger was greatly excited against him—"This Richard of Bordeaux will ruin everything; his head is so thoroughly French that he cannot disguise it; however, a day must come when he shall pay for all." Things continued in this state in England.

The King of France and his council were dissatisfied that King Richard had not instantly determined that his country should be neutral, but in truth he could not prevail with his clergy to do so; and shortly after there fell out such horrible events that the like are not to be found in the whole of this history, nor in that of any other Christian king, except that noble prince, Lusignan, King of Cyprus and Jerusalem, whom his brother and the Cypriots villanously murdered.

The answer of the Duke of Lancaster to his son the Earl of Derby was, that he would not advise him to go into Hungary, but when tired of France to visit Castille and Portugal, and amuse himself at the courts of his brothers-in-law and sisters.

It happened about Christmas-tide that John, Duke of Lancaster, fell dangerously ill of a disorder which to the great grief of all his friends ended his life. He had been for some time very low-spirited on account of the banishment of his son, and also in consequence of the manner in which his nephew Richard governed the kingdom, which, if persevered in, he foresaw must be its ruin. The King of England, as it seemed, was little affected by his uncle's death, and he was soon forgotten. The news of the death of the Duke of Lancaster was soon made public in France; King Richard wrote to the King an account of it, but he did not notice it to his cousin the Earl of Derby. The earl, however, knew of it as soon as, if not sooner than, the King of France; he clothed himself and his attendants in deep mourning, and had his father's obsequies performed on a very grand scale. The Earl of Derby was now Duke of Lancaster—the most potent baron in England, and second to none but the King himself; and if King Richard had acted prudently, remembering how very unpopular he himself was, he would instantly on the death of his father have recalled him. But he had no such inclination; on the contrary, he sent officers to take possession of his lands, and to seize his rents, declaring that during his banishment neither the earl nor his family should receive any of his revenues in England; also, to the great vexation of such as were attached to the earl and his children, he disposed of several estates in the duchy of Lancaster to some of his knights.

In France as well as in England this conduct on the part of King Richard was deemed strange and unjustifiable: in truth the King of France and his family were perfectly well disposed toward the Earl of Derby, whom they greatly respected; moreover, it was considered that he was a widower, likely to marry again, and that the Duke of Berry had a daughter who, though so young, was a widow of two husbands. Mary of Berry, for such was her name, was not more than twenty-three years old, and this marriage between her and the Earl of Derby was talked of and nearly concluded. The Duke of Berry well knew that the Earl of Derby was the greatest heir-apparent in England, as also did the King of France, who was anxious that this match should take place on account of his daughter being Queen of England. It was natural to imagine that two such ladies, so nearly related, would be agreeable companions to each other, and that the kingdoms of France and England would on this account enjoy longer peace, and be more intimately connected: all this would probably have been true, if it could have been accomplished; but King Richard and his council broke off all these measures. Whatever misfortunes fate has decreed, must have their course; those which befell King Richard are wonderful to reflect upon. He might have avoided them, but what must be will be.

I, John Froissart, author of these chronicles, will truly say what in my younger days I heard at a mansion called Berkhampstead, thirty miles from London, and which, in the year of grace 1361, at the time I am speaking of, belonged to the Prince of Wales, father to King Richard. As the prince and princess were about to leave England for Aquitaine, the King of England, Queen Philippa, my mistress; the dukes of Clarence and Lancaster; the Lord Edmund, who was afterward Earl of Cambridge and Duke of York, with their children, came to the mansion to visit the prince and take leave of him. I was at the time twenty-four years old, and one of the clerks of the chamber to my lady the Queen. During this visit, as I was seated on a bench, I heard the following conversation from a knight to some of the ladies of the Queen: "There was in that country," said the knight, "a book called 'Brut,' which many say contains the prophecies of Merlin. According to its contents, neither the Prince of Wales nor the Duke of Clarence, though sons to King Edward, will wear the crown of England; but it will fall on the house of Lancaster." When the knight said this, the Earl of Derby was not born: his birth took place seven years after. This prophecy, however, has been verified, for I have since seen Henry, Earl of Derby, King of England.

The moment King Richard heard that a treaty of marriage was going on between the Earl of Derby and the Lady Mary of Berry, he became much displeased thereat, and resolved to send the Earl of Salisbury to Paris, to entreat the King to beware of allowing such an alliance to be formed, as the Earl of Derby was a traitor to his sovereign. The Earl of Salisbury was by no means pleased at being appointed to so delicate and difficult an office; however, the King would receive no excuses, and he went. On his arrival at Paris, he lodged at the White Horse in the square of the Greve, and lost no time in waiting on the King and Queen; to whom he related very minutely everything with which he had been charged by the King of England, and called the Earl of Derby a traitor to his natural lord. The King on hearing this expression was much angered, and gave back to the earl the letters he had brought, saying, "Earl of Salisbury, our son of England bears too great hatred to our cousin of Derby; we wonder he has continued it so long, for we think that his court would be adorned if the Earl of Derby were near his person." "Very dear sire," replied the Earl of Salisbury, "I can only act as I have been ordered." "That is true," said the King, "we are not angry with you; execute the commission you have been charged with." The earl then, in compliance with the orders he had received, waited on the Duke of Berry and delivered the same message. The duke made no answer, but went forthwith to the King at the hotel de Saint Pol, and asked if he had received any news from England.

The King told him all that had occurred, and a privy council was summoned on the occasion, at which it was agreed, that as they ought to be more attached to the King of England than to the Earl of Derby, it would be advisable to break off the marriage of the earl with the Countess d'Eu. The Earl of Salisbury, having completed the business on which he was engaged, left Paris after this resolution had been adopted. The King of France, however, showed that he was more displeased than otherwise at the intelligence which the earl had brought, and returned to him his credential letters, refusing to accept them from his partiality to the Earl of Derby. The Earl of Salisbury returned to Calais without once speaking to the Earl of Derby, at which the latter was much displeased, and augured from it nothing favorable. However, about a month after his departure, his commissioners renewed the matter of the marriage with the Lady Mary of Berry; but those on the part of the Duke of Berry replied, "Tell my lord of Derby that when he is in the presence of the King and his brother the Duke of Orleans, he may propose this business himself; we cannot say more on the subject, since it is not agreeable to our employers that we longer interfere in it."

The Earl of Derby at the time suspected nothing more was meant by these words than to hasten the marriage, for the King and his lords had shown outwardly as much eagerness as ever for the match. He remembered what had been told him, and at a proper opportunity, when the King and his lords were together, renewed his proposal for the marriage. The Duke of Burgundy, who had been previously charged with the answer, replied, "Cousin of Derby, we cannot think of marrying our cousin to a traitor." The earl, on hearing this expression, instantly changed color and said, "Sir, I am in the presence of my lord the King, and must interrupt your speech. I never was, and never thought of being a traitor; and if anyone dare to charge me with treason, I am ready to answer him now or at whatever time it may please the King to appoint." "No, cousin," said the King, "I don't believe that you will find any man in France that will challenge your honor. The expression my uncle has used comes from England." The Earl of Derby, casting himself on his knees, replied, "I willingly believe you; may God preserve all my friends, and confound mine enemies." The King made the earl rise, and said, "Be appeased, this matter will end well; and when you shall be on good terms with everyone, we will then talk of the marriage. It will be first necessary for you to take possession of your duchy of Lancaster; for it is the custom of France and of many countries on this side the sea, that when a lord marries with the consent of his lord paramount, should he have one, he settles a dower on his wife." Wine and spices were brought, and thus the conversation ended. The Earl of Derby, on his return to the hotel de Clisson, was bitterly enraged, and not without reason. He had been accused of treason when he prided himself upon being one of the most loyal knights in the universe, and that in the presence of the King of France, who had shown him so much affection and courtesy. Moreover, that this accusation should have been brought from

England by the Earl of Salisbury galled him much. His knights endeavored to pacify him; but he was more cast down than man ever was.

It was known in England that the Earl of Salisbury had been sent to France, and the Londoners especially were exceedingly enraged against the King and his ministers for their conduct toward the Earl of Derby. "Ah, gallant and courteous Earl of Derby," they said, " how great are the jealousies and hatreds against thee: to overwhelm thee with disgrace and vexation, they charge thee with treason! It was not enough for the King and his minions to force thee out of the kingdom, but they must add this charge also; however, all things have an end, and their turn may come." "Alas," cried some, "what have his children done? when the King seizes their inheritance—an inheritance which ought to be theirs by direct succession from grandfather to father. There must be some change in public measures; we neither can nor will suffer them to go on longer."

Soon after the return of the Earl of Salisbury, King Richard had proclaimed throughout his realm and in Scotland, that a tournament would be held at Windsor by forty knights and forty squires (clothed in green, with the device of a white falcon), against all comers; and that the Queen of England, well attended by ladies and damsels, would be at the feast. When the day came, the Queen, indeed, was present at the tournament in magnificent array, but very few of the barons attended, so disgusted were they with the King for the banishment of the Earl of Derby, the injuries he was doing the earl's children, the murder of the Duke of Gloucester, which had been committed in the castle of Calais; the death of the Earl of Arundel, whom he had butchered in London, and the perpetual exile of the Earl of Warwick.

After this tournament, King Richard prepared to go to Ireland: and although many knights and squires made ready to join him, none took part in this expedition with good-will. The Earl of Northumberland, and his son Sir Henry Percy, after a special summons, sent excuses, for which they were banished from England, never to return until recalled by the King. This sentence caused the greatest astonishment throughout England, and tended much to increase the general discontent. The earl and his son consulted their friends as to how they should act under the disgrace which the King had so undeservedly heaped upon them, and it was agreed that they should seek an asylum in Scotland until affairs should mend or the King's anger be pacified. King Robert of Scotland and his barons readily granted the request, and moreover assured the earl that five or six hundred lances were at his service whenever he might require them. Things, however, remained as they were; for King Richard and his advisers in a short time had so much to do that they had no leisure to attend to the earl nor to enforce his banishment.

The King on his way to Ireland held his court at Bristol; and while he was there a general insurrection of the people of England took place. The courts of justice were closed, and a stop was put to all traffic; plunder and robbery prevailed, farmers' houses were pillaged of grain, and their beeves, pigs, and sheep carried away. Nothing but complaints were heard throughout the land. The citizens of London, who, being rich from trade, and by whom the other parts of England are generally governed, foresaw that most dangerous consequences would ensue, unless they stepped forward as they had formerly done against King Edward and the d'Espencers, who had forced Queen Isabella and the Prince of Wales out of the kingdom. Their remedy on the present occasion they believed to be in the Earl of Derby. "We must send for him," they said, "and on his arrival appoint him regent of the kingdom. Richard of Bordeaux must be arrested and confined in the Tower of London; his acts are so infamous, that they will condemn him." Many councils were held among the citizens on this subject, and it was at last agreed to request the Archbishop of Canterbury[b] to go over to France and communicate with the earl. The archbishop willingly undertook the office, and as secretly as possible prepared for his journey: in order to escape observation, he travelled not as an archbishop, but as a simple monk on a pilgrimage; and on arriving at Paris, had a private interview with the earl, to whom he explained the real object of his coming.

The Earl of Derby listened attentively to all that the archbishop told him, and to the request of the citizens of London,

[b] Thomas Fitz-alan, son of the Earl of Arundel.

that he would come over and be their king. He did not, however, immediately reply, but leaning in a window that looked into the garden he mused awhile, and then said, "My lord, your speech requires much consideration. I should be unwilling to begin an enterprise and be forced to leave it unfinished. Should I accept the offers and kind promises which you and my good friends the citizens of London make, I must subject myself to their will, arrest King Richard and put him to death. For this I shall be universally blamed: and I would not willingly do it, if other means can be adopted."

"My lord," replied the archbishop, "I am sent hither with every good disposition toward you; call in your council, and lay before them the propositions I have made." To this the earl consented, and when his knights and squires came together, they were unanimous in persuading him to accept the offer of the archbishop.

Matters were soon arranged; but in everything the greatest secrecy was observed; and the earl took leave of the King of France, under pretence of paying a visit to the Duke of Brittany, and staying some time at his court. His stay in Brittany, however, was not many days; for after he had explained his plans to the duke, and received his offer of assistance of men-at-arms and cross-bows, he set out for England, and landed at Plymouth. The next day he took the road to London, accompanied by the archbishop, Sir Peter de Craon, who had attended him from Brittany, and also by the escort which the duke had given him.

The mayor of London and the chief citizens went out to meet the earl on the road; and as they approached London, multitudes came out to receive him, shouting, "Welcome! long-wished-for Earl of Derby and Duke of Lancaster, may all joy and prosperity attend you." The mayor rode by the side of the earl, and in this manner they entered the city. So great indeed was the public rejoicing on the occasion, that every shop was shut, and no more work done than if it had been Easter Day.

To bring this matter to a conclusion, it was determined to march against the King, whom the citizens of London and the other towns now so hated, that they would call him by no other title than Richard of Bordeaux. Indeed, the Earl of Derby was already treated as king, and he engaged to undertake the government on condition that the crown was settled on him and his heirs for ever. An army was collected, chiefly of Londoners, who, with the earl at their head, marched without delay to Bristol, prepared to make King Richard a prisoner. Richard was thunderstruck when the information first reached him; and at the advice of those who were about him, he quietly left Bristol, and retired to Flint Castle. Thither, however, the Earl of Derby followed him with two hundred lances, being determined to have possession of his person by surrender or by force.

The earl and his men on arriving at Flint Castle knocked loudly. "Who is there?" asked the guard. "I am Henry of Lancaster," replied the earl, "and I am come to demand of the King my inheritance of the duchy of Lancaster: tell him so for me."

This message was instantly conveyed to the King, who, on hearing it, looked at his knights, and asked how he was to act. "Sire," replied they, "this request is by no means an improper one; you may allow him to come into your presence with eleven others, and then you can hear what he has to say." The King consented, and the Earl of Derby was conducted into his presence. Richard on seeing the earl changed color, and appeared very uneasy; but the earl, without paying him and reverence or honor, spoke aloud: "Have you broken your fast?" he said. "No," replied the King; "why do you ask?" "Because," continued the earl, "you have a long way to ride." "What road?" said the King. "You must come to London," answered the earl, "and I advise you to eat and drink heartily, that you may perform the journey gayly." The King becoming alarmed, said, "I am not hungry, nor have I any desire to eat." Upon this his knights, perceiving that things were taking a serious turn, said, "Sire, have confidence in my lord of Lancaster, your cousin, he can but wish your good." "Well, well," said the King, "I am willing so to have it; let the tables be prepared." The earl ate nothing, and the King made a most uneasy breakfast, after which he was told that the intention was to carry him to London, and place him as a prisoner in the Tower; to which, as resistance was useless, he quietly submitted.

Richard had not long been confined in the Tower when he expressed a desire to speak with the Earl of Derby, who was now styled Duke of Lancaster. The duke came to him without loss of time, when Richard addressed him thus: "Fair cousin, I have been considering my situation, which is miserable enough, and I have no longer any thought of wearing my crown, or governing my people. As God may have my soul, I wish I were this moment dead, and the King of France had his daughter again; for since I brought her hither, I have lost the love of my people. All things therefore considered, I freely resign to you the crown of England." The duke replied, "It will be necessary that the three estates of the realm hear this. I have issued summonses for assembling the nobles, prelates, and deputies from the principal towns, and within three days you can make your resignation in due form before them. The common report in this country is, that I have a better right to the crown than you have; for it is believed that the Princess of Wales, your mother, was not faithful to her husband; but, however this may be, I will guard and preserve you as long as you like, and will likewise entreat the Londoners on your behalf." "Many thanks," replied the King, "I have greater confidence in you than in any other person in England." "You are right," added the duke, "for had I not stepped forward between you and the people, they would have most disgracefully killed you, in return for all your wicked acts."

Upward of two hours did the duke continue this conversation with the King, and on taking his leave he returned at once to his own house, and renewed his orders for the assembly of the three estates of the realm.

When the day arrived, Richard was released from his prison, and having entered the hall which had been prepared for the occasion, royally dressed, the sceptre in his hand, and the crown on his head, he addressed the company as follows: "I have reigned King of England, Duke of Aquitaine, and Lord of Ireland, about twenty-two years, which royalty, lordship, sceptre, and crown I now freely and willingly resign to my cousin, Henry of Lancaster, and entreat of him, in the presence of you all, to accept this sceptre." He then tendered the sceptre to the duke, who, taking it, gave it to the Archbishop of Canterbury. King Richard next raised his crown from off his head, and placing it before him, said, " Henry, fair cousin, and Duke of Lancaster, I present and give to you this crown, and all the rights dependent on it." And the duke receiving it, delivered it also to the Archbishop of Canterbury.

This done, and the resignation having been accepted, the duke called a public notary to him, and had an authentic account of the proceedings drawn up, and witnessed by the lords and prelates present. Richard was then conducted back to his prison, and the assembly broke up.

On Wednesday, the last day of September, 1399, a Parliament was held at Westminster, at which the Duke of Lancaster challenged the crown of England, and claimed it for his own, for three reasons—first, by conquest; second, from being heir to it; and third, from the pure and free resignation which King Richard had made of it. The Parliament then declared, that it was their will he should be king, and the day of coronation was fixed for the Feast of Saint Edward, which fell on a Monday, the thirteenth day of October.

On Saturday before the coronation, the new King went from Westminster to the Tower of London, attended by great numbers, and those squires who were to be knighted watched their arms that night; they amounted to forty-six; each squire had his chamber and bath. The next day after mass the duke created them knights, and presented them with long green coats with straight sleeves lined with minever, after the manner of the prelates. These knights had on their left shoulder a double cord of white silk, with white tufts hanging down.

This Sunday after dinner the duke left the Tower on his return to Westminster; he was bare-headed, and had round his neck the order of the King of France. The Prince of Wales, six dukes, six earls, and eighteen barons accompanied him; and of other nobility there were from 800 to 900 horse in the procession. The duke, after the German fashion, was dressed in a jacket of cloth of gold, and mounted on a white courser, with a blue garter on his left leg. He passed through the streets of London, which were at the time all handsomely decorated with tapestries and other rich hangings; there were nine fountains in Cheapside and other streets through which he passed, and these perpetually ran with white and red wine.

He was escorted by prodigious numbers of gentlemen, with their servants in livery and badges; and the different companies of London were led by their wardens, clothed in their proper livery, and with the ensigns of their trade: the whole cavalcade amounted to 6,000 horse. That same night the duke bathed, and on the morrow confessed himself, and according to his custom heard three masses.

The prelates and clergy who had been assembled then came in procession from Westminster Abbey, to conduct the King to the Tower, and back again in the same manner. The dukes, earls, and barons wore long scarlet robes, with mantles trimmed with ermine, and large hoods of the same; the dukes and earls had three bars of ermine on the left arm a quarter of a yard long, or thereabout; the barons had but two; all the knights and squires had uniform cloaks of scarlet lined with minever. In the procession to the church the duke had borne over his head a rich canopy of blue silk, supported on silver staves, with four golden bells at the corners. This canopy was borne by four burgesses of Dover, who claimed it as their right. On either side of the duke were the sword of mercy and the sword of justice; the first being borne by the Prince of Wales, and the other by the Earl of Northumberland, constable of England; the Earl of Westmoreland, the marshal of England, carried the sceptre. The procession entered the church about nine o'clock. In the middle of the church was erected a scaffold covered with crimson cloth, in the centre of which was the royal throne of cloth of gold. When the duke entered the church, he seated himself on the throne and was thus in regal state, except having the crown on his head. The Archbishop of Canterbury proclaimed from the four corners of the scaffold how God had given them a man for their lord and sovereign, and then asked the people if they were consenting parties to his being consecrated and crowned king. Upon which the people unanimously shouted " Ay," and held up their hands, promising fealty and homage.

The duke then descended from the throne and advanced to the altar to be consecrated. Two archbishops and ten bishops performed the ceremony. He was stripped of all his royal state before the altar, naked to his shirt, and was then anointed and consecrated at six places: *i.e.*, on the head, the breast, the two shoulders, before and behind; on the back, and hands; a bonnet was then placed on his head, and while this was being done, the clergy chanted the litany, or the service that is performed to hallow a font. The King was now dressed in a churchman's clothes, like a deacon; and they put on him shoes of crimson velvet, after the manner of a prelate. Then they added spurs with a point, but no rowel; and the sword of justice was drawn, blessed, and delivered to the King, who put it again into the scabbard, when the Archbishop of Canterbury girded it about him. The crown of St. Edward, which is arched over like a cross, was next brought and blessed, and placed by the archbishop on the King's head. When mass was over the King left the church, and returned to the palace, in the same state as before. In the court-yard of the palace there was a fountain that ran constantly with red and white wine. The King went first to his closet, and then returned to the hall to dinner. At the first table sat the King; at the second, five great peers of England; at the third, the principal citizens of London; at the fourth, the newly created knights; at the fifth, all knights and squires of honor. The King was served by the Prince of Wales, who carried the sword of mercy; and on the opposite side, by the constable, who bore the sword of justice. At the bottom of the table was the Earl of Westmoreland with the sceptre. At the King's table there were only the two archbishops and seventeen bishops.

When dinner was half over, a knight of the name of Dymock entered the hall completely armed, and mounted on a handsome steed, richly barbed with crimson housings. The knight was armed for wager of battle, and was preceded by another knight bearing his lance. He himself had his drawn sword in one hand, and his naked dagger by his side. The knight presented the King with a written paper, the contents of which were, that if any knight or gentleman should dare to maintain that King Henry was not a lawful sovereign, he was ready to offer him combat in the presence of the King, when and where he should be pleased to appoint.

The King ordered this challenge to be proclaimed by heralds, in six different parts of the town and the hall; and to it no answer was made.

**King Henry having dined and partaken of wine and spices**

in the hall, retired to his private apartments, and all the company separated. Thus passed the coronation day of King Henry.

Intelligence of the imprisonment of King Richard, and of the coronation of Henry, Duke of Lancaster, was soon conveyed to France.

The Lady of Coucy, who was of the household of the young Queen, had been forced to leave her when Richard was conveyed to the Tower; and as she escaped to France, by her means King Charles was informe of all that was being done in England. Greatly was he displeased at the account; indeed, he threw himself into such a rage on the occasion, that he brought back his frenzy, of which he had now been free for some time. The council of the King of France, perceiving the King so greatly affected at what had befallen his son-in-law, determined to send to England some lord of high rank, to see and inquire into the situation of Queen Isabella. King Henry readily consented, and the Lord d'Albreth had an interview with the Queen, at Havering-at-the-Bower, where she resided.

A conspiracy was now set on foot by the earls of Huntingdon and Salisbury, the object of which was to murder King Henry; the attempt, however, completely failed, and the two earls lost their heads.

About this time John, Duke of Brittany, departed this life, leaving issue two sons and a daughter. The Bretons undertook the wardship of the eldest son, who had been betrothed to the second daughter of the King of France; and themselves agreed, also, to be on friendly terms with the French people. The angry feeling excited in France against King Henry did not die away; on the contrary, great preparations were everywhere made as if for hostilities against England.

While things were in this state, a true report was current in London, of the death of Richard of Bordeaux. I could not learn the particulars of it,[c] nor how it happened, the day I wrote these chronicles. When dead, Richard of Bordeaux was placed on a litter covered with black, and having a canopy of the same. Four black horses were harnessed to it, and two varlets in mourning conducted the litter, followed by four knights

[c] The manner of Richard's death is to this day a mystery; it is not certain whether he died by voluntary or compulsory starvation, or whether he was murdered by Piers Exton.

dressed also in mourning. Thus they left the Tower of London, where he had died, and paraded the streets at a foot's pace, until they came to Cheapside, where they halted for upward of two hours. After this they continued their journey until they came to a village, where there is a royal mansion, called Langley, about thirty miles from London. There Richard was interred: God pardon his sins, and have mercy upon his soul!

The news of Richard's death soon spread abroad; indeed, it had for some time been expected, for it was well known that he would never come out of the Tower alive. His death was concealed from his queen, as orders had been given for that purpose.

All these transactions were well known in France, and such knights and squires as wished for war were anxiously looking for orders to attack the frontiers. However, the councils of the two kingdoms thought it would be for the advantage of both countries that the truces should continue.

In consequence of the bad state of health into which the King of France had fallen, the Duke of Burgundy took the chief government of the realm. Negotiators were appointed on both sides; and by their management it was resolved, that the peace should continue for the original term of thirty years, four of which were already gone, so that it had now to last twenty-six years.

# HISTORY OF CHARLES XII

BY
VOLTAIRE
(FRANÇOIS MARIE AROUET)

TRANSLATED FROM THE FRENCH BY
TOBIAS SMOLLETT, M.D.

WITH A SPECIAL INTRODUCTION BY
JUSTIN McCARTHY

REVISED EDITION

NEW YORK
P. F. COLLIER & SON

Copyright, 1901
By THE COLONIAL PRESS

# SPECIAL INTRODUCTION

A STUDY of the life and character of Charles XII by the greatest writer of French prose must of itself be an event in history. Charles XII was one of the most brilliant and, if the word be not an anti-climax, one of the most interesting figures in the story of modern Europe. The age when Charles XII began, from his very boyhood, to astonish the world and to captivate the attention of civilized mankind was an age rich in fascinating figures.

It was the age of Marlborough, of Bolingbroke, of Swift, of Peter the Great, of Eugene, " Der Edle Ritter," and of Vendôme. It was an age which saw the breaking up of old systems all over Europe. The last princess of the Stuart family had come to the throne of England, and the exiled Stuarts were yet maintaining at intervals a struggle for their lost cause. The Russian Empire, after having been long regarded as a mere piece of uncouth Orientalism, out of its place in Europe, was beginning at last to make a recognized and an important figure in European politics. The United Provinces of the Netherlands, which had but lately achieved, after a struggle unsurpassed in history, their independence from the sovereignty of Spain, were beginning to play a momentous part in the politics, the trade, the education, and the armies and navies of Europe.

The despotism of Spain as a conquering and controlling power was breaking up, and there were already indications that Germany was not destined for long to bow before the dictation of imperial Austria. Even in the systems of war on sea and on land new principles and new methods were forcing themselves into prominence. The European stage was already so crowded with striking and commanding figures that it might have been thought there was not much chance for any new actor to rivet public attention on himself. Yet it is certain that Charles XII of Sweden, from the moment of his first appearance in the arena of politics and war, was recognized as one who must take his place among the foremost, and who from time to time could monopolize the attention and the interest of the world. Rare, indeed, is the good-fortune of any public man, even of any great sovereign and general, who could be enshrined in history by such a biographer as Voltaire.

Voltaire's position as a writer of French prose may be fairly described as unique. There was some discussion lately in English journalism about the work of a critical writer who laid it down as his doctrine that the three great masters of prose in the civilized world were Cicero, Voltaire, and Goethe. So far as I was able to observe at the time the position of Voltaire was not challenged by anyone during that critical controversy. The versatility of Voltaire's genius could not perhaps be more effectively illustrated than by his choice of Charles XII for the hero to whose life and actions he would turn his attention as a fascinating subject of study, and whose biographer he was determined to become.

The attraction of contrast must certainly have had an important part in this resolve. Charles was above all things a man of action, a conqueror, ready-made; a man inspired with indomitable energy, and from his very childhood given up to physical exercises, the display of strength, and the subjugation of difficulties. Voltaire was from his very infancy a poor and feeble creature; a sickly child, he had for some time after his entrance into the world to be kept in a swathing of cotton-wool to guard him against the effects of chill air and sudden draughts. His whole life was that of an invalid, and it was only by constant care and watchfulness that he was enabled to keep himself in existence. His strong will, however, maintained its power and himself, and he lived on to what would have been called, even in our long-living times, an advanced old age. He had undergone imprisonments; he had been confined in the Bastille, he had to make more than one rapid flight from danger in his own country, and all the while his tastes were for books, for writing, for bright companionship, for the theatres, for a peaceful and happy life of literature and society. Voltaire visited England and made a long stay there, a remarkable event in the career of a French author and courtier of that time, and the friends whose acquaintance he sought in England were poets and men of letters like himself. He had among his intimates Pope, Chesterfield, Thomson, Young, and Gay. Through Bolingbroke he was introduced at first into this literary companionship, and even to Bolingbroke he seems to have been attracted more by Bolingbroke's gifts as a writer than by his position as a political leader and great parliamentary orator.

All this would not have seemed a very natural preparation for the study of such a career as that of Charles XII, and yet there is, perhaps, hardly any work of Voltaire's which has been more widely read and is more likely to be long remembered than the book which we are now including in our edition of The World's Classics. Voltaire tried his hand at almost everything which a literary man could attempt. He wrote poems; he wrote plays; he wrote essays on philosophy and metaphysics; he loved to regard himself as a man of advanced views on science; he wrote romances—we should hardly regard them as romances according to the modern interpretation of the word, and might rather regard them as humorous fables with satirical application; he burlesqued in a poem of marvellous wit and phrase-power the life-story of one of the noblest women the world has ever known—Joan of Arc—a poem which his warmest admirers might well wish that he had never written. He was for a time regarded as one of the great tragic poets of France, but his tragedies have long since been consigned to obscurity. He wrote an epic poem by which he fondly hoped to win immortality, but which probably no one reads now except out of mere curiosity and as a study of a great man's misdirected enterprise.

There are some of us who think that the romances, as they are called, of Voltaire illustrate within their compass some of Voltaire's finest qualities as a wit, a satirist, an observer of human nature, and an advanced thinker, striving, after his own fashion, for the enlightenment and the advancement of his fellow-men. I do not care to enter into controversial questions in this essay, but I may, perhaps, be allowed to say that those who have been taught to regard Voltaire as an unbeliever in religion, as a mere impious scoffer at all true religious feeling, would find their preconceived opinions curiously disestablished by a study of these marvellous little stories.

To return, however, to the life of Charles XII, I may say that the more inclined we feel to regard Voltaire as a writer little qualified by nature, by tastes, by social influences, and by habits to become the biographer of the great Swedish King, the more we shall have to wonder over the signal success with which he has accomplished his task. The life of Charles XII is a marvellous study, complete and consistent in itself from first to last. For the time Voltaire seems to have thrown himself into a thorough association and affinity with the purposes, the genius, and the daring of the man whom according to Dr. Johnson no dangers could frighten and no labors tire. It might seem, if such a thing were possible, that Voltaire had studied the character of the marvellous Swedish prince from the inside rather than from the outside.

There is much in the career of Charles which might appear to the ordinary reader of history absolutely to defy explanation. The character of the man shows like a hopeless puzzle of contradictions. One is impressed now with a sense of utter recklessness in Charles's daring feats, and again by the extraordinary quality of cool and almost mechanical calculation which he brought to bear on the arrangement of his plans. In many cases it is plain that Charles accomplished a success on the assumption that an extravagant display of utterly reckless audacity would drive his antagonists to the conclusion that he must have some invisible forces within his call, and convince them in a moment of bewildered alarm that it would be idle to make any attempt at resistance.

It is easy to understand how some Rupert of the battle-field might be carried away by his own daring into some seemingly desperate enterprise, and how by its very impetuosity it might have carried all before it for the time. But it is hard, indeed, to understand how such a Rupert could have deliberately planned it all out in advance and composedly calculated the chances of success in a mere attempt to frighten his opponents out of their senses. Rupert, as we know, seldom succeeded in winning more than half the battle, for his antagonists soon rallied, retrieved their lost ground, and made the day their own in the end. But the most complete successes won by Charles XII were achieved by just this marvellous combination of cool preliminary calculating power and what seemed extravagant and unthinking audacity. Voltaire has the marvellous art of enabling his readers to realize the union of the two apparently contradictory qualities in the one man. He could not only understand to the full a nature and temper utterly unlike his own, but he could also construct an artistic realization of that nature and character, and set the man who owned them in living presentment before us.

Voltaire had, indeed, above all things, the art of the story-teller. The history of Charles XII, as told by him, has all the living fascination which is to be found in the stirring romances of the elder Dumas. Yet there is nothing superficial in the book, nor does it give us merely a series of brilliant pictures illustrating the military adventures of his hero. Everything is made clear; everything is explained. There are historical dissertations, not long, indeed, certainly never too long, but always quite long enough to make the reader fully acquainted with the whole conditions of each event. There are symmetrically arranged geographical descriptions, there are rapidly sketched pictures of social life, and every remarkable man or woman who appears in the scenes stands out as a living figure. Voltaire does not allow his hero to monopolize the interest of the reader. The character of Peter the Great, as it showed itself to Voltaire, is set out with as much care and as much vividness as he gives to the character of Charles XII. Figures of less importance passing now and then across the scene are described in vigorous and life-like touches which make each of them real, natural, distinct, and familiar.

The whole book is an animated story, while Voltaire never fails to the utmost of his power and knowledge in keeping close to historical accuracy. He even takes some pains to explain to his readers that the title of " czar " is not, as was then generally supposed, a mere corruption of the word " Cæsar," but is taken from early Russian dialects with which the titles of imperial Rome could have had no possible affinity. I believe there have been more recent disputations on this point, but I mention it only to illustrate the minuteness with which Voltaire endeavors to make his work historically accurate. If we can imagine the possibility of an intelligent modern reader coming to study the book, who had never before heard of the existence of Charles XII, and who assumed the work to be a mere piece of romance, we may be sure that that intelligent reader would find himself carried away by the genuine fascination of the narrative, with its adventurous hero and its pictures of scenes and characters, and would follow it to its end with enraptured attention. I do not know of any character in pure romance which is made more attractive, and at the same time more life-like, than the character of Charles XII in this delightful piece of history. The very contradictions in the temperament and the moods of Charles are made to lend an additional fascination to the story, and at the same time are brought home to the recognition of the reader as component parts of a real and living whole. The heroic magnanimity of one mood and the self-centred personal impulses of another; the reckless unsparing pursuit of ambition or of vengeance up to a certain point, and then the sudden impulse to generosity and to mercy—all these are illustrated with an easy effect which makes them natural, and even realistic, as the essential parts of one extraordinary but not extravagant picture.

Historical critics have found fault here and there with some of Voltaire's statements, descriptions, and inferences, but there has not been more discussion of that kind than the reader will find to have been called up by almost every great biographical work of any time. Many biographies and histories dealing with the men and the events of our own times—with men and events about which we are all supposed to know a good deal—have called forth far more questioning and more controversy than any of Voltaire's accounts and descriptions of what happen among far-off and little-known Tartar regions during the life of Charles XII. Voltaire, it may be added, is especially anxious to vindicate the accuracy of every passage in his narrative, and he is proud to support himself by more than one authentic confirmation from men who bore an actual part in the scenes which he describes. He has, moreover, the artistic capacity to surround each scene with its own peculiar atmosphere, and we may feel that we are in Sweden or in Poland or in Russia as he transports his fascinated reader from place to place.

Undoubtedly at one time Voltaire's ambition was to be regarded as a great epic poet or a great tragedian, but he never succeeded in entering into the very soul of any character in his epic or his tragedies as he has to all appearance succeeded in comprehending and realizing the soul and the impulses of " Swedish Charles." We are generally inclined to regard Voltaire as a man chiefly possessed by critical and cynical instincts, who loved to show up the meanness and the hypocrisies of the human character and to teach that the objects of our hero-worship are, after all, only mean and pitiful creatures like too many of ourselves. Many critics have said, and with much seeming reason, that Voltaire did not succeed in his epic and his tragedies because his temperament did not allow him to take much interest in the deep elementary emotions of human love, heroic passion, and profound suffering.

I think, however, that to maintain this opinion is to take too much account of one side merely of Voltaire's character. It is beyond question that he had deep sympathy with human suffering when the suffering was due to oppression or to wrong of any kind which could be righted. But it certainly is somewhat strange to find that Voltaire could enter into the spirit of a man with whose inclinations, ambitions, and passions he must have been so little in natural sympathy. Voltaire's admiration for his hero never degenerates into mere hero-worship. Some modern English authors have shown us how the tendency to mere hero-worship can utterly mar the true usefulness of a work which has genuine literary charm to recommend it. Into that sort of hero-worship Voltaire never descends. He understands and analyzes the weaknesses of his hero as well as his strength; he exposes and condemns the faults of Charles XII; and he does not glorify even his noblest qualities.

Charles XII always stands before us as a man: we are never allowed to mistake him for a demi-god. Voltaire enters into calm analysis of his hero's intellect as well as of his soldierly qualities, and quietly sets forth the reasons which compel us to believe with him that certain historians were mistaken when they described Charles XII as a master of mathematical science. Voltaire distinguishes him in one remarkable sentence from other great conquerors: he describes Charles XII as "the first who had the ambition to be a conqueror without having the desire to aggrandize his States; he wished to gain empires in order to give them away." In another passage he sums up the character of Charles as that of a man unique rather than a great man. Nor does he ever fail to point what may be called the moral of Charles's career—of that Charles who, as Dr. Johnson sums him up, "left a name at which the world grew pale to point a moral or adorn a tale." "His great qualities," says Voltaire, "any single one of which might have immortalized another prince, brought misfortune on his country." "The lesson which the life of Charles XII ought to teach to kings is that a pacific and happy government is far better worth than so much glory."

These words, indeed, express the spirit of the whole book. But, of course, Voltaire did not write his book merely to give illustration to the old and well-worn moral that the ambition of a sovereign often means the depression and misery of his subjects. Voltaire did not set about his task because he thought that the career of Charles XII would make a new and striking object-lesson in the promulgation of his favorite gospel of peace. He wrote the book because he was fascinated by the man and by the story. The further he goes on with his task, the more he seems to be filled by it and to warm to it. The reader will find the same process working itself out in his own mind. With each succeeding chapter he will feel his interest growing stronger in the hero of the biography and also in its author. We feel a sensation of pleasure, very much like that which may be felt by one who watches the work of a great sculptor whose chisel brings out more and more some form of heroic proportions and beauty. The looker-on is, indeed, enchanted by the noble form of the statue, but he is not so wholly absorbed in his admiration for it as to forget the workman in the work. The more he admires the created work of art, the more he admires the artist who has created it.

I do not think there is anything extravagant or even overwrought in this illustration of the feeling which comes into the reader's mind as he studies Voltaire's life of Charles XII. The career which it pictures is from first to last one of the most romantic interest. The hero of the narrative is almost, as Voltaire says, unique in the story of heroes in or out of romance, but the reader of the book, although often breathlessly carried away by the story, has always some thought for the marvellous skill of the author who with so light and yet so firm a touch has made the whole a living reality for us. A series of "The World's Great Classics" would, indeed, be incomplete without Voltaire's history of Charles XII.

*Justin McCarthy.*

# CONTENTS

### BOOK I

An Abridgment of the History of Sweden to the Reign of Charles XII—The Education of that Prince, and an Account of His Enemies—Character of the Czar Peter Alexiovitch—Curious Anecdotes Relative to that Prince and the Russian Nation—Muscovy, Poland, and Denmark Unite Against Charles XII............ 1

### BOOK II

A Sudden and Surprising Change in the Character of Charles XII—At Eighteen Years of Age He Undertakes a War Against Denmark, Poland, and Muscovy; Finishes the Danish War in Six Weeks; with Eight Thousand Swedes Defeats Eighty Thousand Russians, and then Penetrates into Poland—A Description of Poland, and its Form of Government—Charles Gains Several Battles, and Becomes Master of Poland, where he Prepares to Nominate a King............................... 23

### BOOK III

Stanislaus Leszezynski Elected King of Poland—Death of the Cardinal-Primate—Skilful Retreat of General Schulenburg—Exploits of the Czar—Foundation of Petersburg—Battle of Fraustadt—Charles Enters Saxony—Peace of Altranstädt—Augustus Abdicates the Crown in Favor of Stanislaus—General Patkul, the Czar's Plenipotentiary, is Broken upon the Wheel and Quartered—Charles Receives the Ambassadors of Foreign Princes in Saxony—He Goes alone to Dresden to Visit Augustus before His Departure ................... ........................ 62

### BOOK IV

Charles Quits Saxony in a Victorious Manner; Pursues the Czar; and Shuts Himself up in the Ukraine—His Losses; His Wound—The Battle of Poltava—Consequences of that Battle—Charles Obliged to Fly into Turkey—His Reception in Bessarabia...... 94

## CONTENTS

### BOOK V

State of the Ottoman Porte—Charles Resides near Bender—His Employments—His Intrigues at the Porte—His Designs—Augustus Restored to His Throne—The King of Denmark Makes a Descent upon Sweden—All the Other Dominions of Charles are Invaded—The Czar Enters Moscow in Triumph—Affair of the Pruth—History of the Czarina, Who from a Country-girl Became Empress...................................... 119

### BOOK VI

Intrigues at the Porte—The Khan of Tartary and the Pasha of Bender Endeavor to Force Charles to Depart—He Defends Himself with Forty Domestics against the Whole Army—He is Taken, and Treated as a Prisoner................................... 148

### BOOK VII

The Turks Convey Charles to Demirtash—King Stanislaus is Taken at the Same Time—Bold Undertaking of M. de Villelongue—Revolutions in the Seraglio—Battle in Pomerania—Altona Burnt by the Swedes—Charles at Last Sets out on His Return to His Own Dominions—His Strange Manner of Travelling—His Arrival at Stralsund—His Misfortunes—Successes of Peter the Great—His Triumphant Entry into Petersburg............... 172

### BOOK VIII

Charles gives His Sister in Marriage to the Prince of Hesse—He is Besieged in Stralsund, and Escapes to Sweden—Schemes of Baron Görtz, His Prime Minister—Plan of a Reconciliation with the Czar, and of a Descent upon England—Charles Besieges Frederickshald, in Norway—He is Killed—His Character—Görtz is Beheaded........................................... 198

# THE HISTORY OF CHARLES XII

## BOOK I

An Abridgment of the History of Sweden to the Reign of Charles XII—The Education of that Prince, and an Account of His Enemies—Character of the Czar Peter Alexiovitch—Curious Anecdotes Relative to that Prince and the Russian Nation—Muscovy, Poland, and Denmark Unite against Charles XII.

SWEDEN and Finland constitute a kingdom 200 leagues broad and 300 long. This country reaches from the fifty-fifth degree of latitude, or thereabout, to the seventieth. It lies under a very severe climate, which is hardly ever softened either by the return of spring or of autumn. The winter prevails there nine months in the year. The scorching heats of the summer succeed immediately to the excessive cold of the winter. The frost begins in the month of October, without any of those imperceptible gradations which in other countries usher in the seasons and render the change more agreeable. Nature, in return, has given to this cold climate a clear sky and a pure air. The almost constant heat of the summer produces flowers and fruits in a very short time. The long nights of the winter are tempered by the evening and morning twilights, which last for a greater or less time, in proportion as the sun is nearer to, or farther removed from, Sweden; and the light of the moon, unobscured by clouds, and increased by the reflection of the snow that covers the ground, and frequently by the aurora borealis, makes it as convenient to travel in Sweden by night as by day. For want of pasture, the cattle there are smaller than in the more southern parts of Europe; but the men are of a large stature, healthful from the purity of the air, and strong from the severity of the climate; they live to a great age, unless enfeebled by the immoderate use of wines and strong liquors, of which the northern nations seem to be the more fond, the less nature has indulged them with these commodities.

The Swedes are well made, strong and active, and capable of enduring the greatest fatigue, want, and hunger. Born with a military genius and high spirit, they are more brave than industrious, having long neglected, and even at present but little cultivating, the arts of commerce, which alone can supply them with those productions in which their country is deficient. They say it was chiefly from Sweden, one part of which is still called Gothland, that those swarms of Goths issued forth, who, like a deluge, overran Europe, and wrested it from the Romans, who had usurped the dominion of that vast country, which they continued for the space of 500 years to harass by their tyranny and to civilize by their laws.

The northern countries were much more populous at that time than they are at present. Religion, by allowing the men a plurality of wives, gave them an opportunity of furnishing the State with more subjects. The women themselves knew no reproach but that of sterility or idleness; and being as strong and as laborious as the men, they bore children faster and for a longer time. Sweden, however, with that part of Finland which it still retains, does not contain above 4,000,000 of inhabitants. The soil is poor and barren; Scania [Schonen or Skane] is the only province that bears wheat. The current coin of the kingdom does not exceed 9,000,000 of livres. The public bank, which is the oldest in Europe, was at first established from mere necessity; the copper and iron, in which their payments were formerly made, being too heavy to be transported.

Sweden preserved its freedom without interruption to the middle of the fourteenth century. During that long period the form of government was more than once altered; but all these alterations were in favor of liberty. The first magistrate was invested with the name of King, a title which, in different countries, is attended with very different degrees of power. In France and Spain it signifies an absolute monarch: in Poland, Sweden, and England it means the first man of the republic. This King could do nothing without the Senate, and the Senate depended upon the States-General, which were frequently assembled. The representatives of the nation, in these grand assemblies, were the gentry, the bishops, and the deputies of the towns; and in process of time, the very peasants, a class of people unjustly despised in other places, and subject to slavery in almost all the northern countries, were admitted to a share in the administration.

About the year 1492, this nation, so jealous of its liberty, and which still piques itself on having conquered Rome about 1,300 years ago, was subjected to the yoke by a woman, and by a people less powerful than the Swedes.

Margaret of Valdemar, the Semiramis of the North, and Queen of Denmark and Norway, subdued Sweden by force and stratagem, and united these three extensive kingdoms into one mighty monarchy. After her death Sweden was rent by civil wars; it alternately threw off and submitted to the Danish yoke; was sometimes governed by kings and sometimes by administrators. About the year 1520 this unhappy kingdom was horribly harassed by two tyrants: the one was Christiern II, King of Denmark, a monster whose character was entirely composed of vices, without the least ingredient of virtue; the other an archbishop of Upsala and primate of the kingdom, as barbarous as the former. These two, by mutual agreement, caused the consuls and the magistrates of Stockholm, together with ninety-four senators, to be seized in one day, and to be executed by the hand of the common hangman, under the frivolous pretence that they were excommunicated by the Pope, for having dared to defend the rights of the State against the encroachments of the archbishop.

While these two men, unanimous in their oppressive measures, and disagreeing only about the division of the spoil, domineered over Sweden with all the tyranny of the most absolute despotism, and all the cruelty of the most implacable revenge, a new and unexpected event gave a sudden turn to the state of affairs in the North.

Gustavus Vasa, a young man, sprung from the ancient kings of Sweden, arose from the forests of Dalecarlia, where he had long lain concealed, and came to deliver his country from bondage. He was one of those great souls whom nature so seldom produces, and who are born with all the qualifications necessary to form the accomplished monarch. His handsome and stately person, and his noble and majestic air, gained him followers at first sight. His eloquence, recommended by an engaging manner, was the more persuasive the less it was artful. His enterprising genius formed those projects which, though to the vulgar they may appear rash, are considered only as bold in the eyes of great men, and which his courage and perseverance enabled him to accomplish. Brave with circumspection, and mild and gentle in a fierce and cruel age, he was as virtuous as it is possible for the leader of a party to be.

Gustavus Vasa had been the hostage of Christiern, and had been detained a prisoner contrary to the law of nations. Having found means to escape from prison, he had dressed himself in the habit of a peasant, and in that disguise he wandered about in the mountains and woods of Dalecarlia, where he was reduced to the necessity of working in the copper-mines, at once to procure a livelihood, and to conceal himself from his enemies. Buried as he was in these subterraneous caverns, he had the boldness to form the design of dethroning the tyrant. With this view he discovered himself to the peasants, who regarded him as one of those superior beings to whom the common herd of mankind are naturally inclined to submit. These savage boors he soon improved into hardy and warlike soldiers. He attacked Christiern and the archbishop, beat them in several encounters, banished them both from Sweden, and, at last, was justly chosen by the States King of that country of which he had been the deliverer.

Hardly was he established on the throne, when he undertook an enterprise still more difficult than his conquests. The real tyrants of the State were the bishops, who, having engrossed almost all the riches of Sweden, employed their ill-gotten wealth in oppressing the subjects, and in making war upon the King. This power was the more formidable, as, in the opinion of the ignorant populace, it was held to be sacred. Gustavus punished the Catholic religion for the crimes of its ministers; and, in less than two years, introduced Lutheranism into Sweden, rather by the arts of policy than by the influence of authority. Having thus conquered the kingdoms, as he was wont to say, from the Danes and the clergy, he reigned a happy and an absolute monarch to the age of seventy, and then died full of glory, leaving his family and religion in quiet possession of the throne.

One of his descendants was that Gustavus Adolphus, who is commonly called the "Great Gustavus." He conquered Ingria [Ingermannland], Livonia, Bremen, Verden, Wismar, and Pomerania, not to mention above 100 places in Germany, which, after his death, were yielded up by the Swedes. He shook the throne of Ferdinand II, and protected the Lutherans in Germany, an attempt in which he was secretly assisted by the Pope himself, who dreaded the power of the Emperor much more than the prevalence of heresy. He it was that by his victories effectually contributed to humble the house of Austria; though the glory of that enterprise is usually ascribed to Cardinal Richelieu, who well knew how to procure himself the reputation of those great actions which Gustavus was contented with simply performing. He was just upon the point of extending the war beyond the Danube, and perhaps of dethroning the Emperor, when he was killed, in the thirty-seventh year of his age, at the battle of Lützen, which he gained over Wallenstein, carrying along with him to his grave the name of "Great," the lamentations of the North, and the esteem of his enemies.

His daughter Christina, a lady of an extraordinary genius, was much fonder of conversing with men of learning than of reigning over a people whose knowledge was entirely confined to the art of war. She became as famous for quitting the throne as her ancestors had been for obtaining or securing it. The Protestants have loaded her memory with many injurious aspersions, as if it were impossible for a person to be possessed of great virtues without adhering to Luther; and the papists have piqued themselves too much on the conversion of a woman who had nothing to recommend her but her taste for philosophy. She retired to Rome, where she passed the rest of her days in the midst of those arts of which she was so passionately fond, and for the sake of which she had renounced a crown at twenty-seven years of age.

Before her abdication, she prevailed upon the States of Sweden to elect her cousin, Charles Gustavus X, son of the Count Palatine, and Duke of Deux-Ponts, as her successor. This prince added new conquests to those of Gustavus Adolphus. He presently carried his arms into Poland, where he gained the famous battle of Warsaw, which lasted for three days. He waged a long and successful war with the Danes;

besieged them in their capital; reunited Scania to Sweden; and confirmed the Duke of Holstein in the possession of Sleswick, at least for a time. At last, having met with a reverse of fortune, and concluded a peace with his enemies, he turned his ambition against his subjects, and formed the design of establishing a despotic government in Sweden. But, like the great Gustavus, he died in the thirty-seventh year of his age, without being able to finish his project, the full accomplishment of which was reserved for his son, Charles XI.

Charles XI was a warrior, like all his ancestors, and more despotic than any of them. He abolished the authority of the Senate, which was declared to be the Senate of the King, and not of the kingdom. He was prudent, vigilant, indefatigable; qualities that must certainly have secured him the love of his subjects, had not his despotic measures been more adapted to excite their fear than to gain their affections.

In 1680, he married Ulrica Eleonora, daughter to Frederick III, King of Denmark, a princess eminent for her virtue, and worthy of greater confidence than her husband was pleased to repose in her. Of this marriage, on the twenty-seventh of June, 1682, was born King Charles XII, the most extraordinary man, perhaps, that ever appeared in the world. In him were united all the great qualities of his ancestors; nor had he any other fault or failing, but that he possessed all these virtues in too high a degree. This is the prince whose history we now purpose to write, and concerning whose person and actions we shall relate nothing but what is founded upon the best authority.

The first book which was put into his hands was the work of Samuel Puffendorf, that from thence he might acquire an early knowledge of his own dominions, and of those of his neighbors. He next learned the German language, which he continued to speak for the future, with the same fluency as his mother-tongue. At seven years of age he could manage a horse; and the violent exercises in which he delighted, and which discovered his martial disposition, soon procured him a vigorous constitution, capable of supporting the incredible fatigues which his natural inclination always prompted him to undergo.

Though gentle in his infancy, he betrayed an inflexible obstinacy. The only way to influence him was to awaken his sense of honor; by mentioning the word "glory" you might have obtained anything from him. He had a great aversion to the Latin tongue; but as soon as he heard that the kings of Poland and Denmark understood it, he learned it with great expedition, and retained so much of it as to be able to speak it all the rest of his life. The same means were employed to engage him to learn the French; but he could never be persuaded to make use of that tongue, not even with the French ambassadors themselves, who understood no other.

As soon as he had acquired a tolerable knowledge of the Latin, his teacher made him translate Quintus Curtius; a book for which he conceived a great liking, rather on account of the subject than the style. The person who explained this author to him having asked him what he thought of Alexander, "I think," said the prince, "I could wish to be like him." "But," resumed the preceptor, "he only lived two-and-thirty years." "Ah!" he replied, "and is not that enough when one has conquered kingdoms?" The courtiers did not fail to carry these answers to the King, his father, who would often cry out, "This child will excel me, and will even go beyond the great Gustavus." One day he happened to be diverting himself in the royal apartment, in viewing two plans: the one of a town in Hungary, which the Turks had taken from the Emperor; the other of Riga, the capital of Livonia, a province conquered by the Swedes about a century before. Under the plan of the town of Hungary were written these words, taken from the book of Job: "The Lord hath given it to me, and the Lord hath taken it from me; blessed be the name of the Lord." The young prince having read this inscription, immediately took a pencil and wrote under the plan of Riga: "The Lord hath given it to me, and the devil shall not take it from me." * Thus, in the most indifferent actions of his childhood, his unconquerable spirit would frequently show some traces of those heroic qualities which characterize great souls, and which plainly indicated what sort of a man he would one day prove to be.

He was but eleven years of age when he lost his mother, who expired on August 5, 1693. The disease of which she died was supposed to be owing to the bad usage she had received from

---

* This anecdote I give from the information of two French ambassadors who resided at the Court of Sweden.

her husband, and to her own endeavors to conceal her vexation. Charles XI had, by means of a certain court of justice, which was called the Chamber of Liquidations, and erected by his sole authority, deprived a great number of his subjects of their wealth. Crowds of citizens, ruined by this chamber—nobility, merchants, farmers, widows, and orphans—filled the streets of Stockholm, and daily repaired to the gate of the palace to pour forth their unavailing complaints. The Queen succored these unhappy people as much as lay in her power; she gave them her money, her jewels, her furniture, and even her clothes; and when she had no more to give them, with tears in her eyes, she threw herself at her husband's feet, beseeching him to have pity on his wretched subjects. The King gravely answered her: "Madam, we took you to bring us children, not to give us advice." And from that time he treated her with a severity that is said to have shortened her days.

He died four years after her, on April 15, 1697, in the fifty-second year of his age, and the thirty-seventh of his reign, at a time when the empire, Spain, and Holland, on the one side, and France on the other, had referred the decision of their quarrels to his arbitration, and when he had already concerted the terms of accommodation between these different powers.

He left to his son, who was then fifteen years of age, a throne well established and respected abroad; subjects poor, but valiant and loyal, together with a treasury in good order, and managed by able ministers.

Charles XII, at his accession to the throne, found himself the absolute and undisturbed master, not only of Sweden and Finland, but also of Livonia, Carelia, Ingria, Wismar, Viborg, the Islands of Rügen and Oesel, and the finest part of Pomerania, together with the Duchy of Bremen and Verden—all of them the conquests of his ancestors, secured to the Crown by long possession, and by the solemn treaties of Munster and Oliva, and supported by the terror of the Swedish arms. The peace of Ryswyk, which was begun under the auspices of the father, being fully concluded under those of the son, he found himself the meditator of Europe from the first moment of his reign.

The laws of Sweden fix the majority of their kings at the age of fifteen; but Charles XI, who was entirely absolute, put off, by his last will, the majority of his son to the age of eighteen. In this he favored the ambitious views of his mother, Edwiga Eleonora of Holstein, dowager of Charles X, who was appointed by the King her son, guardian to the young King her grandson, and regent of the kingdom, in conjunction with a Council of five persons.

The regent had a share in the menagament of public affairs during the reign of her son. She was now advanced in years; but her ambition, which was greater than her abilities, prompted her to entertain the pleasing hopes of possessing authority for a long time under the King her grandson. She kept him at as great a distance as possible from all concern with the affairs of state. The young prince passed his time either in hunting or in reviewing his troops, and would even sometimes exercise with them; which amusement seemed only to be the natural effect of his youthful vivacity. He never betrayed any dissatisfaction sufficient to alarm the regent, who flattered herself that the dissipation of mind occasioned by these diversions would render him incapable of application, and leave her in possession of the supreme power for a considerable time.

One day in the month of November, and in the same year in which his father died, when he had been taking a review of several regiments, and Piper the counsellor was standing by him, he seemed to be absorbed in a profound reverie. "May I take the liberty," said Piper to him, " of asking your Majesty what you are thinking of so seriously?" " I am thinking," replied the prince, "that I am capable of commanding those brave fellows; and I don't choose that either they or I should receive orders from a woman." Piper immediately seized this opportunity of making his fortune; but, conscious that his own interest was not sufficient for the execution of such a dangerous enterprise as the removal of the Queen from the regency, and the hastening of the King's majority, he proposed the affair to Count Axel Sparr, a man of a daring spirit, and fond of popularity. Him he cajoled with the hopes of being the King's confidant. The count readily swallowed the bait, and undertook the management of the whole matter, while all his labors only tended to promote the interest of Piper. The counsellors of the regency were soon drawn into the scheme, and forthwith proceeded to the execution of it, in order to recommend themselves the more effectually to the King.

They went in a body to propose it to the Queen who little expected such a declaration. The counsellors of the regency laid the matter before the States-General, who were then assembled, and who were all unanimous in approving the proposal. The point was carried with a rapidity that nothing could withstand; so that Charles XII had only to signify his desire of reigning, and, in three days, the States bestowed the government upon him. The Queen's power and credit fell in an instant. She afterward led a private life, which was more suitable to her age, though less agreeable to her humor. The King was crowned on the twenty-fourth of December following. He made his entry into Stockholm on a sorrel horse shod with silver, having a sceptre in his hand and a crown upon his head, amid the acclamations of a whole people, passionately fond of every novelty, and always conceiving great hopes from the reign of a young prince.

The ceremony of the consecration and coronation belongs to the Archbishop of Upsala. This is almost the only privilege that remains to him of the great number that were claimed by his predecessors. After having anointed the prince, according to custom, he held the crown in his hand, in order to put it upon his head: Charles snatched it from him and crowned himself, regarding the poor prelate all the while with a stern look. The people, who are always dazzled by everything that has an air of grandeur and magnificence, applauded this action of the King. Even those who had groaned most severely under the tyranny of the father were foolish enough to commend the son for this instance of arrogance, which was a sure pledge of their future slavery.

As soon as Charles was master of the kingdom he made Piper his chief confidant, intrusting him at the same time with the management of public affairs, and giving him all the power of a prime minister, without the odium of the name. A few days after he created him a count, which is a dignity of great eminence in Sweden, and not an empty title that may be assumed without any manner of importance, as in France.

The beginning of the King's reign gave no very favorable idea of his character. It was imagined that he had been more ambitious of obtaining the supreme power than worthy of possessing it. True it is, he had no dangerous passion; but his conduct discovered nothing but the sallies of youth and the freaks of obstinacy. He seemed to be equally proud and lazy. The ambassadors who resided at his court took him even for a person of mean capacity, and represented him as such to their respective masters.* The Swedes entertained the same opinion of him: nobody knew his real character: he did not even know it himself, until the storm that suddenly arose in the North gave him an opportunity of displaying his great talents, which had hitherto lain concealed.

Three powerful princes, taking the advantage of his youth, conspired his ruin almost at the same time. The first was his own cousin, Frederick IV, King of Denmark: the second, Augustus, Elector of Saxony and King of Poland; Peter the Great, Czar of Muscovy, was the third, and most dangerous. It will be necessary to unfold the origin of these wars, which produced such great events. Let us begin with Denmark.

Of the two sisters of Charles XII, the eldest was married to the Duke of Holstein, a young prince of an undaunted spirit and of a gentle disposition. The duke, oppressed by the King of Denmark, repaired to Stockholm with his spouse, and throwing himself into the arms of the King, earnestly implored his assistance. This he hoped to obtain, as Charles was not only his brother-in-law, but was likewise the sovereign of a people who bore an irreconcilable hatred to the Danes.

The ancient house of Holstein, sunk in that of Oldenburg, had been advanced by election to the throne of Denmark in 1449. All the kingdoms of the North were at that time elective; but the Kingdom of Denmark soon after became hereditary. One of its kings, called Christiern III, had such a tender affection for his brother Adolphus, or, at least, such a regard for his interest, as is seldom to be met with among princes. He was desirous of investing him with sovereign power, and yet he could not dismember his own dominions. He therefore divided with him the duchies of Holstein-Gottorp and Sleswick, by an odd kind of agreement, the substance of which was that the descendants of Adolphus should ever after govern Holstein in conjunction with the kings of Denmark; that those two duchies should belong to both in common; and that the **King of Denmark should be able to do nothing in Holstein**

* This is confirmed by original letters.

without the duke, nor the duke without the King. A union so strange, of which, however, we have had within these few years a similar instance in the same family, was, for nearly eighty years, the source of perpetual disputes between the Crown of Denmark and the house of Holstein-Gottorp—the kings always endeavoring to oppress the dukes, and the dukes to render themselves independent. A struggle of this nature had cost the last duke his liberty and sovereignty, both which, however, he recovered at the conferences of Altona in 1689, by the interposition of Sweden, England, and Holland, who became guarantees for the execution of the treaty. But as a treaty between princes is frequently no more than a giving way to necessity, till such times as the stronger shall be able to crush the weaker, the contest was revived with greater virulence than ever between the new King of Denmark and the young duke. And while the duke was at Stockholm, the Danes had already committed some acts of hostility in the country of Holstein, and had entered into a secret agreement with the King of Poland to attack the King of Sweden himself.

Frederick Augustus, Elector of Saxony, whom neither the eloquence nor negotiations of the Abbé de Polignac, nor the great qualities of the Prince of Conti, his competitor for the throne, had been able to prevent from being chosen King of Poland about two years before, was a prince still less remarkable for his incredible strength of body than for his bravery and gallantry of soul. His court, next to that of Louis XIV, was the most splendid of any in Europe. Never was prince more generous or munificent, or bestowed his favors with a better grace. He had purchased the votes of one-half of the Polish nobility, and overawed the other by the approach of a Saxon army. As he thought he should have need of his troops in order to establish himself the more firmly on the throne, he wanted a pretext for retaining them in Poland; and he therefore resolved to employ them in attacking the King of Sweden, which he did on the following occasion.

Livonia, the most beautiful and the most fruitful province of the North, belonged formerly to the knights of the Teutonic Order. The Russians, the Poles, and the Swedes had severally disputed the possession of it. The Swedes had carried it from all the rest about 100 years before; and it had been formerly ceded to them by the peace of Oliva.

The late King, Charles XI, amid his severities to his subjects in general, had not spared the Livonians. He had stripped them of their privileges, and of part of their estates. Patkul, who unhappily has since become famous for his tragical death, was deputed by the nobility of Livonia to carry to the throne the complaints of the province. He addressed his master in a speech, respectful indeed, but bold, and full of that manly eloquence which calamity, when joined to courage, never fails to inspire. But kings too frequently consider these public addresses as no more than vain ceremonies, which it is customary to suffer, without paying them any regard. Charles XI, however, who could play the hypocrite extremely well, when he was not hurried away by the violence of his passion, gently struck Patkul on the shoulder and said to him: " You have spoken for your country like a brave man, and I esteem you for it; go on." Notwithstanding, in a few days after, he caused him to be declared guilty of high treason, and as such to be condemned to death. Patkul, who had hid himself, made his escape, and carried his resentment with him to Poland, where he was afterward admitted into the presence of King Augustus. Charles XI was now dead; but Patkul's sentence was still in force, and his indignation still unabated. He represented to his Polish Majesty the facility of conquering Livonia, the people of which were mad with despair, and ready to throw off the Swedish yoke; while the King was a child and unable to make any resistance. These representations were well received by a prince, who already flattered himself with the agreeable hopes of this important conquest. Augustus had engagd at his coronation to exert his most vigorous efforts, in order to recover the provinces which Poland had lost; and he imagined that, by making an irruption into Livonia, he should at once please the people and establish his own power; in both which particulars, however promising of success, he at last found himself fatally disappointed. Everything was soon got ready for a sudden invasion, which he resolved to make without having recourse to the vain formalities of declarations of war and manifestoes. The storm thickened, at the same time, on the side of Muscovy. The monarch who governed that kingdom merits the attention of posterity.

Peter Alexiovitch, Czar of Russia, had already made himself

formidable by the battle he had gained over the Turks in 1697, and by the reduction of Azof, which opened to him the dominion of the Black Sea. But it was by actions still more glorious than even his victories that he aspired to the name of " Great." Muscovy, or Russia, comprehends the northern parts of Asia and of Europe, and from the frontiers of China extends, for the space of 1,500 leagues, to the borders of Poland and Sweden. This immense country, however, was hardly known to Europe before the time of the Czar Peter. The Muscovites were less civilized than the Mexicans, when discovered by Cortez: born the slaves of masters as barbarous as themselves, they were sunk into a state of the most profound ignorance, into a total want of all the arts and sciences, and into such an insensibility of that want as effectually suppressed every exertion of industry. An ancient law, which they held to be sacred, forbade them, under pain of death, to leave their native country without permission of their patriarch. This law, made with a view to preclude them from all opportunities of becoming sensible of their slavery, was very acceptable to a people, who, in the depth of their misery and ignorance, disdained all commerce with foreign nations.

The era of the Muscovites began at the creation of the world: they reckoned up 7,207 years to the beginning of the last century, without being able to assign any reason for this computation. The first day of their year answered to the thirteenth of our month of November. The reason they allege for this regulation is that it is probable that God created the world in autumn, the season when the fruits of the earth are in their full maturity. Thus, the only appearance of knowledge which they had was founded upon gross errors; not one of them ever dreamed that the autumn of Muscovy might possibly be the spring of another country, situated in an opposite climate. Nor is it long since the people at Moscow were going to burn the secretary of a Persian ambassador, who had foretold an eclipse of the sun. They did not so much as know the use of figures, but in all their computations made use of little beads strung upon brass wires. They had no other manner of reckoning in their counting-houses, not even in the treasury of the Czar.

Their religion was, and still is, that of the great Church, intermixed with many superstitious rites, to which they are more strongly attached, in proportion as they are the more ridiculous, and their burden the more intolerable. Few Muscovites would venture to eat a pigeon, because the Holy Ghost is painted in the form of a dove. They regularly observed four lents in the year; and during those times of abstinence, they never presumed to eat either eggs or milk. God and St. Nicholas were the objects of their worship, and next to them the Czar and the patriarch. The authority of the last was as unbounded as the people's ignorance. He pronounced sentences of death, and inflicted the most cruel punishments, without any possibility of an appeal from his tribunal. Twice a year he made a solemn procession on horseback, attended by all his clergy in order. The Czar on foot held the bridle of his horse, and the people prostrated themselves before him in the streets, as the Tartars do before their Grand Lama. Confession was in use among them, but it was only in cases of the greatest crimes. In these absolution was necessary, but not repentance. They thought themselves pure in the sight of God as soon as they received the benediction of their priests. Thus they passed, without remorse, from confession to theft and murder; and what among other Christians is a restraint from vice, with them was an encouragement to wickedness. On a fast-day they would not even venture to drink milk; but on a festival, masters of families, priests, married women and maids, would not scruple to intoxicate themselves with brandy. However, there were religious disputes among them as well as in other countries; but their greatest controversy was, whether laymen should make the sign of the cross with two fingers or with three. One Jacob Nursuff, in the preceding reign, had raised a sedition in Astrakhan about this very quarrel. There were even some fanatics among them, as there are in those civilized nations where everyone is a theologian; and Peter, who always carried justice to the extreme of cruelty, caused some of these wretched creatures, who were called vosko-jesuits, to be committed to the flames.

The Czar, in his vast dominions, had many other subjects who were not Christians. The Tartars, inhabiting the western coasts of the Caspian Sea and the Palus Mæotis,* were Mahometans; the Siberians, the Ostiacks, and the Samoyedes, who lie toward the Frozen Sea, were savages, some of whom were idol-

* Sea of Azof.

aters, and others had not the least knowledge of a god; and yet the Swedes, who were sent prisoners among them, were better pleased with their manners than with those of the ancient Muscovites.

Peter Alexiovitch had received an education that tended still more to increase the barbarity of this part of the world. His natural disposition led him to caress strangers, before he knew what advantages he might derive from their acquaintance. Lefort, as has been already observed, was the first instrument he employed to change the face of affairs in Muscovy. His mighty genius, which a barbarous education had hitherto checked but not destroyed, broke forth all of a sudden. He resolved to be a man, to command men, and to create a new nation. Many princes before him had renounced crowns, wearied out with the intolerable load of public affairs; but no man had ever divested himself of the royal character, in order to learn the art of governing better: this was a stretch of heroism which was reserved for Peter the Great alone.

He left Russia in 1698, having reigned as yet but two years, and went to Holland, disguised under a common name, as if he had been a menial servant of that same Lefort, whom he sent in quality of ambassador-extraordinary to the States-General. As soon as he arrived at Amsterdam, he enrolled his name among the shipwrights of the admiralty of the Indies, and wrought in the yard like the other mechanics. At his leisure hours he learned such parts of the mathematics as are useful to a prince—fortification, navigation, and the art of drawing plans. He went into the workmen's shops and examined all their manufactures: nothing could escape his observation. From thence he passed over into England, where, having perfected himself in the art of ship-building, he returned to Holland, carefully observing everything that might turn to the advantage of his country. At last, after two years of travel and labor, to which no man but himself would have willingly submitted, he again made his appearance in Russia, with all the arts of Europe in his train. Artists of every kind followed him in abundance. Then were seen, for the first time, large Russian ships in the Baltic, and on the Black Sea and the ocean. Stately buildings, of a regular architecture, were raised among the Russian huts. He founded colleges, academies, printing-houses, and libraries. The cities were brought under a regular police. The dress and customs of the people were gradually changed, though not without some difficulty; and the Muscovites learned by degrees the true nature of a social state. Even their superstitious rites were abolished; the dignity of the patriarch was suppressed; and the Czar declared himself the head of the Church. This last enterprise, which would have cost a prince less absolute than Peter both his throne and his life, succeeded almost without opposition, and insured to him the success of all his other innovations.

After having humbled an ignorant and a barbarous clergy, he ventured to make a trial of instructing them, though, by that means, he ran the risk of rendering them formidable; but he was too conscious of his own power to entertain any apprehension from that quarter. He caused philosophy and theology to be taught in the few monasteries that still remained. True it is, this theology still savors of that barbarous period in which Peter civilized his people. A gentleman of undoubted veracity assured me that he was present at a public disputation, where the point of controversy was, whether the practice of smoking tobacco was a sin? The respondent alleged that it was lawful to get drunk with brandy, but not to smoke, because the holy Scripture saith, "That which proceedeth out of the mouth defileth a man, and that which entereth into it doth not defile him."

The monks were not satisfied with this reformation. Hardly had the Czar erected his printing-houses, when these pious drones made use of them to publish declamations against their sovereign. One of them affirmed in print that Peter was Antichrist; and his arguments were, that he deprived the living of their beards, and allowed the dead to be dissected in his academy. But another monk, who had a mind to make his fortune, refuted this book, and proved that Peter could not be Antichrist, because the number 666 was not to be found in his name. The libeller was broken upon the wheel, and the author of the refutation was made Bishop of Riazan.

The reformer of Muscovy enacted a very wholesome law, the want of which reflects disgrace upon many civilized nations. By this law, no man engaged in the service of the State, no citizen established in trade, and especially no minor was allowed to retire into a convent.

Peter knew of what infinite consequences it was to prevent useful subjects from consecrating themselves to idleness, and to hinder young people from disposing of their liberty, at an age when they are incapable of disposing of the least part of their patrimony. This law, however, so plainly calculated for the general interest of mankind, is daily eluded by the industry of the monks; as if they, forsooth, were gainers by peopling their convents at the expense of their country.

The Czar not only subjected the Church to the State, after the example of the Turkish Emperors, but, what was a more masterly stroke of policy, he dissolved a militia of much the same nature with that of the janizaries: and what the sultans had attempted in vain, he accomplished in a short time: he disbanded the Russian janizaries, who were called strelitz, and who kept the czars in subjection. These troops, more formidable to their masters than to their neighbors, consisted of about 30,000 foot, one-half of which remained at Moscow, while the other was stationed upon the frontiers. The pay of a strelitz was no more than four roubles a year; but this deficiency was amply compensated by privileges and extortions. Peter at first formed a company of foreigners, among whom he enrolled his own name, and did not think it below him to begin the service in the character of a drummer, and to perform the duties of that mean office; so much did the nation stand in need of examples! By degrees he became an officer. He gradually raised new regiments; and, at last, finding himself master of a well-disciplined army, he broke the strelitz, who dare not disobey.

The cavalry were nearly the same with that of Poland, or France, when this last kingdom was no more than an assemblage of fiefs. The Russian gentlemen were mounted at their own expense, and fought without discipline, and sometimes without any other arms than a sabre or a bow, incapable of obeying, and consequently of conquering.

Peter the Great taught them to obey, both by the example he set them, and by the punishments he inflicted; for he served in the quality of a soldier and subaltern officer, and as Czar he severely punished the Boyards; that is, the gentlemen, who pretended that it was the privilege of their order not to serve but by their own consent. He established a regular body to serve the artillery, and took 500 bells from the churches to found cannon. In the year 1714 he had 13,000 brass cannon. He likewise formed some troops of dragoons, a kind of militia very suitable to the genius of the Muscovites, and to the size of their horses, which are small. In 1738 the Russians had thirty regiments of dragoons, consisting of 1,000 men each, and well accoutred.

He likewise established the Russian hussars; and had even a school of engineers, in a country where, before his time, no one understood the elements of geometry.

He was himself a good engineer; but his chief excellence lay in his knowledge of naval affairs: he was an able sea-captain, a skilful pilot, a good sailor, an expert shipwright, and his knowledge of these arts was the more meritorious, as he was born with a great dread of the water. In his youth he could not pass over a bridge without trembling: on all these occasions he caused the wooden windows of his coach to be shut; but of this constitutional weakness he soon got the better by his courage and resolution.

He caused a beautiful harbor to be built at the mouth of the Don, near Azof, in which he proposed to keep a number of galleys; and some time after, thinking that these vessels, so long, light, and flat, would probably succeed in the Baltic, he had upward of 300 of them built at his favorite city of Petersburg. He showed his subjects the method of building ships with fir only, and taught them the art of navigation. He had even learned surgery, and, in a case of necessity, has been known to tap a dropsical person. He was was well versed in mechanics, and instructed the artists.

Indeed, the revenue of the Czar, when compared to the immense extent of his dominions, was very inconsiderable. It never amounted to 24,000,000 francs of French money, reckoning the mark at about fifty livres, as we do to-day, though perhaps we may do otherwise to-morrow. But a man may always be accounted rich who has it in his power to accomplish great undertakings. It is not the scarcity of money that weakens a State; it is the want of hands, and of able men.

Russia, notwithstanding the women are fruitful and the men robust, is far from being populous. Peter himself, in civilizing his dominions, unhappily contributed to their depopulation. Frequent levies in his wars, which were long unsuccessful; nations transported from the coasts of the Caspian Sea to those of the Baltic, destroyed by fatigue, or cut off by diseases; three-fourths of the Muscovite children dying of the small-pox, which is more dangerous in those climates than in any other; in a word, the melancholy effects of a government savage for a long time, and even barbarous in its policy; to all these causes it is owing, that in this country, comprehending so great a part of the continent, there are still vast deserts. Russia, at present, is supposed to contain 500,000 families of gentlemen; 200,000 lawyers; something more than 5,000,000 of citizens and peasants, who pay a sort of tax; 600,000 men who live in the provinces conquered from the Swedes: the Cossacks in the Ukraine, and the Tartars that are subject to Muscovy, do not exceed 2,000,000: in fine, it appears that in this immense country there are not above 14,000,000 of men; that is, a little more than two-thirds of the inhabitants of France.

While Peter was employed in changing the laws, the manners, the militia, and the very face of his country, he likewise resolved to increase his greatness by encouraging commerce, which at once constitutes the riches of a particular State, and contributes to the interest of the world in general. He resolved to make Russia the centre of trade between Asia and Europe. He determined to join the Düna [Dvina], the Volga, and the Don, by canals, of which he drew the plans; and thus to open a new passage from the Baltic to the Euxine and Caspian seas, and from these seas to the Northern Ocean.

The port of Archangel, frozen up for nine months in the year, and which could not be entered without making a long and dangerous circuit, he did not think sufficiently commodious. From the year 1700, he had formed a design of building a fort upon the Baltic Sea that should become the magazine of the North, and of raising a city that should prove the capital of his empire.

He was already attempting to find out a northeast passage to China; and the manufactures of Pekin and Paris were designed to embellish his new city.

A road 754 versts long, running through marshes that were to be drained, led from Moscow to his new city. Most of these projects were executed by his own hands; and the two empresses who have successively followed him have even improved upon his schemes, when they were practicable, and abandoned none but such as it was impossible to accomplish.

He was always travelling up and down his dominions, as much as his wars would allow him; but he travelled like a legislator and natural philosopher, examining nature everywhere, endeavoring to correct or perfect her; sounding with his own hands the depths of seas and rivers, repairing sluices, visiting docks, causing mines to be searched for, assaying metals, ordering accurate plans to be drawn, in the execution of which he himself assisted.

He built, upon a wild and uncultivated spot, the imperial city of Petersburg, which now contains 60,000 houses, and is the residence of a splendid court, where all the refined pleasures are known and enjoyed. He built the harbor of Cronstadt, on the Neva, and Sainte-Croix, on the frontiers of Persia; erected forts in the Ukraine and Siberia; established offices of admiralty at Archangel, Petersburg, Astrakhan, and Azof; founded arsenals, and built and endowed hospitals. All his own houses were mean, and executed in a bad taste; but he spared no expenses in rendering the public buildings grand and magnificent.

The sciences, which in other countries have been the slow product of so many ages, were, by his care and industry, imported into Russia in full perfection. He established an academy on the plan of the famous societies of Paris and London. The Delisles, the Bulfingers, the Hermanns, the Bernouillis, and the celebrated Wolf, a man who excelled in every branch of philosophy, were all invited and brought to Petersburg at a great expense. This academy still subsists; and the Muscovites, at length, have philosophers of their own nation.

He obliged the young nobility to travel for improvement, and to bring back into Russia the politeness of foreign countries; and I have seen some young Russians who were men of genius and of knowledge. Thus it was that a single man changed the face of the greatest empire in the universe. It is, however, a shocking reflection that this reformer of mankind should have been deficient in that first of all virtues, the virtue of humanity. Brutality in his pleasures, ferocity in his manners, and cruelty in his punishments, sullied the lustre of so many virtues. He civilized his subjects, and yet remained himself a barbarian. He would sometimes, with his own hands, execute sentences of death upon the unhappy criminals; and, in the midst of a revel, would show his dexterity in cutting off heads.

There are princes in Africa, who, with their own hands, shed the blood of their subjects; but these kings are always detested as barbarians. The death of a son, whom he ought to have corrected, or at most disinherited, would render the memory of Peter the object of universal hatred, were it not that the great and many blessings he bestowed upon his subjects were almost sufficient to excuse his cruelty to his own offspring.

Such was the Czar Peter; and his great projects were little more than in embryo when he joined the kings of Poland and Denmark against a child whom they all despised. The founder of the Russian Empire was ambitious of being a conqueror; and such he thought he might easily become by the prosecution of a war, which, being entered into with so much prudence, could not fail, he imagined, of proving advantageous to his subjects. The art of war was a new art, which it was necessary to teach his people.

Besides, he wanted a port on the east side of the Baltic, to facilitate the execution of all his schemes. He wanted the province of Ingria, which lies to the northeast of Livonia. The Swedes were in possession of it, and from them he resolved to take it by force. His predecessors had had claims upon Ingria, Esthonia, and Livonia; and the present seemed a favorable opportunity for reviving these claims, which had lain buried for 100 years, and had been cancelled by the sanction of treaties. He therefore made a league with the King of Poland, to wrest from young Charles XII all the territories that are bounded by the Gulf of Finland, the Baltic Sea, Poland, and Muscovy.

# BOOK II

A Sudden and Surprising Change in the Character of Charles XII—At Eighteen Years of Age He Undertakes a War against Denmark, Poland, and Muscovy—Finishes the Danish War in Six Weeks—With Eight Thousand Swedes Defeats Eighty Thousand Russians, and then Penetrates into Poland—A Description of Poland and its Form of Government—Charles Gains Several Battles, and Becomes Master of Poland, where He Prepares to Nominate a King.

IN this manner did three powerful sovereigns menace the infancy of Charles XII. The news of these preparations struck the Swedes with consternation and alarmed the Council. All the great generals were now dead, and everything was to be feared under the reign of a young king, who had hitherto given no very favorable impressions of his character. He hardly ever assisted at the Council; and when he did, it was only to sit cross-legged on the table, absent, inattentive, and seemingly regardless of everything that passed.

The Council happened to hold a deliberation in his presence concerning the dangerous situation of affairs; some of the members proposed to avert the storm by negotiations, when all of a sudden Charles rose, with an air of gravity and assurance, like a man of superior consequence who has chosen his side: "Gentlemen," said he, "I am resolved never to begin an unjust war, nor ever to finish a just one but by the destruction of my enemies. My resolution is fixed. I will attack the first that shall declare against me; and, after having conquered him, I hope I shall be able to strike terror into the rest." All the old councillors were astonished at this declaration, and looked at one another without daring to reply. Agreeably surprised to find their King possessed of such noble sentiments, and ashamed to be less sanguine in their expectations than he, they received his orders for the war with admiration.

They were still more surprised when they saw him at once

bid adieu to the most innocent amusements of youth. The moment he began to make preparations for the war, he entered on a new course of life, from which he never afterward deviated in one single instance. Full of the idea of Alexander and Cæsar, he proposed to imitate those two conquerors in everything but their vices. No longer did he indulge himself in magnificence, sports, and recreations: he reduced his table to the most rigid frugality. He had formerly been fond of gayety and dress; but from that time he was never clad otherwise than a common soldier. He was supposed to have entertained a passion for a lady of his court: whether there was any foundation for this supposition does not appear; certain it is, he ever after renounced all commerce with women, not only for fear of being governed by them, but likewise to set an example of continence to his soldiers, whom he resolved to confine within the strictest discipline; perhaps, too, from the vanity of being thought the only king that could conquer a passion so difficult to be overcome. He likewise determined to abstain from wine during the rest of his life. Some people have told me that his only reason for taking this resolution was to subdue his vicious inclinations in everything, and to add one virtue more to his former stock; but the greater number have assured me that it was to punish himself for an excess he had committed, and an affront he had offered to a lady at table, even in presence of the Queen-mother. If that be true, this condemnation of his own conduct, and this abstinence which he imposed upon himself during the remainder of his life, is a species of heroism no less worthy of admiration.

He began by assuring the Duke of Holstein, his brother-in-law, of a speedy assistance. Eight thousand men were immediately sent into Pomerania, a province bordering upon Holstein, in order to enable the duke to make head against the Danes. The duke, indeed, had need of them. His dominions were already laid waste, the castle of Gottorp taken, and the city of Tönningen pressed by an obstinate siege, to which the King of Denmark had come in person, in order to enjoy a conquest which he held to be certain. This spark began to throw the empire into a flame. On the one side, the Saxon troops of the King of Poland, those of Bradenburg, Wolfenbüttel, and Hesse Cassel advanced to join the Danes. On the other, the King of Sweden's 8,000 men, the troops of Hanover and Zell, and three Dutch regiments came to the assistance of the duke. While the little country of Holstein was thus the theatre of war, two squadrons, the one from England and the other from Holland, appeared in the Baltic. These two States were guarantees of the Treaty of Altona, which the Danes had broken, and were eager to assist the Duke of Holstein, because it was for the interest of their trade to check the growing power of the King of Denmark. They knew that should he once become master of the Sound, he would impose the most rigorous laws upon the commercial nations as soon as he should be able to do it with impunity. This consideration has long induced the English and the Dutch to maintain, as much as they can, a balance of power between the princes of the North. They joined the young King of Sweden, who seemed to be in danger of being crushed by such a powerful combination of enemies, and assisted him for the very same reason that the others attacked him—namely, because they thought him incapable of defending himself.

He was taking the diversion of bear-hunting, when he received the news of the Saxons having invaded Livonia. This pastime he enjoyed in a manner equally new and dangerous. No other weapons were used but sharp-pointed sticks, with which the hunters defended themselves behind a cord stretched between two trees. A bear of a huge size came straight against the King, who after a long struggle, by the help of the cord and stick, levelled him with the ground. It must be acknowledged that in reading of such adventures as these, in considering the surprising strength of King Augustus, and reviewing the travels of the Czar, we are almost tempted to think that we live in the times of Hercules and Theseus.

Charles set out for his first campaign on the eighth day of May, new style, in the year 1700, and left Stockholm, whither he never returned. An innumerable company of people attended him to the port of Carlscrona, offering up their prayers for his safety, bedewing the ground with their tears, and expressing their admiration of his virtue. Before he left Sweden, he established at Stockholm a Council of Defence, composed of several senators, who were to take care of whatever concerned the navy, the army, and the fortifications of the country. The body of the Senate were provisionally to regulate everything besides, in the interior government of the kingdom. Having thus settled the administration of public affairs, and freed his mind from every other care, he devoted himself entirely to war. His fleet consisted of three-and-forty vessels: that in which he sailed, named the King Charles, and the largest ship that had ever been seen, was a ship of 120 guns. Count Piper, his first minister, General Rehnskiöld, and the Count de Guiscard, the French ambassador in Sweden, embarked along with him. He joined the squadrons of the allies. The Danish fleet declined the combat, and gave the three combined fleets an opportunity of approaching so near to Copenhagen as to throw some bombs into it.

Certain it is, it was the King himself that first proposed to General Rehnskiöld to make a descent, and to besiege Copenhagen by land, while it should be blocked up by sea. Rehnskiöld was surprised to receive a proposal that discovered as much prudence as courage, from such a young and inexperienced prince. Everything was soon made ready for the descent. Orders were given for the embarkation of 5,000 men, who lay upon the coast of Sweden, and who were joined to the troops they had on board. The King quitted his large ship and went into a frigate, and they then began to dispatch toward the shore 300 grenadiers in small shallops. Among the shallops were some flat-bottomed boats that carried fascines, *chevaux-de-frise,* and the instruments of the pioneers. Five hundred chosen men followed in other shallops. Last of all came the King's men-of-war, with two English and two Dutch frigates, which were to favor the landing of the troops under cover of their cannon.

Copenhagen, the capital of Denmark, is situated in the Isle of Zealand, in the midst of a beautiful plain, having the Sound on the northeast, and on the east the Baltic, where the King of Sweden then lay. At the unexpected movement of the vessels, which threatened a descent, the inhabitants were struck with consternation. Alarmed at the inactivity of their own fleet, and the motion of the Swedish ships, they looked round with terror, to observe where the storm would fall. Charles's fleet stopped over against Humblebek, within seven miles of Copenhagen. In that place the **Danes** immediately drew up their cavalry. Their foot were posted behind thick intrenchments; and what artillery they could bring thither was pointed against the Swedes.

The King then quitted his frigate to throw himself into the first shallop, at the head of his guards. The French ambassador was at his side. "Sir," said the King to him, in Latin (for he would never speak French), "you have no quarrel with the Danes; you need go no farther, if you please." "Sir," answered the Count de Guiscard, in French, "the King my master has ordered me to attend your Majesty. I hope you will not this day banish me from your court, which never before appeared so splendid." So saying, he gave his hand to the King, who leaped into the shallop, whither he was followed by Count Piper and the ambassador. They advanced under shelter of the cannon of the ships that favored the landing. The small boats were still about 300 paces from the shore. Charles, impatient to land, jumped into the sea, sword in hand, the water reaching above his waist. His ministers, the French ambassador, the officers and soldiers, immediately followed his example, and marched up to the shore, amid a shower of musket-shot from the enemy. The King, who had never in his life before heard a discharge of muskets loaded with ball, asked Major Stuart, who stood next to him, what meant that whistling which he heard. "It is the noise of the musket-balls which they fire upon you," replied the major. "Very well," said the King, "henceforward that shall be my music." At that instant the major received a shot in his shoulder, and a lieutenant on the other side of him fell dead at his feet.

It is usual for troops that are attacked in their trenches to be beaten, because the assailants have always an impetuosity of courage, which the defenders cannot have; and besides, to wait for the enemy in our lines is frequently a confession of our own weakness and of their superiority. The Danish horse and foot took to their heels, after a feeble resistance. The King, having become master of their intrenchments, fell upon his knees to return thanks to God for the first success of his arms. He forthwith caused redoubts to be raised toward the town, and himself marked out the place for the encampment. Meanwhile he sent back his vessels to Scania, a port of Sweden opposite to Copenhagen, for a reinforcement of 9,000 men. Everything conspired to favor the ardor of Charles's courage. The 9,000 men were upon the shore ready to embark, and next day a favorable wind brought them safe to the place of their destination.

All this passed within sight of the Danish fleet, which did not venture to advance. Copenhagen, struck with terror, immediately sent deputies to the King, beseeching him not to bombard the city. He received them on horseback, at the head of his regiment of guards, and the deputies fell upon their knees before him. He exacted from the citizens 400,000 rix-dollars, commanding them, at the same time, to supply his camp with all kinds of provisions, for which he assured them they should be honestly paid. They brought the provisions, because they dared not disobey; but they little expected that conquerors would condescend to pay for them; and those who brought them were surprised to find that they were generously and instantly paid, even by the meanest soldier in the army. There had long prevailed among the Swedish troops a strict discipline, which had greatly contributed to the success of their arms; and the King rendered it still more rigid. No soldier dared refuse to pay for what he had bought, still less to go marauding, or even out of the camp. What is more, he would not allow his troops, after a victory, to strip the bodies of the dead, until they had obtained his permission; and he easily brought them to the observance of this injunction. Prayers were regularly said in his camp twice a day, at seven in the morning and four in the afternoon; and he never failed to attend them himself, in order to give his soldiers an example of piety as well as of valor. His camp, which was better regulated than Copenhagen, had everything in abundance—the peasants choosing much rather to sell their provisions to their enemies, the Swedes, than to the Danes, who did not pay them so well. Even the citizens were more than once obliged to come to the Swedish camp to purchase those provisions which they could not find in their own markets.

The King of Denmark was then in Holstein, whither he seemed to have gone for no other purpose than to raise the siege of Tönningen. He saw the Baltic covered with the enemy's ships, and a young conqueror already master of Zealand, and just upon the point of taking possession of his capital. He caused an edict to be published throughout all his dominions, promising liberty to everyone that should take up arms against the Swedes. This declaration was of great weight in a country which was formerly free, but where all the peasants, and even many of the citizens, are now slaves. Charles sent word to the King of Denmark that his only intention in making war was to oblige him to come to a peace; and that he must either resolve to do justice to the Duke of Holstein or see Copenhagen levelled with the ground, and his dominions laid waste with fire and sword. The Dane was too happy in having to do with a conquerer who valued himself on his regard for justice. A congress was held in the town of Travendahl, which lies on the frontiers of Holstein. The King of Sweden would not allow the negotiations to be protracted by the arts of ministers, but determined to have the treaty finished with the same rapidity with which he had made his descent upon Zealand. In effect, a peace was concluded, on the fifth of August, to the advantage of the Duke of Holstein, who was indemnified for all the expenses of the war and delivered from oppression. The King of Sweden, fully satisfied with having succored his ally and humbled his enemy, would accept of nothing for himself. Thus Charles XII, at eighteen years of age, began and finished this war in less than six weeks.

Exactly at the same time the King of Poland invested Riga, the capital of Livonia; and the Czar was advancing on the east at the head of nearly 100,000 men. Riga was defended by the old Count Dalberg, a Swedish general, who, at the age of eighty, joined all the fire of youth to the experience of sixty campaigns. Count Flemming, afterward Minister of Poland, a man of distinguished abilities as well in the field as the Cabinet, and Patkul the Livonian, pushed the siege with great vigor, under the direction of the King; but notwithstanding several advantages which the besiegers had gained, the experience of old Count Dalberg baffled all their efforts, and the King of Poland began to despair of being able to take the town. At last he laid hold of an honorable pretext for raising the siege. Riga was full of merchants' goods belonging to the Dutch. The States-General ordered their ambassador at the Court of Augustus to represent the matter to his Majesty. The King of Poland did not long resist their importunities, and agreed to raise the siege rather than occasion the least damage to his allies, who were not greatly surprised at this stretch of complaisance, to the real cause of which they were no strangers.

The only thing that Charles had now to do toward the finishing of his first campaign was to march against his rival in glory, Peter Alexiovitch. He was the more exasperated against him, as there were still at Stockholm three Muscovite ambassadors, who had lately sworn to the renewal of an inviolable peace. Possessed of the most incorruptible integrity, he could not conceive how a legislator, like the Czar, should make a jest of what ought to be held so sacred. The young prince, whose sense of honor was extremely refined, never imagined that there could be one system of morality for kings and another for private persons. The Emperor of Muscovy had just published a manifesto, which he had much better have suppressed. He there alleged, as the reason of the war, the little respect that had been shown him when he went incognito to Riga, and the extravagant prices his ambassadors had been obliged to pay for provisions. Such were the mighty injuries for which he ravaged Ingria with 80,000 men!

At the head of this great army, he appeared before Narva on the first of October, a season more severe in that climate than the month of January is at Paris. The Czar, who in such weather would sometimes ride post for 400 leagues to see a mine or a canal, was not more sparing of his troops than of himself. He knew, moreover, that the Swedes, ever since the time of Gustavus Adolphus, could make war in the depth of winter as well as in summer; and he wanted to accustom the Russians likewise to forget all distinction of seasons, and to render them, one day, equal to the Swedes. Thus, in a time when frost and snow compel other nations in more temperate climates to agree to a suspension of arms, the Czar Peter besieged Narva, within thirty degrees of the pole, and Charles XII advanced to its relief. The Czar had no sooner arrived before the place, than he immediately put in practice what he had learned in his travels. He marked out his camp, fortified it on all sides, raised redoubts at certain distances, and opened the trenches himself. He had given the command of his troops to the Duke de Croy, a German, and an able general, but who at that time was little assisted by the Russian officers. As for himself, he had no other rank in the army than that of a private lieutenant. He thereby gave an example of military obedience to his nobility, hitherto unacquainted with discipline, and accustomed to march at the head of ill-armed slaves, without experience and without order. There was nothing strange in seeing him who had turned carpenter at Amsterdam, in order to procure himself fleets, serve as lieutenant at Narva, to teach his subjects the art of war.

The Muscovites are strong and indefatigable, and perhaps as courageous as the Swedes; but it requires time and discipline to render troops warlike and invincible. The only regiments that could be depended upon were commanded by some German officers; but their number was very inconsiderable. The rest were barbarians, forced from their forests, and covered with the skins of wild beasts—some armed with arrows and others with clubs. Few of them had guns; none of them had ever seen a regular siege; and there was not one good cannoneer in the whole army. A hundred and fifty cannon, which one would have thought must have soon reduced the little town of Narva to ashes, were hardly able to make a breach, while the artillery of the city mowed down at every discharge whole ranks of the enemy in their trenches. Narva was almost without fortifications: Baron Horn, who commanded there, had not 1,000 regular troops; and yet this immense army could not reduce it in six weeks.

It was now the fifteenth of November, when the Czar learned that the King of Sweden had crossed the sea with 200 transports, and was advancing to the relief of Narva. The Swedes were not above 20,000 strong. The Czar had no advantage but that of numbers. Far, therefore, from despising his enemy, he employed every art in order to crush him. Not content with 80,000 men, he resolved to oppose to him another army still, and to check his progress at every step. He had already given orders for the march of about 30,000 men, who were advancing from Pleskov with great expedition. He then took a step that would have rendered him contemptible, could a legislator who had performed such great and glorious actions incur that imputation. He left his camp, where his presence was necessary, to go in quest of this new army, which might have arrived well enough without him, and seemed by this conduct to betray his

Chronicles (Vol. II).—12

fear of engaging in his intrenchments a young and inexperienced prince who might come to attack him.

Be that as it may, he resolved to shut up Charles XII between two armies. Nor was this all: a detachment of 30,000 men from the camp before Narva were posted at a league's distance from the city, directly in the King of Sweden's road; 20,000 strelitz were placed farther off, upon the same road; and 5,000 others composed an advanced guard; and he must necessarily force his way through all these troops before he could reach the camp, which was fortified with a rampart and double fosse. The King of Sweden had landed at Pernau, in the Gulf of Riga, with about 16,000 foot and little more than 4,000 horse. From Pernau he made a flying march to Revel, followed by all his cavalry, and only by 4,000 foot. He always marched in the van of his army, without waiting for the rear. He soon found himself, with his 8,000 men only, before the first posts of the enemy. He immediately resolved, without the least hesitation, to attack them, one after another, before they could possibly learn with what a small number they had to engage. The Muscovites, seeing the Swedes come upon them, imagined they had a whole army to encounter. The advanced guard of 5,000 men, posted among rocks, a station where 100 resolute men might have stopped the march of a large army, fled at their first approach. The 20,000 men that lay behind them, perceiving the flight of their fellow-soldiers, took the alarm, and carried their terror and confusion with them into the camp. All the posts were carried in two days; and what upon other occasions would have been reckoned three distinct victories, did not retard the King's march for the space of one hour. He appeared then at last with his 8,000 men, exhausted by the fatigues of so long a march, before a camp of 80,000 Muscovites, defended by 150 pieces of cannon; and, scarcely allowing his troops any time for rest, he instantly gave orders for the attack.

The signal was two musket-shots, and the watchword in German—"With the aid of God." A general officer having represented to him the greatness of the danger, "What," said he, "do you not think that with my 8,000 brave Swedes I may easily beat 80,000 Russians?" But soon after, fearing that what he had said might savor too much of gasconade, he ran after the officer, and said to him: "Are you not of the same opinion? Have not I a double advantage over the enemy—one, that their cavalry can be of no service to them; the other, that the place being narrow, their number will only incommode them, and thus in reality I shall be stronger than they?" The officer did not care to differ from him, and thus they marched against the Muscovites about midday, on November 30, 1700.

As soon as their cannon had made a breach in the intrenchments, the Swedes advanced with fixed bayonets, having a furious shower of snow on their backs, which drove full in the face of the enemy. The Russians stood the shock for half an hour without flinching. The King made his attack upon the right of the camp, where the Czar's quarter lay, hoping to come to an encounter with him, as he did not know that he had gone in quest of the 40,000 men, who were daily expected to arrive. At the first discharge of the enemy's muskets, he received a shot in his neck; but as it was a spent ball, it lodged in the folds of his black neckcloth and did him no harm. His horse was killed under him. M. de Sparr told me that the King mounted another horse with great agility, saying, "These fellows make me go through my exercises," and continued to fight and give orders with the same presence of mind. After an engagement of three hours, the intrenchments were forced on all sides. The King pursued the right of the enemy as far as the River Narva, with his left wing; if we may be allowed to call by that name about 4,000 men, who were in pursuit of nearly 40,000. The bridge broke under the fugitives, and the river was immediately filled with dead carcasses. The rest returned to their camp, without knowing whither they went; and finding some barracks, they took post behind them. There they defended themselves for a while, as they were not able to make their escape; but at last their generals, Dolgorovki, Golovkin, and Federovitch, surrendered themselves to the King, and laid their arms at his feet; and while they were presenting them to him, the Duke de Croy came up and surrendered himself with thirty officers.

Charles received all these prisoners of distinction with as much civility and politeness as if he had been paying them the honors of an entertainment in his own court. He detained none but the general officers. All the subalterns and common soldiers were disarmed and conducted to the River Narva, where they were supplied with boats for passing over, and allowed to return to their own country. In the mean time night came on, and the right wing of the Muscovites still continued the fight. The Swedes had not lost above 600 men. Eight thousand Muscovites had been killed in their intrenchments; many were drowned; many had crossed the river; and yet there still remained in the camp a sufficient number to cut off the Swedes to the last man. But the loss of battles is not so much owing to the number of the killed as to the timidity of those who survive. The King employed the small remains of the day in seizing upon the enemy's artillery. He took possession of an advantageous post between the camp and the city, where he slept a few hours upon the ground, wrapped up in his cloak, intending, at daybreak, to fall upon the left wing of the enemy, which was not yet entirely routed. But at two o'clock in the morning, General Vede, who commanded that wing, having heard of the gracious reception the King had given to the other generals, and of his having dismissed all the subaltern officers and soldiers, sent a messenger to him, begging he would grant him the same favor. The conqueror replied that he should have it, provided he would come at the head of his troops, and make them lay their arms and colors at his feet. Soon after, the general appeared with his Muscovites, to the number of about 30,000. They marched, both soldiers and officers, with their heads uncovered, through less than 7,000 Swedes. The soldiers, as they passed the King, threw their guns and swords upon the ground, and the officers presented him with their ensigns and colors. He caused the whole of this multitude to be conducted over the river, without detaining a single soldier. Had he kept them, the number of prisoners would at least have been five times greater than that of the conquerors.

After this, he entered victorious into Narva, accompanied by the Duke de Croy and other general officers of the Muscovites. He ordered their swords to be restored to them all; and knowing that they wanted money, and that the merchants of Narva would not lend them any, he sent 1,000 ducats to the Duke de Croy, and 500 to every Muscovite officer, who could not sufficiently admire the civility of this treatment, of which they were incapable of forming the least conception. An account of the victory was immediately drawn up at Narva, in order to be sent to Stockholm, and to the allies of Sweden; but the King expunged with his own hand every circumstance in the relation that tended too much to his own honor or seemed to reflect upon the Czar. His modesty, however, could not hinder them from striking at Stockholm several medals to perpetuate the memory of these events. Among others they struck one which represented the King on one side, standing on a pedestal, to which were chained a Muscovite, a Dane, and a Pole; and on the reverse a Hercules, holding his club, and treading upon a Cerberus, with this inscription: *Tres uno contudit ictu.*

Among the prisoners taken at the battle of Narva, there was one whose fate exhibited a remarkable instance of the great inconstancy of fortune. He was the eldest son and heir of the King of Georgia; his name the Czarevitch Artschelov. This title of czarevitch, among the Tartars, as well as in Muscovy, signifies prince, or son of the Czar; for the word *czar,* or *tsar,* signified king among the ancient Scythians, from whom all these people are descended, and is not derived from the *Cæsars* of Rome, so long unknown to these barbarians. His father Mittelleski, czar, and master of the most beautiful part of the country lying between the mountains of Ararat and the eastern coasts of the Black Sea, having been expelled from his kingdom by his own subjects, in 1688, had rather chosen to throw himself into the arms of the Emperor of Muscovy than to apply to the Turks for assistance. His son, a youth of nineteen years of age, followed Peter the Great in his expedition against the Swedes, and was taken fighting by some Finland soldiers, who had already stripped him, and were upon the point of killing him. Count Rehnskiöld rescued him from their hands, supplied him with clothes, and presented him to his master. Charles sent him to Stockholm, where the unfortunate prince died a few years after. The King, upon seeing him depart, could not help making, in the hearing of his officers, a very natural reflection on the strange fate of an Asiatic prince, born at the foot of Mount Caucasus, and going to live prisoner among the snows of Sweden. " It is just," said he, " as if I were one day to be a prisoner among the Crim Tartars." These words made no impression at that time; but, in the sequel, there was but too much occasion to remember them, when the event had proved them to be a prediction.

The Czar was advancing, by long marches, with a body of 40,000 Russians, in full hopes of surrounding his enemy on all sides; but before he had proceeded half way, he received intelligence of the battle of Narva, and of the dispersion of his whole army. He was not so foolish as to think of attacking, with his 40,000 raw and undisciplined troops, a conqueror who had lately defeated 80,000 men in their intrenchments. He returned home, with a determined resolution of disciplining his troops at the same time that he civilized his subjects. "I know," said he, "that the Swedes will teach us to beat them." Moscow, his capital, was in the utmost terror and consternation at the news of this defeat. Such was the pride and ignorance of the people that they actually imagined they had been conquered by a power more than human, and that the Swedes were so many magicians. This opinion was so general that public prayers were ordered to be put up to St. Nicholas, the patron of Muscovy, on the occasion. The form of these prayers is too singular to be omitted. It runs thus:

"O thou, who art our perpetual comforter in all our adversities, great St. Nicholas, infinitely powerful, by what sin have we offended thee, in our sacrifices, kneelings, bowings, and thanksgivings, that thou hast thus abandoned us? We implored thy assistance against these terrible, insolent, enraged, dreadful, unconquerable destroyers, when, like lions and bears robbed of their young, they fell upon, terrified, wounded, and slew, by thousands, us who are thy people. As it is impossible that this should have happened without sorcery and witchcraft, we beseech thee, O great St. Nicholas, to be our champion and standard-bearer, to deliver us from this troop of sorcerers, and to drive them far from our frontiers, with the recompense they deserve."

While the Muscovites were thus complaining of their defeat to St. Nicholas, Charles XII returned thanks to God and prepared himself for new victories.

The King of Poland had reason to fear that his enemy, already victorious over the Danes and the Muscovites, would soon turn his arms against him. He entered into a closer alliance with the Czar than ever he had done before. These two princes agreed upon an interview, in order to concert their measures. They met at Birzen, a small town in Lithuania, without any of those formalities which serve only to retard business, and neither suited their situation nor their humor. The princes of the North visit one another with a familiarity that has not yet taken place in the more southern parts of Europe. Peter and Augustus spent fifteen days together, in the enjoyment of pleasures, which were even somewhat extravagant; for the Czar, amid his cares for the reformation of his subjects, could never correct his dangerous inclination to debauchery.

The King of Poland engaged to furnish the Czar with 50,000 German troops, which were to be hired from several princes, and for which the Czar was to pay. Peter, on the other hand, was to send 50,000 Russians into Poland, to learn the art of war, and promised to pay to Augustus 3,000,000 rix-dollars in two years. This treaty, had it been carried into execution, might have proved fatal to the King of Sweden: it was a sure and ready method of rendering the Muscovites good soldiers; perhaps it was forging chains for a part of Europe.

Charles XII exerted his utmost endeavors to prevent the King of Poland from reaping any benefit from this league. After having passed the winter at Narva, he appeared in Livonia in the neighborhood of Riga, the very town which Augustus had in vain besieged. The Saxon troops were posted along the River Düina, which is very broad in that place: and Charles, who lay on the other side of the river, was obliged to dispute the passage. The Saxons were not commanded by their own prince, who was then sick, but were headed by Marshal Steinau, who acted as general, under whom commanded Prince Ferdinand, Duke of Courland, and that same Patkul who had formerly, at the hazard of his life, vindicated the privileges of his country against Charles XI, by his pen, and now defended the same cause against Charles XII, by his arms. The King of Sweden had caused some large boats to be built of a new construction, whose sides were much higher than ordinary, and could be raised or let down, like a drawbridge. When raised, they covered the troops on board, and when let down, they served as a bridge to land them. He likewise made use of another artifice. Having observed that the wind blew from the north, where he lay, to the south, where the enemy were encamped, he set fire to a large heap of wet straw, which, diffusing a thick smoke over the river, prevented the Saxons from seeing his troops, or observing what he was going to do. Under cover of this cloud he despatched some barks filled with more of the same smoking straw; so that the cloud, always increasing, and being driven by the wind directly to the face of the enemy, rendered it impossible for them to know whether the King was passing or not. Meanwhile he alone conducted the execution of his stratagem; and when he had reached the middle of the river, " Well," said he to General Rehnskiöld, " the Düina will be as favorable to us as the Sea of Copenhagen; take my word for it, general, we shall beat them." He arrived at the other side in a quarter of an hour, and was sorry to find that he was only the fourth person that leaped on shore. He forthwith landed his cannon, and drew up his troops in order of battle, while the enemy, blinded with smoke, could make no opposition, except by a few random shots. At last the mist being dispersed by the wind, the Saxons saw the King of Sweden already advancing against them.

Marshal Steinau lost not a moment. As soon as he observed the Swedes, he rushed upon them with the flower of his cavalry. The violent shock of this body falling upon the Swedes just as they were forming threw them into confusion. They gave way, were broken, and pursued even into the river. The King of Sweden rallied them in a moment, in the midst of the water, with as much composure as if he had been making a review; then the Swedes, marching more compact than before, repulsed Marshal Steinau, and advanced into the plain. Steinau, finding his troops beginning to stagger, acted like an able general. He made them retire into a dry place, flanked with a morass and a wood, where his artillery lay. The advantage of the ground, and the time which the Saxons had thus obtained, of recovering from their first surprise, restored to them their former courage. Charles immediately began the attack. He had 15,000 men; Steinau and the Duke of Courland about 12,000, with no other artillery than one dismounted cannon. The battle was obstinate and bloody. The duke had two horses killed under him: he penetrated thrice into the heart of the King's guards; but at length, being unhorsed by a blow with the butt-end of a musket, his army was thrown into confusion and no longer disputed the victory. His cuirassiers carried him off with great difficulty, all bruised and half dead, from the thickest of the fight, and from under the horses' heels, which trampled on him.

Immediately after this victory the King of Sweden advanced to Mittau, the capital of Courland. All the towns of the duchy surrendered to him at discretion; it was rather a journey than a conquest. From thence he passed without delay into Lithuania, conquering wherever he came; and he felt a pleasing satisfaction, as he himself owned, when he entered triumphant into the town of Birzen, where the King of Poland and the Czar had plotted his destruction but a few months before.

It was in this place that he formed the design of dethroning the King of Poland by the hands of the Poles themselves. One day when he was at table, full of this enterprise, and observing, as usual, the strictest temperance, wrapped in profound silence, and seeming, as it were, absorbed in the greatness of his conceptions, a German colonel who waited upon him said, with an audible voice, that the meals which the Czar and the King of Poland had made in the same place were somewhat different from those of his Majesty. "Yes," said the King, rising, "and I shall the more easily spoil their digestion." In short, by intermixing a little policy with the force of his arms, he resolved to hasten the execution of this mighty project.

Poland, a part of the ancient Sarmatia, is somewhat larger than France, but less populous, though it is more so than Sweden. The inhabitants were converted to Christianity only about 750 years ago. It is somewhat surprising that the Roman language, which never penetrated into that country, is now spoken in common nowhere but in Poland; there all speak Latin, even the servants. This extensive country is very fertile; but the natives are only, on that account, so much the less industrious. The artists and tradesmen in Poland are Scotch, French, and especially Jews. The last have, in this country, nearly 300 synagogues; and multiplying too fast, they will in time be banished from it, as they have already been from Spain. They buy the corn, the cattle, and the commodities of the country at a low rate, dispose of them at Dantzic and in Germany, and sell to the nobles at a high price wherewithal to gratify the only species of luxury which they know and love. Thus Poland, watered with the finest rivers in the world, rich in pastures and in mines of salt, and covered with luxuriant crops, remains poor in spite of its plenty, because the people are slaves and the nobles are proud and indolent.

The constitution of Poland is the most perfect model of the ancient government of the Goths and Celts, which has been corrected or altered everywhere else. It is the only State that has preserved the name of republic together with the royal dignity.

Every gentleman has a right to give his vote in the election of a king, and may even be elected himself. This inestimable privilege is attended with inconveniences proportionately great. The throne is almost always exposed to sale; and as a Pole is seldom able to make the purchase, it has frequently been sold to strangers. The nobility and clergy defend their liberties against the King, and deprive the rest of the nation of theirs. The body of the people are slaves. Such is the unhappy fate of mankind, that in every country the greater number are, one way or another, enslaved by the lesser. There the peasant sows not for himself, but for his lord, to whom his person, his lands, and even the labor of his hands belong; and who can sell him, or cut his throat, with the same impunity as he kills the beasts in the field. Every gentleman is independent. He cannot be tried in a criminal cause but by an assembly of the whole nation; he cannot be arrested till once he is condemned; so that he is hardly ever punished. There are great numbers of poor among them. These engage in the service of the more wealthy, receive wages from them, and perform the meanest offices. They rather choose to serve their equals than to enrich themselves by commerce; and while they are dressing their masters' horses they give themselves the title of electors of kings and destroyers of tyrants.

To see a king of Poland in the pomp of royal majesty, one would take him to be the most absolute prince in Europe; and yet he is the least so. The Poles really make with him that contract which, in other nations, is only supposed to be made between the King and the subjects. The King of Poland, even at his consecration, and in swearing to the *Pacta Conventa*, absolves his subjects from the oath of allegiance, should he ever violate the laws of the republic.

He nominates to all offices and confers all honors. Nothing

is hereditary in Poland but the lands and rank of the nobility. The son of a palatine, or of a king, has no claim to the dignity of his father. But there is this great difference between the King and the republic, that the former cannot strip any person of an office after he has bestowed it upon him; whereas the latter may deprive him of the crown if he transgresses the laws of the State.

The nobility, jealous of their liberty, frequently sell their votes, but seldom their affections. They have no sooner elected a king than they begin to fear his ambition and to oppose him by their cabals. The grandees whom he has made, and whom he cannot unmake, often become his enemies, instead of remaining his creatures. Those who are attached to the court are hated by the rest of the nobility, which always forms two parties—a division unavoidable, and even necessary in those countries that must needs have kings and yet preserve their liberties.

Whatever concerns the nation is regulated in the assemblies of the States-General, which are called diets. These States are composed of the body of the Senate and of several gentlemen. The senators are the palatines and the bishops; the gentlemen, the deputies of the particular diets in each palatinate. In these great assemblies presides the Archbishop of Gnesen, primate of Poland, vicar of the kingdom during an interregnum, and, next to the King, the first person in the State. Beside him there is seldom any other cardinal in Poland; because, the Roman purple giving no precedence in the Senate, a bishop who should be made a cardinal would be obliged either to take his rank as senator or to renounce the substantial rights of the dignity he enjoys in his own country to support the vain pretensions of a foreign honor.

These diets, by the laws of the kingdom, must be held alternately in Poland and Lithuania. The deputies frequently transact their business sabre in hand, like the ancient Sarmatians, from whom they are sprung; and sometimes, too, intoxicated with liquor, a vice to which the Sarmatians were utter strangers. Every gentleman deputed to the States-General enjoys the same right which the tribunes of the people had at Rome, of opposing themselves to the laws of the Senate. Any one gentleman who says "I protest," stops by that single word the unanimous resolution of all the rest; and if he quits the place where the diet is held, the assembly is, of course, dissolved.

To the disorders arising from this law they apply a remedy still more dangerous. Poland is seldom without two factions. Unanimity in their diets being rendered thus impossible, each party forms confederacies, in which they decide by a plurality of voices, without any regard to the protestation of the lesser number. These assemblies, condemned by the laws, but authorized by custom, are held in the King's name, though frequently without his consent, and even against his interest; in much the same manner as the League in France made use of the name of Henry III to ruin him; and as the Parliament in England, that brought Charles I to the block, began by prefixing his Majesty's name to all the resolutions they took to destroy him. When the public commotions are ended, it belongs to the general diets either to confirm or repeal the acts of these confederacies. A diet can even cancel the acts of a former diet; for the same reason that, in absolute monarchies, a king can abolish the laws of his predecessor, or even those which have been made by himself.

The nobility, who make the laws of the republic, likewise constitute its strength. They appear on horseback, completely armed, upon great emergencies, and are able to make up a body of 100,000 men. This great army, which is called *pospolite,* moves slowly and is ill governed. It cannot continue assembled for any length of time, for want of provisions and forage: it has neither discipline, subordination, nor experience; but that love of liberty by which it is animated will always make it formidable.

These nobles may be conquered, or dispersed, or even held in subjection for a time; but they soon shake off the yoke. They compare themselves to the reeds, which the storm may bend to the ground, but which rise again the moment the storm is over. It is for this reason that they have no places of strength; they will have themselves to be the only bulwarks of the republic, nor do they ever suffer their king to build any forts, lest he should employ them less for their defence than their oppression. Their country is entirely open, excepting two or three frontier places, so that if in a war, whether civil or foreign, they resolve to sustain a siege, they are obliged to raise fortifications of earth in a hurry, to repair the old walls that are half ruined, and to enlarge the ditches that are almost filled up; and the town is commonly taken before the intrenchments are finished.

The *pospolite* are not always on horseback to defend their country; they never mount but by order of the diets, or sometimes in imminent dangers, by the simple orders of the King.

The usual guard of Poland is an army, which ought to be maintained at the expense of the republic. It is composed of two bodies, under two grand generals. The first body is that of Poland, and should consist of 36,000 men; the second, to the number of 12,000, is that of Lithuania. The two grand generals are independent of each other: though nominated by the King, they are accountable for their conduct to the republic alone, and have an unlimited power over their troops. The colonels are absolute masters of their regiments; and it is their business to maintain and pay them as well as they can. But as they are seldom paid themselves, they ravage the country, ruin the peasants, to satisfy their own avidity, and that of their soldiers. The Polish lords appear in these armies with more magnificence than they do in the towns; and their tents are more elegant than their houses. The cavalry, which makes up two-thirds of the army, is composed almost entirely of gentlemen, and is remarkable for the beauty of their horses and the richness of the accoutrements and harness.

The gendarmes especially, whom they distinguish into hussars and pancernes, never march without several valets in their retinue, who lead their horses; those are furnished with bridles that are ornamented with plates and nails of silver, embroidered saddles, saddle-bows, and gilt stirrups, or stirrups made of massive silver, with large housings trailing on the ground, after the manner of the Turks, whose magnificence the Poles endeavor to imitate as much as they can.

But if the cavalry are fine and gorgeous, the infantry are proportionately wretched, ill clothed, and ill armed, without regimentals, or anything uniform. Such at least was their condition till toward the year 1710: and yet these infantry, who resemble the wandering Tartars, support hunger, cold, fatigue, and all the hardships of war with surprising resolution.

One may still discern in the Polish soldiers the character of their ancestors, the ancient Sarmatians, the same want of discipline, the same fury in the assault, the same readiness to fly and to return to the charge, and the same cruel disposition to slaughter when they conquer.

The King of Poland flattered himself at first, that in this pressing necessity, these two bodies would support his cause; that the Polish *pospolite* would take up arms at his orders; and that these forces, joined to his Saxon subjects, and to his Russian allies, would compose an army, before which the small number of the Swedes would not dare to appear. But he found himself, almost in an instant, deprived of these succors by means of that very eagerness he discovered to have them all at once.

Accustomed, in his hereditary dominions, to the exercise of absolute power, he too fondly imagined that he might govern in Poland as he did in Saxony. The beginning of his reign raised malcontents. His first proceedings provoked the party that had opposed his election, and alienated almost all the rest of the nation. The Poles murmured to see the towns filled with Saxon garrisons, and their frontiers lined with Saxon troops. This nation, more anxious to preserve its liberty than to attack its neighbors, considered the war with Sweden and the irruption into Livonia as enterprises by no means advantageous to the republic. It is very difficult to hinder a free people from seeing their true interest. The Poles were sensible that if this war, undertaken without their consent, should prove unsuccessful, their country, open on all sides, would become a prey to the King of Sweden; and that, should it be crowned with success, they would be enslaved by their own King, who, being master of Livonia, as well as of Saxony, would shut up Poland between these two States. In this alternative, either of becoming slaves to the King whom they had elected, or of being pillaged by Charles XII, who was justly incensed, they raised a clamor against the war, which they believed to be declared rather against themselves than against Sweden. They considered the Saxons and the Muscovites as the forgers of their chains; and observing soon after that the King of Sweden had overcome everything that opposed his progress, and was advancing with a victorious army into the heart of Lithuania, they loudly exclaimed against their sovereign, and with so much the greater freedom as he was unfortunate.

Lithuania was at that time divided into two parties, that of the princes of Sapieha and that of Oginski. The animosity between these two factions, occasioned at first by private quarrels, had at last been inflamed into a civil war. The King of Sweden engaged the princes of Sapieha in his interest; and Oginski being poorly supported by the Saxons, found his party almost annihilated. The Lithuanian army, reduced by these troubles and the want of money to an inconsiderable number, was partly dispersed by the conquerors. The few that still held out for the King of Poland were separated into small bodies of fugitive troops, who wandered up and down the country, and subsisted by spoil. Augustus beheld nothing in Lithuania but the weakness of his own party, the hatred of his subjects, and a hostile army, conducted by a young king, incensed, victorious, and implacable.

There was indeed an army in Poland; but instead of 36,000 men, the number prescribed by the law, it did not amount to 18,000; and it was not only ill-paid and ill-armed, but the generals were as yet undetermined what course to take.

The only resource of the King was to order the nobility to follow him; but he dare not expose himself to the mortification of a refusal, which, by discovering his weakness too plainly, would consequently have increased it.

In this state of trouble and uncertainty, all the palatinates of the kingdom desired the King to call a diet; in the same manner as in England, during times of danger, all the bodies of the State present addresses to the sovereign, entreating him to convoke a parliament. Augustus had more need of an army than a diet, in which the actions of kings are severely canvassed. However, that he might not incense the nation beyond the possibility of reconciliation, he found it necessary to assemble a diet, which was accordingly appointed to be held at Warsaw on December 2, 1701. He soon perceived that Charles XII had, at least, as much power in this assembly as himself. Those who favored the Sapieha, the Lubomirski and their friends, the Palatine Leszczynski, treasurer of the Crown, and especially the partisans of the princes Sobieski, were all of them secretly attached to the King of Sweden.

The most considerable of these partisans, and the most dangerous to the King of Poland, was Cardinal Radjouski, Archbishop of Gnesen, primate of the kingdom, and president of the diet. He was a man full of artifice and cunning, and entirely under the influence of an ambitious woman, who was called by the Swedes Madame Cardinaless, and who was inciting him on to intrigue and faction. King John Sobieski, the predecessor of Augustus, had first made him Bishop of Warmia and vice-chancellor of the kingdom. Radjouski, when no more than a bishop, had obtained the cardinal's hat by the favor of the same prince. This dignity soon opened his way to the primacy; and thus by uniting in his own person whatever can impose upon mankind, he was able to undertake the most arduous enterprises without incurring the least danger.

After the death of John, he employed all his interest to raise Prince James Sobieski to the throne; but the torrent of public hatred ran so strong against the father, notwithstanding the eminent qualities of which he was possessed, that it entirely excluded the son from that dignity. After this, the cardinal-primate joined his endeavors with those of the Abbé de Polignac, the French ambassador, to procure the crown to the Prince of Conti, who was actually elected. But the money and troops of Saxony defeated all his negotiations. At last he suffered himself to be drawn over to the party that crowned the Elector of Saxony, and patiently waited for an opportunity of sowing dissension between the new King and the nation.

The victories of Charles XII, the protector of Prince James Sobieski, the civil war in Lithuania, the general alienation of men's minds from King Augustus—all these circumstances made the cardinal-primate believe that the time had now come when he might safely send back Augustus into Saxony and open for King John's son the way to the throne. This prince, formerly the innocent object of the hatred of the Poles, had now become their darling, ever since the time that Augustus had lost the public favor; but he dare not as yet entertain the most distant hopes of so great a revolution, of which, however, the cardinal was already laying the foundation.

At first he seemed desirous of effecting a reconciliation between the King and the republic, and despatched circular letters, dictated in appearance by the spirit of charity and concord—a common and well-known snare, in which, however, the people are always caught. He wrote an affecting letter to the King of Sweden, conjuring him, in the name of that Saviour whom all Christians adore, to give peace to Poland and her King. Charles XII answered the intentions of the cardinal rather than his words. Meanwhile he remained with his victorious army in the great Duchy of Lithuania, declaring that he would not disturb the Diet; that he made war against Augustus and the Saxons, and not against the Poles; and that, far from attacking, he came only to deliver them from oppression. These letters and these answers were calculated for the public. The emissaries that were continually going and coming between the cardinal and Count Piper, and the secret meetings held at the prelate's house, were the springs that regulated the motions of the Diet. They proposed to despatch an embassy to Charles XII, and unanimously required of the King that he should bring no more Muscovites upon their frontiers, and that he should send back his Saxon troops.

The bad fortune of Augustus had already done what the Diet demanded of him. The league, secretly concluded with the Muscovites at Birzen, was now become as useless as it had once appeared formidable. He was far from being able to send to the Czar the 50,000 Germans whom he had promised to raise in the empire. The Czar himself, a dangerous neighbor to Poland, was in no haste to assist a divided kingdom, from whose misfortunes he hoped to derive some advantage. He contented himself with sending 20,000 Muscovites into Lithuania, who did more mischief than the Swedes, flying everywhere before the conqueror, and ravaging the lands of the Poles; till at last, being pursued by the Swedish generals, and finding no more to pillage, they returned in shoals to their own country. With regard to the shattered remains of the Saxon army that was beaten at Riga, Augustus sent them to winter and recruit in Saxony, hoping by this sacrifice, involuntary as it was, to regain the affection of the Poles who were so highly incensed against him.

The war now was turned into intrigues. The Diet was split into almost as many factions as there were palatines. One day the interests of King Augustus prevailed, the next they were disregarded. Everyone called out for liberty and justice, and yet no one knew what liberty and justice were. The time was spent in private cabals and public harangues. The Diet neither knew what they would be at nor what they ought to do. Great companies seldom steer the right course in times of public commotions, because the factions are bold and the virtuous are commonly diffident. The Diet broke up in a tumultuous manner on February 17, 1702, after having spent three months in cabals, without coming to any fixed resolution. The senators, consisting of the palatines and bishops, remained at Warsaw. The Senate of Poland has a right of making laws provisionally, which the diets seldom disannul. This body being less numerous, and accustomed to business, was far less tumultuous, and decided with greater dispatch.

They decreed that the embassay, which was proposed in the Diet, should be sent to the King of Sweden; and that the *pospolite* should take to arms and hold themselves in readiness at all events. They made several regulations for quelling the commotions in Lithuania, and for diminishing the authority of the King, though less to be dreaded than that of Charles XII.

Augustus rather chose to receive hard laws from his conqueror than from his subjects. He resolved to sue for a peace to the King of Sweden, and to conclude a secret treaty with that monarch. This was a step which he was obliged to conceal from the Senate, whom he considered as an enemy still more untractable than Charles. As the affair was of a very delicate nature, he intrusted it to the Countess of Königsmark, a Swedish lady of high birth, to whom he was at that time attached. This is the lady whose brother became so famous by his unfortunate death, and whose son commanded the French armies with so much glory and success. Celebrated as she was for her wit and beauty, she was more capable than any minister of bringing a negotiation to a happy period. Moreover, as she had an estate in the dominions of Charles XII, and had resided a long time at his court, she had a very plausible pretext for waiting upon him. Accordingly she repaired to the Swedish camp in Lithuania and immediately applied to Count Piper, who too rashly promised her an audience of his master. The countess, among those perfections which rendered her the most amiable woman in Europe, possessed the happy talent of speaking the language of several countries she had never seen, with as much ease and propriety as if she had been a native. She even amused herself sometimes in writing French verses, which one might have easily mistaken for the production of a person born at Versailles. Those which she composed on Charles XII are not beneath the dignity of history to mention. She introduced the heathen gods praising him for his different virtues. The piece concluded thus:

> *Enfin, chacun des Dieux discourant à sa gloire,*
> *Le plaçait par avance au Temple de Mémoire;*
> *Mais Vénus ni Bacchus n'en dirent pas un mot.*

> "The hero's acts while other gods proclaim,
> And praise, and promise him immortal fame;
> Silent sit Bacchus and the queen of love."

All her wit and charms were lost upon such a man as the King of Sweden, who constantly refused to see her. She therefore resolved to throw herself in his way, as he rode out to take the air, which he frequently did. In this attempt she at last succeeded. She met him one day in a very narrow path; and, the moment she observed him, came down from her coach. The King made her a low bow, without speaking a word to her, turned about his horse, and rode back in an instant. And thus the only advantage which the Countess of Königsmark gained from her journey was the pleasure of seeing that the King of Sweden feared nobody but her.

The King of Poland was therefore obliged to throw himself into the arms of the Senate. He made them two proposals, which were laid before them by the Palatine of Marienburg: the one, that they should leave to him the disposal of the republic, in which case he would engage to pay the soldiers two quarters' advance out of his own revenue; the other, that they should allow him to bring back 12,000 Saxons into Poland. The cardinal-primate returned him an answer as severe as the King of Sweden's refusal. He told the Palatine of Marienburg, in the name of the Assembly, "that they had resolved to send an embassy to Charles XII, and that he would not advise him to bring back any Saxons."

In this extremity, the King was desirous of preserving at least the appearance of the royal authority. He sent one of his chamberlains to wait upon Charles, and to learn from him where, and in what manner, his Swedish Majesty would be pleased to receive the embassy of the King his master, and of the republic. Unhappily they had forgotten to ask from the Swedes a passport for the chamberlain. The King of Sweden, instead of giving an audience, caused him to be thrown into prison, saying "that he expected to receive an embassy from the republic, and not from Augustus."

After this, Charles having left garrisons in some towns in Lithuania, advanced beyond Grodno, a city well known in Europe for the diets that are held there, but ill-built, and worse fortified.

A few miles on the other side of Grodno he met the embassy of the republic, which consisted of five senators. They desired, in the first place, to have the ceremony of their introduction properly regulated, a thing with which the King was utterly unacquainted. They demanded that the Senate should be complimented with the title of Most Serene, and that the coaches of the King and senators should be sent to meet them. They were told in answer, "that the republic should be styled Illustrious, and not Most Serene; that the King never used any coaches; that he had plenty of officers in his retinue, but no senators; that a lieutenant-general should be sent to meet them; and that they might come on their own horses."

Charles XII received them in his tent, with some appearance of military grandeur. Their conversation was full of caution and reserve. They said they were afraid of Charles XII and did not love Augustus; but that it would be a shame for them to take the crown, in obedience to the orders of a stranger, from the head of that prince whom they had elected. Nothing was finally concluded, and Charles XII gave them to understand that he would settle all disputes at Warsaw.

His march was preceded by a manifesto, which the cardinal and his party spread over Poland in the space of eight days. By this writing, Charles invited all the Poles to join him in revenging their own quarrel, and endeavored to persuade them that his interest and theirs were the same. They were, however, very different; but the manifesto, supported by a powerful army, by the disorder of the Senate, and by the approach of the conqueror, made a deep impression on the minds of the people. They were obliged to own Charles for their protector, because he was resolved to be so; and happy was it for them that he contented himself with this title.

The senators who opposed Augustus published this manifesto aloud, even in the royal presence. The few who adhered to him observed a profound silence. At length, intelligence being brought that Charles was advancing by long marches, everyone prepared to depart in a hurry. The cardinal left Warsaw among the first. The greatest part fled with precipitation; some retired to their country-seats, there to wait the unravelling of this perplexed and intricate affair; others went to arm their friends. Nobody remained with the King but the ambassadors of the Emperor and the Czar, the Pope's nuncio, and a few bishops and palatines who were attached to his fortunes. He was forced to fly, though nothing as yet decided in his favor. Before his departure he hastened to hold a council with the small body of senators who still represented the Senate. Zealous as these were for his interest, they were nevertheless Poles; they had all conceived such an utter aversion to the Saxon troops, that they dared not grant him a liberty of recalling more than 6,000 of them for his defence; and they even voted that these 6,000 should be commanded by the grand general of Poland, and be immediately sent back upon the conclusion of a peace. The armies of the republic they left entirely to his disposal.

After this decree of the Senate, the King left Warsaw, too weak to resist his enemies, and but little satisfied even with the conduct of his friends. He immediately published orders for assembling the *pospolite* and the two armies, which were little more than empty names. He had nothing to hope for in Lithuania, of which the Swedes were in possession. The army of Poland, reduced to a handful of men, was in want of arms and provisions, and had no great inclination for the war. Most of the nobility, intimidated, irresolute, and disaffected, remained at their country-seats. In vain did the King, authorised by the laws of the land, command every gentleman, under pain of death, to take up arms and follow him. It had even become a problematical point whether they ought to obey him or not. His chief dependence was upon the troops of the electorate, where the form of government being wholly despotic, he was under no apprehensions of being disobeyed. He had already given secret orders for the march of 12,000 Saxons, who were advancing with great expedition. He likewise recalled the

8,000 men whom he had promised to the Emperor in his war against France, and whom the necessity of his affairs now obliged him to withdraw. To introduce so many Saxons into Poland was, in effect, to alienate the affections of all his subjects, and to violate the law made by his own party, which allowed only of 6,000. But he well knew that if he proved victorious, they would not dare to complain, and if he should be conquered, they would never forgive him for having introduced even the 6,000. While the soldiers were arriving in troops, and while he was flying from one palatinate to another, and assembling the nobility who adhered to him, the King of Sweden reached Warsaw, on May 5, 1702. The gates were opened to him at the first summons. He dismissed the Polish garrison, disbanded the city guard, posted guards of his own in all the convenient places, and ordered the inhabitants to deliver up their arms. Satisfied with having disarmed them, and unwilling to provoke them by any unnecessary severities, he demanded a contribution of no more than 100,000 livres. Augustus was then assembling his forces at Cracow, and was greatly surprised to see the cardinal-primate arrive among the rest. This man affected to maintain the decorum of his character to the last, and to dethrone his king with all the appearance of the most respectful behavior. He gave him to understand that the King of Sweden seemed very well inclined to come to a reasonable accommodation, and humbly begged leave to wait upon that monarch. Augustus granted him what he could not refuse, that is, the liberty of hurting himself.

The cardinal-primate immediately repaired to the King of Sweden, before whom he had not as yet ventured to appear. He saw him at Prague, not far from Warsaw, but without any of those ceremonies which had been observed in introducing the ambassadors of the republic. He found the conqueror clad in a coat of coarse blue cloth, with gilt brass buttons, jack-boots, and buff-skin gloves that reached up to his elbows. He was in a room without hangings, attended by the Duke of Holstein, Count Piper, his first minister, and several general officers. The King advanced a few steps to meet the cardinal; they talked together standing for about a quarter of an hour; Charles put an end to the conference, by saying aloud, "I will never give the Poles peace till they have elected a new king." The cardinal, who expected such a declaration, caused it to be immediately notified to all the palatinates, assuring them that he was extremely sorry for it, but represented to them at the same time the absolute necessity they were under of complying with the conqueror's request.

Upon receiving this intelligence, the King of Poland plainly perceived that he must either lose his crown or preserve it by a battle; and he exerted his utmost efforts in order to succeed in the decision of this important quarrel. All his Saxon troops had arrived from the frontiers of Saxony. The nobility of the Palatinate of Cracow, where he still remained, came in a body to offer him their service. He exhorted them to remember the oaths they had taken; and they promised to shed the last drop of their blood in support of his cause. Strengthened by these succors, and by the troops which bore the name of the army of the Crown, he went, for the first time, in quest of the King of Sweden; nor was he long in finding him, for that prince was already advancing toward Cracow.

The two kings met on July 13, 1702, in a spacious plain near Clissow, between Warsaw and Cracow. Augustus had near 24,000 men; Charles XII had not above 12,000. The battle began by a general discharge of the artillery. At the first volley of the Saxons, the Duke of Holstein, who commanded the Swedish cavalry, a young prince of great courage and virtue, received a cannon-ball in his reins. The King asked if he was killed, and was answered in the affirmative. He made no reply; a few tears fell from his eyes; he covered his face with his hands for a moment; and then, of a sudden, spurring on his horse with all his might, he rushed into the thickest of the enemy at the head of the guards.

The King of Poland did everything that could be expected from a prince who fought for his crown. Thrice in person did he rally his troops and lead them up to the charge; but the Saxons only could be said to fight for him; the Poles, who formed his right wing, fled to a man, at the very beginning of the battle, some through fear, and others through disaffection. The good-fortune of Charles XII carried all before it; he gained a complete victory. He took possession of the enemy's camp, their colors, and artillery, and Augustus's military-chest fell into his hands. He halted not a moment on the field of battle, but marched directly to Cracow, pursuing the King of Poland, who fled before him.

The citizens of Cracow were bold enough to shut the gates upon the conqueror. He caused them to be burst open. The garrison did not venture to fire a single gun, but were driven with whips and canes into the castle, into which the King entered pell-mell with them. Charles observing an officer of the artillery going to fire a cannon, ran up to him and snatched the match out of his hand. The commander fell on his knees before him. Three Swedish regiments were lodged at free quarters among the citizens, and the town was taxed with a contribution of 100,000 rix-dollars. Count Stenbock, who was appointed governor of the city, being informed that some treasures were hid in the tombs of the Polish kings, in St. Nicholas's Church, at Cracow, caused them to be opened. Nothing was found there but some ornaments of gold and silver, belonging to the churches. Of these he took a part; and Charles XII even sent a golden cup to one of the Swedish churches— an action that might have raised the Polish Catholics against him, had anything been able to withstand the terror of his arms.

He left Cracow with a determined resolution to pursue Augustus without intermission. At the distance of a few miles from the city his horse fell and broke his thigh-bone. They were obliged to carry him back to Cracow, where he remained confined to his bed for six weeks, in the hands of the surgeons. This accident gave Augustus a little respite. He forthwith caused it to be spread abroad through Poland and Germany that Charles XII was killed by the fall. This report, which gained credit for some time, filled the minds of all men with doubt and apprehension. During this interval, he assembled at Marienburg and then at Lublin all the orders of the kingdom, which had been already convoked at Sandomir. The Assembly was very full, as few palatinates refused to send their deputies thither. He regained the affections of most of them by presents and promises, and by that affability without which absolute kings cannot be beloved nor elective kings maintain themselves on the throne. The Diet was soon undeceived concerning the false report of the King of Sweden's death; but that large body was already put in motion, and suffered itself to be carried along by the impulse it had received; all the members swore to continue faithful to their sovereign: so subject to change are all great companies! Even the cardinal-primate himself, who still pretended a regard for Augustus, repaired to the Diet of Lublin, where he kissed the King's hands and readily took the oath as well as the other members. The substance of the oath was, that they had never attempted, nor ever would attempt, anything prejudicial to the interest of Augustus. The King excused the cardinal from the first part of the oath, and the prelate blushed while he swore to the last. The result of all the deliberations of this diet was, that the Republic of Poland should maintain an army of 50,000 men at their own expense for the service of their sovereign; that they should allow the Swedes six weeks' time to declare whether they were for peace or war; and the same time to the princes of Sapieha, the original authors of the troubles of Lithuania, to come and ask pardon from the King of Poland.

In the meantime Charles XII, being cured of his wound, overturned all their deliberations. Unalterably fixed in his resolution of forcing the Poles to dethrone their king with their own hands, he caused a new assembly to be convoked at Warsaw, by the intrigues of the cardinal, in opposition to that of Lublin. His generals represented to him that this negotiation might possibly be involved in endless delays, and by that means be rendered ineffectual; that, in the meantime, the Muscovites were every day becoming a more equal match for his troops which he had left in Livonia and Ingria; that the skirmishes which frequently happened between the Swedes and Russians in these provinces did not always turn out to the advantage of the former; and, finally, that his own presence might soon be necessary in those quarters. Charles, as steady in the prosecution of his schemes as he was brisk and vigorous in action, replied: "Should it oblige me to remain here for fifty years, I will not depart till I have dethroned the King of Poland."

He left the Assembly of Warsaw to combat that of Lublin, by their speeches and writings, and to justify their proceedings by the laws of the kingdom—laws always equivocal, which each party interprets according to their pleasure, and which success alone can render incontestable. As for himself, having reinforced his victorious troops with 6,000 horse and 8,000 foot, which he had received from Sweden, he marched against the remains of the Saxon army, which he had beaten at Clissow, and which had found time to rally and recruit, while his fall from his horse had confined him to his bed. This army shunned his approach and retired toward Prussia, to the northwest of Warsaw. The River Bug lay between him and the enemy. Charles swam across it at the head of his cavalry; the infantry went to look for a ford somewhat higher. He came up with the Saxons on May 1, 1703, at a place called Pultusk. General Steinau commanded them to the number of about 10,000. The King of Sweden, in his precipitate march, had brought no more than the same number along with him, confident that a less number would be sufficient. So great was the terror of his arms that one-half of the Saxon troops fled at his approach, without waiting for the battle. General Steinau, with two regiments, kept his ground for a moment, but was soon hurried along in the general flight of the army, which was dispersed before it was vanquished. The Swedes did not take above 1,000 prisoners, nor kill above 600 men, having more difficulty in pursuing than in defeating the enemy.

Augustus having now nothing left him but the shattered remains of his Saxons, who were everywhere defeated, retired in haste to Thorn, an ancient city of royal Prussia, situated on the Vistula, and under the protection of the Poles. Charles immediately prepared to besiege it. The King of Poland, not thinking himself secure in this place, withdrew from it, and flew into every corner of Poland where he could possibly find any soldiers, and into which the Swedes had not as yet penetrated. Meanwhile Charles, amid so many rapid marches, swimming across rivers, and hurried along with his infantry mounted behind his cavalry, had not been able to bring up his cannon to Thorn; he was therefore obliged to wait till a train of artillery should be brought from Sweden by sea.

While he tarrried here, he fixed his quarters at the distance of a few miles from the city, in reconnoitring which he frequently approached too near the ramparts. In these dangerous excursions, the plain dress which he wore was of greater service to him than he imagined, as it prevented his being distinguished and marked out by the enemy, who would not have failed to fire upon him. One day, having advanced too near the fortifications, attended by one of his generals called Lieven, who was dressed in a blue coat * trimmed with gold, and fearing lest the general should be too easily distinguished, he ordered him to walk behind him. To this he was prompted by that greatness of soul which was so natural to him that it even prevented his reflecting on the imminent danger to which he exposed his own life, in order to preserve that of his subject. Lieven perceiving his error too late, in having put on a remarkable dress, which endangered all those who were near him, and being equally concerned for the King wherever he was, hesitated for a moment whether or not he should obey him. In the midst of this contest the King took him by the arm, put himself before him, and screened him with his body. At that instant, a cannon-ball taking them in flank, struck the general dead upon the very spot which the King had scarcely left. The death of this man, killed exactly in his stead, and because he had endeavored to save him, contributed not a little to confirm him in the opinion, which he always entertained, of absolute predestination; and made him believe that his fate, which had preserved him in such a singular manner, reserved him for the execution of greater undertakings.

Everything succeeded with him: his negotiations and his arms were equally fortunate. He was present, as it were, in every part of Poland. His grand general, Rehnskiöld, was in the heart of the kingdom with a large body of troops. About 30,000 Swedes, under different generals, were posted toward the north and east upon the frontiers of Muscovy, and withstood the united efforts of the whole Russian Empire; and Charles was in the west, at the other end of Poland, with the flower of his army.

The King of Denmark, tied up by the Treaty of Travendahl, which his weakness had hindered him from breaking, remained quiet. That prudent monarch did not venture to discover the disgust he felt at seeing the King of Sweden so near his dominions. At a greater distance toward the southwest, between the Rivers Elbe and Weser, lay the Duchy of Bremen, the most remote of all the ancient conquests of the Swedes. This country was filled with strong garrisons, and opened to the con-

* In the former editions we gave this officer a scarlet coat; but the Chaplain Norberg has so incontestably proved it to have been a blue one that we have thought proper to correct the error.

queror a free passage into Saxony and the empire. Thus, from the German Ocean almost to the mouth of the Borysthenes [Dnieper], comprehending the whole breadth of Europe, and even to the gates of Moscow, all was in consternation; and everyone was daily expecting a general revolution. Charles's ships, which were now masters of the Baltic, were employed in transporting to Sweden the prisoners he had taken in Poland. Sweden, undisturbed in the midst of these mighty commotions, enjoyed the sweets of peace and shared in the glory of its King, without bearing the burden of the war; inasmuch as its victorious troops were paid and maintained at the expense of the conquered.

While all the northern powers were thus kept in awe by the arms of Charles XII, the town of Dantzic ventured to incur his displeasure. Fourteen frigates and forty transports were bringing the King a reinforcement of 6,000 men, with cannon and ammunition, to complete the siege of Thorn. These succors must necessarily pass up the Vistula. At the mouth of this river stands Dantzic, a free and wealthy town, which, together with Thorn and Elbing, enjoys the same privileges in Poland as the imperial towns possess in Germany. Its liberty has been alternately attacked by the Danes, the Swedes, and some German princes; and nothing has preserved it from bondage but the mutual jealousy of these rival powers. Count Stenbock, one of the Swedish generals, assembled the magistrates in the King's name and demanded a passage for the troops and ammunition. The magistrates were guilty of a piece of imprudence very common with those who treat with people more powerful than themselves; they dared neither refuse nor grant his demands. General Stenbock obliged them to grant more than he had at first demanded. He exacted from the city a contribution of 100,000 crowns, as a punishment for their imprudent refusal. At last the recruits, the cannon, and ammunition, having arrived before Thorn, the siege was begun on September 22d.

Robel, governor of the place, defended it for a month with a garrison of 5,000 men. At the expiration of that term he was obliged to surrender at discretion. The garrison were made prisoners of war and transported to Sweden. Robel was presented to the King unarmed. That prince, who never lost an opportunity of honoring merit in his enemies, gave him a sword with his own hand, made him a handsome present in money, and dismissed him on his parole. But the poor and paltry town was condemned to pay 40,000 crowns; an excessive contribution for such a place.

Elbing, built on an arm of the Vistula, founded by the Teutonic knights, and annexed likewise to Poland, did not profit by the misconduct of the Dantzicers, but hesitated too long about granting a passage to the Swedish troops. It was more severely punished than Dantzic. On December 13th Charles entered it at the head of 4,000 men, with bayonets fixed to the ends of their muskets. The inhabitants, struck with terror, fell upon their knees in the streets and begged for mercy. He caused them all to be disarmed, quartered his soldiers upon them, and then, having assembled the magistrates, exacted that same day a contribution of 260,000 crowns. There were in the town 200 pieces of cannon and 400,000 weight of powder, which he likewise seized. A battle gained would not have procured him so many advantages. All these successes paved the way for the dethroning of Augustus.

Hardly had the cardinal taken an oath that he would make no attempts against his sovereign, when he repaired to the Assembly of Warsaw, always under the specious pretence of peace. When he arrived there, he talked of nothing but obedience and concord, though he was accompanied by a number of soldiers whom he had raised on his own estate. At last he threw off the mask, and, on February 14, 1704, declared, in the name of the Assembly, " that Augustus, Elector of Saxony, was incapable of wearing the crown of Poland." All the members with one voice pronounced the throne to be vacant. It was the intention of the King of Sweden, and consequently of the Diet, to raise Prince James Sobieski to the throne of King John, his father. James Sobieski was then at Breslau, in Silesia, waiting with impatience for the crown which his father had worn. While he was one day hunting a few leagues from Breslau, in company with Prince Constantine, one of his brothers, thirty Saxon horsemen, sent privately by King Augustus, issued suddenly from a neighboring wood, surrounded the two princes, and carried them off without resistance. They had prepared fresh horses, upon which they conducted them to Leipsic and committed them to close custody. This stroke disconcerted the measures of Charles, the cardinal, and the Assembly of Warsaw.

Fortune, which sports with crowned heads, exposed Augustus, almost at the same time, to the danger of being taken himself. He was at table, three leagues from Cracow, relying upon an advanced guard which was posted at some distance, when, all of a sudden, General Rehnskiöld appeared, after having carried off the guard. The King of Poland had but just time to get on horseback, with ten others. General Rehnskiöld pursued him for four days, just upon the point of seizing him every moment. The King fled to Sandomir; the Swedish general pursued him thither, and it was only by a piece of good-fortune that he made his escape.

Meanwhile the King's party and that of the cardinal treated each other as traitors to their country. The army of the Crown was divided between the two factions. Augustus, being at last obliged to accept of assistance from the Russians, was sorry that he had not applied to them sooner. One while he flew into Saxony, where his resources were exhausted; at another he returned to Poland, where no one dared to serve him; while in the meantime the King of Sweden, victorious and unmolested, ruled in Poland with uncontrolled authority.

Count Piper, who was as great a politician as his master was a hero, advised Charles XII to take the crown of Poland to himself. He represented how easy it would be to accomplish such a scheme with a victorious army and a powerful party in the heart of the kingdom, which was already subdued. He tempted him with the title of " Defender of the Evangelical Religion," a name which flattered the ambition of Charles. It would be easy, he said, to effect in Poland what Gustavus Vasa had effected in Sweden—to establish the Lutheran religion, and to break the chains of the people, who were now held in slavery by the nobility and clergy. Charles yielded to the temptation for a moment; but glory was his idol. To it he sacrificed his own interest, and the pleasure he would have enjoyed in taking Poland from the Pope. He told Count Piper that he was much happier in bestowing than in gaining kingdoms; and added, with a smile, " You were made to be the minister of an Italian prince."

Charles was still near Thorn, in that part of royal Prussia which belongs to Poland. From thence he extended his views to what was passing at Warsaw, and kept all the neighboring powers in awe. Prince Alexander, brother of the two Sobieskis who were carried into Silesia, came to implore his aid in revenging his wrongs. Charles granted his desire the more readily as he thought he could easily gratify it, and that, at the same time, he should be avenging himself. But being extremely desirous of giving Poland a king, he advised Prince Alexander to mount the throne, from which fortune seemed determined to exclude his brother. Little did he expect a refusal. Prince Alexander told him that nothing should ever induce him to make an advantage of his elder brother's misfortune. The King of Sweden, Count Piper, all his friends, and especially the young palatine of Posnania, Stanislaus Leszczynski, pressed him to accept of the crown; but he remained unmoved by all their importunities. The neighboring princes were astonished to hear of this uncommon refusal, and knew not which to admire most—a king of Sweden, who, at twenty-two years of age, gave away the crown of Poland, or Prince Alexander, who refused to accept it.

# BOOK III

Stanislaus Leszczynski Elected King of Poland—Death of the Cardinal-Primate—Skilful Retreat of General Schulenburg—Exploits of the Czar—Foundation of Petersburg—Battle of Fraustadt—Charles Enters Saxony — Peace of Altranstädt — Augustus Abdicates the Crown in Favor of Stanislaus—General Patkul, the Czar's Plenipotentiary, is Broken upon the Wheel and Quartered—Charles Receives the Ambassadors of Foreign Princes in Saxony—He Goes Alone to Dresden to Visit Augustus Before his Departure.

YOUNG Stanislaus Leszczynski was then deputed by the Assembly of Warsaw to go to the King of Sweden and give him an account of several differences which had arisen among them since the time that Prince James was carried off. Stanislaus had a very engaging aspect, full of courage and sweetness, with an air of probity and frankness, which, of all external advantages, is certainly the greatest, and gives more weight to words than even eloquence itself. Charles was surprised to hear him talk with so much judgment of Augustus, the Assembly, the cardinal-primate, and the different interests that divided Europe. King Stanislaus did me the honor to inform me that he said to the King of Sweden, in Latin, " How can we elect a king, if the two princes, James and Constantine Sobieski, are held in captivity? " and that Charles replied, " How can we deliver the republic, if we don't elect a king? " This conversation was the only intrigue that placed Stanislaus on the throne. Charles prolonged the conversation, on purpose that he might the better sound the genius of the young deputy. After the audience, he said aloud, that he had not seen a man so fit to reconcile all parties. He immediately made inquiry into the character of the Palatine Leszczynski, and found that he was a man of great courage and inured to labor; that he always lay on a kind of straw mattress, requiring no service from his domestics; that he was temperate to a degree rarely known in that climate; liberal, with economy;

adored by his vassals; and perhaps the only lord in Poland who had any friends, at a time when men acknowledged no ties but those of interest and faction. This character, which in many particulars resembled his own, determined him entirely. After the conference, he said aloud, "There is the man that shall always be my friend"—the meaning of which words was soon perceived to be, "There is the man that shall be king."

As soon as the Primate of Poland understood that Charles XII had nominated the Palatine Leszczynski, in much the same manner as Alexander nominated Abdolonimus, he hastened to the King of Sweden, to try, if possible, to divert him from his resolution; being desirous that the Crown should involve on one Lubomirski. "But what have you to object against Stanislaus Leszczynski?" said the conqueror. "Sir," said the primate, "he is too young." "He is much about my age," replied the King dryly; and, turning his back upon the prelate, immediately despatched Count Horn to acquaint the Assembly of Warsaw that they must choose a king in five days, and that Stanislaus Leszczynski must be the man. Count Horn arrived on the seventh of July, and fixed the twelfth for the day of election, with as much ease and indifference as if he had been ordering the decampment of a battalion. The cardinal-primate, disappointed of the fruit of so many intrigues, returned to the Assembly, where he left no stone unturned to defeat an election in which he had no share. But the King of Sweden having come incognito to Warsaw, he was obliged to hold his peace. All that the primate could do was to absent himself from the election: unable to oppose the conqueror, and unwilling to assist him, he confined himself to a useless neutrality.

On Saturday, the twelfth of July, the day fixed for the election, the Assembly met, at three in the afternoon, at Kolo, the place appointed for the ceremony, the Bishop of Posnania acting as president, in the room of the cardinal-primate. He came attended by several gentlemen of the party. Count Horn and two other general officers assisted publicly at the solemnity, as ambassadors-extraordinary from Charles to the republic. The session lasted till nine in the evening; and the Bishop of Posnania put an end to it by declaring, in the name of the Assembly, that Stanislaus was elected King of Poland. They all threw up their hats in the air, and the shouts of acclamation stifled the cries of the opposers.

It was of no service to the cardinal-primate, or to the others who had resolved to continue neutral, that they had absented themselves from the election; they were all obliged next day to come and do homage to the new king; but the greatest mortification to which they were subjected, was their being compelled to follow him to the King of Sweden's quarters. Charles paid the sovereign he had made all the honors due to a king of Poland; and, to add the greater weight to his new dignity, he furnished him with a considerable sum of money and a sufficient number of troops.

Immediately after this, Charles XII departed from Warsaw, in order to finish the conquest of Poland. He had ordered his army to rendezvous before Lemberg [Leopold], the capital of the great palatinate of Russia, a place important in itself, and still more so on account of the riches which it contained. It was supposed it would hold out for fifteen days, by means of the fortifications with which Augustus had strengthened it. The conqueror sat down before it on the fifth of September, and next day took it by assault. All those who presumed to make resistance were put to the sword. The victorious troops, though masters of the city, did not break their ranks to go pillaging, notwithstanding the immense treasures that were said to be concealed in Lemberg. They drew up in order of battle in the great square, where the remaining part of the garrison came and surrendered themselves prisoners of war. The King published his orders by sound of trumpet, commanding, under pain of death, all the inhabitants who had any effects belonging to Augustus or his adherents to produce them before night. The measures he took were so wisely concerted that few ventured to disobey; and accordingly 400 chests of gold and silver coin, of plate and other valuable effects, were brought to his Majesty.

The beginning of Stanislaus's reign was distinguished by an event of a very different nature. Some business, which absolutely required his presence, had obliged him to remain at Warsaw. He had with him his mother, his wife, and his two daughters. The cardinal-primate, the Bishop of Posnania, and some grandees of Poland, composed his new court. It was guarded by 6,000 Poles, of the army of the Crown, who had lately entered into his service, but whose fidelity had not yet been put to the trial. General Horn, governor of the town, had not above 1,500 Swedes. The citizens of Warsaw were in a profound tranquillity, and Stanislaus proposed setting out in a few days for the conquest of Lemberg, when, all on a sudden, he was informed that a numerous army was approaching the city. This was King Augustus, who, by a fresh effort, and by one of the most dexterous marches that ever general made, had eluded the King of Sweden, and was now coming with 20,000 men to fall upon Warsaw and carry off his rival.

Warsaw was unfortified; the Polish troops, who defended it, were not to be relied on; Augustus held a correspondence with some of the citizens, so that, had Stanislaus remained in it, he must certainly have been ruined. He sent back his family into Posnania, under a guard of Polish troops in whom he could most confide. In this confusion, he thought he had lost his second daughter, who was about a year old, and who had been carried by her nurse into a neighboring village, where she was soon after found in a manger, as Stanislaus himself has since informed me. This is the same child whom fortune, after a variety of the most surprising vicissitudes, at last made Queen of France.* Several gentlemen took different roads. The new King immediately set out for the camp of Charles XII, learning thus betimes to suffer disgrace, and forced to quit his capital six weeks after he had been advanced to the sovereignty.

Augustus entered the capital like a provoked and victorious sovereign. The inhabitants, already fleeced by the King of Sweden, were entirely ruined by Augustus. The cardinal's palace, and all the houses of the confederate lords, with all their effects both in town and country, were given to plunder. What was most extraordinary in this sudden revolution, the Pope's nuncio, who attended Augustus, demanded, in the name of his master, that the Bishop of Posnania should be delivered into hands, as subject to the jurisdiction of the Court of Rome, both as a bishop and as the favorer of a prince who had been advanced to the throne by the arms of a Lutheran.

The Court of Rome, which has always been endeavoring to increase its temporal power by means of the spiritual, had, long before this, established a kind of jurisdiction in Poland, at the head of which was the Pope's nuncio. Its ministers never failed

* Maria Leszczynski, born in 1703, was married to Louis XV in 1725, and died in 1768.

to avail themselves of every favorable opportunity to extend their power, which is revered by the multitude, but always contested by men of sense. They claimed a right of judging in all ecclesiastical causes; and in times of trouble had usurped several other privileges, in which they maintained themselves till about the year 1728, when these abuses were corrected—abuses which are never reformed till they have become absolutely intolerable.

Augustus, glad of an opportunity of punishing the Bishop of Posnania in a decent manner, and willing to gratify the Court of Rome, whose pretensions, however, he would have opposed on any other occasion, delivered the Polish prelate into the hands of the nuncio. The bishop, after having seen his house pillaged, was carried by the soldiers to the lodgings of the Italian Minister, and from thence sent into Saxony, where he ended his days. Count Horn bore the continual fire of the enemy in the castle, where he was shut up, till at last, the place being no longer tenable, he surrendered himself with his 1,500 Swedes. This was the first advantage which Augustus gained, amid the torrent of his bad-fortune, over the victorious arms of his enemy.

This last effort was the blaze of a fire that was just going out. His troops, which had been assembled in haste, consisted either of Poles, ready to forsake him on the first disgrace, or of Saxon recruits, who had never seen a campaign; or of vagabond Cossacks, more fit to distress the conquered than to conquer: and all of them trembled at the bare mention of the King of Sweden's name.

That conqueror, accompanied by Stanislaus, went in quest of his enemy, at the head of his best troops. The Saxon army fled everywhere before him. The towns for thirty miles around sent him the keys of their gates. Not a day passed that was not distinguished by some advantage. Success began to grow too familiar to Charles. He said it was rather like hunting than fighting, and complained that he was not obliged to purchase a victory on harder terms.

Augustus gave the command of his army, for some time, to Count Schulenburg, a very able general, and who had need of all his experience at the head of dispirited troops. He was more anxious to preserve his master's troops than to conquer. He acted by stratagem, and the two kings with vigor. He stole some marches upon them, took possession of some advantageous posts, sacrificed a few horse in order to give his infantry time to retire; and thus, by a glorious retreat, saved his troops in the face of an enemy, in contending with whom it was impossible, at that time, to acquire any other kind of glory.

He had scarcely arrived in the Palatinate of Posnania when he learned that the two kings, who, he imagined, were at the distance of fifty leagues, had marched these fifty leagues in nine hours. He had only 8,000 foot and 1,000 horse; and yet, with this handful of men he was obliged to make head against a superior army, against the name of the King of Sweden, and against that terror with which so many defeats had naturally inspired the Saxons. He had always affirmed, contrary to the opinion of the German generals, that infantry were able to resist cavalry in open field, even without the assistance of *chevaux-de-frise*, and he this day ventured to put the matter to test of experience, against the victorious cavalry commanded by two kings and by the best Swedish generals. He took possession of such an advantageous post, that he could not possibly be surrounded. The soldiers of the first rank, armed with pikes and muskets, bent one knee upon the ground, and, standing very close together, presented to the enemy's horse a kind of pointed rampart with pikes and bayonets; the second rank, inclining a little on the shoulders of the first, fired over their heads; and the third, standing upright, fired at the same time, from behind the other two. The Swedes, with their usual impetuosity, rushed upon the Saxons, who waited the assault without flinching: the discharge of the muskets and the points of the pikes and bayonets maddened the horses, and made them rear instead of advancing. By these means the attack of the Swedes was rendered disorderly, and the Saxons defended themselves by keeping their ranks.

Though he had received five wounds, he drew up his men in an oblong square, and in this form made an orderly retreat about midnight toward the small town of Gurau, three leagues distant from the field of battle. But he had hardly begun to breathe in this place, when the two kings suddenly appeared at his heels.

Beyond Gurau, toward the River Oder, lay a thick wood, by

marching through which the Saxon general saved his fatigued infantry. The Swedes, who were not to be checked by such a trivial interruption, pursued them even through the wood, advancing with great difficulty through paths hardly passable by foot-travellers; and the Saxons had not crossed the wood above five hours before the Swedish horse. On the other side of the wood runs the River Bartsch, hard by a village called Rutzen. Schulenburg had taken care to send orders for having the boats in readiness, and he now transported his troops, which were diminished by one-half. Charles arrived the very moment that Schulenburg reached the opposite bank. Never conqueror pursued his enemy with greater celerity. The reputation of Schulenburg depended upon his escaping from the King of Sweden: the King, on the other hand, thought his glory concerned in taking Schulenburg and the remains of his army. He lost not a moment, but immediately caused his cavalry to cross at a ford. And thus the Saxons found themselves shut up between the River Parts, and the greater River Oder, which takes its rise in Silesia, and at this place is very deep and rapid.

Though the destruction of Schulenburg seemed to be inevitable, yet with the loss of a few soldiers he passed the Oder in the night. Thus he saved his army, and Charles could not help saying, " Schulenburg has conquered us to-day."

This is the same Schulenburg who was afterward general of the Venetians, and to whom the republic erected a statue in Corfu, for having defended that bulwark of Italy against the Turks. Such honors are conferred by republics only; kings give nothing but rewards.

But what contributed so much to the glory of Schulenburg was of no service to King Augustus, who once more abandoned Poland to his enemies, retired into Saxony, and instantly repaired the fortifications of Dresden, being already afraid, and not without reason, for the capital of his hereditary dominions.

Charles XII now beheld Poland reduced to subjection. His generals, after his example, had beaten in Courland several small bodies of the Muscovites, who ever since the battle of Narva had appeared only in small companies, and made war in those parts like the vagrant Tartars, who pillage, fly, and then reappear, in order to fly again.

Wherever the Swedes came, they thought themselves sure

of victory, when they were only twenty to 100. At this happy conjuncture Stanislaus prepared for his coronation. Fortune, to which he owed his election at Warsaw, and his expulsion from thence, now recalled him thither, amid the acclamations of a numerous nobility, attached to him by the fate of war. A diet was immediately convoked, where all obstacles were removed, except such as were raised by the Court of Rome, which alone endeavored to traverse the project.

It was natural for Rome to declare in favor of Augustus, who from a Protestant had become a Catholic, in order to mount the throne of Poland, and to oppose Stanislaus, who had been placed upon the same throne by the great enemy of the Catholic religion. Clement XI, the then Pope, sent briefs to all the prelates of Poland, and particularly to the cardinal-primate, threatening them with excommunication, if they presumed to assist at the consecration of Stanislaus, or attempt anything against the rights of Augustus.

Should these briefs be delivered to the bishops, who were at Warsaw, it was believed that some of them would be weak enough to obey them, and that the majority would avail themselves of this pretext to become more troublesome in proportion as they were more necessary. Every possible precaution was therefore taken to prevent these letters of the Pope from being admitted into Warsaw. But a Franciscan received briefs secretly, promising to deliver them into the bishop's own hands. He presently gave one to the suffragan of Chelm. This prelate, who was strongly attached to Stanislaus, carried it to the King unopened. The King sent for the monk, and asked him how he dared undertake to deliver a writing of that nature. The Franciscan answered that he did it by order of his general. Stanislaus desired him for the future to pay a greater regard to the orders of his King than to those of the general of the Franciscans, and forthwith banished him the city.

The same day a placard was published by the King of Sweden, forbidding, under the most severe penalties, all the ecclesiastics in Warsaw, both secular and regular, to interfere in affairs of state; and, for the greater security, he caused guards to be placed at the gates of all the prelates, and forbade any stranger to enter the city. These little severities he took upon himself, in order to prevent any rupture between the clergy and Stanislaus at his accession to the throne. He said he relaxed himself from the fatigues of war in giving a check to the intrigues of the Romish Court, and that he must fight against it with paper, whereas he was obliged to attack other sovereigns with real arms.

The cardinal-primate was solicited by Charles and Stanislaus to come and perform the ceremony of the coronation. He did not think himself obliged to leave Dantzic, and to consecrate a king who had been chosen against his will. But as it was his maxim never to do anything without a pretext, he resolved to provide a lawful excuse for his refusal. He caused the Pope's brief to be fixed in the night-time to the gate of his own house. The magistrates of Dantzic took fire at this indignity, and caused strict search to be made for the authors, who, nevertheless, could not be found. The primate affected to be highly incensed, but in reality was very well pleased, as it furnished him with a reason for refusing to consecrate the new King; and thus at one and the same time he kept on good terms with Charles XII, Augustus, Stanislaus, and the Pope. He died a few days after, leaving his country involved in confusion, and having reaped no other fruit from all his intrigues but that of embroiling himself with the three kings, Charles, Augustus, and Stanislaus, and with the republic and the Pope, who had ordered him to repair to Rome to give an account of his conduct. But, as even politicians are sometimes touched with remorse in their last moments, he wrote to King Augustus on his death-bed, and begged his pardon.

The consecration was performed with equal tranquillity and magnificence on October 4, 1705, in the city of Warsaw, notwithstanding the usual custom of the Poles of crowning the kings at Cracow. Stanislaus Leszczynski and his wife, Charlotta Opalinska, were consecrated King and Queen of Poland by the hands of the Archbishop of Lemberg, assisted by several other prelates. Charles XII saw the ceremony incognito, the only advantage he reaped from his conquests.

While he was thus giving a king to the conquered Poles, and Denmark dared not disturb him; while the King of Prussia courted his friendship, and Augustus had retired to his hereditary dominions, the Czar was every day becoming more and more formidable. Though he had given but little assistance to

Augustus in Poland, he had nevertheless made powerful diversions in Ingria.

He now began to grow not only a good soldier himself, but likewise instructed his subjects in the art of war. Discipline was established among his troops. He had good engineers, and well-served artillery, and several good officers; and he understood the great secret of subsisting his armies. Some of his generals had learned both how to fight, and, as occasion required, to decline fighting; and he had beside formed a respectable navy, capable of making head against the Swedes in the Baltic.

Strengthened by all these advantages, which were entirely owing to his own genius, and by the absence of the King of Sweden, he took Narva by assault on August 21, 1704, after a regular siege, during which he had prevented its receiving any succors either by sea or land. The soldiers were no sooner masters of the city, than they ran to pillage and abandoned themselves to the most enormous barbarities. The Czar flew from place to place, to stop the disorder and carnage. He snatched the women from the hands of the soldiers, who, after having ravished them, were going to cut their throats. He was even obliged to kill some Muscovites who did not obey his orders. They still show you, in the town-house of Narva, the table upon which he laid his sword as he entered, and repeat the words which he spoke to the citizens who were there assembled: "It is not with the blood of the inhabitants that this sword is stained, but with that of the Muscovites, which I have shed to save your lives."

Had the Czar always observed these humane maxims, he would have been the greatest man in the world. He aspired to a nobler character than that of a destroyer of towns. He was, at that time, laying the foundation of a city not far from Narva, in the middle of his new conquests. This was the city of Petersburg, which he afterward made the place of his residence and the centre of his trade. It is situated between Finland and Ingria, on a marshy island, around which the Neva divides itself into several branches before it falls into the Gulf of Finland. With his own hands he drew the plan of the city, the fortress, and the harbor—the quays which embellished it, and the forts which defended its entrance. This desert and uncultivated island, which, during the short summer in those climates, was only a heap of mud, and in winter a frozen pool, into which there was no entry by land but through pathless forests and deep morasses, and which had hitherto been the haunt of wolves and bears, was filled in 1703 with above 300,-000 men, whom the Czar had brought thither from his other dominions. The peasants of the Kingdom of Astrakhan, and those who inhabit the frontiers of China, were transported to Petersburg. He was obliged to clear forests, to make roads, to drain marshes, and to raise banks, before he could lay the foundation of the city. The whole was a force put upon nature. The Czar was determined to people a country which did not seem designed for the habitation of men. Neither the inundation which razed his works, nor the sterility of the soil, nor the ignorance of the workmen, nor even the mortality which carried off about 200,000 men in the beginning of the undertaking, could divert him from his firm resolution. The town was founded amid the obstacles which nature, the genius of the people, and an unsuccessful war, conspired to raise against it. Petersburg had become a city in 1705, and its harbor was filled with ships. The Emperor, by a proper distribution of favors, drew many strangers thither — bestowing lands upon some, houses upon others, and encouraging all the artists that came to civilize this barbarous climate. Above all, he had rendered it proof against the utmost effort of his enemies. The Swedish generals, who frequently beat his troops in every other quarter, were never able to hurt his infant colony. It enjoyed a profound tranquillity in the midst of the war with which it was surrounded.

While the Czar was thus creating, as it were, new dominions to himself, he still held out a helping hand to Augustus, who was losing his. He persuaded him, by means of General Patkul, who had lately entered into the service of Muscovy, and was then the Czar's ambassador in Saxony, to come to Grodno to confer with him once more on the unhappy situation of his affairs. Thither Augustus repaired with some troops, and accompanied by General Schulenburg, who had now become famous over all the North for his passage across the Oder, and in whom the King reposed his last hopes. The Czar arrived at the same place, followed by an army of 70,000 men. The two monarchs concerted new measures for carrying on the war. Augustus, being now dethroned, was no longer afraid of provoking the Poles, by abandoning their country to the Muscovite troops. It was resolved that the army of the Czar should be divided into several bodies, to check the progress of the King of Sweden at every step. It was at this time that Augustus renewed the order of the White Eagle, a weak expedient for attaching to his interest some Polish lords, who were more desirous of real advantages than of an empty honor, which becomes ridiculous when it is held of a prince possessed of nothing but the name of king. The conference of the two kings ended in a very extraordinary manner. The Czar departed suddenly, left his troops to his ally, and went to extinguish a rebellion with which he was threatened in Astrakhan. Immediately after his departure, Augustus ordered Patkul to be arrested at Dresden. All Europe was surprised at his conduct in presuming, contrary to the law of nations, and even, in appearance, to his own interest, to imprison the ambassador of the only prince from whom he could expect any assistance.

The secret spring of this transaction, as I had the honor to be informed by Marshal Saxe, son of King Augustus, was as follows: Patkul, proscribed in Sweden for having defended the privileges of Livonia, his native country, had been general to Augustus; but his high and lofty spirit being unable to brook the haughty behavior of General Flemming, the King's favorite, more imperious and lofty than himself, he had passed into the service of the Czar, whose general he then was, and his ambassador at the Court of Augustus. Endowed as he was with a penetrating genius, he had observed that Flemming and the Chancellor of Saxony intended to purchase a peace from the King of Sweden at any price. He forthwith formed a design to anticipate them, and to effect an accommodation between the Czar and Sweden. The chancellor discovered his project, and obtained leave to seize him. Augustus told the Czar that Patkul was a perfidious wretch, and would betray them both. And yet he was no further culpable than in having served his new master too well; but an ill-timed piece of service frequently meets with the punishment due to treason.

Meanwhile, the 60,000 Russians, divided into several small bodies, were burning and ravaging the lands of Stanislaus's adherents on one side, and on the other Schulenburg was advancing with fresh troops. The fortune of the Swedes dispersed these two armies in less than two months. Charles XII and Stanislaus attacked the separate bodies of the Muscovites, one after another, and with so much vigor and despatch that one Muscovite general was beaten before he heard of the defeat of his companion.

Nothing could stop the progress of the conqueror. If a river intervened between him and the enemy, Charles XII and his Swedes swam across it. A party of Swedes took the baggage of Augustus, in which were found 200,000 crowns of silver. Stanislaus seized 800,000 ducats belonging to Prince Mentchikof, the Russian general. Charles, at the head of his cavalry, marched thirty leagues in four-and-twenty hours, every soldier leading a horse in his hand to mount when his own was weary. The Muscovites, struck with terror, and reduced to a small number, fled in disorder beyond the Borysthenes.

While Charles was driving the Muscovites before him into the heart of Lithuania, Schulenburg at last repassed the Oder and came at the head of 20,000 men to give battle to the Grand Marshal Rehnskiöld, who was reckoned the best general that Charles had, and was called the Parmenion of this Alexander of the North. These two illustrious generals, who seemed to share the fate of their masters, met near Punitz, in a place called Fraustadt, a spot already fatal to the troops of Augustus. Rehnskiöld had only thirteen battalions and two-and-twenty squadrons, amounting in all to about 10,000 men. Schulenburg had double that number. It is worthy of remark, that there was in his army a body of 6,000 or 7,000 Muscovites, who had been long disciplined and were esteemed good soldiers. The battle of Fraustadt was fought on February 12, 1706. But this very General Schulenburg, who, with 24,000 men, had, in some measure, baffled the good-fortune of the King of Sweden, sunk under that of Rehnskiöld. The combat did not last a quarter of an hour; the Saxons made no resistance, and the Muscovites threw down their arms the moment they saw the Swedes. The panic was so sudden, and the confusion so great, that the conquerors found on the field of battle 7,000 loaded muskets, which the enemy had thrown away without firing. No defeat was ever more sudden, more complete, or more disgraceful; and yet no general ever made a finer disposition of his troops than Schulenburg, even by the confession of the Saxon and Swedish generals themselves, who this day saw how little human prudence is able to command events.

Among the prisoners there was an entire regiment of Frenchmen. These unhappy men had been taken by the Saxons in 1704, at the famous battle of Hochstädt, so fatal to the grandeur of Louis XIV. They had afterward passed into the service of Augustus, who had formed them into a regiment of dragoons, the command of which he had given to a Frenchman of the family of Joyeuse. The colonel was killed at the first, or rather the only, charge of the Swedes, and the whole regiment were made prisoners of war. That very day the French begged to be admitted into the service of Charles XII, into which they were accordingly received by a strange caprice of fortune, which reserved them once more to change their master and their conqueror.

With regard to the Muscovites, they begged their lives on their knees; but the Swedes cruelly put them to death above six hours after the battle, in order to revenge on them the outrages which their countrymen had committed, and to rid their hands of those prisoners whom they did not know how to dispose of.

Augustus now saw himself deprived of all resources. He had nothing left at Cracow, where he was shut up with two regiments of Muscovites, two of Saxons, and some troops of the army of the Crown, by whom he was even afraid of being delivered up to the conqueror; but his misfortunes were completed when he heard that Charles XII had at last entered Saxony, on September 1, 1706.

He had marched through Silesia, without so much as deigning to apprise the Court of Vienna of his motions. Germany was struck with consternation. The Diet of Ratisbon, which represents the empire, and whose resolutions are frequently as ineffectual as they are solemn, declared the King of Sweden an enemy of the empire if he should pass the Oder with his army, a step which only determined him to march the sooner into Germany.

At his approach the villages were deserted and the inhabitants fled on all sides. Charles behaved in the same manner as he had done at Copenhagen; he caused a declaration to be fixed up in all public places, importing "that his only intention in coming was to procure peace; that all those who should return home and pay the contributions he demanded, should be treated as his own subjects, and the rest punished without mercy." This declaration from a prince who was never known to break his word made all those who had fled through fear return home. He pitched his camp at Altranstädt, near the plain of Lützen, a field famous for the victory and death of Gustavus Adolphus. He went to see the place where that great man fell. When he reached the spot, "I have endeavored," said he, "to live like him; God, perhaps, will one day grant me as glorious a death."

From this camp he sent orders to the States of Saxony to assemble, and to transmit to him, without delay, the registers of the electoral finances. As soon as he got them in his power, and was exactly informed how much Saxony could supply, he taxed it at 625,000 rix-dollars a month. Over and above this contribution, the Saxons were obliged to furnish every Swedish soldier with two pounds of flesh, two pounds of bread, two pots of beer, and four pence a day, with forage for the horse. The contributions being thus regulated, the King established a new police, to protect the Saxons from the insults of his soldiers. In all the towns where he placed garrisons, he ordered the innkeepers, in whose houses the soldiers were quartered, to deliver every month certificates of their behavior, without which the soldiers were to have no pay. Beside, inspectors were appointed, who, once in every fifteen days, went from house to house to make inquiry whether the Swedes had committed any outrage; in which case, care was taken to indemnify the innkeepers and to punish the delinquents.

It is well known under what severe discipline the troops of Charles XII were kept; that they never plundered the towns which they took by assault till they had received permission, and that they even plundered in a regular manner, and left off at the first signal. The Swedes pique themselves to this day on the strict discipline which they observed in Saxony; and yet the Saxons complain of the terrible ravages they committed, contradictions which it would be impossible to reconcile, did we not know in what very different lights the same objects appear to different men. It could hardly happen but that the conquerors must have sometimes abused their rights; and the conquered have taken the slightest injuries for the most enormous outrages. One day as the King was taking the air on horseback, in the neighborhood of Leipsic, a Saxon peasant threw himself at his feet, begging he would do him justice on a grenadier, who had just taken from him what was designed for his family's dinner. The King ordered the soldier to be brought before him. "And is it true," said he, with a stern countenance, "that you have robbed this man?" "Sir," said the soldier, "I have not done him so much harm as you have done to his master; you have taken a kingdom from him, and I have only taken a turkey from this fellow." The King gave the peasant ten ducats with his own hand, and pardoned the soldier for the wit and boldness of the reply; adding, "Remember, friend, that if I have taken a kingdom from Augustus, I have kept nothing to myself."

The great fair of Leipsic was held as usual. The merchants came thither in perfect security. Not one Swedish soldier was to be seen at the fair. One would have said that the army of the King of Sweden was in Saxony for no other reason than to watch over the safety of the country. He commanded throughout all the electorate with a power as absolute, and a tranquillity as profound, as if he had been in Stockholm.

Augustus, wandering up and down Poland, and deprived at once of his kingdom and electorate, at last wrote a letter with his own hand to Charles XII, in which he humbly sued for peace. This letter he sent secretly by Baron Imhof and M. Fingsten, referendary of the Privy Council, to which two gentlemen he gave full power, and a blank signed: "Go, and endeavor to procure me reasonable and Christian conditions." He was obliged, however, to conceal these overtures, and to decline the meditation of any prince; for, being then in Poland, at the mercy of the Muscovites, he had reason to fear that that dangerous ally, whom he was now going to abandon, would punish him for his submission to the conqueror. His two plenipotentiaries came to Charles's camp in the night-time and had a private audience. The King having read the letter, told them they should have his answer in a moment; and accordingly, retiring to his closet, he wrote as follows:

"I consent to give peace on the following conditions, in

which it must not be expected that I will ever make the least alteration.

"I. That Augustus renounce the Crown of Poland forever; that he acknowledge Stanislaus as lawful King; and that he promises never to remount the throne, not even after the death of Stanislaus.

"II. That he renounce all other treaties, and particularly those he has made with Muscovy.

"III. That he send back to my camp, in an honorable manner, the Princes Sobieski, and all the prisoners he has taken.

"IV. That he deliver into my hands all the deserters that have entered into his service, and particularly John Patkul; and that he stop all proceedings against such as have passed from his service into mine."

This paper he gave to Count Piper, with orders to transact the rest with the plenipotentiaries of Augustus. These gentlemen were shocked at the cruelty of the proposals, and used all the little arts that men without power can employ, to soften, if possible, the rigor of the King of Sweden. They had several conferences with Count Piper; but that minister answered all their arguments with this short reply: "Such is the will of the King, my master, and he never alters his resolution."

While these negotiations were going on in Saxony, fortune seemed to put Augustus in a condition to obtain more honorable terms, and of treating with his conqueror on a more equal footing.

Prince Mentchikof, generalissimo of the Muscovite army, brought into Poland a body of 30,000 men, at a time when Augustus not only did not desire their assistance, but even feared it. He had with him some Polish and Saxon troops, making in all about 6,000 men. Surrounded with this small body by the army of Prince Mentchikof, he had everything to fear, in case the negotiation should be discovered. He saw himself at once dethroned by his enemy, and in danger of being arrested by his ally. In this delicate conjuncture, one of the Swedish generals named Meyerfeldt, at the head of 10,000 men, appeared at Kalisch, near the Palatinate of Posnania. Prince **Mentchikof** pressed Augustus to give them battle. The King, who was greatly embarrassed, delayed the engagement under various pretexts; for, though the enemy had but one-third of his number, there were 4,000 Swedes in Meyerfeldt's army, and that alone was sufficient to render the event doubtful. To give battle to the Swedes during the negotiation, and to lose it, was, in effect, to deepen the abyss in which he was already plunged. He therefore resolved to send a trusty servant to the general of the enemy, to give him some distant hints with regard to the peace, and advise him to retreat. But this advice produced an effect quite contrary to what he expected. General Meyerfeldt thought they were laying a snare to intimidate him; and for that reason resolved to hazard a battle.

The Russians, now for the first time, conquered the Swedes in a pitched battle. This victory, which Augustus gained almost against his will, was entire and complete. In the midst of his bad-fortune, he entered triumphant into Warsaw, formerly his flourishing capital, but then a dismantled and ruined town, ready to receive any conqueror, and to acknowledge the strongest for king. He was tempted to seize upon this moment of prosperity to go and attack the King of Sweden, in Saxony, with the Muscovite army. But when he reflected that Charles XII was at the head of a Swedish army, hitherto invincible; that the Russians would abandon him on the first intelligence of the treaty he had begun; that his Saxon dominions, already drained of men and money, would be equally ravaged by the Swedes and Muscovites; that the empire, engaged in a war with France, could afford him no assistance; and that, in the end, he should be left without dominions, money, or friends, he thought it most advisable to comply with the terms which the King of Sweden should impose. These terms became still more hard when Charles heard that Augustus had attacked his troops during the negotiation. His resentment, and the pleasure of further humbling an enemy who had just vanquished his forces, made him inflexible upon all the articles of the treaty. Thus the victory of Augustus served only to render his situation the more miserable; a thing which perhaps never happened to any but himself.

He had just caused a *Te Deum* to be sung at Warsaw, when Fingsten, one of his plenipotentiaries, arrived from Saxony with the treaty of peace which deprived him of his crown. Augustus hesitated for a little, but at last signed it; and then set out for Saxony, vainly hoping that his presence would soften the King of Sweden, and that his enemy would perhaps remember the ancient alliances of their families, and the common blood that ran in both their veins.

These two princes met for the first time in Count Piper's tent, at a place called Gutersdorf, without any ceremony. Charles XII was in jack-boots, with a piece of black taffety tied round his neck instead of a cravat; his clothes, as usual, were of coarse blue cloth, with gilt-brass buttons. He had a long sword by his side, which had served him in the battle of Narva, and upon the pummel of which he frequently leaned. The conversation turned wholly upon these jack-boots; Charles XII told Augustus that he had not laid them aside for these six years past, except when he went to bed. These trifles were the only subject of discourse between two kings, one of whom had deprived the other of a crown. Augustus, especially, spoke with an air of complaisance and satisfaction, which princes, and men accustomed to the management of great affairs, know how to assume amid the most cruel mortifications. The two kings dined together two several times. Charles XII always affected to give Augustus the right hand; but, far from mitigating the rigor of his demands, he rendered them still more severe. It was certainly a very mortifying thing for a sovereign to be forced to deliver up a general officer and a public minister. It was still a greater debasement to be obliged to send the jewels and archives of the Crown to his successor Stanislaus. But what completed his degradation was his being at last compelled to congratulate, on his accession to the throne, the man who was going to usurp his place. Charles required Augustus to write a letter to Stanislaus. The dethroned King endeavored to evade the demand; but Charles insisted upon his writing the letter, and he was at last obliged to comply. Here follows an exact copy of it, which I have seen. It is transcribed from the original, which is still in the possession of King Stanislaus:

" SIR AND BROTHER:

"We little imagined it would have been necessary to enter into a literary correspondence with your Majesty; nevertheless, in order to please his Swedish Majesty, and to avoid the suspicion of our being unwilling to gratify his desire, we hereby congratulate you on your accession to the throne, and wish you may find in your native country more faithful subjects than we have left there. All the world will do us the justice to believe that we have received nothing but the most ungrateful returns for our good offices, and that the greater part of our subjects seemed to have no other aim than to hasten our ruin. Wishing that you may never be exposed to the like misfortunes, we commit you to the protection of God.

"Your brother and neighbor,
"AUGUSTUS, KING."

DRESDEN, April 8, 1707.

Augustus was obliged to give orders to all his magistrates no longer to style him King of Poland, and to erase this title, which he now renounced, out of the public prayers. He was less averse to the releasing of the Sobieskis; but the sacrifice of Patkul was the severest of all. The Czar, on the one hand, loudly demanded him back as his ambassador; and, on the other, the King of Sweden, with the most terrible menaces in case of a refusal, insisted that he should be delivered up to him. Patkul was then confined in the castle of Königstein, in Saxony. Augustus thought he might easily gratify Charles XII and save his own honor. He sent his guards to deliver this unhappy man to the Swedish troops; but he previously dispatched a secret order to the governor of Königstein to let his prisoner escape. The bad-fortune of Patkul defeated the pains that were taken to save him. The governor, knowing that Patkul was very rich, had a mind to make him purchase his liberty. The prisoner still relying on the law of nations, and informed of the intentions of Augustus, refused to pay for that which he thought he had a title to obtain for nothing. During this interval, the guards who were commissioned to seize the prisoner arrived, and immediately delivered him to four Swedish captains, who carried him forthwith to the general quarters at Altranstädt, where he remained for three months, tied to a stake with a heavy iron chain, and from thence was conducted to Casimir.

Charles XII, forgetting that Patkul was the Czar's ambassador, and considering him only as his own subject, ordered a council of war to try him with the utmost rigor. He was condemned to be broken alive and quartered. A chaplain having come to inform him of the fatal sentence, without acquainting him with the manner in which it was to be executed, Patkul, who had braved death in so many battles, finding himself shut up with a priest, and his courage being no longer supported by glory or passion, the only sources of human intrepidity, poured out a flood of tears into the chaplain's bosom. He was affianced to a Saxon lady, called Madame von Einsiedel, a woman of birth, of merit, and of beauty, and whom he had intended to marry about the time that he was now condemned to die. He entreated the chaplain to wait upon her, to give her all the consolation he could, and to assure her that he died full of the most tender affection for his incomparable mistress. When he was brought to the place of punishment, and beheld the wheels and stakes prepared for his execution, he fell into convulsions and threw himself into the arms of the minister, who embraced him, covered him with his cloak, and wept over him. Then a Swedish officer read aloud a paper to the following effect:

"This is to declare, that it is the express order of his Majesty, our most merciful lord, that this man, who is a traitor to his country, be broken upon the wheel and quartered, in order to atone for his crimes and to be an example to others; that everyone may beware of treason, and faithfully serve his king." At the words "most merciful prince," Patkul cried out, "What mercy?" and at those of "traitor to his country," "Alas!" said he, "I have served it but too well." He received sixteen blows, and suffered the longest and most excruciating tortures that can be imagined. Thus died the unfortunate John Reinhold Patkul, ambassador and general of the Emperor of Russia.

Those that looked upon him only as a rebel, said that he deserved death; but those who considered him as a Livonian, born in a province that had privileges to defend, and remembered that he had been banished from Livonia for no other reason than his having defended those privileges, called him a martyr to the liberty of his country. But all agreed that the title of ambassador to the Czar ought to have rendered his person sacred. The King of Sweden alone, brought up in the principles of arbitrary power, thought that he had only performed an act of justice, while all Europe condemned his cruelty.

His mangled limbs remained exposed upon gibbets till 1713, when Augustus, having regained his throne, caused these testimonies of the necessity to which he was reduced at Altranstädt to be gathered together. They were brought to Warsaw in a box, and delivered to him in presence of the French envoy. The King of Poland, showing the box to this minister, only said, " These are the limbs of Patkul," without adding anything, either to blame his conduct or to bewail his memory, and without anyone daring to speak on so delicate and mournful a subject.

About this time, a Livonian called Paykul, an officer in the Saxon troops, who had been taken prisoner in the field, was condemned at Stockholm by a decree of the Senate; but his sentence was only to lose his head. This difference of punishments in the same case made it but too plain that Charles, in putting Patkul to such a cruel death, was more anxious to avenge himself than to punish the criminal. Be that as it may, Paykul, after his condemnation, proposed to the Senate to impart to the King the secret of making gold, on condition that he should obtain his pardon. He made the experiment in prison, in presence of Colonel Hamilton and the magistrates of the town; and whether he had actually discovered some useful secret, or, what is more probable, had only acquired the art of deceiving with a plausible air, they carried the gold which was found in the crucible to the mint at Stockholm and gave the Senate such a full and seemingly such an important account of the matter, that the queen-dowager, Charles's grandmother, ordered the execution to be suspended till the King should be informed of this uncommon affair, and should send his orders accordingly.

The King replied " that he had refused the pardon of the criminal to the entreaties of his friends, and that he would never grant to interest what he had denied to friendship." This inflexibility had something in it very heroical in a prince, especially as he thought the secret practicable. Augustus, upon hearing this story, said, " I am not surprised at the King of Sweden's indifference about the philosopher's stone; he has found it in Saxony."

When the Czar was informed of the strange peace which Augustus had, notwithstanding their former treaties, concluded at Altranstädt, and that Patkul, his ambassador-plenipotentiary, was delivered up to the King of Sweden, in contempt of the law of nations, he loudly complained of these indignities to the Courts of Europe. He wrote to the Emperor of Germany, to the Queen of England, and to the States-General of the United Provinces. He gave the terms of cowardice and treachery to the sad necessity to which Augustus had been obliged to submit. He conjured all these powers to interpose their mediation to procure the restoration of his ambassador, and to prevent the affront, which, in his person, was going to be offered to all crowned heads. He pressed them, by the motive of honor, not to demean themselves so far as to become guarantees of the Treaty of Altranstädt—a concession which Charles XII meant to extort from them by his threatening and imperious behavior. These letters had no other effect than to set the power of the King of Sweden in a stronger light. The Emperor, England, and Holland, were then engaged in a destructive war against France, and thought it a very unseasonable juncture to exasperate Charles XII by refusing the vain ceremony of being guarantees to a treaty. With regard to the unhappy Patkul, there was not a single power that interposed its good offices in his behalf; from whence it appears what little confidence a subject ought to put in princes, and how much all the European powers at that time stood in awe of the King of Sweden.

It was proposed in the Czar's Council to retaliate on the Swedish officers who were prisoners at Moscow; but the Czar would not consent to a barbarity which would have been attended with fatal consequences, as there were more Muscovites prisoners in Sweden than Swedes in Muscovy.

He resolved to take a more advantageous revenge. The main body of his enemy's army lay idle in Saxony. Löwenhaupt [Levenhaupt], the King of Sweden's general, who was left in Poland with about 20,000 men, was not able to guard the passes into a country without forts, and full of factions. Stanislaus was in the camp of Charles XII. The Emperor of Muscovy seized this opportunity, and re-entered Poland with above 60,000 men. These he divided into several bodies and marched with a flying camp to Lemberg, where there was no Swedish garrison. All the towns of Poland yielded to anyone who appeared before their gates at the head of an army. He caused an assembly to be convoked at Lemberg of much the same nature with that which had dethroned Augustus at Warsaw.

At that time Poland had two primates as well as two kings, the one nominated by Augustus, the other by Stanislaus. The primate nominated by Augustus summoned the Assembly of Lemberg, to which resorted all those whom that prince had abandoned by the peace of Altranstädt, and those that the Czar's money had gained. Here it was proposed to elect a new sovereign; so that Poland was almost upon the point of having three kings at once, without being able to say which was the real one.

During the conferences at Lemberg, the Czar, whose interest was closely connected with that of the Emperor of Germany, on account of the common dread which they both entertained of the power of the King of Sweden, secretly obtained from him a number of German officers, who, daily arriving, increased his strength in a considerable degree by bringing along with them discipline and experience. These he engaged in his service by several instances of liberality; and the more to encourage his own troops, he gave his picture set round with diamonds to all the general officers and colonels who had fought at the battle of Kalisch: the subaltern officers had medals of gold, and every private soldier a medal of silver. These monuments of the victory at Kalisch were all struck in the new city of Petersburg, where the improvement of the arts kept pace with the desire of glory and spirit of emulation which the Czar had infused into his troops.

The confusion, the multiplicity of factions, and the continual ravages prevailing in Poland, hindered the Diet of Lemberg from coming to any resolution. The Czar transferred it to Lublin; but the change of place did not lessen the disorder and perplexity in which the whole nation was involved. The Assembly contented themselves with declaring that they neither acknowledged Augustus, who had abdicated the throne, nor Stanislaus, who had been elected against their will; but they were neither sufficiently united, nor had resolution enough to nominate another king. During these fruitless deliberations, the party of the Princes Sapieha, that of Oginski, those who secretly adhered to Augustus and the new subjects of Stanislaus, all made war upon one another, and, by pillaging each other's estates, completed the ruin of their country. The Swedish troops, commanded by Löwenhaupt, one part of which lay in

Livonia, another in Lithuania, and a third in Poland, were daily in pursuit of the Russians, and set fire to everything that opposed Stanislaus. The Russians ruined their friends and foes without distinction; and nothing was to be seen but towns reduced to ashes, and wandering troops of Poles, deprived of all their substance, and detesting alike their two kings, the Czar, and Charles XII.

To quell these commotions, and to secure the possession of the throne, Stanislaus set out from Altranstädt on July 15, 1707, accompanied by General Rehnskiöld and sixteen Swedish regiments and furnished with a large sum of money. He was acknowledged wherever he came. The strict discipline of his troops, which made the barbarity of the Muscovites to be more sensibly felt, conciliated the affections of the people. His extreme affability, in proportion as it was better known, reconciled to him almost all the different factions; and his money procured him the greatest part of the army of the Crown. The Czar, apprehensive of wanting provisions in a country which his troops had laid waste, retired into Lithuania, where he had fixed the general rendezvous of his army, and where he resolved to establish magazines. This retreat left Stanislaus the undisturbed sovereign of the greater part of Poland.

The only person that gave him any uneasiness was Count Siniawski, grand general of the Crown, by the nomination of Augustus. This man, who was possessed of no contemptible talents, and entertained the most ambitious views, was at the head of a third party. He neither acknowledged Augustus nor Stanislaus; and after having used his utmost efforts in order to procure his own election, he contented himself with being the head of a party, since he could not be king. The troops of the Crown, which continued under his command, had no other pay but the liberty of pillaging their fellow-subjects with impunity. And all those who had either suffered, or were apprehensive of suffering, from the rapacity of these free-booters, soon submitted to Stanislaus, whose power was gathering strength every day.

The King of Sweden was then receiving, in his camp at Altranstädt, ambassadors from almost all the princes in Christendom. Some entreated him to quit the empire, others desired him to turn his arms against the Emperor; and it was then the general report that he intended to join with France, in humbling the house of Austria. Among these ambassadors was the famous John, Duke of Marlborough, sent by Anne, Queen of Great Britain. This man, who never besieged a town which he did not take, nor fought a battle which he did not gain, was at St. James's a perfect courtier, in Parliament the head of a party, and in foreign countries the most able negotiator of his time. He did France as much mischief by his politics as by his arms. M. Fagel, secretary of the States-General, and a man of great merit has been heard to say that when the States-General had more than once resolved to oppose the schemes which the duke was about to lay before them, the duke came, spoke to them in French, a language in which he expressed himself but very indifferently, and brought them all over to his opinion. This account I had from Lord Bolingbroke.

In conjunction with Prince Eugene, the companion of his victories, and Heinsius, the grand-pensionary of Holland, he supported the whole weight of the war which the allies waged against France. He knew that Charles was incensed against the empire and the Emperor; that he was secretly solicited by the French; and that if this conqueror should espouse the cause of Louis XIV, the allies must be entirely ruined.

True it is, Charles had given his word in 1700, that he would not intermeddle in the quarrel between Louis XIV and the allies; but the Duke of Marlborough could not believe that any prince would be so great a slave to his word as not to sacrifice it to his grandeur and interest. He therefore set out from The Hague, with a resolution to sound the intentions of the King of Sweden. Fabricius, who then attended upon Charles XII, assured me that the Duke of Marlborough, on his arrival, applied secretly, not to Count Piper, the prime minister, but to Baron Görtz, who now began to share with Piper the confidence of the King. He even went to the quarters of Charles XII in the coach of this gentleman, between whom and the Chancellor Piper, together with Robinson, the English Minister, he spoke to the King in French. He told him that he should esteem it a singular happiness could he have an opportunity of learning, under his command, such parts of the art of war as he did not yet understand. To this polite compliment the King made no return, and seemed to forget that it was Marlborough who was speaking to him. He even thought, as I have been credibly informed, that the dress of this great man was too fine and costly, and that his air had in it too little of a soldier. The conversation was tedious and general—Charles XII speaking in the Swedish tongue, and Robinson serving as an interpreter. Marlborough, who was never in haste to make proposals, and who, by a long course of experience, had learned the art of diving into the real characters of men, and discovering the connection between their most secret thoughts and their actions, gestures, and discourse, regarded the King with the utmost attention. When he spoke to him of war in general, he thought he perceived in his Majesty a natural aversion to France; and remarked that he talked with pleasure of the conquests of the allies. He mentioned the Czar to him, and observed that his eyes always kindled at the name, notwithstanding the calmness of the conversation. Besides, he saw a map of Muscovy lying before him upon the table. He wanted no more to convince him that the real design and the sole ambition of the King of Sweden was to dethrone the Czar, as he had already done the King of Poland. He was sensible that if Charles remained in Saxony, it was only to impose some hard conditions on the Emperor of Germany. He knew the Emperor would make no resistance, and that thus all disputes would be easily accommodated. He left Charles XII to follow the bent of his own mind; and satisfied with having discovered his intentions, he made him no proposals. These particulars I had from the Duchess of Marlborough, his widow, who is still alive.*

As few negotiations are finished without money, and as ministers are sometimes seen to sell the hatred or favor of their masters, it was the general opinion throughout all Europe that the Duke of Marlborough would not have succeeded so well with the King of Sweden had he not made a handsome present to Count Piper, whose memory still labors under the imputation. For my own part, after having traced this report to its source, with all the care and accuracy of which I am master, I have found that Piper received a small present from the Emperor, by the hands of the Count Wratislau, with the consent of his master, and not a farthing from the Duke of Marlbor-

---

* The author wrote in 1727, since which time, as appears from other dates, the work has undergone several corrections.

ough. Certain it is, Charles was so firmly resolved to dethrone the Emperor of Russia, that he asked nobody's advice on that subject, nor needed the instigation of Count Piper to prompt him to wreak his long-meditated vengeance on the head of Peter Alexiovitch.

But what vindicates the chaacter of that minister beyond all probability and cavil, was the honor which, long after this period, was paid to his memory by Charles XII, who, having heard that Piper was dead in Russia, caused his corpse to be transported to Stockholm, and gave him a magnificent funeral at his own expense.

The King, who had not as yet experienced any reverse of fortune, nor even met with any interruption in his victories, thought one year would be sufficient for dethroning the Czar, after which he imagined he might return in peace and erect himself into the arbiter of Europe. But, first of all, he resolved to humble the Emperor of Germany.

Baron Stralheim, the Swedish envoy at Vienna, had had a quarrel at a public entertainment with Count Zobor, chamberlain of the Emperor. The latter having refused to drink the health of Charles XII, and having bluntly declared that that prince had used his master ill, Stralheim gave him at once the lie and a box on the ear, and, besides this insult, boldy demanded a reparation from the imperial court. The Emperor, afraid of displeasing the King of Sweden, was obliged to banish his subject, whom he ought rather to have avenged. Charles, not satisfied even with this condescension, insisted that Count Zobor should be delivered up to him. The pride of the Court of Vienna was forced to stoop. The count was put into the hands of the King, who sent him back, after having kept him for some time as a prisoner at Stettin.

He further demanded, contrary to all the laws of nations, that they should deliver up to him 1,500 unhappy Muscovites, who, having escaped the fury of his arms, had fled for refuge into the empire. The Emperor was obliged to yield even to this unreasonable demand; and had not the Russian envoy at Vienna given these unhappy wretches an opportunity of escaping by different roads, they must have been delivered into the hands of their enemies.

The third and last of his demands was the most daring. He

declared himself the protector of the Emperor's Protestant subjects in Silesia, a province belonging to the house of Austria, and not to the empire. He insisted that the Emperor should grant them the liberties and privileges which had been established by the treaties of Westphalia, but which were extinguished, or at least eluded, by those of Ryswyk. The Emperor, who wanted only to get rid of such a dangerous neighbor, yielded once more, and granted all that he desired. The Lutherans of Silesia had above 100 churches, which the Catholics were obliged to cede to them by this treaty; but of these advantages, which were now procured them by the King of Sweden's good fortune, they were afterward deprived, when that prince was no longer in a condition to impose laws.

The Emperor who made these forced concessions, and complied in everything with the will of Charles XII, was called Joseph, and was the eldest son of Leopold, and brother of Charles VI, who succeeded him. The Pope's inter-nuncio, who then resided at the Court of Joseph, reproached him in very severe terms, alleging that it was a most shameful condescension for a Catholic emperor like him, to sacrifice the interest of his own religion to that of heretics. "You may think yourself very happy," replied the Emperor, with a smile, " that the King of Sweden did not propose to make me a Lutheran; for if he had, I do not know what I might have done."

Count Wratislau, his ambassador to Charles XII, brought to Leipsic the treaty in favor of the Silesians, signed with his master's hand; upon which Charles said he was the Emperor's very good friend. He was far from being pleased, however, with the Court of Rome, which had employed all its arts and intrigues, in order to traverse his scheme. He looked with the utmost contempt upon the weakness of that court, which, having one-half of Europe for its irreconcilable enemy, and placing no confidence in the other, can only support its credit by the dexterity of its negotiations; and he therefore resolved to be revenged on his Holiness. He told Count Wratislau that the Swedes had formerly subdued Rome, and had not degenerated like her. He sent the Pope word that he would one day redemand the effects which Queen Christina had left at Rome. It is hard to say how far this young conqueror might have carried his resentment and his arms, had fortune favored his designs. At that time nothing appeared impossible to him. He had even sent several officers privately into Asia and Egypt, to take plans of the towns and to examine into the strength of those countries. Certain it is, that if ever prince was able to overturn the Empire of the Turks and Persians, and from thence pass into Italy, it was Charles XII. He was as young as Alexander, as brave, as enterprising, more indefatigable, more robust, and more temperate; and the Swedes, perhaps, were better soldiers than the Macedonians. But such projects, which are called divine when they succeed, are regarded only as chimeras when they prove abortive.

At last, having removed every difficulty, and accomplished all his designs; having humbled the Emperor, given laws in the Empire, protected the Lutheran religion in the midst of the Catholics, dethroned one king, crowned another, and rendered himself the terror of all the princes around him, he began to prepare for his departure. The pleasures of Saxony, where he had remained inactive for a whole year, had not made the least alteration in his manner of living. He mounted his horse thrice a day, rose at four in the morning, dressed himself with his own hands, drank no wine, sat at table only a quarter of an hour, exercised his troops every day, and knew no other pleasure but that of making Europe tremble.

The Swedes were still uncertain whither their King intended to lead them. They had only some slight suspicion that he meant to go to Moscow. A few days before his departure, he ordered the grand-marshal of his household to give him in writing the route from Leipsic—. . . At that word he paused a moment; and lest the marshal should discover his project, he added with a smile—to all the capital cities of Europe. The marshal brought him a list of all these routes, at the head of which he placed, in great letters, " The route from Leipsic to Stockholm." The generality of the Swedes were extremely desirous of returning home, but the King was far from the thoughts of carrying them back to their native country. " Marshal," said he, " I plainly see whither you would lead me; but we shall not return to Stockholm so soon."

The army was already on its march, and was passing by Dresden. Charles was at the head of his men, always riding, as usual, 200 or 300 paces before his guards. All of a sudden he vanished from their sight. Some officers advanced at full gallop to see where he was. They ran in all directions, but could not find him. In a moment the alarm spread over the whole army. The troops were ordered to halt; the generals assembled together, and were already in the utmost consternation. At last they learned from a Saxon, who was passing by, what had become of the King.

As he was passing so near Dresden, he took it into his head to pay a visit to Augustus. He entered the town on horseback, followed by three or four general officers. The sentries at the gates asked them their names. Charles said his name was Karl, and that he was a Draban; and all the rest took fictitious names. Count Flemming, seeing them pass through the town, had only time to run and inform his master. All that could possibly be done on such an occasion immediately presented itself to the mind of that Minister, who laid it before Augustus. But Charles entered the chamber in his boots, before Augustus had time to recover from his surprise. Augustus was then sick, and in his night-gown, but dressed himself in a hurry. Charles breakfasted with him, as a traveller who comes to take leave of his friend; and then expressed his desire of viewing the fortifications. During the short time he employed in walking around them, a Livonian, who had been condemned in Sweden, and now served in the Saxon army, imagining that he could never find a more favorable opportunity of obtaining his pardon, entreated Augustus to ask it of Charles, being fully convinced that his Majesty would not refuse so small a favor to a prince from whom he had taken a crown, and in whose power he now was. Augustus readily undertook the charge. He was then at some distance from the King, and was conversing with Hord, a Swedish general. "I believe," said he, smiling, "your master will not refuse me." "You do not know him," replied General Hord; "he will rather refuse you here than anywhere else." Augustus, however, did not fail to prefer the petition, in very pressing terms; and Charles refused it in such a manner as to prevent a repetition of the request. After having passed some hours in this strange visit, he embraced Augustus and departed. Upon rejoining his army, he found all his generals still in consternation. They told him they had determined to besiege Dresden in case his Majesty had been detained a prisoner. "Right," said the King, "they dare not." Next day, upon hearing the news that Augustus held an extraordinary council at Dresden, "You see," said Baron Stralheim, "they are deliberating upon what they should have done yesterday." A few days later, Rehnskiöld, coming to wait upon the King, expressed his surprise at this unaccountable visit to Augustus. "I confided," said Charles, "in my good-fortune; but I have seen the moment that might have proved prejudicial to me. Flemming had no mind that I should leave Dresden so soon."

# BOOK IV

Charles Quits Saxony in a Victorious Manner—Pursues the Czar—And Shuts Himself up in the Ukraine—His Losses—His Wound—The Battle of Poltava—Consequences of that Battle—Charles Obliged to Fly into Turkey—His Reception in Bessarabia.

CHARLES at last took leave of Saxony, in September, 1707, followed by an army of 43,000 men, formerly covered with steel, but now shining with gold and silver, and enriched with the spoils of Poland and Saxony. Every soldier carried with him fifty crowns in ready money. Not only were all the regiments complete, but in every company there were several supernumeraries. Besides this army, Count Löwenhaupt, one of his best generals, waited for him in Poland with 20,000 men. He had another army of 15,000 in Finland; and fresh recruits were coming to him from Sweden. With all these forces it was not doubted but that he would easily dethrone the Czar.

That Emperor was then in Lithuania, endeavoring to reanimate a party which Augustus seemed to have abandoned. His troops, divided into several bodies, fled on all sides at the first report of the King of Sweden's approach. He himself had enjoined his generals never to wait for the conqueror with unequal forces; and he was punctually obeyed.

The King of Sweden, in the midst of his victorious march, received an ambassador from the Turks. The ambassador had his audience in Count Piper's quarters, for it was always in that minister's tent that ceremonies of pomp were performed. On these occasions he supported the dignity of his master by an appearance which had in it something magnificent; and the King, who was always worse lodged, worse served, and more plainly dressed than the meanest officer in his army, was wont to say that his palace was Piper's quarters. The Turkish ambassador presented Charles with 100 Swedish soldiers, who, having been taken by the Calmucks, and sold in Turkey, had been purchased by the Grand Seignior, and sent back by their emperor as the most acceptable present he could make to his Majesty; not that the Ottoman pride condescended to pay homage to the glory of Charles XII, but because the Sultan, the natural enemy of the Russian and German emperors, was willing to fortify himself against them by the friendship of Sweden and the alliance of Poland. The ambassador complimented Stanislaus upon his accession to the throne; so that this King was acknowledged by Germany, France, England, Spain, and Turkey. There remained only the Pope, who, before he would acknowledge him, resolved to wait till time should have settled on his head that crown of which a reverse of fortune might easily deprive it.

Charles had no sooner given audience to the ambassador of the Ottoman Porte, than he went in pursuit of the Muscovites. The Russians, in the course of the war, had quitted Poland and returned to it above twenty different times. That country, which is open on all sides, and has no places of strength to cut off the retreat of an army, gave the Muscovites an opportunity of sometimes revisiting the very spot where they had formerly been beaten, and even of penetrating as far into the heart of the kingdom as the conqueror himself. While Charles remained in Saxony, the Czar had advanced as far as Lemberg, situated at the southern extremity of Poland. Charles was then at Grodno, in Lithuania, 100 leagues to the northward of Lemberg.

He left Stanislaus in Poland to defend his new kingdom, with the assistance of 10,000 Swedes and that of his own subjects, against all his enemies, both foreign and domestic. He then put himself at the head of his cavalry, and marched amid frost and snow to Grodno, in the month of January, 1708.

He had already passed the Niemen, about two leagues from the town, and the Czar as yet knew nothing of his march. Upon the first news of the approach of the Swedish army, the Czar quitted the town by the north gate, and Charles entered it by the south. Charles had only 600 of his guards with him, the rest not being able to keep pace with his rapid march. The Czar fled with above 2,000 men, from an apprehension that a whole army was entering Grodno. That very day he was informed by a Polish deserter that he had abandoned the place to no more than 600 men, and that the main body of the army was still at the distance of five leagues. He lost no time; he detached 1,500 horse of his own troops, in the evening, to surprise the King of Sweden in the town. This detachment, under favor of darkness, arrived undiscovered at the first Swedish guard, which, though consisting only of thirteen men, sustained for half a quarter of an hour the efforts of the whole 1,500. The King, who happened to be at the other end of the town, flew to their assistance with the rest of his 600 men; upon which the Russians fled with precipitation. In a short time his army arrived, and he then set out in pursuit of the enemy. All the corps of the Russian army, dispersed through Lithuania, retired hastily into the Palatinate of Minsk, near the frontiers of Muscovy, where their general rendezvous was appointed. The Swedes, who were likewise divided into several bodies, continued to pursue the enemy for more than thirty leagues. The fugitives and the pursuers made forced marches almost every day, though in the middle of winter. For a long time past, all seasons of the year had become the same to Swedes and Russians; and the only difference between them now arose from the terror of Charles's arms.

From Grodno to the Borysthenes, eastward, there is nothing but morasses, deserts, and immense forests. In the cultivated spots there are no provisions to be had, the peasants burying under ground all their grain, and whatever else can be preserved in their subterranean receptacles. In order to discover these hidden magazines, the earth must be pierced with long poles pointed with iron. The Muscovites and the Swedes alternately made use of these provisions; but they were not always to be found, and even then they were not sufficient.

The King of Sweden, who had foreseen these difficulties, had provided biscuit for the subsistence of his army, and nothing could stop him in his march. After having traversed the forest of Minsk, where he was every moment obliged to cut down trees in order to clear the road for his troops and baggage, he found himself, on June 25, 1708, on the banks of the River Beresina, opposite to Borizof.

In that place the Czar had assembled the best part of his forces, and intrenched himself to great advantage. His design was to hinder the Swedes from crossing the river. Charles posted some regiments on the banks of the Beresina, over against Borizof, as if he meant to attempt a passage in the face of the enemy. Meanwhile he led his army three leagues higher up the river, threw a bridge across it, cut his way through a body of 3,000 men who defended that pass, and, without halting, marched against the main body of the enemy. The Russians did not wait his approach, but decamped and retreated toward the Borysthenes, spoiling all the roads and destroying everything in their way, in order, at least, to retard the progress of the Swedes.

Charles surmounted every obstacle, and still advanced toward the Borysthenes. In his way he met with 20,000 Muscovites, intrenched in a place called Holowczyn, behind a morass, which could not be approached without passing a river. Charles did not delay the attack till the rest of his infantry should arrive. He plunged into the water at the head of his foot-guards, and crossed the river and the morass, the water frequently reaching above his shoulders. While he was thus pressing forward to the enemy, he ordered his cavalry to go round the morass and take them in flank. The Muscovites, surprised that no barrier could defend them, were instantly routed by the King, who attacked them on foot, and by the Swedish cavalry.

The horse, having forced their way through the enemy, joined the King in the midst of the battle. He then mounted on horseback; but some time after, observing in the field a young Swedish gentleman, named Gyllenstiern, for whom he had a great regard, wounded and unable to walk, he forced him to take his horse, and continued to command on foot at the head of his infantry. Of all the battles he had ever fought, this was perhaps the most glorious; this was the one in which he encountered the greatest dangers and displayed the most consummate skill and prudence. The memory of it is still preserved by a medal, with this inscription on one side: *Sylvæ, paludes, aggeres, nostes victi;* and on the other this verse of Lucan: *Victrices copias alium laturus in orbem.*

The Russians, chased from all their posts, repassed the Borysthenes, which divides Poland from Muscovy. Charles did not give over the pursuit, but followed them across the Borysthenes, which he passed at Mohilev, the last town of Poland, and which sometimes belongs to the Poles, and sometimes to the Russians—a fate common to frontier places.

The Czar thus seeing his empire, where he had lately established the fine arts and a flourishing trade, exposed to a war, which, in a short time, might overturn all his mighty projects, and perhaps deprive him of his crown, began to think seriously of peace, and accordingly ventured to make some proposals for that purpose, by means of a Polish gentleman, whom he sent to the Swedish army. Charles XII, who had not been used to grant peace to his enemies, except in their own capitals, replied, "I will treat with the Czar at Moscow." When this haughty answer was reported to the Czar, "My brother Charles," said he, "always affects to act the Alexander; but, I flatter myself, he will not find in me another Darius."

From Mohilev, the place where the King passed the Borysthenes, as you advance toward the north, along the banks of the river, and always on the frontiers of Poland and Muscovy, you meet with the country of Smolensk, through which lies the great road that leads from Poland to Muscovy. This way the Czar directed his flight; and the King pursued him by long marches. Part of the Russian rear-guard was frequently engaged with the dragoons of the Swedish vanguard. The latter had generally the advantage; but they weakened themselves even by conquering in these small skirmishes, which were never decisive, and in which they always lost a number of men.

On September 22, 1708, the King attacked, near Smolensk, a body of 10,000 horse and 6,000 Calmucks.

These Calmucks are Tartars, living between the Kingdom of Astrakhan, which is subject to the Czar, and that of Samarcand, belonging to the Usbeck Tartars, and the country of Timur, known by the name of Tamerlane. The country of the Calmucks extends eastward to the mountains which divide Mongolia from western Asia. Those who inhabit that part of the country which borders upon Astrakhan, are tributary to the Czar, who pretends to an absolute authority over them; but their vagrant life hinders him from making good his claim, and obliges him to treat them in the same manner in which the Grand Seignior treats the Arabs, sometimes conniving at and sometimes punishing their robberies. There are always some of these Calmucks in the Russian army; and the Czar had even reduced them to a regular discipline, like the rest of his soldiers.

The King attacked these troops with only six regiments of

horse and 4,000 foot; broke their ranks at the first onset, at the head of his Ostrogothic regiment, and obliged them to fly. He pursued them through rugged and hollow ways, where the Calmucks lay concealed, who soon began to show themselves and cut off the regiment in which the King fought from the rest of the Swedish army. In an instant the Russians and Calmucks surrounded this regiment, and penetrated even to the King. Two aides-de-camp who fought near him fell at his feet. The King's horse was killed under him; and as one of his equerries was presenting him with another, both the equerry and horse were struck dead upon the spot. Charles fought on foot, surrounded by some of his officers, who instantly flocked around him.

Many of them were taken, wounded or slain, or pushed to a great distance from the King by the crowds that assailed them; so that he was left at last with no more than five attendants. With his own hand he had killed above a dozen of the enemy, without receiving a single wound, owing to that surprising good-fortune which had hitherto attended him, and upon which he always relied. At length a colonel, named Dahldorf, forced his way through the Calmucks, with a single company of his regiment, and arrived in time to save the King. The rest of the Swedes put the Tartars to the sword. The army recovered its rank; Charles mounted his horse, and, fatigued as he was, pursued the Russians for two leagues.

The conqueror was still in the great road to the capital of Muscovy. The distance from Smolensk, near which the battle was fought, to Moscow, is about 100 French leagues; and the army began to be in want of provision. The officers earnestly entreated the King to wait till General Löwenhaupt, who was coming up with a reinforcement of 15,000 men, should arrive. The King, who seldom indeeed took counsel of anyone, not only rejected this wholesome advice, but, to the great astonishment of all the army, quitted the road to Moscow, and began to march southward toward the Ukraine, the country of the Cossacks, lying between Little Tartary, Poland, and Muscovy. This country extends about 100 French leagues from south to north, and almost as many from east to west. It is divided into two parts, almost equal, by the Borythenes, which runs from the northwest to the southeast. The chief town is called Baturim, and is situated upon the little River Sem. The northern part of the Ukraine is rich and well cultivated. The southern, lying in the forty-eighth degree of latitude, is one of the most fertile countries in the world, and yet one of the most desolate. Its bad form of government stifles in embryo, as it were, all the blessings which nature, if properly encouraged, would shower down upon the inhabitants. The people of these cantons, neighboring Little Tartary, neither sow nor plant, because the Tartars of Budziack[?] and Perekop, and the Moldavians, all of them brigands, would rob them of their harvests.

The Ukraine has always aspired to liberty, but being surrounded by Muscovy, the dominions of the Grand Seignior, and Poland, it has been obliged to choose a protector, and, consequently, a master, in one of these three States. The Ukrainians at first put themselves under the protection of the Poles, who treated them with great severity. They afterward submitted to the Russians, who governed them with despotic sway. They had originally the privilege of electing a prince under the name of general; but they were soon deprived of that right, and their general was nominated by the Court of Moscow.

The person who then filled that station was a Polish gentleman, named Mazeppa, and born in the Palatinate of Podolia. He had been brought up as a page to John Casimir, and had received some tincture of learning in his court. An intrigue, which he had had in his youth with the lady of a Polish gentleman, having been discovered, the husband caused him to be bound stark-naked upon a wild horse, and let him go in that condition. The horse, which had been brought out of the Ukraine, returned to its own country, and carried Mazeppa along with it, half dead with hunger and fatigue. Some of the country people gave him assistance; and he lived among them for a long time, and signalized himself in several excursions against the Tartars. The superiority of his knowledge gained him great respect among the Cossacks; and his reputation daily increasing, the Czar found it necessary to make him Prince of the Ukraine.

While he was one day at the table with the Czar at Moscow, the Emperor proposed to him to discipline the Cossacks, and to render them more dependent. Mazeppa replied that the situation of the Ukraine and the genius of the nation were insuperable obstacles to such a scheme. The Czar, who began to be overheated with wine, and who had not always the command of his passions, called him a traitor, and threatened to have him impaled.

Mazeppa, on his return to the Ukraine, formed the design of a revolt; and the execution of it was greatly facilitated by the Swedish army, which soon after appeared on his frontiers. He resolved to render himself independent, and to erect the Ukraine and some other ruins of the Russian Empire into a powerful kingdom. Brave, enterprising, and indefatigable, though advanced in years, he entered into a secret league with the King of Sweden, to hasten the downfall of the Czar, and to convert it to his own advantage.

The King appointed the rendezvous near the River Desna. Mazeppa promised to meet him there at the head of 30,000 men, with ammunition and provisions, and all his treasures, which were immense. The Swedish army therefore continued its march on that side, to the great grief of all the officers, who knew nothing of the King's treaty with the Cossacks. Charles sent orders to Löwenhaupt to bring his troops and provisions with all possible despatch into the Ukraine, where he proposed to pass the winter, that, having once secured that country, he might the more easily conquer Muscovy in the ensuing spring; and, in the meantime, he advanced toward the River Desna, which falls into the Borysthenes at Kiev.

The obstructions they had hitherto found in their march were but trifling, in comparison with what they encountered in this new road. They were obliged to cross a marshy forest fifty leagues in length. General Lagercrona, who marched before with 5,000 soldiers and pioneers, led the army astray to the eastward, thirty leagues from the right road. It was not till after a march of four days that the King discovered the mistake. With great difficulty they regained the main road; but almost all their artillery and wagons were lost, being either stuck fast or quite sunk in the mud.

At last, after a march of twelve days, attended with so many vexations and untoward circumstances, during which they had consumed the small quantity of biscuit that was left, the army, exhausted with hunger and fatigue, arrived on the banks of the Desna, in the very spot which Mazeppa had marked out as the place of rendezvous; but instead of meeting with that prince, they found a body of Muscovites advancing toward the other bank of the river. The King was astonished, but resolved immediately to pass the Desna and attack the enemy. The banks of the river were so steep that they were obliged to let the soldiers down with ropes. They crossed it in their usual manner, some on floats, which were made in haste, and others by swimming. The body of Muscovites which arrived at the same time did not exceed 8,000 men; so that it made but little resistance, and this obstacle was also surmounted.

Charles advanced farther into this desolate country, alike uncertain of his road and of Mazeppa's fidelity. That Cossack appeared at last, but rather like a fugitive than a powerful ally. The Muscovites had discovered and defeated his design; they had fallen upon the Cossacks and cut them in pieces. His principal friends, being taken sword in hand, had, to the number of thirty, been broken upon the wheel; his towns were reduced to ashes; his treasures plundered; the provisions he was preparing for the King of Sweden seized; and it was with great difficulty that he himself made his escape with 6,000 men, and some horses laden with gold and silver. However, he gave the King some hopes that he should be able to assist him by his intelligence in that unknown country, and by the affection of all the Cossacks, who, being enraged against the Russians, flocked to the camp and supplied the army with provisions.

Charles hoped that General Löwenhaupt at least would come and repair this misfortune. He was to bring with him about 15,000 Swedes, who were better than 100,000 Cossacks, together with ammunition and provisions. At length he arrived, in much the same condition, with Mazeppa.

He had already passed the Borysthenes above Mohilev, and advanced twenty leagues beyond it, on the road to the Ukraine. He was bringing the King a convoy of 8,000 wagons, with the money which he had levied in his march through Lithuania. As he approached the town of Liesna, near the conflux of the rivers Pronia and Sossa, which fall into the Borysthenes far below, the Czar appeared at the head of nearly 40,000 men.

The Swedish general, who had not 16,000 complete, scorned to shelter himself in a fortified camp. A long train of victories had inspired the Swedes with so much confidence that they never informed themselves of the number of their enemies, but only of the place where they lay. Accordingly, on October 7, 1708, in the afternoon, Löwenhaupt advanced against them with great resolution. In the first attack the Swedes killed 1,500 Russians. The Czar's army was thrown into confusion and fled on all sides. The Emperor of Russia saw himself upon the point of being entirely defeated. He was sensible that the safety of his dominions depended upon the success of this day, and that he would be utterly ruined should Löwenhaupt join the King of Sweden with a victorious army.

The moment he saw his troops begin to flinch, he ran to the rear-guard, where the Cossacks and Calmucks were posted. "I charge you," said he to them, "to fire upon everyone that runs away, and even to kill me should I be so cowardly as to fly." From thence he returned to the vanguard, and rallied his troops in person, assisted by the princes Mentchikof and Gallitzin. Löwenhaupt, who had received strict orders to rejoin his master, chose rather to continue his march than renew the battle, imagining he had done enough to prevent the enemy from pursuing him.

Next morning, about eleven o'clock, the Czar attacked him near a morass and extended his lines with a view to surround him. The Swedes faced about on all sides; and the battle was maintained for the space of two hours with equal courage and obstinacy. The loss of the Muscovites was three times greater than that of the Swedes; the former, however, still kept their ground, and the victory was left undecided.

At four in the afternoon, General Bayer brought the Czar a reinforcement of troops. The battle was then renewed for the third time with more fury and eagerness than ever, and lasted till night put an end to the combat. At last superior numbers prevailed, the Swedes were broken, routed, and driven back to their baggage. Löwenhaupt rallied his troops behind the wagons. The Swedes were conquered, but disdained to fly. They were still about 9,000 in number, and not so much as one of them deserted. The general drew them up with as much ease as if they had not been vanquished. The Czar, on the other side, remained all night under arms, and forbade his officers, under pain of being cashiered, and his soldiers, under pain of death, to leave their ranks for the sake of plunder.

Next morning, at daybreak, he ordered a fresh assault. Löwenhaupt had retired to an advantageous situation, at the distance of a few miles, after having spiked part of his cannon and set fire to his wagons.

The Muscovites arrived in time to prevent the whole convoy from being consumed by the flames. They seized about 6,000 wagons, which they saved. The Czar, desirous of completing the defeat of the Swedes, sent one of his generals, named Phlug, to attack them again for the fifth time. That general offered them an honorable capitulation. Löwenhaupt refused it, and fought a fifth battle, as bloody as any of the former. Of the 9,000 soldiers he had left, he lost about one-half in this action and the other remained unbroken. At last, night coming on, Löwenhaupt, after having sustained five battles against 40,000 * men, passed the Sossa with about 5,000 soldiers that remained. The Czar lost about 10,000 men in these five engagements, in which he had the glory of conquering the Swedes, and Löwenhaupt that of disputing the victory for three days and of effecting a retreat, without being obliged to surrender. Thus he arrived in his master's camp with the honor of having made such a noble defence, but bringing with him neither ammunition nor an army.

By these means Charles found himself destitute of provisions, cut off from all communication with Poland, and surrounded with enemies, in the heart of a country where he had no resource but his own courage.

In this extremity, the memorable winter of 1709, which was still more terrible in those quarters of the world than in France, destroyed part of his army. Charles resolved to brave the seasons, as he had done his enemies, and ventured to make long marches with his troops during this mortal cold. It was in one of these marches that 2,000 men fell dead with cold before his eyes. The dragoons had no boots and the foot-soldiers were without shoes and almost without clothes. They were forced to make stockings of the skins of wild beasts in the best manner they could. They were frequently in want of bread. They were obliged to throw almost all their cannon into the marshes and rivers, for want of horses to draw them; so that this army, which was once so flourishing, was reduced to 24,000 men ready

---

* In his History of Russia, Voltaire reduces this number to 20,000.

to perish with hunger. They no longer received any news from Sweden nor were able to send any thither. In this condition only one officer complained. "What," said the King to him, " are you uneasy at being so far from your wife? If you are a good soldier I will lead you to such a distance that you shall hardly be able to receive news from Sweden once in three years."

The Marquis de Brancas, afterward ambassador in Sweden, told me that a soldier ventured, in presence of the whole army, to present to the King, with an air of complaint, a piece of bread that was black and mouldy, made of barley and oats, which was the only food they then had, and of which they had not even a sufficient quantity. The King received the bit of bread without the least emotion, ate it up, and then said coldly to the soldier, " It is not good, but it may be eaten." This incident, trifling as it is, if, indeed, anything that increases respect and confidence can be said to be trifling, contributed more than all the rest to make the Swedish army support those hardships which would have been intolerable under any other general.

While he was in this situation he at last received a packet from Stockholm by which he was informed of the death of his sister, the Duchess of Holstein, who was carried off by the small-pox, in the month of December, 1708, in the twenty-seventh year of her age. She was a princess as mild and gentle as her brother was imperious in his disposition and implacable in his revenge. He had always entertained a great affection for her, and was the more afflicted with her death, that now beginning to taste of misfortunes himself, he had become the more susceptible of tender impressions.

By this packet he was likewise informed that they had raised money and troops, in obedience to his orders; but nothing could reach his camp, as between him and Stockholm there were nearly 500 leagues to travel and an enemy superior in number to engage.

The Czar, who was as active as the King of Sweden, after having sent some fresh troops to the assistance of the confederates in Poland, who, under the command of General Siniawski, exerted their joint efforts against Stanislaus, immediately advanced into the Ukraine in the midst of this severe winter, to make head against his Swedish Majesty. Then he continued to pursue the political scheme he had formed of weakening his enemy by petty rencounters, wisely judging that the Swedish army must, in the end, be entirely ruined, as it could not possibly be recruited. The cold must certainly have been very severe, as it obliged the two monarchs to agree to a suspension of arms. But on the first of February they renewed their military operations, in the midst of frost and snow.

After several slight skirmishes and some losses the King perceived, in the month of April, that he had only 18,000 Swedes remaining. Mazeppa, the prince of the Cossacks, supplied them with provisions; without his assistance the army must have perished with want and hunger. At this conjuncture, the Czar made proposals to Mazeppa for submitting again to his authority. But whether it was that the terrible punishment of the wheel, by which his friends had perished, made the Cossack apprehend the same danger for himself, or that he was desirous of revenging their death, he continued faithful to his new ally.

Charles, with his 18,000 Swedes, had neither laid aside the design nor the hopes of penetrating to Moscow. Toward the end of May he laid siege to Poltava, upon the River Vorskla, at the eastern extremity of the Ukraine, and thirty leagues from the Borysthenes. This country is inhabited by the Zaporogues, the most remarkable people in the universe. They are a collection of ancient Russians, Poles, and Tartars, professing a species of Christianity and exercising a kind of freebooting somewhat akin to that of the buccaneers. They choose a chief, whom they frequently depose or strangle. They allow no women to live among them, but they carry off all the children for twenty or thirty leagues around and bring them up in their own manners. The summer they always pass in the open fields; in winter they shelter themselves in large barns, containing 4,000 or 5,000 men. They fear nothing; they live free; they brave death for the smallest booty, with as much intrepidity as Charles XII did, in order to obtain the power of bestowing crowns. The Czar gave them 60,000 florins, hoping by this means to engage them in his interest. They took his money, and, influenced by the powerful eloquence of Mazeppa, declared in favor of Charles XII; but their service was of very little consequence, as they think it the most egregious folly to fight for anything but plunder. It was no small advantage, however, that they were prevented from doing harm. The number of their troops was, at most, but about 2,000. One morning ten of their chiefs were presented to the King; but it was with great difficulty they could be prevailed upon to remain sober, as they commonly begin the day by getting drunk. They were brought to the intrenchments, where they showed their dexterity in firing with long carbines; for being placed upon the mounds, they killed such of the enemy as they picked out at the distance of 200 paces. To these banditti Charles added some thousands of Wallachians, whom he had hired from the Khan of Little Tartary, and thus laid siege to Poltava, with all these troops of Zaporogues, Cossacks, and Wallachians, which, joined to his 18,000 Swedes, composed an army of about 30,000 men; but an army in a wretched condition and in want of everything. The Czar had formed a magazine in Poltava. If the King should take it, he would open himself a way to Moscow, and be able, at least, amid the great abundance he would then possess, to wait the arrival of the succors which he still expected from Sweden, Livonia, Pomerania, and Poland. His only resource, therefore, being in the conquest of Poltava, he pressed the siege of it with great vigor. Mazeppa, who carried on a correspondence with some of the citizens, assured him that he would soon be master of it; and his assurance revived the hopes of the soldiers, who considered the taking of Poltava as the end of all their miseries.

The King perceived, from the beginning of the siege, that he had taught his enemies the art of war. In spite of all his precautions, Prince Mentchikof threw some fresh troops into the town; by which means the garrison was rendered almost 5,000 strong.

They made several sallies, and sometimes with success. They likewise sprung a mine; but what saved the town from being taken was the approach of the Czar, who was advancing with 70,000 men. Charles went to reconnoitre them on June 27th, which happened to be his birthday, and beat one of their detachments; but as he was returning to his camp he received a shot from a carbine, which pierced his boot and shattered the bone of his heel. There was not the least alteration observable in his countenance, from which it could be suspected that he had received a wound. He continued to give orders with great composure, and after this accident remained almost six hours on horseback. One of his domestics observing that the sole of the King's boot was bloody, made haste to call the surgeons; and the pain had now become so severe that they were obliged to assist him in dismounting and to carry him to his tent. The surgeons examined the wound, and were of opinion that the leg must be cut off, which threw the army into the utmost consternation. But one of the surgeons, named Newman, who had more skill and courage than the rest, affirmed that, by making deep incisions, he could save the King's leg. "Fall to work then presently," said the King to him: "cut boldly and fear nothing." He himself held the leg with both his hands and beheld the incisions that were made in it as if the operation had been performed upon another person.

As they were laying on the dressing, he ordered an assault to be made the next morning; but he had hardly given these orders when he was informed that the whole army of the enemy was advancing against him; in consequence of which he was obliged to alter his resolution. Charles, wounded and incapable of acting, saw himself cooped up between the Borysthenes and the river that runs to Poltava, in a desert country, without any places of security or ammunition, in the face of an army which at once cut off his retreat and prevented his being supplied with provisions. In this extremity he did not assemble a council of war, as, considering the perplexed situation of his affairs, he ought to have done, but on the seventh or eighth of July, in the evening, he sent for Field Marshal Rehnskiöld to his tent, and without deliberation or the least discomposure ordered him to make the necessary dispositions for attacking the Czar next day. Rehnskiöld made no objections and went to carry his orders into execution. At the door of the King's tent he met Count Piper, with whom he had long lived on very bad terms, as frequently happens between the minister and the general. Piper asked him whether he had any news. "No," said the general, coldly, and passed on to give his orders. As soon as Count Piper had entered the tent, "Has Rehnskiöld told you nothing?" the King said. "Nothing," replied Piper. "Well, then," resumed he, "I tell you that we shall give battle to-morrow." Count Piper was astonished at such a desperate resolution, but well knowing that it was impossible to make his master change his mind, he expressed his surprise only by his silence and left Charles to sleep till break of day.

It was on July 8, 1709, that the decisive battle of Poltava was fought between the two most famous monarchs that were then in the world: Charles XII, illustrious for nine years of victories; Peter Alexiovitch, for nine years of pains taken to form troops equal to those of Sweden: the one glorious for having given away dominions, the other for having civilized his own: Charles, fond of dangers, and fighting for glory alone; Alexiovitch, scorning to fly from danger, and never making war but from interested views: the Swedish monarch, liberal from an innate greatness of soul; the Muscovite, never granting favors but in order to serve some particular people: the former a prince of uncommon sobriety and continence, naturally magnanimous, and never cruel but once; the latter having not yet worn off the roughness of his education or the barbarity of his country, as much the object of terror to his subjects as of admiration to strangers, and too prone to excesses, which even shortened his days. Charles had the title of "Invincible," of which a single moment might deprive him; the neighboring nations had already given Peter Alexiovitch the name of "Great," which, as he did not owe it to his victories, he could not forfeit by a defeat.

In order to form a distinct idea of this battle and the place where it was fought we must figure to ourselves Poltava on the north, the camp of the King of Sweden on the south, stretching a little toward the east, his baggage about a mile behind him, and the river of Poltava on the north of the town, running from east to west.

The Czar had passed the river about a league from Poltava, toward the west, and was beginning to form his camp.

At break of day the Swedes appeared before the trenches with four iron cannon for their whole artillery; the rest were left in the camp, with about 3,000 men, and 4,000 remained with the baggage; so that the Swedish army which advanced against the enemy consisted of about 21,000 men, of which about 16,000 only were regular troops.

The generals Rehnskiöld, Roos, Löwenhaupt, Schlippenbach, Horn, Sparr, Hamilton, the Prince of Würtemberg, the

King's relation, and some others, who had most of them seen the battle of Narva, put the subaltern officers in mind of that day, when 8,000 Swedes defeated an army of 80,000 Muscovites in their intrenchments. The officers exhorted the soldiers by the same motive, and as they advanced they all encouraged one another.

Charles, carried in a litter at the head of his infantry, conducted the march. A party of horse advanced by his orders to attack that of the enemy, and the battle began with this engagement at half an hour past four in the morning. The enemy's horse was posted toward the west, on the right side of the Russian camp. Prince Mentchikof and Count Gollovin had placed them at certain distances between redoubts lined with cannon. General Schlippenbach, at the head of the Swedes, rushed upon them. All those who have served in the Swedish troops are sensible that it is almost impossible to withstand the fury of their first attack. The Muscovite squadrons were broken and routed. The Czar ran up to rally them in person; his hat was pierced with a musket-shell; Mentchikof had three horses killed under him; and the Swedes cried out, "Victory!"

Charles did not doubt that the battle was gained. About midnight he had sent General Creutz with 5,000 horse or dragoons to take the enemy in flank while he attacked them in front; but as his ill-fortune would have it, Creutz mistook his way and did not make his appearance. The Czar, who thought he was ruined, had time to rally his cavalry, and in his turn fell upon that of the King, which, not being supported by the detachment of Creutz, was likewise broken. Schlippenbach was taken prisoner in this engagement. At the same time seventy-two pieces of cannon played from the camp upon the cavalry, and the Russian foot, opening their lines, advanced to attack Charles's infantry.

After this the Czar detached Prince Mentchikof to go and take post between Poltava and the Swedes. Prince Mentchikof executed his master's orders with dexterity and expedition. He not only cut off the communication between the Swedish army and the camp before Poltava, but, having met with a corps of reserve, he surrounded them and cut them to pieces. If Mentchikof performed this exploit of his own accord Russia is indebted to him for its preservation: if it was by the orders of the Czar he was an adversary worthy of Charles XII. Meanwhile the Russian infantry came out of their lines and advanced into the plain in order of battle. On the other hand, the Swedish cavalry rallied within a quarter of a league from the enemy, and the King, assisted by Field Marshal Rehnskiöld, made the necessary dispositions for a general engagement.

He ranged the few troops that were left him in two lines, his infantry occupying the centre and his cavalry forming the two wings. The Czar disposed his army in the same manner. He had the advantage of numbers and of seventy-two pieces of cannon, while the Swedes had no more than four to oppose him and began to be in want of powder.

The Emperor of Muscovy was in the centre of his army, having then only the title of major-general, and seemed to obey General Sheremetef. But he rode from rank to rank in the character of emperor, mounted on a Turkish horse, which had been given him as a present by the Grand Seignior, animating the captains and soldiers, and promising rewards to them all.

At nine in the morning the battle was renewed. One of the first discharges of the Russian cannon carried off the two horses of Charles's litter. He caused two others to be immediately put to it. A second discharge broke the litter in pieces and overturned the King. Of four-and-twenty Drabans, who mutually relieved each other in carrying him, one-and-twenty were killed. The Swedes, struck with consternation, began to stagger; and the cannon of the enemy continuing to mow them down, the first line fell back upon the second and the second began to fly. In this last action it was only a single line of 10,000 Russian infantry that routed the Swedish army: so much were matters changed!

All the Swedish writers allege that they would have gained the battle if they had not committed several blunders; but all the officers affirm that it was a great blunder to give battle at all, and a greater still to shut themselves up in a desert country, against the advice of the most prudent generals, in opposition to a warlike enemy three times stronger than Charles, both in number of men and in the many resources from which the Swedes were entirely cut off. The remembrance of Narva was the chief cause of Charles's misfortune at Poltava.

The Prince of Würtemberg, General Rehnskiöld, and several principal officers, were already made prisoners; the camp before Poltava was stormed, and all was thrown into a confusion which it was impossible to rectify. Count Piper, with some officers of the chancery, had left the camp, and neither knew what to do nor what had become of the King, but ran about from one corner of the field to another. A major, called Bere, offered to conduct them to the baggage, but the clouds of dust and smoke which covered the plain and the dissipation of mind so natural amid such a desolation brought them straight to the counterscarp of the town, where they were all made prisoners by the garrison.

The King scorned to fly, and yet was unable to defend himself. General Poniatowski happened to be near him at that instant. He was a colonel of Stanislaus's Swedish guards, a man of extraordinary merit, and had been induced, from his strong attachment to the person of Charles, to follow him into the Ukraine, without any post in the army. He was a man who, in all the occurrences of life and amid those dangers when others would at most have displayed their courage, always took his measures with despatch, prudence, and success. He made a sign to two Drabans, who took the King under the arm and placed him on his horse, notwithstanding the excruciating pain of his wounds.

Poniatowski, though he had no command in the army, became, on this occasion, a general through necessity and drew up 500 horse near the King's person—some of them Drabans, others officers, and a few private troopers. This body being assembled and animated by the misfortune of their prince, forced their way through more than ten Russian regiments and conducted Charles through the midst of the enemy for the space of a league to the baggage of the Swedish army.

Charles, being closely pursued in his flight, had his horse killed under him; and Colonel Gierta, though wounded and spent with loss of blood, gave him his. Thus in the course of the flight they twice put this conqueror on horseback, though he had not been able to mount a horse during the engagement.

This surprising retreat was of great consequence in such distressful circumstances, but he was obliged to fly a still greater distance. They found Count Piper's coach among the baggage, for the King had never used one since he left Stockholm. They put him into this vehicle and fled toward the Borysthenes with great precipitation. The King, who, from the time of his being set on horseback till his arrival at the baggage, had not spoken a single word, at length inquired what had become of Count Piper? They told him he was taken prisoner, with all the officers of the chancery. "And General Rehnskiöld and the Duke of Würtemberg?" added the King. "Yes," said Poniatowski. "Prisoners to the Russians!" resumed Charles, shrugging up his shoulders. "Come, then, let us rather go to the Turks." They could not perceive, however, the least mark of dejection in his countenance; and had anyone seen him at that time, without knowing his situation, he would never have suspected that he was conquered and wounded.

While he was getting off, the Russians seized his artillery in the camp before Poltava, his baggage, and his military chest, in which they found 6,000,000 in specie, the spoils of Poland and Saxony. Nine thousand men, partly Swedes and partly Cossacks, were killed in the battle and about 6,000 taken prisoners. There still remained about 16,000 men, including the Swedes, Poles, and Cossacks, who fled toward the Borysthenes, under the conduct of General Löwenhaupt. He marched one way with these fugitive troops and the King took another road with some of his horse. The coach in which he rode broke down by the way and they again set him on horseback; and, to complete his misfortune, he wandered all night in a wood, where, his courage being no longer able to support his exhausted spirits, the pain of his wound becoming more intolerable through fatigue and his horse falling under him through excessive weariness, he lay some hours at the foot of a tree, in danger of being surprised every moment by the conquerors, who were searching for him on all sides.

At last on the ninth or tenth of July, at night, he found himself on the banks of the Borysthenes. Löwenhaupt had just arrived with the shattered remains of the army. It was with an equal mixture of joy and sorrow that the Swedes again beheld their King, whom they thought to be dead. The enemy was approaching. The Swedes had neither a bridge to pass the river, nor time to make one, nor powder to defend themselves, nor provisions to support an army, which had eaten nothing for two days. But the remains of this army were Swedes and the conquered king was Charles XII. Most of the officers imagined that they were to halt there for the Russians, without flinching, and that they would either conquer or die on the banks of the Borysthenes. Charles would undoubtedly have taken this resolution had he not been exhausted with weakness. His wound had now come to a suppuration, attended with a fever; and it has been remarked that men of the greatest intrepidity, when seized with the fever that is common in a suppuration, lose that impulse to valor, which, like all other virtues, requires the direction of a clear head. Charles was no longer himself. This, at least, is what I have been well assured of, and what, indeed, is extremely probable. They carried him along like a sick person in a state of insensibility. Happily there was still left a sorry calash, which by chance they had brought along with them: this they put on board of a little boat and the King and General Mazeppa embarked in another. The latter had saved several coffers full of money; but the current being rapid, and a violent wind beginning to blow, the Cossack threw more than three-fourths of his treasures into the river to lighten the boat. Muller, the King's chancellor, and Count Poniatowski, a man more necessary to the King than ever, on account of his admirable dexterity in finding expedients in difficulties, crossed over in other barks with some officers. Three hundred troopers of the King's guard and a great number of Poles and Cossacks, trusting to the goodness of their horses, ventured to cross the river by swimming. Their troop, keeping close together, resisted the current and broke the waves; but all those who attempted to pass separately, a little below, were carried down by the stream and sunk in the river. Of all the foot who attempted to pass, there was not a single man that reached the other side.

While the shattered remains of the army were in this extremity, Prince Mentchikof came up with 10,000 horsemen, having each a foot-soldier behind him. The carcasses of the Swedes who had died by the way, of their wounds, fatigue, and hunger, showed Prince Mentchikof but too plainly the road which the fugitive army had taken. The prince sent a trumpet to the Swedish general to offer him a capitulation. Four general officers were presently despatched by Löwenhaupt to receive the commands of the conqueror. Before that day, 16,000 soldiers of King Charles would have attacked the whole forces of the Russian Empire, and would have perished to a man rather than surrender. But after the loss of a battle and a flight of two days—deprived of the presence of their prince, who was himself constrained to fly—the strength of every soldier being exhausted, and their courage no longer supported by the least prospect of relief, the love of life overcame their natural intrepidity. Colonel Troutfetre alone, observing the Muscovites approach, began to advance with one Swedish battalion to attack them, hoping, by this means, to induce the rest of the troops to follow his example. But Löwenhaupt was obliged to oppose this unavailing ardor. The capitulation was settled and the whole army were made prisoners of war. Some soldiers, reduced to despair at the thoughts of falling into the hands of the Muscovites, threw themselves into the Borysthenes. Two officers of the regiment commanded by the brave Troutfetre killed each other and the rest were made slaves. They all filed off in the presence of Prince Mentchikof, laying their arms at his feet, as 30,000 Muscovites had done nine years before at those of the King of Sweden, at Narva. But whereas the King sent back all the Russians whom he did not fear, the Czar retained the Swedes that were taken at Poltava.

These unhappy creatures were afterward dispersed through the Czar's dominions, particularly in Siberia, a vast province of Great Tartary, which extends eastward to the frontiers of the Chinese Empire. In this barbarous country, where even the use of bread was unknown, the Swedes, who had become ingenious through necessity, exercised the trades and employments of which they had the least notion. All the distinctions which fortune makes among men were there banished. The officer who could not follow any trade was obliged to cleave and carry wood for the soldier, now turned tailor, clothier, joiner, mason, or goldsmith, and who got a subsistence by his labor. Some of the officers became painters and others architects. Some of them taught the languages and mathematics. They even established some public schools, which, in time, became so useful and famous that the citizens of Moscow sent their children thither for education.

Count Piper, the King of Sweden's first minister, was for a

long time confined in prison at Petersburg. The Czar was persuaded, as well as the rest of Europe, that this minister had sold his master to the Duke of Marlborough and drawn on Muscovy the arms of Sweden, which might have given peace to Europe; for which reason he rendered his confinement the more severe. Piper died in Muscovy a few years after, little assisted by his own family, which lived in opulence at Stockholm, and vainly lamented by his sovereign, who would never condescend to offer a ransom for his minister, which he feared the Czar would not accept; for no cartel of exchange had ever been settled between them.

The Emperor of Muscovy, elated with a joy which he was at no pains to conceal, received upon the field of battle the prisoners, whom they brought to him in crowds, and asked every moment, " Where, then, is my brother Charles? "

He did the Swedish generals the honor of inviting them to dine with him. Among other questions which he put to them, he asked General Rehnskiöld what might be the number of his master's troops before the battle? Rehnskiöld answered that the King always kept the muster-roll himself, and would never show it to anyone; but that, for his own part, he imagined the whole might be about 30,000, of which 18,000 were Swedes and the rest Cossacks. The Czar seemed to be surprised, and asked how they dared venture to penetrate into so distant a country and lay siege to Poltava with such a handful of men? " We were not always consulted," replied the Swedish general; " but, like faithful servants, we obeyed our master's orders, without ever presuming to contradict them." The Czar, upon receiving this answer, turned about to some of his courtiers, who were formerly suspected of having engaged in a conspiracy against him: " Ah," said he, " see how a king should be served; " and then taking his glass of wine, " To the health," said he, " of my masters in the art of war." Rehnskiöld asked him who were the persons whom he honored with so high a title? " You, gentlemen, the Swedish generals," replied the Czar. " Your Majesty, then," resumed the count, " is very ungrateful to treat your masters with so much severity." After dinner the Czar caused their swords to be restored to all the general officers, and behaved to them like a prince who had a mind to give his subjects a lesson of generosity and politeness, with which he was well acquainted. But this same prince, who treated the Swedish generals with so much humanity, caused all the Cossacks that fell into his hands to be broken upon the wheel.

Thus the Swedish army, which left Saxony in such a triumphant manner, was now no more. One half of them had perished with hunger and the other half were either massacred or made slaves. Charles XII had lost in one day the fruit of nine years' labor and of almost a hundred battles. He made his escape in a wretched calash, attended by Major-General Hord, who was dangerously wounded. The rest of his troop followed, some on foot, some on horseback, and others in wagons, through a desert, where neither huts, tents, men, beasts, nor roads were to be seen; everything was wanting, even to water itself. It was now the beginning of July; the country lay in the forty-seventh degree of latitude; the dry sand of the desert rendered the heat of the sun more insupportable; the horses fell by the way; and the men were ready to die with thirst. A brook of muddy water which they found toward evening was all they met with; they filled some bottles with this water, which saved the lives of the King's little troop. After a march of five days, he at last found himself on the banks of the River Hypanis, now called Bog by the barbarians, who have spoiled not only the general face, but even the very names of those countries, which once flourished so nobly in the possession of the Greek colonies. This river joins the Borysthenes some miles lower and falls along with it into the Black Sea.

On the other side of the Bog, toward the south, stands the little town of Otchakov, on the frontier of the Turkish Empire. The inhabitants seeing a body of soldiers approach, to whose dress and language they were entire strangers, refused to carry them over the river without an order from Mehemet Pacha, Governor of Otchakov. The King sent an express to the governor, demanding a passage; but the Turk not knowing what to do, in a country where one false step frequently costs a man his life, dared not venture to take anything upon himself, without having first obtained permission of the Seraskier of the province, who resided at Bender in Bessarabia. While they were waiting for this permission, the Russians who had made the King's army prisoners had crossed the Borysthenes and were approaching to take him also. At last the Pacha of Otchakov sent word to the King that he would furnish him with one small boat, to transport himself and two or three of his attendants. In this extremity the Swedes took by force what they could not obtain by gentle means: some of them went over to the further side in a small skiff, seized on some boats, and brought them to the hither bank of the river. And happy it was for them that they did so; for the masters of the Turkish barks, fearing they should lose such a favorable opportunity of getting a good freight, came in crowds to offer their service. At that very instant arrived the favorable answer of the Seraskier of Bender; and the King had the mortification to see 500 of his men seized by the enemy, whose insulting bravadoes he even heard. The Pasha of Otchakov, by means of an interpreter, asked his pardon for the delays which had occasioned the loss of these 500 men, and humbly entreated him not to complain of it to the Grand Seignior. Charles promised him that he would not; but, at the same time, gave him a severe reprimand, as if he had been speaking to one of his own subjects.

The commander of Bender, who was likewise seraskier, a title which answers to that of general, and Pasha of the province, which signifies governor and intendant, forthwith sent an aga to compliment the King, and to offer him a magnificent tent, with provision, baggage, wagons, and all the conveniences, officers, and attendants necessary to conduct him to Bender in a splendid manner; for it is the custom of the Turks, not only to defray the charges of ambassadors to the place of their residence, but likewise to supply, with great liberality, the necessities of those princes who take refuge among them during the time of their stay.

# BOOK V

State of the Ottoman Porte—Charles Resides near Bender—His Employments—His Intrigues at the Porte—His Designs—Augustus Restored to his Throne—The King of Denmark makes a Descent upon Sweden—All the Other Dominions of Charles are Invaded—The Czar Enters Moscow in Triumph — Affair of the Pruth — History of the Czarina, who, from a Country Girl, became Empress.

ACHMET III was at that time Emperor of the Turks. He had been placed upon the throne in 1703, by a revolution not unlike that which transferred the crown of England from James II to his son-in-law William. Mustapha being governed by his mufti, who was hated by all the Turks, provoked the whole empire to rise against him. His army, by the assistance of which he hoped to punish the malcontents, went over to the rebels. He was seized, and deposed in form, and his brother taken from the seraglio and advanced to the throne, almost without a drop of blood being spilled. Achmet shut up the deposed sultan in the seraglio at Constantinople, where he lived for several years, to the great astonishment of Turkey, which had been wont to see the dethronement of her princes always followed by their death.

The new Sultan, as the only recompense for a crown which he owed to the ministers, to the generals, to the officers of the Janizaries, and, in a word, to those who had any hand in the revolution, put them all to death one after another, fearing lest they should one day attempt a second revolution. By sacrificing so many brave men, he weakened the strength of the nation, but established his throne, at least, for some years. The next object of his attention was to amass riches. He was the first of the Ottoman race that ventured to make a small alteration in the current coin and to impose new taxes; but he was obliged to drop both these enterprises, through fear of an insurrection. The rapacity and tyranny of the Grand Seignior are seldom felt by any but the officers of the empire, who, whatever they may be in other respects, are domestic slaves to the Sultan; but the rest of the Mussulmans live in profound tranquillity, secure of their liberty, their lives, and fortunes.

Such was the Turkish Emperor to whom the King of Sweden fled for refuge. As soon as he set foot on the Sultan's territories, he wrote him a letter, which bears the date of July 13, 1709. Several copies of this letter were spread abroad, all of which are now held to be spurious; but of all those I have seen, there is not one which does not sufficiently indicate the natural haughtiness of the author and is more suitable to his courage than his condition. The Sultan did not return him an answer till toward the end of September. The pride of the Ottoman Porte made Charles sensible what a mighty difference there was between a Turkish emperor and a king of a part of Scandinavia, a conquered and fugitive Christian. For the rest, all those letters, which kings seldom write themselves, are but vain formalities, which neither serve to discover the characters of princes nor the state of their affairs.

Though Charles XII was in reality no better than a prisoner honorably treated in Turkey, he yet formed the design of arming the Ottoman Empire against his enemies. He flattered himself that he should be able to reduce Poland under the yoke and subdue Russia. He had an envoy at Constantinople, but the person that served him most effectually in his vast projects was the Count Poniatowski, who went to Constantinople without a commission and soon rendered himself necessary to the King, agreeable to the Porte, and at last dangerous even to the grand-viziers.*

One of those who seconded his designs with the greatest activity was the physician Fonseca,† a Portuguese Jew, settled at Constantinople—a man of knowledge and address, well qualified for the management of business, and perhaps the only philosopher of his nation. His profession procured him a free access to the Ottoman Porte, and frequently gained him the confidence of the viziers. With this gentleman I was very well acquainted at Paris; and all the particulars I am going to relate

---

* It was from this nobleman I received not only the remarks which have been published, and of which the Chaplain Norberg has made use, but likewise several other manuscripts relating to this history.
† He was a renegade Frenchman, named Goin, first physician to the seraglio.

were, he assured me, unquestionable truths. Count Poniatowski has informed me, both by letters and by word of mouth, that he had the address to convey some letters to the Sultana Valide, the mother of the reigning Emperor, who had formerly been ill-used by her son, but now began to recover her influence in the seraglio. A Jewess, who was often admitted to this princess, was perpetually recounting to her the exploits of the King of Sweden and charmed her ear by these relations. The Sultana, moved by that secret inclination with which most women feel inspired in favor of extraordinary men, even without having seen them, openly espoused the King's cause in the seraglio. She called him by no other name than that of her lion. "And when will you," she would sometimes say to the Sultan her son—"when will you help my lion to devour this Czar?" She even dispensed with the rules of the seraglio, so far as to write several letters with her own hand to Count Poniatowski, in whose custody they still are, at the time of my writing this history.

Meanwhile the King was honorably conducted to Bender, through the desert that was formerly called the Wilderness of the Getæ. The Turks took care that nothing should be wanting on the road to render his journey agreeable. A great many Poles, Swedes, and Cossacks, who had escaped from the Muscovites, came by different ways to increase his train on the road. By the time he reached Bender he had 1,800 men, who were all maintained and lodged—both they and their horses—at the expense of the Grand Seignior.

The King chose to encamp near Bender rather than lodge in the town. The Seraskier Jussuf, pasha, caused a magnificent tent to be erected for him; and tents were likewise provided for all the lords of his retinue. Some time after, Charles built a house in this place: the officers followed his example and the soldiers raised barracks; so that his camp insensibly became a little town. As the King was not yet cured of his wound, he was obliged to have a carious bone extracted from his foot. But as soon as he could mount a horse, he resumed his wonted labors, always rising before the sun, tiring three horses a day, and exercising his soldiers. By way of amusement, he sometimes played at chess; and, as the characters of men are often discovered by the most trifling incidents, it may not be improper to observe that he always advanced the King first at that game, and made greater use of him than of any of the other men, by which he was always a loser.

At Bender he had all the necessaries of life in great abundance, a felicity that seldom falls to the lot of a conquered and fugitive prince; for, besides the more than sufficient quantity of provisions, and the 500 crowns a day, which he received from the Ottoman munificence, he drew some money from France and borrowed of the merchants at Constantinople. Part of this money was employed in forwarding his intrigues in the seraglio, in buying the favors of the viziers, or procuring their ruin. The rest he squandered away with great profusion among his own officers and the Janizaries who composed his guards at Bender. The dispenser of these acts of liberality was Grothusen, his favorite—a man who, contrary to the custom of persons in that station, was as fond of giving as his master. He once brought him an account of 60,000 crowns in two lines; 10,000 crowns given to the Swedes and Janizaries by the generous orders of his Majesty and the rest eaten up by himself. "It is thus," said the King, "that I would have friends give in their accounts. Muller makes me read whole pages for the sum of 10,000 livres. I like the laconic style of Grothusen much better." One of his old officers, who was suspected of being somewhat covetous, complained that his Majesty gave all to Grothusen. "I give money," replied the King, "to none but those who know how to use it." This generosity frequently reduced him to such a low ebb that he had not wherewithal to give. A better economy in his acts of generosity would have been as much for his honor, and more for his interest; but it was the failing of this prince to carry all the virtues beyond the due bounds.

Great numbers of strangers went from Constantinople to see him. The Turks and the neighboring Tartars came thither in crowds: all respected and admired him. His inflexible resolution to abstain from wine and his regularity in assisting twice a day at public prayers made them say that he was a true Mussulman, and inspired them with an ardent desire of marching along with him to the conquest of Muscovy.

During his abode at Bender, which was much longer than he expected, he insensibly acquired a taste for reading. **Baron**

Fabricius, a gentleman of the bed-chamber to the Duke of Holstein, a young man of an amiable character, who possessed that gayety of temper and easy turn of wit which is so agreeable to princes, was the person who engaged him in these literary amusements. He had been sent to reside with him at Bender in the character of envoy, to take care of the interests of the young Duke of Holstein; and he succeeded in his negotiations by his open and agreeable behavior. He had read all the best French authors. He persuaded the King to read the tragedies of Pierre Corneille, those of Racine, and the works of Despreaux [Boileau]. The King had no relish for the satires of the last author, which, indeed, are far from being his best pieces; but he was very fond of his other writings. When he had read that passage of the Eighth Satire where the author treats Alexander as a fool and a madman, he tore out the leaf.

Of all the French tragedies, Mithridates pleased him most, because the situation of that monarch, who, though vanquished, still breathed vengeance, was so similar to his own. He showed Fabricius the passages that struck him, but would never read any of them aloud nor ever hazard a single word in French. Nay, when he afterward saw M. Désaleurs, the French ambassador at the Porte, a man of distinguished merit, but acquainted only with his mother-tongue, he answered him in Latin; and when M. Désaleurs protested that he did not understand four words of that language, the King, rather than talk French, sent for an interpreter.

Such were the occupations of Charles XII at Bender, where he waited till a Turkish army should come to his assistance. His envoy presented memorials in his name to the grand-vizier, and Poniatowski supported them with all his interest. This gentleman's address succeeded in everything; he was always dressed in the Turkish fashion, and he had free access to every place. The Grand Seignior presented him with a purse of 1,000 ducats, and the grand-vizier said to him: "I will take your King with one hand and a sword in the other; I will lead him to Moscow at the head of 200,000 men." The name of this grand-vizier was Chourlouli Ali Pasha, he was the son of a peasant of the village of Chourlou. Such an extraction is not reckoned a disgrace among the Turks, who have no rank of nobility, neither that which is annexed to certain employments nor that which consists in titles. With them the dignity and importance of a man's character depend entirely upon his personal services. This is a custom which prevails in most of the Eastern countries — a custom extremely natural, and which might be productive of the most beneficial effects if posts of honor were conferred on none but men of merit; but the viziers, for the most part, are no better than the creatures of a black eunuch or a favorite female slave.

The first minister soon changed his mind. The King could do nothing but negotiate, and the Czar could give money, which he distributed with great profusion; and he even employed the money of Charles XII on this occasion. The military-chest, which he took at Poltava, furnished him with new arms against the vanquished King; and it was no longer the question at court, whether war should be made upon the Russians. The interest of the Czar was all-powerful at the Porte, which granted such honors to his envoy as the Muscovite ministers had never before enjoyed at Constantinople. They allowed him to have a seraglio, that is, a place in the quarter of the Franks, who converse with the foreign ministers. The Czar thought he might even demand that General Mazeppa should be put into his hands, as Charles XII had caused the unhappy Patkul to be delivered up to him. Chourlouli Ali Pasha could refuse nothing to a prince who backed his demands with millions. Thus that same grand-vizier, who had formerly promised, in the most solemn manner, to lead the King of Sweden into Muscovy with 200,000 men, had the assurance to make him a proposal of consenting to the sacrifice of General Mazeppa. Charles was enraged at this demand. It is hard to say how far the vizier might have pushed the affair, had not Mazeppa, who was now seventy years of age, died exactly at this juncture. The King's grief and indignation were greatly increased when he understood that Tolstoy, now become the Czar's ambassador at the Porte, was served in public by the Swedes that had been slaves at Poltava, and that the brave soldiers were daily sold in the market at Constantinople. Nay, the Russian ambassador made no scruple of declaring openly that the Mussulman troops at Bender were placed there rather with a view to secure the King's person than to do him any honor.

Charles, abandoned by the grand-vizier, and vanquished by

the Czar's money in Turkey, as he had been by his arms in the Ukraine, saw himself deceived and despised by the Porte, and almost a prisoner among the Tartars. His attendants began to despair. He alone remained firm, and never appeared in the least dejected. Convinced that the Sultan was ignorant of the intrigues of Chourlouli Ali, his grand-vizier, he resolved to acquaint him with them; and Poniatowski undertook the execution of this hazardous enterprise. The Grand Seignior goes every Friday to the mosque, surrounded by his solaks, a kind of guards, whose turbans are adorned with such high feathers as to conceal the Sultan from the view of the people. When anyone has a petition to present to the Grand Seignior, he endeavors to mingle with the guards and holds the petition aloft. Sometimes the Sultan condescends to receive it himself; but, for the most part, he orders an aga to take charge of it, and upon his return from the mosque causes the petition to be laid before him. There is no fear of anyone daring to importune him with useless memorials and trifling petitions, inasmuch as they write less at Constantinople in a whole year than they do at Paris in one day. There is still less danger of any memorials being presented against the ministers, to whom he commonly remits them unread. Poniatowski had no other way of conveying the King of Sweden's complaint to the Grand Seignior. He drew up a heavy charge against the grand-vizier. M. de Fériol, who was then the French ambassador, and who gave me an account of the whole affair, got the memorial translated into the Turkish tongue. A Greek was hired to present it: this Greek, mingling with the guards of the Grand Seignior, held the paper so high for so long a time, and made such a noise, that the Sultan observed him and took the memorial himself.

This method of presenting memorials to the Sultan against his viziers was frequently employed. A Swede, called Leloing, gave in another petition a few days after. Thus, in the Turkish Empire Charles XII was reduced to the necessity of using the same expedients with an oppressed subject.

Some days after this, the Sultan sent to the King of Sweden, as the only answer to his complaints, five-and-twenty Arabian horses, one of which, that had carried his Highness, was covered with a saddle and housing enriched with precious stones, with stirrups of massive gold. This present was accompanied with an obliging letter, but conceived in general terms, and such as gave reason to suspect that the minister had done nothing without the Sultan's consent. Chourlouli, too, who was a perfect master in the art of dissimulation, sent the King five very curious horses. But Charles, with a lofty air, said to the person that brought them: "Go back to your master, and tell him that I don't receive presents from my enemies."

Poniatowski, having already ventured to present a petition against the grand-vizier, he next formed the bold design of deposing him. Understanding that the vizier was disagreeable to the sultana-mother, and that he was hated by the kislar-aga, the chief of the black eunuchs, and by the aga of the Janizaries, he prompted them all three to speak against him. It was something very surprising to see a Christian, a Pole, an uncommissioned agent of the King of Sweden, who had taken refuge among the Turks, caballing almost openly at the Porte against a viceroy of the Ottoman Empire, who, at the same time, was both an able minister and a favorite of his master. Poniatowski could never have succeeded, and the bare attempt would have cost him his life, had not a power superior to all those that operated in his favor given a finishing stroke to the fortune of the grand-vizier, Chourlouli.

The Sultan had a young favorite, who afterward governed the Ottoman Empire, and was killed in Hungary in 1716, at the battle of Peterwardein, which Prince Eugene of Savoy gained over the Turks. His name was Coumourgi Ali Pasha. His birth was much the same with that of Chourlouli, being the son of a coal-heaver, as *Coumourgi* imports; *comour* in the Turkish tongue signifying coal. The Emperor Achmet II, uncle of Achmet III, having met Coumourgi, while yet an infant, in a wood near Adrianople, was struck with his extraordinary beauty, and caused him to be conducted to the seraglio. Mustapha, the eldest son and successor of Mahomet, was very fond of him, and Achmet III made him his favorite. He had then no other place but that of *selictar-aga*, or sword-bearer to the Crown. His extreme youth did not allow him to make any open pretensions to the post of grand-vizier, and yet he had the ambition to aspire to it. The Swedish faction could never draw over this favorite to their side. He had never been a friend to Charles, or to any other Christian prince, or to any

of their ministers; but, on this occasion, he served King Charles
XII without intending to do so. He joined with the Sultana
Valide and the great officers of the Porte to hasten the ruin of
Chourlouli, who was equally hated by them all. This old minister, who had served his master for a long time, and with great
fidelity, fell a victim to the caprice of a boy and the intrigues of
a foreigner. He was stripped of his dignity and riches. His
wife, who was the daughter of the late Sultan Mustapha, was
taken from him, and he was himself banished to Caffa, formerly
called Theodosia, in Crim Tartary. The bull—that is to say,
the seal of the empire—was given to Numan Couprougli
[Kuprili], grandson to the great Couprougli, who took Candia.
This new vizier was, what ill-informed Christians can hardly
believe it possible for a Turk to be, a man of incorruptible virtue, a scrupulous observer of the law, and one who frequently
opposed the rigid rules of justice to the wayward will of the
Sultan. He could not endure to hear of a war against Muscovy, which he considered as alike unjust and unnecessary; but
the same attachment to his law, that prevented his making war
upon the Czar, contrary to the faith of treaties, made him observe the rights of hospitality toward the King of Sweden.
"The law forbids you," he would say to his master, "to attack
the Czar, who has done you no injury; but it commands you
to succor the King of Sweden, who is an unfortunate prince
in your dominions." He sent his Majesty 800 purses (every
purse containing 500 crowns), and advised him to return
peaceably to his own dominions, either through the territories
of the Emperor of Germany, or in some of the French vessels
which then lay in the harbor of Constantinople, and which M.
de Fériol, the French ambassador at the Porte, offered to
Charles to conduct him to Marseilles. Count Poniatowski carried on his negotiations with greater activity than ever, and
acquired such a superiority with an incorruptible vizier as the
gold of the Muscovites was unable to counterbalance. The
Russian faction thought it would be their wisest course to poison such a dangerous negotiator. They gained one of his domestics, who was to give him the poison in a dish of coffee; but
the crime was discovered before it was carried into execution.
The poison **was found** in the hands of the domestic, contained
**in a small phial, which** was carried to the Grand Seignior. The

poisoner was tried in a full divan and condemned to the galleys; the justice of the Turks never inflicting death for those crimes that have not been perpetrated.

Charles, who could not be persuaded but that, sooner or later, he should be able to engage the Turkish Empire in a war against Muscovy, rejected every proposal that was made for his peaceable return home. He was continually representing to the Turks the formidable power of that same Czar, whom he had so long despised. His emissaries were perpetually insinuating that Peter Alexiovitch wanted to make himself master of the navigation of the Black Sea; and that after having subdued the Cossacks, he would carry his arms into Crim Tartary. Sometimes these representations aroused the Porte, sometimes the Russian ministers destroyed all their effect.

While Charles XII made his fate depend upon the caprice of viziers, and while he was alternately receiving favors and affronts from a foreign power, presenting petitions to the Sultan, and subsisting upon his bounty in a desert, all his enemies, awaking from their former lethargy, invaded his domains.

The battle of Poltava was the first signal for a revolution in Poland. Augustus returned to that country, protesting against his abdication, against the peace of Altranstädt, and publicly accusing Charles XII, whom he no longer feared, of robbery and cruelty. He imprisoned Fingsten and Imhof, his plenipotentiaries, who had signed his abdication, as if in so doing they had exceeded their orders and betrayed their master. His Saxon troops, which had been the pretext of his dethronement, conducted him back to Warsaw, accompanied by most of the Polish palatines, who, having formerly sworn fidelity to him, had afterward done the same to Stanislaus, and had now come to do it again to Augustus. Siniawski himself rejoined his party, and laying aside the ambitious hopes of raising himself to the royal dignity, was content to remain grand-general of the Crown. Flemming, his first minister, who had been obliged to leave Saxony, through fear of being delivered up with Patkul, now contributed by his address to bring back to his master's interest a great part of the Polish nobility.

The Pope absolved the people from the oath of allegiance which they had taken to Stanislaus. This step of the holy father, seasonably taken, and supported by the forces of Augustus, was of considerable weight. It strengthened the credit of the Court of Rome in Poland, the natives of which had no inclination at that time to dispute with the sovereign pontiffs their chimerical right of interfering in the temporal concerns of princes. Everyone was ready to submit anew to the authority of Augustus, and willingly received an absolution, which, however useless in itself, the nuncio took care to represent as absolutely necessary.

The power of Charles and the grandeur of Sweden were now drawing toward their last period. Above ten crowned heads had long beheld, with fear and envy, the Swedish power extending itself far beyond its natural bounds, on the other side of the Baltic Sea, from the Düina to the Elbe. The fall of Charles, and his absence, revived the interested views and rekindled the jealousies of all these princes, which had for a long time been laid asleep by treaties and by their inability to break them.

The Czar, who was more powerful than all of them put together, improving his late victory, took Viborg and all Carelia, overrun Finland, laid siege to Riga, and sent a body of forces into Poland to aid Augustus in recovering his throne. The Czar was, at that time, what Charles had been formerly—the arbiter of Poland and the North; but all his measures were directed to the promotion of his own interest; whereas Charles had never been prompted by any other motives than those of revenge and glory. The Swedish monarch had succored his allies and crushed his enemies, without reaping any fruit from his victories. The Czar, behaving more like a prince and less like a hero, would not assist the King of Poland, but on condition that Livonia should be ceded to him; and that this province, for which Augustus had kindled the war, should remain forever in the possession of the Muscovites.

The King of Denmark, forgetting the Treaty of Travendahl, as Augustus had that of Altranstädt, began to entertain thoughts of making himself master of the duchies of Holstein and Bremen, to which he renewed his pretensions. The King of Prussia had ancient claims upon Swedish Pomerania, which he now resolved to revive. The Duke of Mecklenburg was vexed to see that the Swedes were still in possession of Wismar, the finest town in the duchy. This prince was to marry a niece of the Russian Emperor; and the Czar wanted only a pretext for establishing himself in Germany, after the example of the Swedes. George, Elector of Hanover, was likewise desirous of enriching himself with Charles's spoils. The Bishop of Münster too would have been willing enough to avail himself of some of his claims, had he been able to support them.

About 12,000 or 13,000 Swedes defended Pomerania and the other countries which Charles possessed in Germany; and it was there that the war was most likely to begin. This storm alarmed the Emperor and his allies. It is a law of the empire that whoever invades one of its provinces shall be reputed an enemy of the whole Germanic body.

But there was still a greater difficulty. All these princes, except the Czar, were then united against Louis XIV, whose power, for a long time, had been as formidable to the empire as that of Charles.

At the beginning of this century, Germany found itself hard pressed from south to north by the armies of France and Sweden. The French had passed the Danube, and the Swedes the Oder, and had their forces, victorious as they then were, been joined together, the empire had been utterly undone. But the same fatality that ruined Sweden had likewise humbled France. Sweden, however, had still more resources left; and Louis XIV carried on the war with vigor, though without success. Should Pomerania and the Duchy of Bremen become the theatre of the war, it was to be feared that the empire would suffer by such an event; and that being weakened on that side, it would be less able to withstand the arms of Louis XIV. To prevent this danger, the Emperor, the princes of the empire, Anne, Queen of England, and the States-General of the United Provinces, concluded at The Hague, about the end of the year 1709, one of the most singular treaties ever signed.

It was stipulated by these powers that the war against the Swedes should not be in Pomerania, nor in any of the German provinces; and that the enemies of Charles XII should be at liberty to attack him anywhere else. Even the Czar and the King of Poland acceded to this treaty, in which they caused to be inserted an article as extraordinary as the treaty itself; viz., that the 12,000 Swedes who were in Pomerania should not be allowed to leave it in order to defend their other provinces.

To secure the execution of the treaty, and to maintain this imaginary neutrality, it was proposed to assemble an army, which should encamp on the banks of the Oder. An unheard-of novelty, to levy an army in order to prevent a war! nay, the very princes, who were to pay the army, were most of them concerned to commence a war which they thus affected to prevent. The treaty imported that the army should be composed of the troops of the Emperor, of the King of Prussia, of the Elector of Hanover, of the Landgrave of Hesse, and of the Bishop of Münster.

The issue of this project was such as might naturally have been expected: it was not carried into execution. The princes who were to have furnished their contingents for completing the army contributed nothing. There were not two regiments formed. Everybody talked of a neutrality, but nobody observed it; and the princes of the North, who had any quarrel with the King of Sweden, were left at full liberty to dispute with each other the spoils of that prince.

During these transactions, the Czar having quartered his troops in Lithuania and given orders for pushing the siege of Riga, returned to Moscow to show his people a sight as new as anything he had hitherto done in the kingdom: this was a triumph of nearly the same nature with that of the ancient Romans. He made his entry into Moscow on January 1, 1710, under seven triumphal arches erected in the streets and adorned with everything which the climate could furnish or which a flourishing commerce (rendered such by his care) could import. The procession began with a regiment of guards, followed by the pieces of artillery taken from the Swedes at Liesna and Poltava, each of which was drawn by eight horses, covered with scarlet housings hanging down to the ground. Next came the standards, kettle-drums, and colors won at these two battles, carried by the officers and soldiers who had taken them. All these spoils were followed by the finest troops of the Czar. After they had filed off, there appeared, in a chariot made on purpose,* the litter of Charles XII, found on the field of battle at Poltava, all shattered with two cannon-shots. Behind the litter marched all the prisoners two and two, among whom was

* Here M. Norberg, the chaplain of Charles XII, finds fault with the author, and affirms that the litter was carried by the soldiers. With regard to these circumstances (which are of great importance, to be sure), we appeal to those who saw them.

Count Piper, first minister of Sweden, the famous Marshal Rehnskiöld, Count Löwenhaupt, the generals Schlippenbach, Stackelberg, and Hamilton, and all the officers and soldiers who were afterward dispersed through Great Russia. Immediately after these appeared the Czar himself, mounted on the same horse which he rode at the battle of Poltava. A little after him came the generals who had had a share in the success of the day. Next followed a regiment of guards, and the whole was closed by the wagons loaded with the Swedish ammunition.

This grand procession was accompanied with the ringing of all the bells in Moscow, with the sound of drums, kettle-drums, trumpets, and an infinite number of musical instruments, which played in concert, together with the volleys of 200 pieces of cannon, amid the acclamations of 500,000 men, who, at every stop the Czar made in this triumphal entry, cried out, "Long live the Emperor, our father!"

This dazzling exhibition augmented the people's veneration for his person, and perhaps made him appear greater in their eyes than all the solid advantages they had derived from his labors. Meanwhile he continued the blockade of Riga, and the generals made themselves masters of the rest of Livonia and part of Finland. At the same time, the King of Denmark came with his whole fleet to make a descent upon Sweden, where he landed 17,000 men, and left them under the command of Count Reventlau.

Sweden was, at that time, governed by a regency, composed of some senators, who were appointed by the King before he left Stockholm. The body of the Senate, imagining that the government of right belonged to them, became jealous of the regency; and the State suffered by these divisions. But when, after the battle of Poltava, the first news was brought to Stockholm that the King was at Bender, at the mercy of the Turks and Tartars, and that the Danes had invaded Scania and taken the town of Helsingborg, all their jealousies immediately vanished, and they bent their whole attention toward the preservation of the kingdom. Sweden was now drained, in a great measure, of regular troops; for though Charles had always made his great expeditions at the head of small armies, yet the innumerable battles he had fought in the space of nine years, the necessity he was under of recruiting his forces with continual supplies, and maintaining his garrisons, and the standing army he was constantly obliged to keep in Finland, Ingria, Livonia, Pomerania, Bremen, and Verden, had cost Sweden, during the course of the war, above 250,000 men; so that there were not 8,000 of the ancient troops remaining, which, together with the newly raised militia, was the only resource Sweden had to trust to for the defence of her territories.

The nation is naturally warlike, and every people insensibly imbibes the spirit of the sovereign. From one end of the country to the other, nothing was talked of but the prodigious achievements of Charles and his generals, and of the old regiments that fought under them at Narva, Düina, Clissow, Pultusk, and Holowczyn. Hence the very lowest of the Swedes were fired with a spirit of emulation and glory; and this heroic impulse was greatly augmented by their affection for their King, their pity for his misfortunes, and their implacable hatred of the Danes. In several other countries the peasants are slaves, or treated as such, but here they compose a part of the State, are considered as citizens, and, of consequence, are capable of more exalted sentiments; so that these newly raised militia became, in a short time, the best troops of the North.

General Stenbock, by order of the Regency, put himself at the head of 8,000 of the ancient troops and about 12,000 of these new militia, to go in pursuit of the Danes, who ravaged all the country about Helsingborg and had already extorted contributions from some of the more inland provinces.

There was neither time nor opportunity to give regimental clothes to the new militia. Most of these boors came in their flaxen frocks, having pistols tied to their girdles with cords. Stenbock, at the head of this strange army, overtook the Danes about three leagues from Helsingborg on the tenth of March, 1710. He had designed to give his troops a few days' rest, to raise intrenchments, and to allow his new soldiers sufficient time to habituate themselves to the face of the enemy; but all the peasants called out for battle the very day on which they arrived.

I have been assured by some of the officers who were present that they saw almost every individual soldier foaming with rage, so great is the national hatred of the Swedes to the Danes. Stenbock availed himself of this ardor of spirit, which, in the day of battle, is of as much consequence as military discipline. He attacked the Danes; and there one might have seen a thing to which, perhaps, the whole history of mankind cannot furnish above two similar examples: the newly raised militia, in their first assault, equalled the intrepidity of veteran soldiers. Two regiments of these undisciplined peasants cut in pieces the regiment of the King of Denmark's guards, of which there remained only ten men alive.

The Danes, being entirely routed, retired under the cannon of Helsingborg. The passage from Sweden to Zealand is so short that the King of Denmark received the news of the defeat of his army in Sweden the same day on which it happened, and sent his fleet to bring off the shattered remains of his army. The Danes quitted Sweden with precipitation five days after the battle; but unable to carry off their horses, and unwilling to leave them to the enemy, they killed them all in the suburbs of Helsingborg, and set fire to their provisions, burning their corn and baggage and leaving in Helsingborg 4,000 wounded, the greater part of whom died with the infection occasioned by so many dead horses, and for want of provision, of which even their countrymen deprived them, in order to prevent the Swedes from enjoying any share of it.

Meanwhile the peasants of Dalecarlia, having heard in the heart of their forests that their King was a prisoner among the Turks, sent a deputation to the Regency of Stockholm, and offered to go at their own expense, to the number of 20,000 men, to rescue their master from the hands of his enemies. This proposal, which was better calculated to express their courage and loyalty than to produce any real advantage, was received with pleasure, though it was not accepted; and the senators took care to acquaint the King with it at the same time that they sent him a circumstantial account of the battle of Helsingborg.

Charles received this agreeable news in his camp near Bender, in July, 1710. And another event that happened soon after contributed still more to strengthen his hopes.

The grand-vizier, Couprougli, who opposed all his designs, was dismissed from his office, after having filled it for two months. The little court of Charles XII, and those who still adhered to him in Poland, gave out that Charles made and unmade the viziers and governed the Turkish Empire from his retreat at Bender. But he had no hand in the disgrace of that favorite. The rigid probity of the vizier was said to have been the sole cause of his fall. His predecessor had paid the Janizaries, not out of the imperial treasury, but with the money which he procured by extortion. Couprougli paid them out of the treasury. Achmet reproached him with preferring the interest of the subject to that of the Emperor. "Your predecessor," said he, "well knew how to find other means of paying my troops." "If," replied the grand-vizier, "he had the art of enriching your Highness by rapine, it is an art of which I am proud to say I am entirely ignorant."

The profound secrecy that prevails in the seraglio seldom allows such particulars to transpire to the public; but this fact was published along with Couprougli's disgrace. The vizier's boldness did not cost him his head, because true virtue is sometimes respected, even while it displeases. He was permitted to retire to the island of Negropont. These particulars I learned from the letters of M. Bru, my relation, first druggist to the Ottoman Porte, and I have retold them in order to display the true spirit of that government.

After this the Grand Seignior recalled from Aleppo, Baltagi [Baltadschi] Mehemet, Pasha of Syria, who had been grand-vizier before Chourlouli. The baltagis of the Seraglio, so called from *balta,* which signifies an *axe,* are slaves employed to cut wood for the use of the princes of the Ottoman blood and the sultanas. This vizier had been a baltagi in his youth and had ever since retained the name of that office, according to the custom of the Turks, who are not ashamed to take the name of their first profession, or of that of their father, or even of the place of their birth.

While Baltagi Mehemet was a valet in the seraglio, he was so happy as to perform some little services to Prince Achmet, who was then a prisoner of state, in the reign of his brother Mustapha. The princes of the Ottoman blood are allowed to keep for their pleasure a few women, who are past the age of child-bearing (and that age arrives very early in Turkey), but still agreeable enough to please. As soon as Achmet became Sultan, he gave one of these female slaves, for whom he had had a great affection, in marriage to Baltagi Mehemet. This woman, by her intrigues, made her husband grand-vizier; another intrigue displaced him; and a third made him grand-vizier again.

When Baltagi Mehemet received the bull of the empire, he found the party of the King of Sweden prevailing in the seraglio. The Sultaness Valide, Ali Coumourgi, the Grand Seignior's favorite, the kislar aga, chief of the black eunuchs, and the aga of the Janizaries, were all for a war against the Czar: the Sultan was fixed in the same resolution, and the first order he gave the grand-vizier was to go and attack the Muscovites with 200,000 men. Baltagi had never made a campaign; yet was he not an idiot, as the Swedes, who were dissatisfied with his conduct, affected to represent him. Upon receiving from the Grand Seignior a sabre, adorned with precious stones, he addressed him in the following terms: "Your Highness knows that I was brought up to handle an axe and cleave wood, not to wield a sword and command your armies. Nevertheless, I will endeavor to serve you to the best of my power; but should I fail of success, remember I have entreated you beforehand not to impute the blame to me." The Sultan assured him he might depend upon his friendship, and the vizier prepared to carry his orders into execution.

The first step of the Ottoman Porte was to imprison the Russian ambassador in the castle of the Seven Towers. It is the custom of the Turks to begin by arresting the ministers of those princes against whom they declare war. Strict observers of hospitality in everything else, in this they violate the most sacred law of nations. This injustice, however, they commit under the pretext of equity, believing themselves, or, at least, desirous of making others believe, that they never undertake any but just wars, because they are consecrated by the approbation of their mufti. Upon this principle they take up arms (as they imagine) to chastise the violators of treaties, and think they have a right to punish the ambassadors of those kings with whom they are at enmity, as being accomplices in the treachery of their masters. Add to this the ridiculous contempt they affect to entertain for Christian princes and their ambassadors, the latter of whom they commonly consider in no other light than as the consuls of merchants.

The Khan of Crim Tartary received orders to hold himself in readiness with 40,000 Tartars. This prince is sovereign of

Nagai[?], Budziack [Badakshan?], part of Circassia, and all of the Crimea, a province anciently known by the name of Taurica Chersonesus, into which the Greeks carried their arms and commerce and founded powerful cities; and into which, in aftertimes, the Genoese penetrated, when they were masters of the trade of Europe. In this country are to be seen the ruins of some Greek cities, and some monuments of the Genoese, which still subsist in the midst of desolation and barbarity.

The Khan is called emperor by his own subjects; but, with this grand title, he is, nevertheless, the slave of the Porte. The Ottoman blood, from which the khans are sprung, and the right they pretend to have to the empire of the Turks, upon the failure of the Grand Seignior's race, render their family respectable, and their persons formidable even to the Sultan himself. It is for this reason that the Grand Seignior dares not destroy the race of the khans of Tartary; though, indeed, he seldom allows any of these princes to live to a great age. Their conduct is closely inspected by the neighboring pachas; their dominions are surrounded with Janizaries, their inclinations thwarted by the grand-viziers, and their designs always suspected. If the Tartars complain of the Khan, the Porte deposes him under that pretext. If he is too popular, it is still a higher crime, for which he suffers a more severe punishment. Thus almost all of them are driven from sovereign power into exile, and end their days at Rhodes, which is commonly their prison and their grave.

The Tartars, their subjects, are the most thievish people on earth, and, what is hardly to be credited, are at the same time the most hospitable. They will go fifty leagues from home to attack a caravan or pillage a town; and yet when any stranger happens to travel through their country, he is not only received, lodged, and maintained everywhere, but, through whatever place he passes, the inhabitants dispute with each other the honor of having him for their guest; and the master of the house, his wife, and daughters are ambitious to serve him. This inviolable regard to hospitality they have derived from their ancestors, the Scythians; and they still preserve it, because the small number of strangers that travel among them, and the low price of all sorts of provisions, render the practice of such a virtue in no way burdensome.

When the Tartars go to war, in conjunction with the Ottoman army, they are maintained by the Grand Seignior, but the booty they get is their only pay; and hence it is that they are much fitter for plundering than fighting.

The Khan, won over to the King of Sweden's interest by presents and promises, at first obtained leave to appoint the general rendezvous of the troops at Bender, and even under the eye of Charles XII, in order the more effectually to convince that monarch that the war was undertaken solely for his sake.

The new vizier, Baltagi Mehemet, who did not lie under the same engagements, would not flatter a sovereign prince so highly. He changed the order, and Adrianople was the place fixed for the rendezvous of this great army. It is always in the vast and fertile plains of Adrianople that the Turks assemble their armies when they are going to make war upon the Christians; there the troops that arrive from Asia and Africa repose and refresh themselves for a few weeks; but the grandvizier, in order to anticipate the preparations of the Czar, allowed the army but three days' rest, and then marched to the Danube, from whence he advanced into Bessarabia.

The Turkish troops at present are not so formidable as they were in former times, when they conquered so many kingdoms in Asia, Africa, and Europe; when, by their great strength of body, their valor, and numbers, they triumphed over enemies less robust and worse disciplined than themselves. But now that the Christians are more expert in the art of war, they seldom fail to beat the Turks in a pitched battle, and even with unequal numbers. If the Ottoman Empire has made some conquests in latter times, it has only been over the Republic of Venice, esteemed more wise than warlike, defended by strangers, and little succored by the Christian princes, who are perpetually at variance among themselves.

The Janizaries and Saphis always attack in a confused and disorderly manner; they are incapable of obeying the commands of their general, or of recovering their ranks. Their cavalry, which, considering the goodness and fleetness of their horses, ought to be excellent, is unable to sustain the shock of the German cavalry. Their infantry cannot, even to this day, make use of fixed bayonets to any purpose. Add to this that the Turks have not had an able general since the time of Couprougli, who conquered the isle of Candia. A slave, brought up in the indolence and silence of a seraglio, made a vizier by interest, and a general against his will, led a raw army, without discipline or experience, against Russian troops, hardened by twelve campaigns, and proud of having conquered the Swedes.

The Czar, in all appearance, must have vanquished Baltagi Mehemet; but he was guilty of the same fault, in regard to the Turks, which the King of Sweden had committed with regard to him: he despised his enemy too much. Upon the first news of the Turkish preparations, he left Moscow, and, having given orders for turning the siege of Riga into a blockade, assembled a body of 80,000 men on the frontiers of Poland.* With this army he took the road through Moldavia and Wallachia, formerly the country of the Dacians, but now inhabited by Greek Christians, who are tributaries to the Grand Seignior.

Moldavia was, at that time, governed by Prince Cantemir, a Grecian by birth, and who united in his person the talents of the ancient Greeks, the knowledge of letters and of arms. He was supposed to have sprung from the famous Timur, known by the name of Tamerlane. This extraction appeared more honorable than a Greek origin; and the reality of the descent is proved by the name of the conqueror. Timur, it is said, resembles Temir; the title of khan, which Timur possessed before he conquered Asia, is included in the word Cantemir; therefore Prince Cantemir is descended from Tamerlane. Such are the foundations of most genealogies!

From whatever family Cantemir was sprung, he owed all his fortune to the Ottoman Porte. Hardly had he received the investiture of his principality, when he betrayed his benefactor, the Turkish Emperor, to the Czar, from whom he expected greater advantages. He fondly imagined that the conqueror of Charles XII would easily triumph over a vizier of so little reputation, who had never made a campaign, and who had chosen for his kiaia, or lieutenant, the superintendent of the customs in Turkey. He made no question but all his subjects would readily follow his standard, as the Greek patriarchs encouraged him in his revolt. The Czar, therefore, having made a secret treaty with this prince and received him into his army,

---

* The chaplain Norberg alleges that the Czar compelled every fourth man in his dominions, able to bear arms, to follow him to the field. Had that been the case, his army would have amounted, at least, to 2,000,000 of men.

advanced further into the country; and in June, 1711, arrived on the northern banks of the River Hierasus, now Pruth, near Jassy, the capital of Moldavia.

As soon as the grand-vizier heard that Peter Alexiovitch was advancing on that side, he immediately decamped, and, following the course of the Danube, resolved to cross the river on a bridge of boats, near a town called Saccia, at the same place where Darius formerly built the bridge that long went by his name. The Turkish army proceeded with so much expedition that it soon came in sight of the Muscovites, the River Pruth being between them.

The Czar, sure of the Prince of Moldavia, never dreamed that the Moldavians would fail him. But it frequently happens that the interest of the prince and that of the subjects are extremely different. The Moldavians liked the Turkish government, which is never fatal to any but the grandees, and affects a great lenity and mildness to its tributary States. They dreaded the Christians, and especially the Muscovites, who had always treated them with inhumanity. They carried all their provisions to the Ottoman army.

The undertakers who had engaged to furnish the Russians with provisions performed that contract with the grand-vizier which they had made with the Czar. The Wallachians, who border upon the Moldavians, showed the same attachment to the Turks, so much had the remembrance of the Russian cruelty alienated all their affections.

The Czar, thus balked of his hopes, which perhaps he had too rashly entertained, saw his army on a sudden destitute of forage and provisions. The soldiers deserted in troops, and the army was soon reduced to less than 30,000 men, ready to perish with hunger. The Czar experienced the same misfortunes upon the banks of the Pruth, in having delivered himself up to Cantemir, that Charles XII had done at Poltava, in relying upon Mazeppa. The Turks meanwhile passed the river, hemmed in the Russians, and formed an intrenched camp before them. It is somewhat surprising that the Czar did not dispute the passage of the river, or, at least, repair this error by attacking the Turks immediately after the passage, instead of giving them time to destroy his army with hunger and fatigue. It would seem, indeed, that Peter did everything in this campaign to hasten his own ruin. He found himself without provision; the River Pruth was behind him; 150,000 Turks were before him; while 40,000 Tartars were continually harassing his army on the right and left. In this extremity, he made no scruple of acknowledging in public that he was at least reduced to as bad a condition as his brother Charles had been at Poltava.

Count Poniatowski, an indefatigable agent of the King of Sweden, was in the grand-vizier's army, together with some Poles and Swedes, all of whom considered the ruin of the Czar as inevitable.

As soon as Poniatowski saw that the armies must infallibly come to an engagement, he sent an express to the King of Sweden, who immediately set out from Bender, accompanied with forty officers, anticipating the mighty pleasure he should have in fighting the Emperor of Muscovy. After many losses, and several marches in which he suffered severely, the Czar was driven back to the Pruth, without any other defence than a chevaux-de-frise and a few wagons. A part of the Janizaries and Saphis attacked his army in this disadvantageous situation; but their attack was disorderly, and the Russians defended themselves with a firmness and resolution which nothing but despair and the presence of their prince could inspire.

The Turks were twice repulsed. Next day Poniatowski advised the grand-vizier to starve the Russian army, which, being in want of everything, would, together with its Emperor, be obliged in a day's time to surrender at discretion.

The Czar, since that time, has more than once acknowledged that, in the whole course of his life, he never felt anything so exquisitely tormenting as the perturbation of mind in which he passed that night. He revolved in his thoughts all that he had been doing for so many years to promote the glory and happiness of his country. He reflected that so many grand undertakings, which had always been interrupted by wars, were now, perhaps, going to perish with him before they were fully accomplished. And he plainly perceived that he must either be destroyed by famine or attack about 180,000 men with feeble and dispirited troops, diminished one-half in their number, the cavalry almost entirely dismounted, and the infantry exhausted with hunger and fatigue.

He sent for General Sheremetef in the evening, and, without the least hesitation, or even so much as asking anyone's advice, ordered him to have everything in readiness next morning for attacking the Turks with fixed bayonets.

He likewise gave express orders that all baggage should be burnt, and that no officer should keep above one wagon; that so, in case of a defeat, the enemy might not obtain the booty they expected.

Having settled everything with the general relating to the battle, he retired to his tent, oppressed with grief, and racked with convulsions, a disease which often attacked him, and always recurred with redoubled violence when he was under any perturbation of mind. He gave peremptory orders that no one should presume, under any pretext whatsoever, to enter his tent in the night, not choosing to receive any remonstrances against a resolution, which, however desperate, was absolutely necessary, and still less that anyone should be a witness of the melancholy condition in which he was.

Meanwhile the greatest part of the baggage was burnt, according to his orders. All the army followed the example, though with much reluctance; and several buried their most valuable effects in the earth. The general officers were already giving orders for the march and endeavoring to inspire the army with that courage which they did not possess themselves. The soldiers, exhausted with hunger and fatigue, advanced without spirit and without hope. The women, with which the army was but too much crowded, set up the most lamentable shrieks and cries, which contributed still more to enervate the men; and the next morning everyone expected death or slavery as the only alternative. This picture is by no means exaggerated; it is exactly according to the accounts that were given by some officers who served in the army.

There was at that time in the Russian camp a woman as extraordinary, perhaps, as the Czar himself. As yet she was known only by the name of Catharine. Her mother was a poor countrywoman, called Erb-Magden, of the village of Ringen, in Estonia, a province where the people are serfs, and which was then subject to the Swedes. She never knew her father, but was baptized by the name of Martha. The vicar of the parish, out of pure charity, brought her up to the age of fourteen, after which she went to service at Marienburg, and hired herself to a Lutheran minister of that country, called Gluk.

In 1702, being then eighteen years of age, she married a Swedish dragoon. The day immediately succeeding her marriage, a party of the Swedish troops having been defeated by the Muscovites, the dragoon, who was in the action, disappeared, and was never heard of more; but whether or not he was taken prisoner his wife could never learn, nor, indeed, from that time could she ever procure the least intelligence about him.

A few days after, being made a prisoner herself by General Bauer, she entered into his service, and afterward into that of Marshal Scheremetef, by whom she was given to Mentchikof, a man who experienced the greatest vicissitudes of fortune, having from a pastry-cook's boy been raised to the rank of a general and a prince, and at last stripped of everything and banished into Siberia, where he ended his days in misery and despair.

The first time the Emperor saw her was one evening as he was at supper with Prince Mentchikof, when he instantly fell in love with her. He married her privately in 1707; not seduced into this step by the artifices of the woman, but because he found her possessed of a strength and firmness of mind capable of seconding his schemes, and even of continuing them after his death. He had long before divorced his first wife Ottokefa, the daughter of a Boyard, who was accused of opposing the alterations which he was introducing into his dominions. This crime, in the eyes of the Czar, was the most heinous of all others. He would have nobody in his family whose thoughts did not exactly correspond with his own. He imagined he could discern in this foreign slave the qualities of a sovereign, though she had none of the virtues of her sex. For her sake he disdained and broke through the prejudices that would have fettered a man of ordinary capacity. He caused her to be crowned Empress. The same talents which made her the wife of Peter Alexiovitch, procured her the empire after the death of her husband; and Europe has seen with surprise a woman who could neither read nor write,* compensating the want of education,

---

* The Sieur de la Motraye pretends that she had a good education, and could both read and write with great facility. The contrary of this, however, is known to all the world. The peasants of Livonia are never allowed to learn either to read or write, owing to an ancient privilege, which is termed *the benefit of clergy*, formerly established among the barbarians who were converted to Christianity, and still subsisting in this country. The memoirs from which we have extracted this anecdote, further add that the princess Elizabeth, afterward empress, always signed for her mother from the time she could write.

and the weakness of her sex, by her invincible courage and resolution, and filling with glory the throne of a legislator.

When she married the Czar, she renounced the Lutheran religion, in which she had been born, and embraced that of Muscovy. She was rebaptized, according to the rules of the Russian Church, and instead of Martha, she took the name of Catharine, by which she was ever after known. This woman, being in the camp of Pruth, held a council with the general officers and the vice-chancellor, Schaffirof, while the Czar was in his tent.

The result of their deliberations was that they must necessarily sue for a peace to the Turks and endeavor to persuade the Czar to agree to such a measure. The vice-chancellor wrote a letter to the grand-vizier in his master's name. This letter the Czarina carried to the Emperor's tent, notwithstanding his prohibition; and having with tears and entreaties prevailed upon him to sign it, she forthwith collected all her jewels, money, and most valuable effects, together with what money she could borrow from the general officers, and having by these means made up a considerable present, she sent it, with the Czar's letter, to Osman aga, lieutenant to the grand-vizier. Mehemet Baltagi replied with the lofty air of a vizier and a conqueror: "Let the Czar send me his prime minister and I shall then consider what is to be done." The vice-chancellor, Schaffirof, immediately repaired to the Turkish camp, with some presents which he publicly offered to the grand-vizier, sufficient to show him that they stood in need of his clemency, but too inconsiderable to corrupt his integrity.

The vizier at first demanded that the Czar, with his whole army, should surrender at discretion. The vice-chancellor replied that his master was going to attack him in a quarter of an hour, and that the Russians would perish to a man rather than submit to such dishonorable conditions. Schaffirof's application was strongly seconded by the remonstrances of Osman.

Mehemet Baltagi was no warrior: he saw that the Janizaries had been repulsed the day before; so that Osman easily prevailed upon him not to risk such certain advantages upon the fate of a battle. He accordingly granted a suspension of arms for six hours, in which time the terms of the treaty might be fully settled.

During the parley there happened a trifling incident, which plainly shows that the Turks often keep their word with a more scrupulous exactness than we imagine. Two Italian gentlemen, relations of M. Brillo, lieutenant-colonel of a regiment of grenadiers in the Czar's service, having gone to some distance in quest of forage, were taken prisoners by some Tartars, who brought them to the camp and offered to sell them to an officer of the Janizaries. The Turk, enraged at their presumption, in having thus violated the truce, arrested the Tartars and carried them himself before the grand-vizier, together with the two prisoners.

The vizier sent back the two gentlemen to the Czar's camp and ordered the Tartars, who had been chiefly concerned in carrying them off, to be beheaded.

Meanwhile the Khan of Tartary opposed the conclusion of the treaty, which would deprive him of all hopes of plunder; and Poniatowski seconded the Khan with the strongest arguments. But Osman carried his point against the importunity of the Tartar and the insinuations of Poniatowski.

The vizier thought that by concluding an advantageous peace he would sufficiently consult the honor and interest of his master. He insisted that the Russians should restore Azof, burn the galleys which lay in that harbor, demolish the important citadels built upon the Palus Mæotis [sea of Azof], and deliver all the cannon and ammunition of these fortresses into the hands of the Grand Seignior; that the Czar should withdraw his troops from Poland, give no further disturbance to the few Cossacks that were under the protection of the Poles, nor to those who were subject to the Turks; and that, for the future, he should pay the Tartars an annual subsidy of 40,000 sequins—an odious tribute long since imposed, but from which the Czar had delivered his country.

At last the treaty was going to be signed, without so much as making mention of the King of Sweden. All that Poniatowski could obtain of the vizier was to insert an article, by which the Czar bound himself not to incommodate the King in his return. And what is very remarkable, it was stipulated in this article that the Czar and Charles should make peace if they thought proper, and could agree upon the terms.

On these conditions the Czar was permitted to retire with

his army, cannon, artillery, colors, and baggage. The Turks supplied him with provisions, and he had plenty of everything in his camp two hours after the signing of the treaty, which was begun, concluded, and signed July 21, 1711.

Just as the Czar, now extricated from this terrible dilemma, was marching off, with drums beating and colors flying, the King of Sweden arrived impatient for the fight, and happy in the thoughts of having his enemy in his power. He had ridden post above fifty leagues from Bender to Jassy. He arrived the very moment that the Russians were beginning to retire in peace; but he could not penetrate to the Turkish camp without passing the Pruth by a bridge, three leagues distant. Charles XII, who never did anything like other men, swam across the river, at the hazard of being drowned, and traversed the Russian camp at the risk of being taken. At length he reached the Turkish army, and alighted at the tent of Poniatowski, who informed me of all these particulars, both by letter and word of mouth. The count came to him with a sorrowful countenance, and told him that he had lost an opportunity which, perhaps, he would never be able to recover.

The King, inflamed with resentment, flew straight away to the tent of the grand-vizier, and, with a stern air, reproached him for the treaty he had made. "I have a right," said the grand-vizier, with a calm aspect, " either to make peace or war." "But," added the King, "have you not the whole Russian army in your power?" "Our law commands us," replied the vizier, with great gravity, "to grant peace to our enemies when they implore our mercy." "And does it command you," resumed the King in a passion, "to make a bad treaty, when you may impose what laws you please? Had you not a fair opportunity, if you would have embraced it, of leading the Czar a prisoner to Constantinople?"

The Turk, driven to this extremity, replied very coldly: "And who would have governed his empire in his absence? It is not proper that all kings should leave their dominions." Charles made no other answer than by a smile of indignation. He then threw himself down upon a sofa, and, eyeing the vizier with an air of contempt and resentment, stretched out his leg, and entangling his spur in the Turk's robe, purposely tore it, after which he rose up, remounted his horse, and with a sorrowful heart returned to Bender. Poniatowski continued some time longer with the grand-vizier, to try if he could not prevail upon him, by more gentle means, to extort greater concessions from the Czar; but the hour of prayer having arrived, the Turk, without answering a single word, went to wash and attend divine service.

# BOOK VI

Intrigues at the Porte—The Khan of Tartary and the Pacha of Bender Endeavor to Force Charles to Depart—He Defends Himself with Forty Domestics against the Whole Army—He is Taken, and Treated as a Prisoner.

THE fortune of the King of Sweden, now so different from what it had formerly been, harassed him even in the most trifling circumstances. On his return, he found his little camp at Bender, and all his apartments, overflowed by the waters of the Dniester. He retired to the distance of a few miles, near the village of Varnitza; and, as if he had had a secret foreboding of what was to befall him, he there built a large house of stone, capable, on occasion, of sustaining an assault for a few hours. He even furnished it in a magnificent manner, contrary to his usual custom, in order the more effectually to attract the respect of the Turks.

He likewise built two other houses—one for his chancery and the other for his favorite Grothusen, who kept a table at the King's expense. While Charles was thus employed in building near Bender, as if he had been always to remain in Turkey, Baltagi Mehemet, dreading more than ever the intrigues and complaints of this prince at the Porte, had sent the resident of the Emperor of Germany into Vienna to demand a free passage for the King of Sweden through the hereditary dominions of the house of Austria. The envoy, in the space of three weeks, brought back a promise from the imperial regency, importing that they would pay Charles XII all due honors and conduct him safely into Pomerania.

Application was made to the Regency of Vienna, because Charles, the Emperor of Germany, who had succeeded Joseph, was then in Spain, disputing the crown of that kingdom with Philip V. While the German envoy was executing this commission at Vienna, the grand-vizier sent three pachas to acquaint the King of Sweden that he must quit the Turkish dominions.

The King, being previously apprised of the orders with which they were charged, caused intimation to be given them that if they presumed to make him any proposals contrary to his honor, or to the respect that was due to his character, he would forthwith have them all strung up on a gallows. The Pacha of Salonica, who delivered the message, disguised the harshness of the commission under the most respectful terms. Charles put an end to the audience, without deigning to give them an answer. His chancellor, Muller, who remained with the three pachas, briefly explained to them his master's refusal, which, indeed, they had sufficiently understood by his profound silence.

The grand-vizier was not to be diverted from his purpose; he ordered Ismael Pacha, the new Seraskier of Bender, to threaten the King with the Sultan's indignation if he did not immediately come to a resolution. The seraskier was a man of mild temper and engaging address, which had gained him the good-will of Charles and the friendship of all the Swedes. The King entered into a conference with him; but it was only to tell him that he would not depart until Achmet had granted him two favors — the punishment of his grand-vizier and 100,000 men to conduct him back to Poland.

Baltagi Mehemet was aware that Charles remained in Turkey only to ruin him. He therefore took care to place guards in all the roads from Bender to Constantinople, to intercept the King's letters. He did more; he retrenched his *thaim;* that is to say, the provision which the Porte allows those princes to whom she grants an asylum. That of the King of Sweden was immense, consisting of 500 crowns a day in money and a profusion of everything necessary to maintain a court in splendor and affluence.

As soon as the King was informed that the vizier had presumed to retrench his allowance, he turned to the steward of his household and said: "Hitherto you have only had two tables; I command you to have four for the future."

The officers of Charles XII had been used to find nothing impossible which their master ordered; at present, however, they had neither money nor provisions. They were forced to borrow at twenty, thirty, and forty per cent. of the officers, domestics, and Janizaries, who had grown rich by the King's profusion. Fabricius, the envoy of Holstein, Jeffreys, the English Minister, and their secretaries and friends gave all that they had. The King, with his usual stateliness, and without any concern about the morrow, lived on these presents, which could not have sufficed him long. It was necessary to elude the vigilance of the guards, and to send privately to Constantinople to borrow money of the European merchants. But everybody refused to lend to a king who seemed to have put himself out of a condition of ever being able to repay them. One English merchant alone, called Cook, ventured to lend him about 40,000 crowns, content to lose that sum if the King of Sweden should happen to die. This money was brought to the King's little camp just as they began to be in want of everything, and even to give over all hopes of any further relief.

During this interval, Poniatowski wrote, even from the camp of the grand-vizier, an account of the campaign at Pruth, in which he accused Baltagi Mehemet of perfidy and cowardice. An old Janizary, provoked at the vizier's weakness, and gained, moreover, by Poniatowski's liberality, undertook the delivery of the letter, and, having obtained leave, presented it with his own hand to the Sultan.

A few days after, Poniatowski left the camp and repaired to the Porte to form cabals, as usual, against the grand-vizier.

Everything favored his project. The Czar, being now at liberty, was in no haste to perform his engagements. The keys of Azof had not yet arrived; the grand-vizier was answerable for them, and justly dreading the indignation of his master, dared not venture to appear in his presence.

At that time the seraglio was filled more than ever with intrigues and factions. These cabals, which prevail in all courts, and which in ours commonly end in the dismission, or, at most, in the banishment of the minister, never fail at Constantinople to occasion the loss of more than one head. The present plot proved fatal to the old vizier, Chourlouli, and to Osman, the lieutenant of Baltagi Mehemet, who had been the principal author of the peace of Pruth, and had afterward obtained a considerable post at the Porte. Among Osman's treasures was found the Czarina's ring, and 20,000 pieces of gold, of Saxon and Russian coin; a plain proof that money alone had extricated the Czar from his dangerous situation and ruined the fortunes of Charles. The vizier, Baltagi Mehemet, was banished to the isle of Lemnos, where he died three years afterward. The Sultan did not seize his effects, either at his banishment or his death. He was far from being rich, and his poverty was a sufficient vindication of his character.

This grand-vizier was succeeded by Jussuf, or Joseph, whose fortune was as singular as that of his predecessors. Born on the frontiers of Muscovy, and taken prisoner at six years of age, with his family, he had been sold to a Janizary. He was long a servant in the seraglio, and at last became the second person in the empire where he had been a slave; but he was only the shadow of a minister. The young selictar, Ali Coumourgi, raised him to that slippery post, in hopes of one day filling it himself; and Jussuf, his creature, had nothing to do but to set the seals of the empire to whatever the favorite desired. From the very beginning of this vizier's ministry, the politics of the Ottoman Court seemed to undergo a total alteration. The Czar's plenipotentiaries, who resided at Constantinople, either as ministers or hostages, were treated with greater civility than ever. The grand-vizier confirmed with them the peace of Pruth; but what mortified the King of Sweden more than all the rest was to hear that the secret alliance, made with the Czar at Constantinople, was brought about by the mediation of the English and Dutch ambassadors.

Constantinople, from the time of Charles's retreat to Bender, had become what Rome has often been, the centre of the negotiations of Christendom. Count Désaleurs, the French ambassador at the Porte, supported the interests of Charles and Stanislaus; the Emperor of Germany's Minister opposed them; and the factions of Sweden and Muscovy clashed, as those of France and Spain have long done at the Court of Rome.

England and Holland seemed to be neuter, but were not so in reality. The new trade which the Czar had opened at Petersburg attracted the attention of these two commercial nations.

The English and the Dutch will always side with that prince who favors their trade the most. There were many advantages to be derived from a connection with the Czar, and therefore it is no wonder that the ministers of England and Holland should serve him privately at the Porte. One of the conditions of this new alliance was that Charles should be immediately obliged to quit the Turkish dominions, whether it was that the Czar hoped to seize him on the road, or that he thought him less formidable in his own kingdom than in Turkey, where he was always on the point of arming the Ottoman troops against the Russian Empire.

Charles was perpetually soliciting the Porte to send him back through Poland with a numerous army. The divan was resolved to send him back with a simple guard of 7,000 or 8,000 men, not as a king whom they meant to assist, but as a guest of whom they wanted to get rid. For this purpose, the Sultan Achmet wrote him the following letter:

> "*Most powerful among the kings that adore Jesus, redresser of wrongs and injuries in the ports and republics of the South and North, shining in majesty, lover of honor and glory, and of our sublime Porte, Charles, King of Sweden, whose enterprises may God crown with success:*

"As soon as the most illustrious Achmet, formerly Chiaoux Pachi, shall have the honor to deliver you this letter, adorned with our imperial seal, be persuaded and convinced of the truth of our intentions therein contained, viz., that though we had proposed once more to march our ever-victorious army against the Czar, yet that prince, in order to avoid the just resentment which he had conceived at his delaying to execute the treaty concluded on the banks of the Pruth, and afterward renewed at our sublime Porte, having surrendered into our hands the castle and city of Azof, and endeavored by the mediation of the English and Dutch ambassadors, our ancient allies, to cultivate a lasting peace with us, we have granted his request, and delivered to his plenipotentiaries, who remain with us as hostages, our imperial ratification, after having received his from their hands.

"We have given to the most honorable and valiant Delvet Gherai, Khan of Cudziack[?], Crimea, Nagai, Circassia, and to our most sage counsellor and noble Seraskier of Bender, Ismael (whom God preserve and increase their magnificence and wisdom), our inviolable and salutary orders for your return through Poland, according to your first intention, which has again been presented to us in your name. You must, therefore, prepare to set out before next winter under the protection of Providence, and with an honorable guard, in order to return to your own territories, taking care to pass through those of Poland in a friendly manner.

"Whatever is necessary for your journey shall be furnished you by my sublime Porte, as well in money as in men, horses, and wagons. Above all things, we advise and exhort you to give the most distinct and express orders to all the Swedes, and other persons in your retinue, to commit no outrage, nor be guilty of any action that may tend either directly or indirectly to break this peace and alliance.

"By these means you will preserve our good-will, of which we shall endeavor to give you as great and as frequent proofs as we shall have opportunities. The troops designed to attend you shall receive orders agreeable to our imperial intentions.

"Given at our sublime Porte of Constantinople, the fourteenth of the moon Rebyul Eurech, 1124, which answers to the 19th of April, 1712."

This letter did not deprive the King of Sweden of all hopes. He wrote to the Sultan that he should ever retain a grateful remembrance of the favors his Highness had bestowed upon him, but that he believed the Sultan was too just to send him back with the simple guard of a flying-camp into a country that still swarmed with the Czar's troops. And indeed the Emperor of Russia, notwithstanding the first article of the Treaty of Pruth, by which he was obliged to withdraw all his troops from Poland, had sent fresh ones into that kingdom; and it is somewhat surprising that the Grand Seignior should be ignorant of this particular.

The bad policy of the Porte, in being so much guided by the motives of vanity as to allow Christian princes to have ambassadors at Constantinople, without ever sending a single agent to any Christian court, gives the latter an opportunity of discovering, and sometimes of directing the most secret resolutions of the Sultan, and keeps the divan in a profound ignorance of what passes in the Christian world.

The Sultan, shut up in his seraglio among his women and eunuchs, can only see with the eyes of his grand-vizier. That minister, as inaccessible as his master, his time **wholly** engrossed with the intrigues of his seraglio, and having no foreign correspondence, is commonly deceived himself, or else deceives the Sultan, who deposes or causes him to be strangled for the first offence, in order to choose another minister as ignorant or as perfidious, who behaves like his predecessors, and soon shares the same fate.

So great, for the most part, is the inactivity and supine negligence of this court, that were the Christian princes to combine against it, their fleets might be at the Dardanelles, and their land forces at the gates of Adrianople, before the Turks would think of taking any measures for their defence; but their jarring interests, that must ever divide the Christian world, will preserve the Turks from a fate to which they seem at present exposed, by their want of policy and by their ignorance of the art of war, both by sea and land.

So little was Achmet acquainted with what passed in Poland that he sent an aga to inquire whether, in reality, the Czar's troops were still in that country. The aga was accompanied by two secretaries of the King of Sweden, who understood the Turkish language, and were to serve as evidences against him, in case he should give in a false report.

The aga saw the Russian forces with his own eyes and informed the Sultan of every particular. Achmet, fired with indignation, was going to strangle the grand-vizier; but the favorite, who protected him, and who thought he should have further occasion for him, obtained his pardon and supported him some time longer in the ministry.

The cause of the Russians was openly espoused by the vizier, and secretly favored by Ali Coumourgi, who had changed sides. But the Sultan was so provoked, the infraction of the treaty was so manifest, and the Janizaries, who often make the ministers, the favorites, and even the sultans tremble, called out for war with so much importunity that no one in the seraglio dared offer a more moderate proposal.

The Grand Seignior immediately committed to the Seven Towers the Russian ambassadors, who were already as much accustomed to go to prison as to an audience. War was declared afresh against the Czar, the standards were displayed, and orders were given to all the pachas to assemble an army of 200,000 men. The Sultan himself quitted Constantinople, and fixed his court at Adrianople, that he might be so much the nearer to the seat of the war.

Meanwhile a solemn embassy, sent to the Grand Seignior by Augustus and the Republic of Poland, was upon the road to Adrianople. The Palatine of Massovia was at the head of this embassy, with a retinue of above 300 persons.

All the members of the embassy were seized and imprisoned in one of the suburbs of the city. Never was the King of Sweden's party more highly flattered than on this occasion; and yet these great preparations were rendered abortive, and all their hopes were again disappointed.

If we may believe a public minister, a man of sagacity and penetration, who then resided at Constantinople, young Coumourgi had already found other designs than that of disputing a desert country with the Czar, by a war, the event of which must have been so uncertain. He had resolved to strip the Venetians of Peloponnesus, now called the Morea, and to make himself master of Hungary.

These grand projects he proposed to carry into execution as soon as he should have attained the post of prime-vizier, from which he was still excluded on account of his youth. In this view, it was more for his advantage to be the ally than the enemy of the Czar. It was neither his interest nor his inclination to keep the King of Sweden any longer, and much less to arm the Turkish Empire in his favor. He not only resolved to dismiss that prince, but he openly declared that, for the future, no Christian minister should be allowed to reside at Constantinople; that all the common ambassadors were, at best, but honorable spies, who corrupted or betrayed the viziers, and had too long influenced the intrigues of the seraglio; and that the Franks settled at Pera and in the seaports of the Levant were merchants who needed a consul only, and not an ambassador. The grand-vizier, who owed his post and even his life to the favorite, and who, beside, stood greatly in awe of him, complied with his intentions with so much the more alacrity, as he had sold himself to the Russians, and hoped by this means to be revenged on the King of Sweden, who had endeavored to ruin him. The mufti, a creature of Ali Coumourgi, was likewise an absolute slave to his will. He had been a keen advocate for a war with Russia when the favorite was of that opinion; but the moment

Coumourgi changed his mind, he pronounced it to be unjust. Thus the army was hardly assembled when they began to listen to proposals of peace. The vice-chancellor, Schaffirof, and young Sheremetef, the Czar's hostages and plenipotentiaries at the Porte, promised, after several negotiations, that their master should withdraw his troops from Poland. The grand-vizier, who well knew that the Czar would never execute this treaty, made no scruple to sign it; and the Sultan, satisfied with having, though only in appearance, imposed laws upon the Russians, continued still at Adrianople. Thus, in less than six months, peace was ratified with the Czar, war declared, and peace renewed again.

The chief article of all these treaties was to oblige the King of Sweden to depart. The Sultan was unwilling to endanger his own honor and that of the Ottoman Empire by exposing the King to the risk of being taken by his enemies on the road. It was stipulated that he should depart, but only on condition that the ambassadors of Poland and Muscovy should be responsible for the safety of his person. Accordingly these ambassadors swore, in the name of their masters, that neither the Czar nor the King of Poland should molest him in his journey; and Charles was to engage, on his side, that he would not attempt to excite any commotions in Poland. The divan having thus settled the fate of Charles, Ismael, Seraskier of Bender, repaired to Varnitza, where the King was encamped, and acquainted him with the resolutions of the Porte, insinuating to him, with great politeness, that there was no time for any longer delay, but that he must necessarily depart.

Charles made no other answer than this, that the Grand Seignior had promised him an army, and not a guard; and that kings ought to keep their word.

Meanwhile General Flemming, the Minister and favorite of Augustus, maintained a secret correspondence with the Khan of Tartary and the Seraskier of Bender. La Mare, a French gentleman, a colonel in the service of Saxony, had made several journeys from Bender to Dresden; and all these journeys were strongly suspected.

At this very time, the King of Sweden caused a courier, whom Flemming had sent to the Prince of Tartary, to be arrested on the frontiers of Wallachia. The letters were brought to him and deciphered, and from them it clearly appeared that a correspondence was carried on between the Tartars and the Court of Dresden; but the letters were conceived in such ambiguous and general terms that it was difficult to discover whether the intention of Augustus was only to detach the Turks from the interest of Sweden, or if he meant that the Khan should deliver Charles to the Saxons as he conducted him back to Poland.

We can hardly imagine that a prince so generous as Augustus would, by seizing the person of the King of Sweden, endanger the lives of his ambassadors, and of 300 Polish gentlemen, who were detained at Adrianople as pledges of Charles's safety.

But it is well known, on the other hand, that Flemming, the Minister of Augustus, and who had an absolute power over his master, was a man devoid of every principle of virtue or honor. The injuries which the Elector had received from the King of Sweden might seem to excuse any kind of revenge; and it might be thought that, if the Court of Dresden could buy Charles from the Khan of Tartary, they would find it no difficult matter to purchase the liberty of the Polish hostages at the Ottoman Porte.

These reasons were carefully canvassed by the King, Muller, his privy chancellor, and Grothusen, his favorite. They read the letters again and again; and their unhappy condition making them more suspicious, they resolved to believe the worst.

A few days after, the King was confirmed in his suspicions by the sudden departure of Count Sapieha, who had taken refuge with him, and now left him abruptly, in order to go to Poland to throw himself into the arms of Augustus. Upon any other occasion he would have considered Sapieha only as a malcontent; but in his present delicate situation, he at once concluded him to be a traitor. The repeated importunities with which he was pressed to depart converted his suspicions into certainty. The inflexible obstinacy of his temper, co-operating with these circumstances, confirmed him in the opinion that they intended to betray him and deliver him up to his enemies, though this plot has never been fully proved.

Perhaps he was mistaken in supposing that Augustus had made a bargain with the Tartars for his person; but he was much more deceived in relying on the assistance of the Ottoman Court. Be that as it may, he resolved to gain time.

He told the Pacha of Bender that he could not depart till he had received money to discharge his debts; for though his *thaim* had for a long time been duly paid, his unbounded liberality had always obliged him to borrow. The pacha asked him how much he wanted? The King replied, at a venture, 1,000 purses, amounting to 1,500,000 livres, full weight. The pacha acquainted the Porte with his request. The Sultan, instead of 1,000 purses which Charles had required, granted him 1,200, and wrote the Pacha the following letter:

### THE GRAND SEIGNIOR'S LETTER TO THE PACHA OF BENDER

"The design of this imperial letter is to acquaint you that upon your representation and request, and upon that of the most noble Delvet Gherai Khan, to our Sublime Porte, our imperial munificence has granted 1,000 purses to the King of Sweden, which shall be sent to Bender under the care and conduct of the most illustrious Mehemet Pacha, formerly Chiaoux Pachi, to remain in your custody till the departure of the King of Sweden, whose steps may God direct, and then to be given him, together with 200 purses more, as an overplus of our imperial liberality, above what he demands.

"With regard to the route of Poland, which he is resolved to take, you and the Khan, who are to attend him, shall be careful to pursue such wise and prudent measures as may, during the whole journey, prevent the troops under your command, as well as those of the King of Sweden, from committing any outrage, or being guilty of any action that may be deemed a violation of the peace which still subsists between our Sublime Porte and the Kingdom and Republic of Poland; so that the King may pass in a friendly manner under our protection.

"By doing this (which you must expressly require him to do), he will receive from the Poles all the honor and respect that are due to his Majesty; as we have been assured by the ambassadors of Augustus and the republic, who, on this condition, have even offered themselves, together with several others of the Polish nobility, if required, as hostages for the security of his passage.

"When the time which you and the most noble Delvet Gherai shall fix for the march arrives, you shall put yourself at the head of your brave soldiers, among whom shall be the Tartars, headed by the Khan, and you shall conduct the King of Sweden and his men.

"And may it please the only God, the Almighty, to direct your steps and theirs. The Pacha of Aulos shall continue at Bender with a regiment of Spahis and another of Janizaries, to defend it in your absence. And in the following our imperial orders and intentions in all these points and articles, you will deserve the continuance of our imperial favor, as well as the praise and recompense due to all those who observe them.

"Done at our imperial residence of Constantinople, the 2d of the moon Cheval, 1124, of the Hegira."

While they were waiting for this answer from the Grand Seignior, Charles wrote to the Porte, complaining of the treachery of which he suspected the Khan of Tartary to be guilty; but all the passages were well guarded, and, moreover, the Minister was against him, so that his letters never reached the Sultan. Nay, the vizier would not allow M. Désaleurs to come to Adrianople, where the Porte then was, lest that Minister, who was then an agent of the King of Sweden, should endeavor to disconcert the plan he had formed for obliging him to depart.

Charles, enraged to see himself thus hunted, as it were, from the Grand Seignior's dominions, resolved not to quit them at all.

He might have desired to return through Germany, or to take ship on the Black Sea, in order to sail to Marseilles by the Mediterranean, but he rather chose to ask nothing, and to await the event.

When the 1,200 purses had arrived, his treasurer Grothusen, who, during his long abode in Turkey, had learned the language of the country, went to wait upon the pacha without an interpreter, hoping to draw the money from him, and afterward to form some new intrigue at the Porte, foolishly supposing, as he always did, that the Swedish party would at last be able to arm the Ottoman Empire against the Czar.

Grothusen told the pacha that the King could not get ready his equipages without money. "But," said the pacha, "we shall defray all the expenses of your departure; your master shall be at no charge while he continues under my protection."

Grothusen replied that the difference between the equipages of the Turks and those of the Franks was so great that they were obliged to apply to the Swedish and Polish artificers at Varnitza.

He assured him that his master was willing to depart, and that this money would facilitate and hasten his departure. The too credulous pacha gave the 1,200 purses, and a few days after came to the King, and, in a most respectful manner, begged to receive his orders for his departure.

He was extremely surprised when the King told him he was not yet ready to go, and that he wanted 1,000 purses more. The pacha, confounded at this answer, stood speechless for a moment; then retiring to a window, he was observed to shed some tears. At last, addressing himself to the King, "I shall lose my head," said he, "for having obliged your Majesty; I have given you the 1,200 purses against the express orders of my sovereign." So saying, he took his leave with a dejected countenance.

The King stopped him, and said that he would make an excuse for him to the Sultan. "Ah," replied the Turk, as he was going away, "my master can punish faults, but cannot excuse them."

Ismael Pacha carried this piece of news to the Khan, who, having received the same orders with the pacha, not to suffer the 1,200 purses to be given to the King before his departure, and having consented to the delivery of the money, was as apprehensive as the pacha of the Grand Seignior's indignation. They both wrote to the Porte in their own vindication, protesting they did not give the 1,200 purses but upon a solemn promise from the King's minister that he would depart without delay, and beseeching his Highness not to impute the King's refusal to their disobedience.

Charles, still persisting in the belief that the Khan and pacha meant to deliver him up to his enemies, ordered Funk, who was then his envoy at the Ottoman Court, to lay his complaints against them before the Sultan, and to ask 1,000 purses more. His great generosity, and the little account he made of money, hindered him from perceiving the meanness of this proposal. He did it with a view to be refused and in order to find a fresh pretext for delaying his departure. But a man must be reduced to strange extremities, to stand in need of such artifices. Savari, his interpreter, an artful and enterprising man, carried the letter to Adrianople, in spite of all the care which the grand-vizier had taken to guard the passes.

Funk was obliged to present this dangerous request. All the answer he received was to be thrown into prison. The Sultan, in a passion, convoked an extraordinary Divan, and, what very seldom happens, spoke himself on the occasion. His speech, according to the translation which was then made of it, was conceived in the following terms:

"I have scarcely known the King of Sweden but by his defeat at Poltava, and by the application he made to me to grant him an asylum in my dominions. I have not, I believe, any need of him, nor any reason either to love or fear him. Nevertheless, without consulting any other motives than the hospitality of a Mussulman, and my own generosity, which sheds the dew of its favors upon the great as well as the small, upon strangers as well as my own subjects, I have received and assisted him, his ministers, officers, and soldiers, and, for the space of three years and a half, have continued to load him with presents.

"I have granted him a considerable guard to conduct him back to his own kingdom. He asked 1,000 purses to defray some expenses, though I pay them all: instead of 1,000, I granted him 1,200. After having got these out of the hands of the Seraskier of Bender, he asks 1,000 purses more, and refuses to depart, under a pretence that the guard is too small, whereas, in fact, it is but too large to pass through the country of a friend.

"I ask you, then, whether it be a violation of the laws of hospitality to send back this prince; and whether foreign powers ought to accuse me of cruelty and injustice, in case I should be obliged to compel him to depart?" All the members of the Divan answered that such conduct would be consistent with the strictest rules of justice.

The mufti declared that Mussulmans were not bound to show any hospitality to infidels, and much less to the ungrateful; and he gave his *fetfa*, a kind of mandate which commonly accompanies the important orders of the Grand Seignior. These fetfas are revered as oracles, though the persons by whom they are given are as much slaves to the Sultan as any others.

The order and the fetfa were carried to Bender by the *Bouyouk Imraour*, grand-master of the horse, and a *Chiaoux Pacha*, first usher. The Pacha of Bender received the order at the lodgings of the Khan of Tartary, from whence ne immediately repaired to Varnitza, to ask the King whether he would depart in a friendly manner or lay him under the necessity of executing the Sultan's orders.

Charles XII being thus menaced, could not restrain his passion. "Obey your master, if you dare," said he to the pacha, "and leave my presence immediately." The pacha, fired with indignation, returned at full gallop, contrary to the common custom of the Turks; and meeting Fabricius by the way, he called out to him, without halting: "The King will not listen to reason; you will see strange things presently." The same day he discontinued the supply of the King's provisions and removed the guard of Janizaries. He caused intimation to be made to the Poles and Cossacks at Varnitza that if they had a mind to have any provisions, they must quit the King of Sweden's camp, repair to Bender, and put themselves under the protection of the Porte. These orders were readily obeyed by all, and the King was left without any other attendants than the officers of his household and 300 Swedish soldiers to make head against 20,000 Tartars and 6,000 Turks.

There was now no provision in the camp either for man or horse. The King ordered twenty of the fine Arabian horses, which had been sent him by the Grand Seignior, to be shot without the camp, adding, "I will have none of their provisions nor their horses." This was an excellent feast to the Tartars, who, as all the world knows, think horse-flesh delicious fare. Meanwhile the Turks and Tartars invested the King's little camp on all sides.

Charles, without the least discomposure, ordered his 300 Swedes to raise regular intrenchments, in which work he himself assisted, as did likewise his chancellor, his treasurer, his secretaries, his *valets-de-chambre*, and all his domestics. Some barricaded the windows and others fastened beams behind the doors in the form of buttresses.

After the house was sufficiently barricaded and the King had rode round his pretended fortifications, he sat down to chess with his favorite, Grothusen, with as much tranquillity as if everything had been perfectly safe and secure. Happily Fabricius, the Envoy of Holstein, did not lodge at Varnitza, but at a small village between Varnitza and Bender, where Jeffreys, the English envoy to the King of Sweden, likewise resided. These two ministers, seeing the storm ready to burst, undertook the office of mediators between the King and the Turks. The Khan, and especially the Pacha of Bender, who had no inclination to offer any violence to the Swedish monarch, received the offers of these two ministers with great satisfaction. They had two conferences at Bender, in which the usher of the seraglio, and the grand-master of the horse, who had brought the Sultan's order, and the mufti's fetfa assisted.

Fabricius * declared to them that his Swedish Majesty had good reason to believe that they designed to deliver him up to his enemies in Poland. The Khan, the pacha, and all the rest swore by their heads, and called God to witness, that they detested such a horrible piece of treachery, and that they would shed the last drop of their blood rather than suffer even the least disrespect to be shown to the King in Poland; adding that they had in their hands the Russian and Polish ambassadors, whose lives should be answerable for any affront that should be offered to the King of Sweden. In fine, they complained bitterly that the King should entertain such injurious suspicions of those who had received and treated him with so much humanity and politeness.

Though oaths are frequently the language of treachery, Fabricius could not help being convinced of their sincerity. He thought he could discern in their protestations such an air of veracity as falsehood can, at best, but imperfectly imitate. He was aware there had been a secret correspondence between the Khan of Tartary and Augustus; but he was firmly persuaded that the only end of their negotiation was to oblige Charles XII to quit the dominions of the Grand Seignior. Whether Fabricius was mistaken or not, he assured them he would represent to the King the injustice of his suspicions. "But," added he, "do you intend to compel him to depart?" "Yes," said the pacha, "for such are the orders of our master." He then entreated them to consider seriously whether that order implied that they should shed the blood of a crowned head. "Yes," replied the Khan, in a passion, "if that crowned head disobeys the Grand Seignior in his own dominions."

In the meantime, everything being ready for the assault, the

* The whole of this account is related by M. Fabricius in his letters.

death of Charles XII seemed inevitable. But as the Sultan had not given them positive orders to kill him in case of resistance, the pacha prevailed upon the Khan to let him despatch an express to Adrianople, where the Grand Seignior then resided, to receive the last orders of his Highness.

Jeffreys and Fabricius, having procured this short respite, hastened to acquaint the King with it. They came with all the eagerness of people who bring good news, but were received very coldly. He called them unsolicited mediators, and still persisted in the belief that the Sultan's order and the mufti's fetfa were both forged, inasmuch as they had sent to the Porte for fresh orders.

The English Minister retired, with a firm resolution to interfere no more in the affairs of a prince so very obstinate and inflexible. Fabricius, beloved by the King, and more accustomed to his humor than the English Minister, remained with him, and earnestly entreated him not to hazard so precious a life on such an unnecessary occasion.

For answer, the King showed him his fortifications, and begged he would employ his good offices in procuring him some provisions. The Turks were easily prevailed upon to allow provisions to be conveyed to the King's camp until the return of the courier from Adrianople. The Khan himself had strictly enjoined his Tartars, who were eager for pillage, not to make any attempt against the Swedes till the arrival of fresh orders; so that Charles XII went sometimes out of his camp with forty horse, and rode through the midst of the Tartars, who, with great respect, left him a free passage. He even marched directly up to their lines, which, instead of resisting, readily opened and allowed him to pass.

At last, the order of the Grand Seignior having arrived, to put to the sword all the Swedes that should make the least resistance, and not even to spare the life of the King, the pacha had the complaisance to show the order to Fabricius, with a view of inducing him to make his last effort to bend, if possible, the obstinacy of Charles. Fabricius went immediately to acquaint him with these sad tidings. "Have you seen the order you mention?" said the King. "I have," replied Fabricius. "Well, then, go tell them in my name that this second order is another forgery of theirs and that I will not depart." Fabricius threw himself at his feet, fell into a passion, and reproached him with his obstinacy; but all to no purpose. "Go back to your Turks," said the King to him, smiling; "if they attack me, I know how to defend myself." The King's chaplains likewise fell upon their knees before him, conjuring him not to expose to certain death the unhappy remains of Poltava, and especially his own sacred person; assuring him, at the same time, that resistance in such a case was altogether unjustifiable, and that it was a direct violation of all the laws of hospitality to resolve to continue with strangers against their will, especially with those strangers who had so long and so generously supported him. The King, who had heard Fabricius with great patience, fell into a passion with his priests, and told them that he had taken them to pray for him, and not to give him advice.

The generals Hord and Dehldorf, who had always declared against hazarding a battle which could not fail to be attended with fatal consequences, showed the King their breasts, covered with wounds, which they had received in his service; and assuring him that they were ready to lay down their lives for his sake, begged that it might be, at least, upon a more necessary occasion. "I know," said Charles XII, "by your wounds and by my own that we have fought valiantly together. You have hitherto done your duty; do it to-day likewise." Nothing now remained but to pay implicit obedience to the King's command. Everyone was ashamed not to court death with his sovereign. Charles, being now prepared for the assault, enjoyed in secret the pleasing thoughts that he should have the honor of sustaining with 300 Swedes the united efforts of a whole army. He assigned to every man his post. His chancellor, Muller, and the secretary, Ehrenpreus, and his clerks were to defend the chancery-house; Baron Fief, at the head of the officers of the kitchen, was stationed at another post. A third place was to be guarded by the grooms of the stable and the cooks, for with him everyone was a soldier. He rode from the intrenchments to his house, promising rewards to everyone, creating officers, and assuring them that he would exalt the very meanest of his servants, who should fight with courage and resolution, to the dignity of captains.

It was not long before they beheld the combined army of the Turks and Tartars advancing to attack this little camp with ten pieces of cannon and two mortars. The banners waved in the air; the clarions sounded; the cries of "*Allah! Allah!*" were heard on all sides. Baron Grothusen, observing that the Turks did not mix in their cries any injurious reflections on the King, but only called him *Demirbash*, i.e., Iron-head, he instantly resolved to go out of the camp alone and unarmed; and having accordingly advanced to the lines of the Janizaries, most of whom had received money from him: "What, then, my friends," said he to them, in their own language, "have you come to massacre 300 defenceless Swedes? You, brave Janizaries, who pardoned 100,000 Russians upon their crying *Amman* [pardon]—have you forgot the many favors you have received from us? and would you assassinate that great King of Sweden for whom you have so great a regard, and from whom you have received so many presents? All he asks, my friends, is but the space of three days; and the Sultan's orders are not so strict as you are made to believe."

These words produced an effect which Grothusen himself could little have expected. The Janizaries swore by their beards that they would not attack the King, but would grant him the three days he demanded. In vain was the signal given for the assault. The Janizaries were so far from obeying that they threatened to fall upon their leaders, unless they would consent to grant three days to the King of Sweden. They came to the Pacha of Bender's tent, crying out that the Sultan's orders were fictitious. To this unexpected sedition the pacha had nothing to oppose but patience.

He affected to be pleased with the generous resolution of the Janizaries, and ordered them to return to Bender. The Khan of Tartary, a man of headstrong and impetuous passions, would have given the assault immediately with his own troops, but the pacha, unwilling that the Tartars should have all the honor of taking the King, while he himself perhaps might be punished for the disobedience of the Janizaries, persuaded the Khan to wait till the next day.

On his return to Bender, the pacha assembled all the officers of the Janizaries, and the oldest soldiers, to whom he both read and showed the Sultan's positive orders and the mufti's fetfa. Sixty of the oldest of them, with venerable gray beards, who had received a thousand presents from the King's hands, proposed to go to him in person, to entreat him to put himself into their hands, and to permit them to serve him as guards.

The pacha agreed to the proposal, as, indeed, there was no expedient he would not willingly have tried, rather than be reduced to the necessity of killing the King. Accordingly these sixty veterans repaired next morning to Varnitza, having nothing in their hands but long white rods, the only arms which the Janizaries wear, except when they are going to fight; for the Turks consider the Christian custom of carrying swords in time of peace, and of entering armed into churches and the houses of their friends, as a barbarous practice.

They addressed themselves to Baron Grothusen and Chancellor Muller. They told them that they had come with a view to serve as faithful guards to the King; and that if he pleased they would conduct him to Adrianople, where he might have a personal interview with the Grand Seignior. While they were making this proposal, the King read the letters which were brought from Constantinople, and which Fabricius, who could no longer attend him in person, had sent him privately by a Janizary. These letters were from Count Poniatowski, who could neither serve him at Bender nor Adrianople, having been detained at Constantinople by order of the Porte, ever since the time of his making the imprudent demand of 1,000 purses. He told the King that the Sultan's orders to seize or massacre his royal person in case of resistance were but too true; that, indeed, the Sultan was imposed upon by his ministers; but the more he was imposed upon, he would, for that very reason, be the more faithfully obeyed; that he must submit to the times and yield to necessity; that he took the liberty to advise him to try every expedient with the ministers by way of negotiations, not to be inflexible in a matter which required the gentlest management, and to expect from time and good policy a cure of that evil, which, by rash and violent measures, would be only rendered incurable.

But neither the proposals of the old Janizaries nor Poniatowski's letters could convince the King that it was consistent with his honor to yield. He rather chose to perish by the hands of the Turks than in any respect to be made a prisoner. He dismissed the Janizaries without condescending to see them, and sent them word that if they did not immediately depart he would shave their beards for them; an affront which, in the Eastern countries, is considered as the most intolerable of all others.

The old men, filled with the highest indignation, returned home, crying out as they went: "Ah! this Iron-head! since he will perish, let him perish." They gave the pacha an account of their commission, and informed their comrades at Bender of the strange reception they had met with; upon which they all swore to obey the pacha's orders without delay, and were as impatient to go to the assault as they had been averse to it the day before.

The word of command was immediately given. The Turks marched up to the fortifications: the Tartars were already waiting for them and the cannon began to play. The Janizaries on the one side and the Tartars on the other instantly forced the little camp. Hardly had twenty Swedes time to draw their swords, when the whole 300 were surrounded and taken prisoners without resistance. The King was then on horseback, between his house and his camp, with the generals Hord, Dehldorf, and Sparr: seeing that all his soldiers had suffered themselves to be taken prisoners before his eyes, he said, with great composure, to these three officers: "Come, let us go and defend the house; we will fight," added he, with a smile, "*pro aris et focis.*"

Accordingly, accompanied by these three generals, he forthwith galloped up to the house, in which he had placed about forty domestics as sentinels, and which he had fortified in the best manner he could.

The generals, accustomed as they were to the dauntless intrepidity of their master, could not help being surprised to see him resolve in cold blood, and even with an air of pleasantry, to defend himself against ten pieces of cannon and a whole army; nevertheless they followed him, with some guards and domestics, making in all about twenty persons.

When they had come to the door, they found it beset by the Janizaries. Beside, 200 Turks and Tartars had already entered by a window and made themselves masters of all the apartments, except a large hall where the King's domestics had retired. Happily, this hall was near the door at which the King designed to enter with his little troop of twenty persons. He threw himself off his horse with pistol and sword in hand, and his followers did the same.

The Janizaries fell upon him on all sides. They were animated with the promise which the pacha had made, of eight ducats of gold to every man who should only touch his clothes, in case they could take him. He wounded and killed all those who came near him. A Janizary whom he wounded clapped a blunderbuss to his face, and had he not been jostled by the arm of a Turk, owing to the crowd that moved backward and forward like waves, the King had certainly been killed. The ball grazed his nose, and carried off part of his ear, and then broke the arm of General Hord, whose constant fate it was to be wounded by his master's side.

The King plunged his sword into the Janizary's breast. At the same time, his domestics, who were shut up in the great hall, opened the door to him. The King, with his little troop, sprung in like an arrow. They instantly shut the door, and barricaded it with whatever they could find. Thus was Charles XII shut up in this hall with all his attendants, consisting of about sixty men, officers, guards, secretaries, *valets-de-chambre*, and domestics of every kind.

The Janizaries and Tartars pillaged the rest of the house and filled the apartments. "Come," said the King, "let us go and drive out these barbarians;" and putting himself at the head of his men, he, with his own hands, opened the door that led to his bed-chamber, rushed into the room, and fired upon the plunderers.

The Turks, loaded with spoil, and terrified at the sudden appearance of the King, whom they had ever been accustomed to respect, threw down their arms, leaped out of the window, or flew to the cellars. The King taking advantage of their confusion, and his own men being animated by the success of this attempt, they pursued the Turks from chamber to chamber, killed or wounded those who had not made their escape, and in a quarter of an hour cleared the house of the enemy.

In the heat of the fight the King perceived two Janizaries, who lay concealed under his bed; one of them he stabbed with his sword; the other asked pardon, by crying, *Amman*. "I give you your life," said the King to him, " on this condition: that you go and give the pacha a faithful account of what you have seen." The Turk readily promised to do as he was bid, and was allowed to leap out at the window like the rest.

The Swedes, having at last made themselves masters of the house, again shut and barricaded the windows. They were in no want of arms. A ground-room full of muskets and powder had escaped the tumultuous search of the Janizaries. These they employed to good purpose. They fired through the windows almost close upon the Turks, of whom, in less than half a quarter of an hour, they killed 200. The cannon still played upon the house, but the stones being very soft, there were only some holes made in the walls, and nothing was demolished.

The Khan of Tartary and the pacha, who were desirous of taking the King alive, being ashamed to lose so many men, and to employ a whole army against sixty persons, thought it most advisable to set fire to the house in order to oblige the King to surrender. They ordered some arrows, to which lighted matches were attached, to be shot upon the roof and against the doors and windows. In a moment the house was in flames. The roof, all on fire, was ready to tumble upon the Swedes. The King, with great calmness, gave orders to extinguish the fire. Finding a small barrel full of liquor, he took it up, and being assisted by two Swedes, threw it upon the place where the fire was most violent. At last he recollected that the barrel was full of brandy; but the hurry, inseparable from such a scene of confusion, hindered him from thinking of it in time. The fire now raged with double fury. The King's apartment was reduced to ashes. The great hall where the Swedes were was filled with a terrible smoke, mixed with sheets of flame that darted in at the doors of the neighboring apartments. One half of the roof sunk within the house; the other fell on the outside, cracking amid the flames.

In this extremity, a sentinel, called Walberg, ventured to cry that there was a necessity for surrendering. "What a strange man is this," said the King, "to imagine that it is not more glorious to be burnt than to be taken prisoner!" Another sentinel, named Rosen, had the presence of mind to observe that the chancery-house, which was not above fifty paces distant, had a stone roof and was proof against fire; that they ought to sally forth, take possession of that house, and then defend themselves to the last extremity. "There is a true

Swede for you!" cried the King; and embracing the sentinel, he made him a colonel upon the spot. "Come on, my friends," said he; "take as much powder and ball with you as you can, and let us take possession of the chancery, sword in hand."

The Turks, who all the while surrounded the house, were struck with fear and admiration to see the Swedes continue in it, notwithstanding it was all in flames; but their astonishment was greatly increased when they saw the doors opened, and the King and his followers rushing out upon them like so many madmen. Charles and his principal officers were armed with sword and pistol. Every man fired two pistols at once, the moment the doors were opened; and in the twinkling of an eye, throwing away their pistols, and drawing their swords, they made the Turks recoil above fifty paces. But in a moment after, this little troop was surrounded. The King, who was booted, as usual, entangled himself with his spurs, and fell. One-and-twenty Janizaries at once sprang upon him. He threw up his sword into the air, to save himself the mortification of surrendering it. The Turks bore him to the pacha's quarters, some taking hold of his arms, and others of his legs, in the same manner as sick persons are wont to be carried, in order to prevent their being hurt.

No sooner did the King see himself in their hands, than the violence of his temper, and the fury which such a long and desperate fight must have naturally inspired, gave place at once to a mild and gentle behavior; not one word of impatience dropped from his lips; not one angry look was to be seen in his face. He eyed the Janizaries with a smiling countenance, and they carried him off, crying *Allah,* with a mixture of respect and indignation. His officers were taken at the same time, and stripped by the Turks and Tartars. It was on February 12, 1713, that this strange event happened—an event that was followed by very remarkable consequences.*

---

* M. Norberg, who was not present at this adventure, has, in this particular part of his history, only copied the account of Voltaire; but he has mangled it. He has suppressed some interesting circumstances, and has not been able to justify the temerity of Charles XII. All that he has been able to advance against Voltaire with regard to the affair of Bender, is reducible to the adventure of the Sieur Frederick, *valet-de-chambre* to the King of Sweden, who, according to some, was burnt in the King's house, and, according to others, was cut in two by the Tartars. La Motraye alleges likewise, that the King of Sweden did not use these words, "We will fight *pro aris et focis.*" But Fabricius, who was present, affirms that the King did pronounce these words; that La Motraye was not near enough to hear them; and that if he had, he was not capable of comprehending their meaning, as he did not understand a word of Latin.

# BOOK VII

The Turks Convey Charles to Demirtash—King Stanislaus is Taken at the Same Time—Bold Undertaking of M. de Villelongue—Revolutions in the Seraglio — Battle in Pomerania — Altona Burnt by the Swedes—Charles at last Sets Out on His Return to His Own Dominions—His Strange Manner of Travelling—His Arrival at Stralsund—His Misfortunes—Successes of Peter the Great—His Triumphant Entry into Petersburg.

THE Pacha of Bender, with great gravity, waited for Charles in his tent, attended by one Marco, an interpreter. He received his Majesty in a most respectful manner, and entreated him to repose himself on a sofa; but the King, who did not so much as take notice of the Turk's civilities, continued standing.

"Blessed be the Almighty," said the Pacha, "that your Majesty is alive. I am extremely sorry that your Majesty obliged me to execute the orders of his Highness." The King, who was only vexed that his 300 soldiers should have suffered themselves to be taken in their intrenchments, said to the pacha: "Ah! had they defended themselves as they ought, you would not have been able to force our camp in ten days." "Alas!" said the Turk, "that so much courage should be so ill employed." He ordered the King to be conducted back to Bender on a horse richly caparisoned. All the Swedes were either killed or taken prisoners. All his equipage, his goods, his papers, and most necessary utensils, were either plundered or burnt. One might have seen in the public roads the Swedish officers, almost naked, and chained together in pairs, following the Tartars or Janizaries on foot. The chancellor and the general officers did not meet with a milder fate; they were the slaves of the soldiers to whose share they had fallen.

Ismael Pacha having conducted Charles to his seraglio at Bender, gave him his own apartment and ordered him to be served like a king; but not without taking the precaution to plant a guard of Janizaries at the chamber door. A bed was prepared for him, but he threw himself down upon a sofa, booted as he was, and fell fast asleep. An officer, that stood near him in waiting, covered his head with a cap; but the King, upon awaking from his first sleep, threw it off, and the Turk was surprised to see a sovereign prince sleeping in his boots and bare-headed. Next morning Ismael introduced Fabricius into the King's chamber. Fabricius found his Majesty with his clothes torn, his boots, his hands, and his whole body covered with dust and blood, and his eyebrows burnt, but still maintaining, in this terrible condition, a placid and cheerful look. He fell upon his knees before him, without being able to utter a word; but soon recovering from his surprise, by the free and easy manner in which the King addressed him, he resumed his wonted familiarity with him, and they began to talk of the battle of Bender with great humor and pleasantry. "It is reported," said Fabricius, "that your Majesty killed twenty Janizaries with your own hand." "Well, well," replied the King, "a story, you know, never loses in the telling." During this conversation the pacha presented to the King his favorite Grothusen, and Colonel Ribbing, whom he had had the generosity to redeem at his own expense. Fabricius undertook to ransom the other prisoners.

Jeffreys, the English envoy, joined his endeavors with those of Fabricius, in order to procure the money necessary for this purpose. A Frenchman, who had come to Bender out of mere curiosity, and who has written a short account of these transactions, gave all that he had; and these strangers, assisted by the interest, and even by the money of the pacha, redeemed not only the officers, but likewise their clothes, from the hands of the Turks and Tartars.

Next day the King was conducted, as a prisoner, in a chariot covered with scarlet, toward Adrianople. His treasurer Grothusen was with him. Chancellor Muller and some officers followed in another carriage. Several were on horseback, and, when they cast their eyes on the King's chariot, they could not refrain from tears. The pacha was at the head of the convoy: Fabricius told him that it was a shame the King should want a sword, and begged he would give him one. "God forbid!" said the pacha; "he would cut our beards for us, if he had a sword." However, he gave him one a few hours after.

While they were conducting this King, disarmed and a prisoner, who, but a few years before, had given law to so many States, and had seen himself the arbiter of the North, and the terror of Europe, there apeared in the same place another instance of the frailty of human greatness.

King Stanislaus had been seized in the Turkish dominions, and they were now carrying him a prisoner to Bender at the very time they were removing Charles from it.

Stanislaus, being no longer supported by the hand which had raised him to the throne, and, finding himself destitute of money, and consequently of interest in Poland, had retired at first into Pomerania; and unable to preserve his own kingdom, he had done all that lay in his own power to defend that of his benefactor: he had even gone to Sweden, in order to hasten the reinforcements that were so much wanted in Livonia and Pomerania. In a word, he had done everything that could be expected from the friend of Charles XII. About this time, the first king of Prussia, a prince of great prudence, being justly apprehensive of danger from the too near neighborhood of the Muscovites, thought proper to enter into a league with Augustus and the Republic of Poland, in order to send back the Russians to their own country, and he hoped to engage the King of Sweden himself in this project. From this plan three great events were expected to result: the peace of the North, the return of Charles to his own kingdom, and the establishment of a strong barrier against the Russians, whose power had already become formidable to Europe. The preliminary article of this treaty, upon which the public tranquillity depended, was the abdication of Stanislaus, who not only accepted the proposal, but even undertook to use his endeavors in bringing about a peace which deprived him of his crown. To this step he was prompted by necessity, the public good, the glory of the sacrifice, and the interest of Charles XII. He wrote to Bender. He explained to the King of Sweden the desperate situation of his affairs, and the only effectual remedy that could be applied. He conjured him not to oppose an abdication which was rendered necessary by the strange conjunctures of the times, and honorable by the noble motive from which it proceeded. He entreated him not to sacrifice the interests of Sweden to those of an unhappy friend, who cheerfully preferred the public good to his own private happiness. Charles XII received these letters at Varnitza. He said to the courier in a passion, in presence of several witnesses: "If my friend will not be a king, I can easily find another that will."

Stanislaus was obstinately bent on making the sacrifice which Charles opposed. These times seem to have been destined to produce strange sentiments, and still stranger actions. Stanislaus resolved to go himself, and endeavor to prevail upon Charles; and thus he ran a greater risk in abdicating the throne than he had run in obtaining it. One evening about six o'clock he stole from the Swedish army which he commanded in Pomerania, and set out, in company with Baron Sparr and another colonel, the former of whom has since been an ambassador in France and England. He assumed the name of a French gentleman, called Haran, who was then a major in the Swedish army, and lately died commander of Dantzic. He passed close by the whole army of the enemy; was sometimes stopped, and as often released by virtue of a passport obtained in the name of Haran. At length, after many perils and dangers, he arrived on the frontiers of Turkey.

As soon as he had reached Moldavia, he sent back Baron Sparr to the army, and entered Jassy, the capital of Moldavia, thinking himself perfectly secure in a country where the King of Sweden had been treated with so much respect, and never entertaining the least suspicion of what had happened.

The Moldavians asked him who he was? He said he was major of a regiment in the service of Charles XII. At the bare mention of that name he was seized, and carried before the Hospodar of Moldavia, who, having already learned from the gazettes that Stanislaus had privately withdrawn from his army, began to suspect that this was probably the man. He had heard the King's figure described so exactly that it was very easy to discover the resemblance—an open and engaging countenance and a very uncommon air of sweetness.

The hospodar examined him, put to him a great many captious questions, and at last asked him what commission he bore in the Swedish army. Their conversation was carried on in Latin. "*Major sum*," said Stanislaus. "*Imo maximus es*," replied the Moldavian; and immediately presenting him with a chair of state, he treated him like a king—but still like a king who was a prisoner, placing a strict guard about a Greek convent, in which he was obliged to remain till such time as the Sultan's orders should arrive. At length these orders came, importing that Stanislaus should be carried to Bender, from which Charles XII had been just removed.

The news of this event was brought to the pacha, at the time he was accompanying the King of Sweden's chariot. The pacha communicated the particulars to Fabricius, who, coming up to Charles's chariot, told him he was not the only king that was a prisoner in the hands of the Turks, and that Stanislaus was but a few miles off, under a guard of soldiers. "Run to him, my dear Fabricius," said Charles, without being in the least disconcerted; "tell him never to make a peace with Augustus, and assure him that our affairs will soon take another turn."

Such was the inflexibility of Charles that, abandoned as he was in Poland, attacked in his own dominions, a captive in a Turkish litter, and led a prisoner without knowing whither they were carrying him, he still reckoned on the favor of fortune, and hoped the Ottoman Porte would assist him with 100,000 men. Fabricius hastened to execute his commission, attended by a Janizary, having first obtained leave from the pacha. At a few miles distance he met the body of soldiers that conducted Stanislaus. He addressed himself to a person that rode in the midst of them, clad in a French dress, and but indifferently mounted, and asked him in the German tongue where the King of Poland was. The person to whom he spoke happened to be Stanislaus himself, whose features he could not recollect under this disguise. "What!" said the King, "don't you know me?" Fabricius then informed him of the wretched condition in which the King of Sweden was, but added that his resolutions, however unsuccessful, were as determined as ever.

As Stanislaus was drawing near to Bender, the pacha, who had returned thither after having accompanied Charles for some miles, sent the King of Poland an Arabian horse, with a magnificent harness.

He was received at Bender amid a discharge of the artillery; and, excepting his confinement, from which he was not as yet

delivered, he had no great cause to complain of his treatment.*
Meanwhile Charles was on his way to Adrianople. Nothing
was talked of in that town but his late battle. The Turks at
once condemned and admired him; but the Divan was so provoked that they threatened to confine him in one of the islands
of the Archipelago.

Stanislaus, King of Poland, from whom I had the honor to
receive the greater part of these particulars, assured me likewise that a proposal was made in the Divan for confining him
in one of the islands of Greece; but the Grand Seignior being
mollified, a few months after allowed him to depart.

Désaleurs, who could have taken his part, and could have prevented the Turks from offering such an affront to all Christian
kings, was at Constantinople; as was likewise Poniatowski,
whose fertile and enterprising genius the Divan had always
dreaded. Most of the Swedes at Adrianople were in prison;
and the Sultan's throne seemed to be inaccessible to any complaints of the King of Sweden.

The Marquis de Fierville, who had resided with Charles at
Bender as a private agent of France, was then at Adrianople.
He undertook to do that prince a piece of service, at a time when
he was abandoned or oppressed by all the world besides. In
this design he was happily assisted by a French gentleman, of
an ancient family in Champagne, called Villelongue, a man of
great courage, but who, not having a fortune equal to his spirit,
and charmed with the fame of the King of Sweden, had repaired to Turkey with a view of entering into the service of
that prince.

With the assistance of this young man M. de Fierville wrote
a memorial in the King of Sweden's name, in which he made
his Majesty demand satisfaction of the Sultan for the insult
which, in his person, had been offered to all crowned heads, and
for the treachery, real or supposed, of the Khan and the Pacha
of Bender.

In this memorial he accused the vizier and other ministers
of having received bribes from the Russians, imposed upon the
Grand Seignior, intercepted the King's letters to his Highness,

* The good chaplain Norberg alleges that we are here guilty of a manifest contradiction, in supposing that King Stanislaus was at once detained a prisoner and treated as a
king at Bender. What! had not the poor man discernment enough to perceive that it is
very possible for a person, at one and the same time, to be loaded with honor and deprived
of his liberty?

and of having, by their artifices, extorted from the Sultan an order so contrary to the hospitality of Mussulmans, by which, in direct violation of the laws of nations, and in a manner so unworthy of a great emperor, they had attacked, with 20,000 men, a king who had none but his domestics to defend him, and who relied upon the sacred word of the Sultan.

When this memorial was drawn up, it was to be translated into the Turkish language, and written in a particular hand, and upon a certain kind of paper, which is always used in addresses to the Sultan.

For this purpose they applied to several French interpreters in the town; but the affairs of the King of Sweden were in such a desperate situation, and the vizier was so much his declared enemy, that not a single interpreter would undertake the task. At last they found a stranger, whose hand was not known at the Porte, who, having received a handsome gratuity, and being fully assured of the most profound secrecy, translated the memorial into the Turkish tongue and wrote it upon the right kind of paper. Baron Arvidson, a Swedish officer, counterfeited the King's subscription; Fierville, who had the royal signet, appended it to the writing; and the whole was sealed with the arms of Sweden. Villelongue undertook to deliver it into the hands of the Grand Seignior as he went to the mosque according to his usual custom. The like methods had been frequently employed for presenting memorials to the Sultan against his ministers; but that very circumstance rendered the success of this enterprise the more precarious and the danger of the attempt the more imminent.

The vizier, who plainly foresaw that the Swedes would demand justice of the Sultan, and who, from the unhappy fate of his predecessors, had but too many warnings to provide for his own safety, had given peremptory orders to allow no one to approach the Grand Seignior's person, but to seize all such as should be about the mosque with petitions in their hands.

Villelongue was well apprised of this order, and, at the same time, knew that, by breaking it, he ran the risk of losing his head. He therefore laid aside his Frankish dress and put on a Grecian habit; and concealing the letter in his bosom, repaired betimes to the neighborhood of the mosque to which the Grand Seignior resorted. He counterfeited the madman, and dancing between two files of Janizaries, through which the Sultan was to pass, he purposely let some pieces of money drop from his pockets, as if by chance, in order to amuse the guards.

When the Sultan was drawing near, the guards endeavored to remove Villelongue out of the way; but he fell on his knees and struggled with the Janizaries. At last his cap fell off, and he was discovered by his long hair to be a Frank. He received several blows and was very roughly handled. The Grand Seignior, who was at no great distance, heard the scuffle, and asked the cause of it. Villelongue cried out with all his might, *Amman! Amman!* Mercy! pulling the letter at the same time out of his bosom. The Sultan ordered the guards to let him approach. Villelongue instantly ran up to him, embraced his stirrup, and presented the memorial, saying, *Suet kral dan,* " The King of Sweden gives it thee." The Sultan put the letter in his bosom and proceeded to the mosque. Meantime Villelongue was secured and imprisoned in one of the exterior apartments of the seraglio.

The Sultan having read the letter upon his leaving the mosque, resolved to examine the prisoner himself. This perhaps will appear somewhat incredible: nothing, however, is here advanced but what is vouched by the letters of Villelongue; and surely, when so brave an officer affirms anything upon his honor, he merits, at least, some credit. He assured me that the Sultan laid aside his imperial garb and turban and disguised himself like an officer of the Janizaries, a thing which he frequently does. He brought along with him an old man of the island of Malta as an interpreter. By favor of this disguise, Villelongue enjoyed an honor which no Christian ambassador ever obtained. He had a private conference with the Turkish Emperor for a quarter of an hour. He did not fail to represent the wrongs which the King of Sweden had suffered, to accuse the ministers, and to demand satisfaction; and all this with so much the more freedom, as in talking to the Sultan he was only supposed to be talking to his equal. He could easily discover, notwithstanding the darkness of the prison, that it was no other than the Grand Seignior himself; but this discovery only made him speak with the greater boldness. The pretended officer of the Janizaries said to Villelongue: " Christian, be assured that the Sultan, my master, has the soul of an emperor, and that your King of Sweden, if he has reason on his side, shall obtain justice." Villelongue was soon set at liberty; and in a few weeks after, a sudden change took place in the seraglio, owing, as the Swedes affirm, to this conference alone. The mufti was deposed; the Khan of Tartary was banished to Rhodes; and the Seraskier Pacha of Bender was confined in one of the islands of the Archipelago.

The Ottoman Porte is so subject to these revolutions that it is hard to say whether the Sultan really meant to gratify the King of Sweden by these sacrifices. From the treatment which that prince received, it cannot surely be inferred that the Porte had any great inclination to oblige him.

The favorite, Ali Coumourgi, was suspected of having brought about all these changes, in order to serve his own particular views. The Khan of Tartary and the Seraskier of Bender were said to have been banished for giving the King the 1,200 purses, in contradiction to the express orders of the Grand Seignior. Coumourgi raised to the throne of Tartary the brother of the deposed Khan, a young man of his own age, who had little regard for his brother, and upon whom the favorite depended greatly in prosecuting the wars he had already planned. With respect to the Grand-vizier Jussuf, he was not deposed till some weeks after; and the title of prime vizier was bestowed on Soliman Pacha.

Truth obliges me to declare that Villelongue and several Swedes assured me that all these great revolutions at the Porte were entirely owing to the letter which was presented to the Sultan in the King's name, whereas M. de Fierville is of a quite contrary opinion. I have sometimes found the like contradictions in such memorials as have been submitted to my perusal. In all these cases it is the duty of a historian honestly to narrate the plain matter of fact, without endeavoring to dive into the motives; and to confine himself to the relation of what he does know, instead of indulging his fancy in vague conjectures about what he does not know.

Meanwhile Charles XII was conducted to the little castle of Demirtash, in the neighborhood of Adrianople. An innumerable multitude of people had crowded to this place to see the arrival of his Majesty, who was carried from his chariot to the castle on a sofa; but Charles, in order to conceal himself from the view of the populace, put a cushion upon his head.

The Porte was strongly solicited to allow him to reside at Demotica, a little town six leagues from Adrianople, and near the famous River Hebrus, now called Merizza; but it was not till after several days that they granted his request. "Go," said Coumourgi to the Grand-vizier Soliman, "and tell the King of Sweden that he may stay at Demotica all his life long if he pleases; but I will answer for him that, in less than a year, he will want to be gone of his own accord: take care, however, not to give him any money."

Thus was the King conveyed to the little town of Demotica, where the Porte allotted him a considerable quantity of provisions for himself and his retinue. But all the money they would grant him was five-and-twenty crowns a day, to buy pork and wine, two kinds of provisions which the Turks never furnish to others. The allowance of 500 crowns a day, which he had enjoyed at Bender, was entirely withdrawn.

Hardly had he reached Demotica with his little court, when the Grand-vizier Soliman was deposed, and his place filled by Ibrahim Molla, a man of high spirit, of great courage, and unpolished manners. It may not be amiss to give a short sketch of his history, that the reader may thus be better acquainted with the characters of all those viceroys of the Ottoman Empire upon whom the fortune of Charles so long depended.

He had been a common sailor till the accession of the Sultan Achmet III. This Emperor frequently disguised himself in the habit of a private man, of a priest, or a dervis, and slipped in the evening into the coffee-houses and other public places of Constantinople, to hear what the people said of him and what were their opinions concerning the affairs of State. One day he overheard this Molla complaining that the Turkish ships never took any prizes, and swearing that if he were captain of a ship he would never enter the port of Constantinople without bringing some vessel of the infidels along with him. Next day the Grand Seignior gave him the command of a ship and sent him on a cruise. The new captain returned in a few days with a Maltese bark and a galley of Genoa. In two years' time he was appointed captain-general of the navy, and at last grand-vizier. As soon as he had attained his new post, he thought he could easily dispense with the interest of the favorite. In order to render himself the more necessary, he formed a scheme for commencing a war against the Russians; and with this view pitched a tent not far from the place where the King of Sweden resided.

He invited his Majesty to come and see him, with the new Khan of Tartary and the French ambassador. The King, whose pride rose with his misfortunes, considered it as a most intolerable affront for a subject to send him an invitation. He ordered his chancellor, Muller, to go in his place; and, lest the Turks should not pay him that respect which was due to his royal person, or oblige him to condescend to anything beneath his dignity, Charles, who was ever in extremes, took to his bed, which he resolved not to leave during his abode at Demotica. This resolution he kept for ten months, under pretence of sickness; Chancellor Muller, Grothusen, and Colonel Duben being the only persons that were admitted to his table. They had none of the conveniences with which the Franks are usually provided; all these they had lost at Bender; consequently it could not be supposed that their meals were served with much pomp or elegance. They were obliged to serve themselves; and, during the whole time, Chancellor Muller was cook-in-ordinary.

While Charles XII was thus passing his time in bed, he received the disagreeable news of the desolation of all his provinces that lay without the limits of Sweden.

General Stenbock [Steenbock?], who had rendered himself illustrious by chasing the Danes out of Scania, and beating their best troops with a parcel of peasants, still maintained the glory of the Swedish arms. He defended Pomerania, Bremen, and the King's possessions in Germany as long as he was able, but could not hinder the combined army of the Danes and Saxons from besieging Stade a town of great strength and importance, situated on the banks of the Elbe, in the Duchy of Bremen. The town was bombarded and reduced to ashes, and the garrison obliged to surrender at discretion, before Stenbock could come to their assistance.

This general, who had about 12,000 men, of whom the one-half was cavalry, pursued the enemy, who were twice as numerous, and at last overtook them in the Duchy of Mecklenburg, at a place called Gadebusch, near a river of the same name. It was on December 12, 1712, that he came in sight of the Danes and Saxons. He was separated from them by a morass. The enemy were so posted as to have this morass in front and a wood in their rear; they had the advantage of number and situation; and their camp was utterly inaccessible, except across the morass, which the Swedes could not pass without being exposed to the fire of the enemy's artillery.

Notwithstanding these difficulties, Stenbock passed the morass at the head of his troops, advanced against the enemy in order of battle, and began one of the most desperate and bloody engagements which ever happened between these rival nations. After a sharp conflict for three hours, the Danes and Saxons were entirely routed and obliged to quit the field of battle.

It was in this battle that a son of Augustus, by the Countess of Königsmark, known by the name of Count Saxe, served his apprenticeship in the art of war. This is the same Count Saxe who had afterward the honor to be chosen Duke of Courland, and who wanted nothing but power to put himself in possession of the most incontestable right which any man can have to sovereignty—I mean the unanimous consent of the people. In fine, this was the man who has since acquired a more solid glory by saving France at the battle of Fontenoy, conquering Flanders, and meriting the character of the greatest general of the age. He commanded a regiment at Gadebusch, and had a horse killed under him. I have heard him say that all the Swedes kept their ranks, and that, even after the victory was gained, and the first lines of these brave troops saw their enemies laying dead at their feet, there was not so much as a single Swede that dared stoop to strip them till prayers had been read on the field of battle, so inflexibly did they adhere to that strict discipline which their King had taught them.

After the victory, Stenbock, remembering that the Danes had laid Stade in ashes, resolved to retaliate on Altona, a town belonging to the King of Denmark. Altona stands below Hamburg, on the banks of the Elbe, which can convey ships of considerable burden into its harbor. The King of Denmark had indulged this town with many privileges, hoping to make it, one day, a place of great trade; and, indeed, the industry of the inhabitants, encouraged by the prudent measures of the King, had already raised them to such opulence that Altona began to be reckoned in the number of rich and commercial cities. Hamburg grew jealous of this rival in trade, and earnestly wished for its destruction. When Stenbock came in sight of Altona, he sent a trumpet to acquaint the inhabitants that they might retire with as many of their effects as they could carry off, for he meant to raze their town to the foundation.

The magistrates came and threw themselves at his feet, and offered him 100,000 crowns by way of ransom. Stenbock demanded 200,000. The inhabitants begged that they might have time, at least, to send to their correspondents at Hamburg, assuring him that the money should be paid him the next day; but the Swedish general replied that they must give it instantly or he would immediately set Altona in flames.

His troops were already in the suburbs, with torches in their hands. The town had no defence but a poor wooden gate and a ditch already filled up. The wretched inhabitants were therefore obliged to leave their houses at midnight, on January 9, 1713. The rigor of the season, which was then excessive, was still further increased by a strong north wind, which served at once to spread the flames through the town with greater violence, and to render the miseries of the poor people, who were exposed in the open fields, the more intolerable. Men and women, weeping and wailing, and bending under their heavy loads, fled to the neighboring hills, which were covered with snow. The palsied old men were transported on the shoulders of the young. Some women, newly delivered, fled with their tender babes in their arms, and perished together on the naked rock, turning their languishing eyes toward their dear country, which was now wrapped in flames. The Swedes set fire to the town before the inhabitants had entirely left it. The conflagration continued from midnight till ten in the morning. The houses, being mostly of wood, were entirely consumed, and next day there was not the least vestige of a town remaining.

The aged, the sick, and women of tender constitutions, who had lodged on the snow while their houses were in flames, at last made a shift to crawl to the gates of Hamburg, where they besought the inhabitants to receive them within the walls, and thereby to save their lives. But this favor was denied them, because some contagious distempers were known lately to have raged in Altona; and the Hamburgers had not so great a regard for the inhabitants as to run the risk of having their own town infected by admitting such dangerous guests. Thus the greater part of these unhappy people expired under the walls of Hamburg, calling on heaven to witness the barbarity of the Swedes, and the still greater inhumanity of the Hamburgers.

All Germany exclaimed against this outrage. The ministers and generals of Poland and Denmark wrote to Count Stenbock, reproaching him with an act of cruelty, committed without necessity, and incapable of any excuse, which could not fail to provoke heaven and earth against him.

Stenbock replied that " he never would have pushed matters to such extremities, had it not been with a view to teach the enemies of the King, his master, not to make war for the future like barbarians, but to pay some regard to the laws of nations; that they had filled Pomerania with their cruelties, laid waste that beautiful province, and sold near 100,000 of its inhabitants to the Turks; and that the torches which had laid Altona in ashes were no more than just reprisals for the red-hot bullets which had destroyed Stade."

Such was the implacable resentment with which the Swedes and their enemies carried on the war. Had Charles appeared in Pomerania at this time, he might possibly have retrieved his ruined fortune. His armies, though removed at so great a distance from his person, were still animated by his spirit; but the absence of a prince is always prejudicial to his affairs, and hinders his subjects from making the proper use of their victories. Stenbock lost by piecemeal what he had gained by those signal actions, which, at a happier juncture, would have been decisive.

Victorious as he was, he could not prevent the junction of the Russians, Danes, and Saxons. The combined army of these allies seized upon his quarters. He lost some troops in several little skirmishes. Two thousand of his men were drowned in passing the Eider, as they were going to their winter quarters in Holstein; and all these losses, in a country surrounded on every side by powerful enemies, were utterly irreparable.

He endeavored to defend the Duchy of Holstein against the Danes; but, notwithstanding all his prudent measures and vigorous efforts, the country was lost, his whole army ruined, and himself taken prisoner.

Pomerania, all but Stralsund, the isle of Rügen, and some neighboring places, being left defenceless, became a prey to the allies, and was sequestered in the hands of the King of Prussia. Bremen was filled with Danish garrisons. At the same time, the Russians overran Finland and beat the Swedes, who, being now dispersed and inferior in point of number, began to lose that superiority over their enemies which they had possessed at the commencement of the war.

To complete the misfortunes of Sweden, the King resolved to stay at Demotica, and still flattered himself with the delusive hopes of obtaining assistance from the Turks, in whom he ought no longer to have reposed any confidence.

Ibrahim Molla, that bold vizier who had been so obstinately bent on a war with the Russians in opposition to the favorite, was strangled in one of the passages of the seraglio.

The place of vizier had become so dangerous that no one would venture to accept of it, and in consequence it continued vacant for six months. At last the favorite, Ali Coumourgi, assumed the title of grand-vizier. This measure gave a fatal blow to all the hopes of the King of Sweden, who knew Coumourgi so much the better that he had really been obliged to him for some friendly offices, when the interest of the favorite and that of his Majesty happened to coincide.

Charles had now been eleven months at Demotica, buried in sloth and oblivion. This extreme indolence succeeding so suddenly to the most violent exercises, had at last given him the disease which he had formerly feigned. The report of his death was spread over all Europe. The Council of Regency, which he had established at Stockholm when he left his capital, no longer received any despatches from him. The Senate came in a body to the Princess Ulrica Eleonora, the King's sister, and entreated her to take the Regency into her own hands during her brother's absence. She accepted the proposal, but, finding that the Senate intended to force her to make a peace with the Czar and the King of Denmark, and well knowing that her brother would never approve of such a measure, she resigned the Regency, and wrote a full and circumstantial account of the whole matter to the King in Turkey.

Charles received his sister's packet at Demotica. The arbitrary principles which he had sucked in with his mother's milk made him forget that Sweden had formerly been a free State, and that, in ancient times, the management of public affairs was conducted by the King and Senate, in conjunction. He considered that respectable body as no better than a parcel of menial servants, who wanted to usurp the command of the house in their master's absence. He wrote to them that if they pretended to assume the reins of government, he would send them one of his boots, from which he would oblige them to receive their orders.

To prevent, therefore, these attempts (as he thought them) upon his authority in Sweden, and to defend his kingdom now in the last extremity, deprived of all hopes of assistance from the Ottoman Porte, and relying on himself alone, he signified to the grand-vizier his desire of departing, and returning by the way of Germany.

Désaleurs, the French ambassador, who was charged with the affairs of Sweden, made the proposal. "Well," said the vizier to Count Désaleurs, "did not I tell you that in less than a year the King of Sweden would beg it as a favor to be allowed to depart? Tell him he may either go or stay, as he pleases; but let him come to a fixed resolution, and appoint the day of his departure, that he may not again bring us into such another scrape as that of Bender."

Count Désaleurs softened the harshness of this answer when he reported it to the King. The day was accordingly fixed. But, before he would quit Turkey, Charles resolved to display the pomp of a great king, though involved in all the difficulties of a fugitive prince. He gave Grothusen the title of his ambassador-extraordinary, and sent him with a retinue of eighty persons, all richly dressed, to take his leave in form at the Porte. The splendor of this embassy was only exceeded by the meanness of the shifts which the King was obliged to employ, in order to collect a sum of money sufficient to defray the expense of it.

M. Désaleurs lent him 40,000 crowns. Grothusen had agents at Constantinople, who borrowed in his name, at the rate of fifty per cent. interest, 1,000 crowns of a Jew, 200 pistoles of an English merchant, and 1,000 livres of a Turk.

By these means they procured wherewithal to enable them to act the splendid farce of the Swedish embassy before the

Divan. Grothusen received, at the Porte, all the honors which are usually paid to ambassadors-extraordinary on the day of their audience. The design of all this parade was only to obtain money from the grand-vizier; but that minister was inexorable.

Grothusen made a proposal for borrowing 1,000,000 from the Porte. The vizier answered coldly that his master knew how to give when he thought proper, but that it was beneath his dignity to lend; that the King should be supplied with plenty of everything necessary for his journey, in a manner worthy of the person that sent him back; and that the Porte, perhaps, might even make him a present in gold bullion, though he would not have him depend upon it for certain.

At last, on October 1, 1714, the King of Sweden set out on his journey. A *capigi pacha*, with his six *chiaoux*, came to attend him from the castle of Demirtash, where he had resided for some days past. The pacha presented him, in the name of the Grand Seignior, with a large tent of scarlet embroidered with gold, a sabre whose handle was set with jewels, and eight beautiful Arabian horses, with fine saddles, and stirrups of massive gold. It is not beneath the dignity of history to observe that the Arabian groom, who took care of the horses, gave the King an account of their genealogy—a custom which has long prevailed among these people, who seem to be more attentive to the nobility of horses than of men; which, after all, perhaps, is not so unreasonable, as these animals, if the breed is kept free from intermixture, are never known to degenerate.

The convoy consisted of sixty loaded wagons and 300 horse. The *capigi pacha* being informed that several Turks had lent money to the King of Sweden's attendants at an immoderate interest, told his Majesty that usury was forbidden by the Mahometan law; he therefore entreated him to liquidate all these debts, and to order his resident at Constantinople to pay no more than the capital. "No," said the King, "if any of my servants have given bills for 100 crowns, I will pay them, though they should not even have received ten."

He made a proposal to his creditors to follow him, assuring them, at the same time, that he would not only pay their debts, but likewise indemnify them for the expense of the journey. Several of them went to Sweden; and Grothusen was commissioned to see them paid.

In order to show the greater deference to their royal guest, the Turks made him travel by very short stages; but this slow and respectful motion was ill suited to the impatient spirit of the King. During the journey he got up at three in the morning, according to his usual custom. As soon as he was dressed, he went himself and awakened the *capigi* and *chiaoux* and began to march in the dark. The Turkish gravity was affronted with this new manner of travelling; but Charles took pleasure in making them uneasy, and said that he should, at least, be a little revenged on them for their behavior to him at Bender.

About the time that Charles reached the frontiers of Turkey, Stanislaus was leaving them, though by a different road, and going into Germany, with a view of retiring into the Duchy of Deux-Ponts, a province bordering on the Palatinate of Alsace and the Rhine, and which has belonged to the kings of Sweden ever since Charles X, the successor of Christina, united it to his crown. Charles assigned Stanislaus the revenue of this duchy, which was then valued at about 70,000 crowns. Such was the final result of so many projects, wars, and expectations. Stanislaus both could and would have concluded an advantageous treaty with Augustus, had not the inflexible obstinacy of Charles made him lose his lands and real estate in Poland, in order to preserve the empty title of king.

This prince continued to reside in the Duchy of Deux-Ponts [Zweibrücken] till the death of Charles XII, when that province returning to a prince of the Palatine family, he chose to retire to Wissembourg, a place belonging to the French in Alsace. M. Sum, Augustus's envoy, entered a complaint on this head to the Duke of Orleans, regent of France. The duke made him this remarkable answer: " Sir, let the King your master know that France has never refused an asylum to kings in distress."

When the King of Sweden arrived on the frontiers of Germany, he had the pleasure to hear that the Emperor had given strict orders to receive him in every part of his dominions with a becoming magnificence. The towns and villages through which the quarter-masters had previously fixed his route made great preparations for receiving him; everyone burned with impatience to see this extraordinary man, whose victories and misfortunes, whose most trifling actions, and even his keeping his bed, had made so great a noise in Europe and Asia. But Charles had no inclination to bear the fatigue of all this pomp and pageantry, or to exhibit as a public spectacle the prisoner of Bender. On the contrary, he had resolved never to re-enter Stockholm until he should have repaired his losses by a change of fortune.

As soon as he arrived at Tergowitz, on the confines of Transylvania, he took leave of his Turkish convoy; and then, assembling his attendants in a barn, he told them not to give themselves any concern about him, but to proceed with all possible expedition to Stralsund in Pomerania, on the coast of the Baltic, distant from Tergowitz about 300 leagues.

He took nobody with him but During, and parted cheerfully with the rest of his attendants, who were filled with astonishment, sorrow, and apprehension. By way of disguise, he put on a black wig, concealing his own hair, which he always wore underneath it, a gold-laced hat, a gray coat, and blue cloak, and, assuming the name of a German officer, rode post with his fellow-traveller.

He shunned, as much as possible, the territories of his secret or declared enemies, taking the road through Hungary, Moravia, Austria, Bavaria, Würtemberg, the Palatinate, Westphalia, and Mecklenburg; by which means he almost made the complete tour of Germany and lengthened his journey by one-half. Having rode the whole first day without intermission, young During, who was not so much inured to these excessive fatigues, fainted away as he was dismounting. The King, who was determined not to halt a moment by the road, asked During, as soon as he had recovered, how much money he had? "About 1,000 crowns in gold," replied During. "Then give me one-half of it," said the King; "I see you are not able to follow me; I shall finish the journey by myself." During begged he would be so good as to tarry but for three hours, assuring him that by that time he should be able to remount his horse and attend his Majesty, and entreated him to reflect on the imminent dangers to which he would expose himself by travelling alone. The King was inexorable. He made him give him the 500 crowns, and called for horses. During, startled at this resolution, bethought himself of an innocent stratagem. He took the postmaster aside, and, pointing to the King, "This gentleman," said he, "is my cousin; we are going together upon the same business; he sees that I am indisposed, and yet he will not wait for me but for three hours; pray give him the worst horse in your stable, and let me have a chariot or post-chaise."

He slipped two ducats into the postmaster's hand, who punctually obeyed his orders. The King had a lame and restive horse, upon which he set out alone at ten at night, amid darkness, snow, wind, and rain. His fellow-traveller, after having slept a few hours, began to follow him in a chariot, with good horses. He had not rode many miles when, at daybreak, he overtook the King, who, not being able to make his beast move on, was travelling on foot to the next stage.

Charles was obliged to get into During's chaise, where he slept upon the straw. Thus they continued the journey without intermission, by day on horseback, and sleeping by night in a chaise.

Having travelled for sixteen days, during which they had more than once been in danger of being taken, they arrived at last, on November 21, 1714, at the gates of Stralsund, about one in the morning.

The King called out to the sentinel, and told him that he was a courier despatched from Turkey by the King of Sweden, and that he must immediately speak with General Dücker, the governor. The sentinel said that it was too late; that the governor had gone to bed; and that he must wait till break of day.

The King replied that he came upon business of importance, and that if they did not instantly go and awaken the governor, they should all be punished next morning. At last a sergeant went and called up the governor. Dücker imagined that it might possibly be one of the King's generals: the gates were opened and the courier introduced into the governor's chamber.

Dücker, who was still half asleep, asked him, "What news of the King of Sweden?" The King, taking him by the arm, "What," said he to Dücker, "have my most faithful subjects forgotten me?" The governor recollected the King, though he could not believe his own eyes; and, jumping out of bed, embraced his master's knees with tears of joy. The news of this happy event were spread through the town in a moment. Everybody got up. The soldiers flocked about the governor's house. The streets were crowded with people, asking each other whether the King had really come. All the windows were illuminated, and the conduits ran with wine, amid the blaze of a thousand flambeaux and the repeated discharges of the artillery.

Meanwhile the King was put to bed, which was more than he had been for sixteen days before. His legs were so much swollen with the great fatigue he had undergone, that, instead of pulling, they were obliged to cut off his boots. As he had neither linen nor clothes, they immediately furnished him with such a wardrobe as the town could afford. After he had slept a few hours, he rose and went directly to review his troops and visit his fortifications. And that very day he despatched orders into all parts, for renewing the war against his enemies with greater vigor than ever. All these particulars, which are so consistent with the extraordinary character of Charles XII, were first communicated to me by Fabricius, and afterward confirmed by Count Croissi, ambassador to the King of Sweden.

Europe was now in a condition very different from that in which it was when Charles left it, in 1709.

The war which had so long raged in the South, that is, in Germany, England, Holland, France, Spain, Portugal, and Italy, was now at an end. The general peace which succeeded was owing to some private intrigues in the Court of England. The Earl of Oxford, an able Minister, and Lord Bolingbroke, one of the greatest geniuses and one of the most eloquent orators of the age, had got the better of the Duke of Marlborough and prevailed upon the Queen to make a peace with Louis XIV. France, being no longer at war with England, soon obliged the other powers to come to an accommodation.

Philip V, the grandson of Louis XIV, began to reign in peace over the ruins of the Spanish monarchy. The Emperor of Germany, now become master of Naples and Flanders, was firmly established in his vast dominions, and Louis XIV seemed to aim at nothing higher than to finish his long career of glory by a peaceable end.

Anne, Queen of England, died on August 10, 1714, hated by half the nation for having given peace to so many kingdoms. Her brother, James Stuart, an unhappy prince, excluded from the throne almost at his birth, not being in England at that time to claim the succession, which new laws would have conferred upon him if his party could have prevailed, George I, Elector of Hanover, was unanimously acknowledged King of Great Britain. The throne devolved to that Elector not by right of blood, though descended from a daughter of James, but by virtue of an act of Parliament.

George, advanced in years when he was called to reign over a people whose language he did not understand, and to whom he was an utter stranger, considered himself rather as Elector of Hanover than King of England. All his ambition was to aggrandize his German dominions. He commonly went once a year to visit his hereditary subjects, by whom he was adored. In other respects, he took more pleasure in living like a private man than like a mighty sovereign. The pomp of royalty appeared to him an insupportable burden. He passed his time with a few old courtiers, with whom he lived in great familiarity. He was not the King that made the greatest figure in Europe, but he was one of the wisest princes of the age, and perhaps the only one that knew how to enjoy on a throne the pleasures of friendship and private life. Such were the principal monarchs and such the situation of the south of Europe.

The changes that happened in the North were of another nature. The kings in that part of the world were engaged in war, and leagued together against the King of Sweden.

Augustus had been long restored to the throne of Poland by the assistance of the Czar, and with the joint consent of the Emperor of Germany, of Anne of England, and of the States-General, who, through guarantees of the Treaty of Altranstädt when Charles XII was able to impose laws, thought themselves absolved from that obligation when they had nothing more to fear from him.

But Augustus did not enjoy an undisturbed authority. No sooner was he restored to the throne than the people's apprehensions of arbitrary power began to revive. The whole nation was in arms to oblige him to conform to the *pacta conventa*, a sacred contract between the King and people, who seemed to have recalled their sovereign for no other purpose than to declare war against him. In the beginning of these troubles the name of Stanislaus was not once mentioned; his party seemed to be annihilated; and the Poles retained no other remembrance of the King of Sweden than as of a torrent, which, in the violence of its course, had occasioned a temporary change in the face of nature.

Poltava, and the absence of Charles XII, had occasioned the fall not only of Stanislaus, but also of the Duke of Holstein, Charles's nephew, who had lately been despoiled of his dominions by the King of Denmark. The King of Sweden had had a sincere regard for the father, and of consequence could not fail to be deeply affected with the misfortunes of the son; the rather, as, glory being the end of all his actions, the fall of those princes whom he had either made or restored, gave him as much pain as the loss of his own provinces.

Everyone was at liberty to enrich himself with the ruins of Charles's fortune. Frederick William, the new King of Prussia, who seemed to be as fond of war as his father had been of peace, was the first who put in for his share of the spoils. He seized Stettin and part of Pomerania, as an equivalent for 400,000 crowns which he had advanced to the Czar and the King of Denmark.

George, Elector of Hanover, now become King of England, had likewise sequestered into his hands the Duchy of Bremen and Verden, which the King of Denmark had assigned to him as a deposit for 60,000 pistoles. In this manner were divided the spoils of Charles XII; and whoever held any of his dominions as pledges, became, from their selfish and interested views, as dangerous enemies as those who had taken them from him.

With regard to the Czar, he was doubtless the most formidable of all his enemies. His former losses, his victories, his very faults, his unremitted perseverance in acquiring knowledge, and in communicating that knowledge to his subjects, and his incessant labors, had justly entitled him to the character of a great man. Riga was already taken; Livonia, Ingria, Carelia, half of Finland, and all the provinces that had been conquered by Charles's ancestors, were now subjected to the Russian yoke.

Peter Alexiovitch, who twenty years before had not a single vessel in the Baltic, now saw himself master of those seas, with a fleet of thirty ships of the line.

One of these ships had been built by his own hands. He was the best carpenter, the best admiral, and the best pilot in the North. There was not a difficult passage from the Gulf of Bothnia to the ocean which he had not sounded. And, having thus joined the labors of a common sailor to the curious experiments of a philosopher and the grand designs of an emperor, he arrived, by degrees and a course of victories, to the rank of admiral, in the same manner as he had become a general in the land service.

While Prince Gallitzin, a general formed under his auspices, and one of those who seconded his enterprises with the greatest vigor, completed the reduction of Finland, took the town of Vasa, and beat the Swedes, the Emperor put to sea, in order to attempt the conquest of Aland, an island in the Baltic about twelve leagues from Stockholm.

He set out on this expedition in the beginning of July, 1714, while his rival, Charles XII, was keeping his bed at Demotica. He embarked at Cronstadt, a harbor which he had built a few years before, about four miles from Petersburg. The new harbor, the fleet, the officers, the sailors, were all the work of his own hands; and wherever he turned his eyes, he could behold nothing but what he himself had, in some measure, created.

On July 15th the Russian fleet, consisting of thirty ships of the line, eighty galleys, and 100 half-galleys, reached the coast of Aland. On board of these ships were 20,000 soldiers; Admiral Apraxin was commander-in-chief and the Russian Emperor served as rear-admiral. On the sixteenth the Swedish fleet, commanded by Vice-Admiral Ehrenskiöld, came up with the enemy, and, though weaker than they by two-thirds, maintained a fight for the space of three hours. The Czar attacked the admiral's ship and took her after a sharp engagement.

The same day he landed 16,000 men on the isle of Aland, and, having taken a number of Swedish soldiers that had not been able to get on board of Ehrenskiöld's fleet, he carried them off in his own ships. He returned to his harbor of Cronstadt with Ehrenskiöld's large ship, three others of a less size, one frigate, and six galleys, all which he had taken in the engagement.

From Cronstadt he set sail for Petersburg, followed by his own victorious fleet and the ships he had taken from the enemy. On his arrival at Petersburg he was saluted by a triple discharge of 150 pieces of cannon. He then made a triumphant entry, which flattered his vanity still more than that at Moscow, as he received these honors in his favorite city, a place where but ten years before there was not a single hut, and where now there were 34,500 houses; in a word, as he saw himself at the head not only of a victorious navy, but what is more, of the first Russian fleet that had ever appeared in the Baltic, and amid the acclamations of a people to whom, before his time, the very name of a fleet was not so much as known.

The entry into Petersburg was accompanied with much the same ceremonies as that into Moscow. The Swedish vice-admiral was the chief ornament of this new triumph. Peter Alexiovitch appeared in the procession as rear-admiral. A Russian nobleman, called Romanodowski, who commonly represented the Czar on these solemn occasions, was seated on a throne, surrounded with senators. To this nobleman the rear-admiral presented an account of his victory; and in reward of his services was declared vice-admiral—an odd ceremony, but extremely necessary in a country where military subordination was one of the novelties which the Czar wanted to introduce.

The Emperor of Russia, now victorious over the Swedes by sea and land, and having assisted in expelling them from Poland, began to domineer there in his turn. He acted as mediator between Augustus and the republic—a glory, perhaps, not inferior to that of creating a king. This honor, and, indeed, all the good-fortune of Charles, had fallen to the share of the Czar, who, it must be owned, made a better use of these advantages; for all his successes were so managed as to contribute to the interest of his country. If he took a town, the best artisans in it carried their families and their industry to Petersburg. The manufactures, the arts and sciences of the provinces which he conquered from Sweden, were transported into Muscovy. Thus were his dominions enriched by his victories, a circumstance that makes him the most excusable of all conquerors.

Sweden, on the contrary, despoiled of almost all her foreign provinces, had neither commerce, money, nor credit. Her veteran troops which were formerly so formidable, had either fallen in battle or perished with hunger. Upward of 100,000 Swedes were slaves in the vast dominions of the Czar, and near the same number had been sold to the Turks and Tartars. The human species seemed visibly to decline in the country; but the King's arrival at Stralsund inspired them with fresh hopes.

The respect and admiration which they had formerly entertained for his sacred person were still so strongly fixed in the minds of his subjects that the youth came from the country in crowds and voluntarily offered to enlist, though there was not a sufficient number of hands left to cultivate the lands.

# BOOK VIII

Charles Gives his Sister in Marriage to the Prince of Hesse—He is Besieged in Stralsund, and Escapes to Sweden—Schemes of Baron Görtz, his Prime Minister—Plan of a Reconciliation with the Czar, and of a Descent upon England—Charles Besieges Frederickshald, in Norway—He is Killed—His Character—Görtz is Beheaded.

IN the midst of these preparations, the King gave his only surviving sister, Ulrica-Eleonora, in marriage to Frederick, Prince of Hesse-Cassel. The queen-dowager, grandmother of Charles XII and the princess, and then in the eightieth year of her age, did the honors of the table at this solemnity, which was celebrated on April 4, 1715, in the palace of Stockholm, where she died soon after.

The marriage was not honored with the presence of the King, who was then employed in finishing the fortifications of Stralsund, a place of great importance, and threatened with a siege by the kings of Prussia and Denmark. Nevertheless, he made his brother-in-law generalissimo of all his forces in Sweden. This prince had served the States-General in their wars with the French, and was esteemed a good general—a qualification which contributed not a little to procure him the sister of Charles XII in marriage.

Charles's misfortunes now came as thick upon him as his victories had formerly done. In the month of June, 1715, the German troops of the King of England, with those of Denmark, invested the strong town of Wismar, while the combined army of the Danes and Saxons, amounting to 36,000 men, marched toward Stralsund, to form the siege of that place. The kings of Prussia and Denmark sunk five Swedish ships a little off Stralsund. The Czar was then in the Baltic with twenty large ships of war, and 150 transports, on board of which were 30,000 men. He threatened a descent upon Sweden, one time approaching the coast of Helsingborg and at another appearing before Stockholm. All Sweden was in arms upon the coasts and every moment expected an invasion. At the same time the Czar's land forces drove the Swedes from post to post until they had dispossessed them of all the places they held in Finland, toward the Gulf of Bothnia, but Peter pushed his conquests no farther.

At the mouth of the Oder, a river that divides Pomerania in two, and, after washing the walls of Stettin, falls into the Baltic, lies the little isle of Usedom, a place of great importance on account of its situation, commanding the Oder both on the right and left; so that whoever is master of the island is likewise master of the navigation of the river. The King of Prussia had dislodged the Swedes from this place, and taken possession of it as well as of Stettin, which he kept sequestered, and all, as he pretended, " for the sake of peace." The Swedes had retaken Usedom in May, 1715. They had two forts in the island; one of which was the fort of Swiene, upon a branch of the Oder, that bore the same name; the other, a place of greater consequence, was called Peenemunde, and situated upon another branch of that river. To defend these two forts, and, indeed, the whole island, there were only 250 Pomeranians, under the command of an old Swedish officer, called Kuze-Slerp, a man whose name deserves to be immortalized.

On the fourth of August the King of Prussia sent 1,500 foot and 800 dragoons to make a descent upon the island. They came and landed without opposition near the fort of Swiene, which, being the least important of the two, the Swedish commander abandoned to the enemy; and as he could not safely divide his men, he retired with his little company to the castle of Peenemunde, determined to hold out to the last extremity.

There was therefore a necessity of besieging it in form; for which purpose a train of artillery was embarked at Stettin, and the Prussian troops were reinforced with 1,000 foot and 400 horse. On the eighteenth the trenches were opened in two places, and the fort was briskly battered with cannon and mortars. During the siege, a Swedish soldier, who was sent privately with a letter from Charles XII, found means to land on the island and to slip into the fort. The letter he delivered to the commander. The purport was as follows: " Do not fire till the enemy come to the brink of the fosse. Defend the place to the last extremity. I commend you to your good fortune. CHARLES."

Slerp, having read the note, resolved to obey, and to lay down his life, as he was ordered, for the service of his master. On the twenty-second at daybreak the assault was given. The besieged having kept in their fire till they saw the enemy on the brink of the fosse, killed an immense number of them. But the ditch was full, the breach large, and the assailants too numerous. They entered the castle at two different places at once. The commander now thought of nothing but of selling his life dear, and obeying his master's orders. He abandoned the breaches through which the enemy entered, intrenched his little company, who had all the courage and fidelity to follow him, behind a bastion, and posted them in such a manner that they could not be surrounded. The enemy came up to him, and were greatly surprised that he did not ask for quarter. He fought for a complete hour; and, after having lost half of his men, was at last killed himself, together with his lieutenant and major. Upon this, the surviving few, amounting to 100 soldiers and one officer, begged their lives, and were made prisoners of war. Charles's letter was found in the commander's pocket and carried to the King of Prussia.

At the time that Charles lost Usedom, and the neighboring isles, which were quickly taken; while Wismar was ready to surrender, and Sweden, destitute of a fleet, was daily threatened with an invasion, he himself was in Stralsund, besieged by an army of 36,000 men.

Stralsund, a town famous over all Europe for the siege which the King of Sweden sustained there, is the strongest place in Pomerania. It is situated between the Baltic and the Lake of Franken, near the straits of Gella. It is inaccessible by land, except by a narrow causeway, defended by a citadel, and by fortifications which were thought to be impregnable. There was in it a garrison of about 9,000 men, and, what was more than all, the King of Sweden himself. The kings of Prussia and Denmark undertook the siege of this place, with an army of 36,000 men, composed of Prussians, Danes, and Saxons.

The honor of besieging Charles XII was so powerful a motive that they soon surmounted every obstacle and opened the trenches in the night between the nineteenth and twentieth of

October, 1715. The King of Sweden declared, at the beginning of the siege, that for his own part, he could not comprehend how a place well fortified, and provided with a sufficient garrison, could possibly be taken: not but that in the course of his past victories he had taken several places himself, but hardly ever by a regular siege. The terror of his arms carried all before it. Beside, he never judged of other people by himself, but always entertained too low an opinion of his enemies. The besiegers carried on their works with surprising vigor and resolution, and were greatly assisted by a very singular accident.

It is well known that the Baltic Sea neither ebbs nor flows. The fortifications which covered the town, and which were defended on the west by an impassable morass, and by the sea on the east, seemed to be secure from any assault. It had hitherto escaped the observation of everyone, that when the west wind blows strong, the waves of the Baltic are driven back in such a manner as to leave but three feet depth of water under the fortifications, which had always been supposed to be washed by a branch of the sea so deep as to be utterly impassable. A soldier having fallen from the top of the fortifications into the sea was surprised to find a bottom; and thinking that this discovery might make his fortune, he deserted, and went to the quarters of Count Wackerbarth, the Saxon general, to inform him that the sea was fordable, and that he might easily penetrate to the Swedish fortifications. It was not long before the King of Prussia availed himself of this piece of intelligence.

The next night, about twelve o'clock, the west wind still continuing to blow, Lieutenant-Colonel Koppen entered the water with 1,800 men. At the same time 2,000 advanced upon the causeway that led to the fort: all the Prussian artillery fired and the Danes and Prussians gave an alarm on the other side.

The Swedes thought they could easily repulse the 2,000 men whom they saw advancing with so much apparent rashness upon the causeway; but all of a sudden, Koppen, with his 1,800 men, entered the fort on the side toward the sea. The Swedes, surrounded and surprised, could make no resistance; and the post was carried after a terrible slaughter. Some of the Swedes fled to the town; the besiegers pursued them thither and entered pell-mell along with the fugitives. Two officers and four Saxon soldiers were already on the drawbridge, which the Swedes had just time to raise; so that the men were taken and the town saved for that time.

There were found in the fort twenty-four pieces of cannon, which were immediately turned against Stralsund. The siege was pushed with such vigor and resolution as this success could not fail to inspire. The town was cannonaded and bombarded without intermission.

Opposite to Stralsund, in the Baltic Sea, lies the isle of Rügen, which serves as a bulwark to that place, and into which the garrison and citizens might have retired, could they have found boats to transport them thither. This island was of the last importance to Charles. He plainly perceived that should it fall into the hands of the enemy, he would be immediately besieged both by sea and land, and perhaps reduced to so great extremities that he must either bury himself in the ruins of Stralsund or else become a prisoner to those very enemies whom he had so long despised and upon whom he had imposed the most severe and rigorous terms. But notwithstanding these gloomy prospects, such was the wretched situation of his affairs that he had not been able to place a sufficient garrison in Rügen, where, in fact, there were no more than 2,000 men.

His enemies had been employed for three months past in making all the necessary preparations for a descent upon this island; and having at last finished a great number of boats, the Prince of Anhalt, favored by the goodness of the weather, landed 12,000 men upon Rügen, on the fifteenth of November. The King, who seemed to be everywhere present, was then in the island, having lately joined his 2,000 men, who were intrenched near a small harbor, three leagues from the place where the enemy had landed. He put himself at the head of this little troop, and, observing the most profound silence, advanced at midnight toward the foe. The Prince of Anhalt had already intrenched his forces, a precaution which seemed altogether unnecessary. The inferior officers never dreamed of being attacked the very first night, as they imagined Charles to be at Stralsund; but the Prince of Anhalt, who well knew what incredible things Charles was capable of attempting, had caused a deep fosse to be sunk, fenced with *chevaux-de-frise*, and, indeed, took all his measures with as much circumspection as if he had had a superior army to contend with.

At two in the morning Charles reached the enemy's camp without making the least noise. His soldiers said to each other, " Come, let us pull up the *chevaux-de-frise.*" These words being overheard by the sentinels, the alarm was instantly given in the camp and the enemy put themselves under arms. The King, taking up the *chevaux-de-frise,* perceived a deep ditch before him. " Ah! " said he, " is it possible? This is more than I expected." However, this unexpected event did not disconcert him. He was alike ignorant of the number of the enemy and they of his. The darkness of the night seemed to favor the boldness of the attempt. He formed his resolution in a moment, and jumped into the ditch, accompanied by the bravest of his men, and instantly followed by all the rest. The *chevaux-de-frise,* which were presently plucked up, the crumbling earth, the trunks and branches of such trees as they could find, and the carcasses of the soldiers that were killed by random shot, served for fascines. The King, the generals, and the bravest of the officers and soldiers, mounted upon the shoulders of others, as in an assault. The fight began in the enemy's camp. The irresistible impetuosity of the Swedes soon threw the Danes and Prussians into confusion; but the numbers were too unequally matched. After a keen dispute for a quarter of an hour the Swedes were repulsed and obliged to repass the fosse. The Prince of Anhalt pursued them into a plain, little thinking it was Charles XII that fled before him. The unhappy monarch rallied his troops in the open field and the battle was renewed with equal fury on both sides. Grothusen, the King's favorite, and General Dehldorf fell dead at his feet. In the heat of the fight Charles passed over the body of the latter, who was still breathing; and During, who had accompanied him in his journey from Turkey to Stralsund, was killed before his face.

In the midst of the fray, a Danish lieutenant, whose name I have not been able to learn, knew the King; and seizing his sword with one hand, and with the other dragging him by the hair, " Surrender yourself," said he, " or you are a dead man." The King drew a pistol from his belt, and with his left hand fired it at the officer, who died of the wound the next morning. The name of King Charles, which the Dane had pronounced, immediately drew a crowd of the enemy together. The King was surrounded, and received a musket-shot below his left breast. The wound, which he called a contusion, was two fingers deep. Charles was on foot, and in the most imminent danger of either being killed or taken prisoner. At that critical moment Count Poniatowski fought near his Majesty's person. He had saved his life at Poltava, and had now the good fortune to save it once more in the battle of Rügen, by putting him on his horse.

The Swedes retired to a part of the island called Alteferre, where there was a fort, of which they were still masters. From thence the King passed over to Stralsund, obliged to abandon his brave troops, who had so courageously assisted him in this daring enterprise, and who, two days after, were all made prisoners of war.

Among the prisoners was that unhappy French regiment, composed of the shattered remains of the battle of Hochstädt, which had entered into the service of Augustus and afterward into that of the King of Sweden. Most of the soldiers were now incorporated in a new regiment, commanded by the Prince of Anhalt's son, who was their fourth master. The commander of this wandering regiment in the isle of Rügen was that same Count de Villelongue, who had so nobly exposed his life at Adrianople to serve King Charles XII. He was taken prisoner with his men, and but poorly rewarded in the sequel for all his services, labors, and sufferings.

After all these prodigies of valor, which tended only to weaken his forces, the King, shut up in Stralsund, which was every moment in danger of being stormed, behaved in much the same manner as he had done at Bender. Unappalled by so many surrounding dangers, he employed the day in making ditches and intrenchments behind the walls, and by night he sallied out upon the enemy. Meanwhile Stralsund was battered in breach; the bombs fell thick as hail upon the houses, and half the town was reduced to ashes. The citizens were so far from complaining that, filled with the highest veneration for their royal master, whose vigilance, temperance, and courage they could not sufficiently admire, they had all become soldiers under him. They accompanied him in all his sallies and served him in place of a second garrison.

One day, as the King was dictating some letters to his

secretary that were to be sent to Sweden, a bomb fell on the house, pierced the roof, and burst near the royal apartment. One-half of the floor was shattered to pieces; but the closet in which the King was, being partly surrounded by a thick wall, received no damage; and, what was remarkably fortunate, none of the splinters that flew about in the air came in at the closet-door, which happened to be open. The report of the bomb, and the crashing noise it occasioned in the house, which seemed ready to tumble about their ears, made the secretary drop his pen. "What is the reason," said the King, with great composure, "that you do not write?" The poor secretary could only utter, with a faltering voice: "The bomb, sir." "Well," replied the King, "and what has the bomb to do with the letter I am dictating? Go on."

There was at that time an ambassador of France shut up with Charles in Stralsund. This was one Colbert, Count de Croissi, a lieutenant-general in the French army, brother to the Marquis de Torci, the famous minister of state, and a relation of the celebrated Colbert, whose name ought never to be forgotten in France. To send a man on an embassy to Charles XII, or into trenches, was much the same thing. The King would talk with Croissi for hours together in places of the greatest danger, while the soldiers were falling on every side of them by the firing of cannon and the bursting of bombs—Charles, to all appearance, insensible of the risk he ran, and the ambassador not choosing to give his Majesty so much as a hint that there were more proper places to talk of business. This Minister exerted his utmost efforts, before the siege commenced, to effect an accommodation between the kings of Sweden and Prussia; but the demands of the latter were too high, and the former would make no concessions: so the Count de Croissi derived no other advantage from his embassy to Charles XII than the pleasure of being intimately acquainted with that extraordinary man. He frequently lay by his Majesty upon the same cloak, and, by sharing with him in all his dangers and fatigues, had acquired a right of talking to him with greater freedom. Charles encouraged this boldness in those he loved, and would sometimes say to the Count de Croissi: *Veni, maledicamus de rege,* "Come now, let us make a little free with the character of Charles XII." This account I had from the ambassador himself.

Croissi continued in the town till the thirteenth of November, when, having obtained from the enemy a passport for himself and his baggage, he took his leave of the King, who still remained amid the ruins of Stralsund, with a garrison diminished by one-half, but firmly resolved to stand an assault.

In fact, two days after, an assault was actually made upon the horn-work. Twice did the enemy take it, and twice were they repulsed. In this encounter the King fought amid his grenadiers, but at last superior numbers prevailed and the enemy remained masters of the place. Charles continued in the town two days after this, expecting every moment a general assault. On the twenty-first he stayed till midnight upon a little ravelin that was entirely demolished by the bombs and cannon. Next day the principal officers conjured him to quit a place which he could no longer defend. But to retreat was now as dangerous as to stay. The Baltic was covered with Russian and Danish ships. There were no vessels in the harbor of Stralsund but one small bark with sails and oars. The great danger, which rendered this retreat so glorious, was the very thing that prompted Charles to attempt it. He embarked at midnight on December 20, 1715, accompanied by ten persons only. They were obliged to break the ice with which the water of the harbor was covered—a hard and laborious task, which they were forced to continue for several hours before the bark could sail freely. The enemy's admirals had strict orders not to allow Charles to escape from Stralsund, but to take him, dead or alive. Happily for him they were under the wind, and could not come near him. He ran a still greater risk in passing by a place called the *Babrette,* on the isle of Rügen, where the Danes had erected a battery of twelve cannon, from which they fired upon him. The mariners spread every sail and plied every oar, in order to get clear of the enemy; but two men were killed at the King's side by one cannon-ball, and the ship's masts were shattered by another. Through all these dangers, however, did the King escape unhurt, and at last came up with two of his own ships that were cruising in the Baltic. The next day Stralsund was surrendered and the garrison made prisoners of war. Charles landed at Ystad, in Scania, and forthwith repaired to Carlscrona, in a condition very different from that in which, about fifteen years before, he set sail from that harbor in a ship of 120 guns to give laws to the North.

As he was so near his capital, it was expected that after such a long absence he would pay it a visit; but he was determined not to enter it again until he had obtained some signal victory. Beside, he could not bear the thought of revisiting a people by whom he was beloved, and whom nevertheless he was obliged to oppress, in order to enable him to make head against his enemies. He wanted only to see his sister, with whom he appointed an interview on the banks of Lake Wetter, in Ostrogothia. Thither he rode post, attended only by one servant, and after having spent a day with her returned to Carlscrona.

From this place, where he passed the winter, he issued orders for raising recruits through the whole kingdom. He thought that his subjects were born for no other purpose than to follow him to the field of battle, and he had actually accustomed them to entertain the same opinion. Some were enlisted who were not above fifteen years of age. In several villages there were none left but old men, women, and children; and in many places the women were obliged to plough the land alone.

It was still more difficult to procure a fleet. In order to supply that defect as well as possible, commissions were granted to the owners of privateers, who, upon obtaining certain privileges unreasonable in themselves and destructive to the community, equipped a few ships; and these poor efforts were the last that the declining state of Sweden was now capable of making. To defray the expenses of all these preparations, there was a necessity for encroaching upon the property of the subject; and every kind of extortion was practised under the specious name of taxes and duties. Strict search was made in every house, and one-half of the provisions there found was conveyed to the King's magazines. All the iron in the kingdom was bought up for his use. This the government paid for in paper, and sold it out for ready money. A tax was laid on all such as had any mixture of silk in their clothes, or wore periwigs or gilded swords; and the duty of hearth-money was immoderately high. The people, oppressed with such a load of taxes, would have revolted under any other king; but the poorest peasant in Sweden knew that his master led a life still more hard and frugal than himself: so that everyone submitted cheerfully to those hardships which the King was the first to suffer.

All sense of private misfortunes was swallowed up in the apprehension of public danger. The Swedes expected every moment to see their country invaded by the Russians, the Danes, the Prussians, the Saxons, and even by the English; and their fear of this hostile visit was so strong and prevalent that those who had money or valuable effects took care to bury them in the earth.

An English fleet had already appeared in the Baltic, though its particular destination was not known; and the Czar had given his word to the King of Denmark that in the spring of 1716 the Russians should join the Danes, in order to make a descent upon Sweden.

But how great was the astonishment of all Europe, ever attentive to the fortune of Charles XII, when, instead of defending his own country, which was threatened with an invasion by so many princes, they saw him, in the month of March, 1716, passing over into Norway with 20,000 men.

From the time of Hannibal to that of Charles XII the world had never seen any general, who, unable to make head against his enemies at home, had boldly carried the war into the heart of their own dominions. The Prince of Hesse, his brother-in-law, attended him in this expedition.

There is no travelling from Sweden to Norway but through the most dangerous by-ways; and when these are passed, one meets with so many flashes of water formed by the sea among the rocks that there is a necessity for making bridges every day. A handful of Danes might have stopped the progress of the whole Swedish army; but this sudden invasion had not been foreseen. Europe was still more astonished to see the Czar, amid all these mighty events, remaining inactive, and not making a descent upon Sweden, as had formerly been stipulated between him and his allies. This inactivity was owing to one of the greatest and most difficult schemes that ever was formed by the mind of man.

Henry of Görtz, a native of Franconia and baron of the empire, having done several good offices to the King of Sweden, during that monarch's abode at Bender, had now become his favorite and first minister.

Never was man at once so bold and so artful, so full of expedients amid misfortunes, so unbounded in his designs, or so active in the prosecution of them; no project was too great for his daring genius to attempt, no means too difficult for his sagacity and penetration to discover; in pursuing his favorite schemes he was equally prodigal of presents and promises, of oaths, of truth and of falsehood.

From Sweden he went to France, England, and Holland, to examine those secret springs which he afterward meant to put in motion. He was capable of throwing all Europe into confusion; and his inclination was equal to his power. What his master was at the head of an army, that was Görtz in the Cabinet; by which means he had acquired a greater ascendancy over Charles XII than any minister had possessed before him.

Charles, who, at twenty years of age, had prescribed orders to Count Piper, was now content to receive instructions from Baron Görtz, resigning himself to the direction of that minister with so much the less reserve, as his misfortunes obliged him to listen to the advice of others, and as Görtz never gave him any but such as was suitable to his undaunted courage. He observed that of all the sovereigns united against Sweden, George, Elector of Hanover and King of England, was the prince against whom Charles was most highly incensed; because he was the only one to whom he had never done the least injury; and because George had engaged in the quarrel under the pretext of compromising matters, but in reality with a view of preserving Bremen and Verden, to which he seemed to have no other right than that of having bought them for a trifle from the King of Denmark, to whom, after all, they did not belong.

Nor was it long before he discovered that the Czar was secretly dissatisfied with his allies, who had all conspired to hinder him from acquiring any possessions in Germany, where that monarch, already too formidable, wanted only to obtain a footing. Wismar, the only town that still remained to the Swedes on the frontiers of Germany, was, on February 14, 1716, surrendered to the Danes and Prussians, who would not so much as allow the Russian troops that were in Mecklenburg to be present at the siege. Such repeated marks of jealousy for two years together had alienated the Czar's mind from the common cause, and perhaps prevented the ruin of Sweden. There are many instances of several States in alliance being conquered by a single power, but hardly any of a great empire subdued by several allies. If it should happen to be humbled by their joint efforts, their intestine divisions soon allow it to retrieve its former grandeur.

Ever since the year 1714 the Czar had had it in his power to make a descent upon Sweden; but whether it was that he could not perfectly agree with the kings of Poland, England, Denmark, and Prussia, allies justly jealous of his growing power, or that he did not as yet think his troops sufficiently disciplined to attack in their own territories a people whose very peasants had beaten the flower of the Danish forces, he still put off the execution of the enterprise.

But what had chiefly interrupted the progress of his arms was the want of money. The Czar, though one of the most powerful monarchs in the world, was far from being one of the richest, his revenues at that time not exceeding 24,000,000 of livres. He had discovered indeed some mines of gold, silver, copper, and iron; but the profits arising from these were still uncertain and the expense of working them was intolerably great. He had likewise established an extensive commerce; but that in its infancy only filled him with the agreeable hopes of what it might one day become; nor did the provinces which he had lately conquered increase his revenues in the same proportion as they augmented his power and glory. It required a long time to heal the wounds of Livonia, a country extremely fertile, but desolated by fire, sword, and distemper, and by a war of fifteen years' continuance, destitute of inhabitants, and as yet chargeable to the conqueror. His finances were further drained by the large fleets he maintained and by the new enterprises which he was daily undertaking. He had even been reduced to the wretched expedient of raising the value of money, a remedy that can never cure the evils of state, and is, in a particular manner, prejudicial to a country whose exports fall short of the imports.

Such was the foundation upon which Görtz had built his scheme of a revolution. He ventured to advise the King of Sweden to purchase a peace from the Russian Emperor at any price, intimating to him, at the same time, that the Czar was highly incensed at the kings of Poland and England, and assuring him that he and Peter Alexiovitch, when joined together, would be able to strike terror into the rest of Europe.

There was no possibility of making a peace with the Czar

without giving up a great many of those provinces which lie to the east and north of the Baltic Sea. But Görtz entreated the King to consider that by yielding up these provinces, which the Czar already possessed, and which Charles at present was unable to recover, he might have the honor of restoring Stanislaus to the throne of Poland, of replacing the son of James II on that of England, and of re-establishing the Duke of Holstein in the peaceable possession of his dominions.

Charles, pleased with these mighty projects, upon which, however, he laid no great stress, gave a *carte blanche* to his minister. Görtz set out from Sweden, furnished with full powers to act without control, and to treat as his master's plenipotentiary with all those princes with whom he should think proper to negotiate. The first step was to sound the Court of Moscow, which he did by means of a Scotchman, named Erskine, first physician to the Czar, and strongly attached to the Pretender's interest, as, indeed, most of the Scots were, except such as subsisted upon favors from the Court of London.

This physician represented to Prince Mentchikof the greatness and importance of the scheme with all the warmth of a man who was so much interested in its success. Prince Mentchikof relished the proposal and the Czar approved of it. Instead of making a descent upon Sweden, as had been stipulated between him and his allies, he sent his troops to winter in Mecklenburg, whither he soon after repaired himself. This he did under the specious pretext of terminating some disputes that had lately arisen between the duke and his nobility; but in reality with a view to prosecute his favorite scheme of obtaining a principality in Germany, and hoping he should be able to persuade the Duke of Mecklenburg to sell him his sovereignty.

The allies were highly provoked at these proceedings; and the more so, as they did not choose to have such a formidable neighbor as Peter Alexiovitch, who, could he once obtain any footing in Germany, might one day procure himself to be elected Emperor, to the great oppression of all the princes of the empire. But the more they were provoked, the more was the grand scheme of Görtz forwarded. This minister, the better to conceal his secret intrigues, affected to negotiate with the confederate princes, who were likewise amused with vain hopes from the Czar. Charles XII and his brother-in-law, the Prince of

Hesse, were all this while in Norway, at the head of 20,000 men. The country was defended by no more than 11,000 Danes, divided into several detached parties, who were all put to the sword by the King and the Prince of Hesse.

Charles advanced toward Christiania, the capital of the kingdom; and fortune began once more to smile upon him in this part of the globe. But he never took sufficient care to provide for the subsistence of his troops. A Danish fleet and army were coming to the relief of Norway; and Charles, being in want of provisions, was obliged to return to Sweden, there to wait the issue of his minister's mighty projects.

The execution of the scheme required at once inviolable secrecy and vast preparations, two things almost incompatible. Görtz even ransacked the Asiatic seas for an assistance, which, however odious in appearance, would, nevertheless, have been extremely proper for making a descent upon Scotland and for furnishing Sweden with ships, men, and money.

The pirates of all nations, and especially those of England, having entered into a mutual association, had long infested the seas of Europe and America. Driven at last from all their wonted haunts, and having no hopes of obtaining any quarter, they had lately retired to the coasts of Madagascar, a large island east of Africa. These men were all of them desperadoes, and most of them famous for actions which wanted nothing but justice to render them truly heroic. They were endeavoring to find a prince that would receive them under his protection; but the laws of nations shut all the harbors in the world against them.

No sooner were they informed that Charles XII had returned to Sweden, than they began to flatter themselves with the agreeable hopes, that this prince, passionately fond of war, obliged at present to be engaged in it, and in great want of ships as well as soldiers, would be glad to make an agreement with them upon reasonable terms. With this view they sent a deputy to Europe on board of a Dutch vessel, to make a proposal to Baron Görtz, that if they were sure of meeting with a favorable reception in the port of Gottenburg, they would instantly repair thither with sixty ships loaded with riches.

The baron prevailed upon the king to agree to the proposal; and next year Cronstrom and Mendal, two Swedish gentlemen, were sent to finish the treaty with the corsairs of Madagascar.

But a more honorable and a more powerful support was soon after found in Cardinal Alberoni, a man of an extraordinary genius, who governed Spain long enough for his own glory, but too short a time for the grandeur and happiness of the kingdom. He readily embraced the proposal of placing the son of James II on the throne of England. Nevertheless, as he had but just entered into the ministry, and had the affairs of Spain to regulate before he could think of throwing other kingdoms into confusion, it was not likely that he would be able for a considerable time to put this grand machine in motion. But in less than two years he changed the face of affairs in Spain, restored that kingdom to her former degree of credit among the other powers of Europe, prevailed upon the Turks, as is commonly supposed, to attack the Emperor of Germany, and attempted, at one and the same time, to deprive the Duke of Orleans of the regency of France, and King George of the crown of England. So dangerous may one man become, when he is vested with absolute authority in a powerful State, and is endowed with courage and greatness of soul.

Görtz, having thus scattered, in the courts of Muscovy and Spain, the first sparks of that flame which he intended to kindle, went privately to France, and from thence to Holland, where he had an interview with some of the Pretender's adherents.

He informed himself more particularly of the strength, the number, and disposition of the malcontents in England, of the money they could furnish, and the troops they could raise. The malcontents required only a reinforcement of 10,000 men, with whose assistance, they said, they should be fully able to effect a revolution.

Count Gyllenborg, the Swedish ambassador in England, being furnished with proper instructions by Baron Görtz, had several conferences at London, with the chiefs of the disaffected party. He encouraged them with the most flattering hopes of success, and readily promised them whatever they could wish to obtain; and they, on their part, were so forward as to furnish considerable sums of money, which Görtz received in Holland. He treated about the purchase of some ships, and bought six in Britain, with all kinds of arms.

He then sent several officers privately into France, and among others the Chevalier Folard, who having made thirty campaigns in the French armies, without any considerable addition to his fortune, had lately offered his services to the King of Sweden, not so much from any interested views, as from a desire of serving under a king of such a glorious reputation. Folard likewise hoped to recommend to that prince the improvements he had made in the art of war, which he had always studied as a philosopher; and he has since published his discoveries in his "Commentaries on Polybius." Charles XII, who had made war himself in a manner entirely new, and was never guided by custom in anything, was pleased with his notions, and resolved to employ him in his projected invasion of Scotland. The secret orders of Baron Görtz were faithfully executed in France by the Chevalier Folard. A great number of French, and a still greater number of Irish officers, engaged in this uncommon conspiracy, which was hatching at one and the same time in England, France, and Muscovy, and the branches of which were secretly extended from one end of Europe to the other.

These preparations, however great, were only a sample of what Görtz intended to do; though it was a matter of no small consequence to have thus set the scheme going. But the point of the greatest importance, and without which nothing could succeed, was to bring about a peace between the Czar and Charles, to accomplish which, many difficulties were to be removed. Baron Ostermann, minister of state in Muscovy, refused at first to come into Görtz's measures. The former was as cautious and circumspect as the latter was bold and enterprising. The one, slow and regular in his politics, was for allowing everything time to ripen; the other, of a daring genius and impatient spirit, had not sooner sown the seed than he was presently for reaping the harvest. Ostermann, fearing that the Emperor, his master, dazzled with the splendor of this enterprise, would grant the

Swedes a too advantageous peace, delayed the conclusion of it by a variety of obstacles and procrastinations.

Happily for Baron Görtz, the Czar himself came to Holland in the beginning of the year 1717. His intention was to go from thence into France. He was desirous of seeing that famous nation, which, for more than a hundred years past, has been censured, envied, and imitated by all its neighbors. He wanted to gratify his insatiable curiosity of seeing and learning everything, and, at the same time, to exercise his politics.

Görtz had two interviews with him at The Hague; and in these he made greater progress than he could have done in six months with the plenipotentiaries. Everything wore a favorable aspect. His mighty projects seemed to be covered under the veil of impenetrable secrecy, and he flattered himself that Europe would know them only by their being carried into execution. Meanwhile he talked of nothing but peace at The Hague; he openly declared that he would always consider the King of England as the pacifier of the North; and he even pressed (in appearance, at least) the holding of a congress at Brunswick, in which the jarring interests of Sweden and her enemies might be amicably adjusted.

These intrigues were first discovered by the Duke of Orleans, regent of France, who had spies in every part of Europe. Men of this character, who made a trade of selling the secrets of their friends, and got their livelihood by being informers, and frequently by inventing and propagating the grossest lies and calumnies, had so much increased in France under his government, that one half of the nation had become spies upon the other. The Duke of Orleans, who was connected with the King of England by personal ties, acquainted him with the secret plot that was hatching against him.

At the same time the Dutch, who began to take umbrage at the behavior of Görtz, communicated their suspicions to the English Minister. Görtz and Gyllenborg were prosecuting their schemes with great vigor, when they were both arrested, the one at Deventer, in Gueldres, and the other at London.

As Gyllenborg, the Swedish ambassador, had violated the

laws of nations, by conspiring against the prince to whom he was sent in a public character, the English made no scruple to violate the same law, by arresting his person. But all the world was surprised to see the States-General imprison Baron Görtz, in order to gratify the King of England, an instance of complaisance hardly to be paralleled in history. They even appointed Count Welderen to examine him. This formality was only an aggravation of their former insult, which, being rendered entirely abortive, produced no other effect than to cover them with confusion. "Do you know me?" said Görtz to Count Welderen. "Yes, sir," replied the Dutchman. "Well, then," said Görtz, "if you know me, you must be aware that I will not speak one word more than I please." The examination was carried no farther. All the foreign ministers, and especially the Marquis de Monteléon, the Spanish ambassador in England, protested against the violence offered to the person of Görtz and Gyllenborg. The Dutch were inexcusable. They had not only violated a most sacred law, by seizing the prime minister of the King of Sweden, who had formed no plots against them; but they acted in direct opposition to the spirit of that inestimable liberty which has drawn so many foreigners into their country, and is the foundation of all their greatness.

With regard to the King of England, he had acted consistently with the strictest principles of justice, in imprisoning his enemy. He published, in his own vindication, the letters of Görtz and Gyllenborg, which were found among the papers of the latter. The King of Sweden was in Scania when he received these printed letters, together with the news of the two ministers being imprisoned. He asked, with a smile, if they had not likewise printed his letters; and gave immediate orders for arresting the English resident at Stockholm, with all his family and domestics. The Dutch resident was forbidden the court, and strictly watched in all his motions. Charles, meanwhile, neither avowed nor disclaimed the proceedings of Görtz. Too proud to deny a scheme which he had once approved, and too wise to acknowledge a plot which had thus been stifled in its birth, he maintained a disdainful silence towards England and Holland.

The Czar took a very different course. As his name was not expressly mentioned, but only obscurely hinted at in the papers of Görtz and Gyllenborg, he wrote a long letter to the King of England, complimenting him upon the discovery of the plot, and assuring him of the most inviolable friendship; and King George received his protestations without believing them, though he thought it most prudent in the present case to pretend that he did. A plot contrived by private men is annihilated the moment it is discovered; but a conspiracy, formed by kings, the more it is known the stronger it grows.

The Czar arrived at Paris in the month of May, 1717. To view the beauties of art and nature, and to visit the academies, public libraries, the cabinets of the curious, and the royal palaces, were not the only ends of his journey. He made a proposal to the Duke of Orleans for concluding a treaty, which, had it taken place, would have completed the greatness of Muscovy. His design was to compromise matters with the King of Sweden, who would yield to him some large provinces, to deprive the Danes of the empire of the Baltic Sea, to weaken the English by a civil war, and to make all the trade of the North centre in Russia. He had even some thoughts of setting up Stanislaus afresh against Augustus, that, the fire being everywhere kindled, he might have it in his power either to quench it or blow it up, as should be most conducive to his interest. With this view he proposed to the regent of France to act as mediator between Sweden and Muscovy, and to make a league, offensive and defensive, with these two crowns and that of Spain. This treaty, seemingly so natural and so advantageous to the several nations concerned, and which would have put the balance of power in Europe into their hands, was nevertheless rejected by the Duke of Orleans. Nay, at that very time, he entered into engagements of a quite opposite nature. He made a league with the Emperor of Germany, and with George, King of England. Reasons of state had so much altered the views and inclinations of all the princes of Europe, that the Czar was ready to declare against his old ally, Augustus, and to espouse the cause of Charles, his mortal enemy, while France, in order to oblige the Germans and the English, was going to make war upon the grandson of Louis XIV, after having so long supported him against these very enemies, at a prodigious expense of blood and treasure. All that the Czar could obtain by these indirect measures was to prevail upon the regent to interpose his good offices to procure the enlargement of Görtz and Gyllenborg. He returned to his own dominions about the end of June, after having shown the French a sight they had never seen before—an emperor travelling for instruction. But too many of that nation were only struck with his rude, unpolished manners, the result of his bad education; while the legislator, the great man, and the creator of a new nation, entirely escaped their notice.

What the Czar sought for in the Duke of Orleans, he soon found in Cardinal Alberoni, who now governed the Spanish councils with unlimited sway. Alberoni desired nothing so much as the restoration of the Pretender, both as the minister of Spain, who had been so ill-treated by the English, and as a personal enemy to the Duke of Orleans, who was leagued with England against Spain; and, in fine, as a priest of that Church for the sake of which the Pretender's father had so foolishly lost his crown.

The Duke of Ormond, as much beloved in England as the Duke of Marlborough was admired, had left his country at the accession of King George, and retired to Madrid. This nobleman was now vested with full powers by the King of Spain and the Pretender; and, accompanied by one Irnegan, another native of England, a man of fine address and an enterprising spirit, he went to meet the Czar on his way to Mittau, in Courland. He demanded the Princess Anne Petrovna, the Czar's daughter, in marriage for the son of James II,* hoping that this alliance would the more strongly attach the Czar to the interests of that unhappy prince. But this proposal, instead of forwarding, retarded, at least for some time, the progress of the negotiations. Baron Görtz, among his other projects, had long set apart this princess for the Duke of Holstein, to whom, in fact, she was soon after mar-

* The truth of all these particulars is confirmed by Cardinal Alberoni himself, in a letter of thanks which he wrote to the author. M. Norberg, whose ignorance of the affairs of Europe can only be equalled by the poverty of his genius, alleges that the Duke of Ormond left England not upon the accession of George I, but immediately after the death of Queen Anne; as if George I had not been the immediate successor of that Queen.

ried. The moment he was informed of the Duke of Ormond's proposal, he became jealous of its success, and employed every art to render it abortive. He, as well as Count Gyllenborg, was set at liberty in the month of August, the King of Sweden not even deigning to offer the least apology to the King of England, nor to express the slightest disapprobation of his Minister's conduct.

At the same time the English resident and all his family were released at Stockholm, where they had been treated with much more severity than Gyllenborg had been at London.

Görtz, being now at liberty, behaved like an implacable enemy, prompted not only by the powerful motives by which he had been formerly actuated, but also animated by a spirit of revenge, on account of his late imprisonment. He instantly posted away to the Czar, and, by his artful insinuations, obtained a greater ascendancy over that prince than ever. He assured him that, in less than three months, he would, in conjunction with a single plenipotentiary from Russia, remove every obstacle that retarded the conclusion of a peace with Sweden. Taking a map in his hand, which had been drawn by the Czar himself, and making a line from Viborg all the way to the frozen sea, and running along the lake Ladoga, he undertook to persuade his master to give up all the country lying to the eastward of that line, as well as Carelia, Ingria, and Livonia. He then hinted at a proposal of marriage between his Czarish Majesty's daughter and the Duke of Holstein, flattering the Czar with the agreeable hopes that the duke might possibly be prevailed upon to yield him up his dominions for an equivalent, by which acquisition he would become a member of the empire; and that either himself or some of his descendants might one day obtain the imperial crown. By these means he gratified the ambitious views of the Russian monarch, and deprived the Pretender of all hopes of marrying the czarinian princess, at the same time that he opened to him a more tempting project in England, and thus accomplished all his own projects at once.

The Czar named the isle of Aland for holding the conference between Ostermann, his minister of state, and Baron Görtz. He desired the Duke of Ormond to return to Spain, that he might not give too great cause of offence to the English, with whom he had no intention of coming to an open rupture till he should be ready to make the projected invasion. But Irnegan, the duke's confidant, was allowed to stay at Petersburg, where he lived with so much privacy and caution that he never went abroad in the daytime, nor ever conversed with any of the Czar's ministers, except in the disguise of a peasant or Tartar.

Immediately after the Duke of Ormond's departure, the Czar acquainted the King of England with the high compliment he had paid him in dismissing the greatest man in the Pretender's faction; and Baron Görtz returned to Sweden, flushed with hopes of success.

Görtz found his master at the head of 35,000 regular troops, and all the coasts guarded by the militia. The King wanted nothing but money. But the public credit, as well at home as abroad, was entirely exhausted. France, which had furnished him with some supplies, under the last years of Louis XIV, refused to contribute any more under the regency of the Duke of Orleans, who pursued a course very different from that of Louis. Spain promised him some remittances; but was not yet in a condition to afford anything considerable.

Görtz therefore carried a scheme into execution which he had tried before his journey to France and Holland. This was to give to copper the value of silver, so that a piece of the former metal, whose intrinsic value was only a halfpenny, should, when stamped with the King's mark, pass for forty pence; as the governors of besieged towns frequently pay the soldiers and citizens in leathern money, in expectation of being one day able to reimburse them in real coin. This fictitious kind of money, which owes its birth to necessity, and can only be rendered current by its being punctually paid in real specie, is like bills of exchange, the imaginary value of which may easily exceed the solid funds that are in a nation.

These expedients are of great use in a free country. They have often saved a republic, but seldom, or never, fail to ruin a monarchy; for, as the people soon begin to grow suspicious, the minister is obliged to break his word: the ideal money multiplies apace: private men bury their money in the earth; and the whole machine of government falls into a confusion which is often productive of the most pernicious consequences, as was but too plainly exemplified in the king of Sweden.

At first, Baron Görtz issued his new coin with equal discretion and reserve; but, by the rapidity of a motion which he could not restrain, he was soon hurried beyond the limits which he had originally prescribed to himself. All kinds of goods and provisions having risen to an immoderate price, he was obliged to increase the quantity of his copper coin. But the more it was increased, the less was its value; and Sweden, deluged as it were by this false money, set up a general cry against the baron. The people, who always regarded their sovereign with a kind of veneration, could not find it in their hearts to hate him, and therefore made the weight of their resentment fall on a minister, who, both as a foreigner and chief director of the finances, was doubly exposed to the public odium.

But what entirely completed his ruin was a tax he attempted to impose on the clergy. The clergy, who are too apt to join their own cause to that of the Supreme Being, called him an atheist, because he demanded their money. Some of the new copper coin being stamped with the figures of the heathen gods, they thence took occasion to call those pieces *the gods of Baron Görtz*.

To this public odium under which he labored was added the jealousy of the ministers; the more implacable in their resentment as their power was the less. The King's sister, and the prince her husband, dreaded him, as a man attached from his birth to the Duke of Holstein, and might one day be able to place the crown of Sweden on his head. In a word, he had incurred the hatred of the whole nation, Charles alone excepted; but this general aversion served only to insure to him the friendship of the King, whose maxim it always was to be the more inflexible the more he was contradicted. Accordingly, he now relied upon the baron with an almost implicit confidence; gave him an absolute power in the interior government of the kingdom; and committed to his care whatever related to the negotiations with the Czar, pressing him above all things to hasten the conference that was to be held in the island of Aland.

And, indeed, Görtz had no sooner regulated the finances (a work which had hitherto detained him at Stockholm), than he set out on his journey for the place appointed, in order to finish, with the Czar's minister, the grand scheme he had projected.

The preliminary articles of that alliance, which was wholly to have changed the face of affairs in Europe, were found among Görtz's papers after his death, and were as follows:

The Czar was to keep the whole of Livonia, and part of Ingria and Carelia, to himself, and to restore the rest to Sweden. He was to join his efforts with those of Charles XII in order to restore Stanislaus to the throne of Poland, and to enter that country with 80,000 Russians, to dethrone the very king in whose defence he had waged a war of ten years' continuance. He was to furnish the King of Sweden with a number of ships sufficient to transport 10,000 Swedes to England, and 30,000 to Germany. The united forces of Peter and Charles were to attack the King of England in his German dominions, especially in Bremen and Verden; and were likewise to be employed in re-establishing the Duke of Holstein, and compelling the King of Prussia to agree to a treaty, by which he would have been deprived of part of those territories which he had seized. From the time that this alliance was made, Charles assumed as lofty airs as if his victorious troops, reinforced by those of the Czar, had already carried all his schemes into execution. He required the Emperor of Germany, in a peremptory manner, to fulfil the treaty of Altranstädt. But the Court of Vienna would hardly deign to give an answer to the proposal of a prince from whom she had nothing to fear.

The King of Poland did not enjoy the same tranquillity, but saw the clouds gathering all around him. The Polish nobility had formed a confederacy against him; and, ever since his restoration, he had perpetually been engaged either in wars or treaties with his subjects. The Czar, who had now become a dangerous mediator, had a hundred galleys near Dantzic, and 40,000 men on the frontiers of Poland. All the North was filled with jealousy and apprehension. Flemming, of all men in the world the most apt to distrust, and himself the most to be distrusted, was the first who suspected the designs of the Czar and the King of Sweden in favor of Stanislaus. He therefore resolved to have this prince seized in the Duchy of Deux-Ponts, as James Sobieski had formerly been in Silesia. A Frenchman, one of those restless and enterprising spirits who wander into foreign parts to try their fortunes, had lately brought a small number of his countrymen, bold and daring like himself, into the service of the King of Poland. He imparted a project to Flemming, by which he undertook, with the assistance of thirty French officers, to seize Stanislaus in his own palace, and carry him a prisoner to Dresden. The project was approved. Enterprises of that nature were not then uncommon. Some of those desperate fellows who are called *bravos* in Italy, had performed the like achievements in the Milanese, during the last war between France and Germany: and, even since that time, several French refugees in Holland had ventured to penetrate to Versailles, in order to carry off the dauphin, and actually had seized the person of the first equerry almost under the windows of the castle where Louis XIV resided.

Accordingly, the adventurer disposed his men and post-horses in the best manner he could contrive, in order to seize and carry off Stanislaus. But the enterprise was discovered the night before it was to have been carried into execution. Several of the desperadoes saved themselves by flight, and the rest were taken prisoners. They had no right to expect to be treated as prisoners of war, but rather as common robbers. Stanislaus, instead of punishing them as their crime deserved, contented himself with reproaching them with their baseness, and even that he did with the greatest politeness and humanity. Nay, what is more, he gave them money to defray the expenses of their return to Poland, and, by that act of generosity, plainly showed that his rival Augustus had but too much reason to fear him.*

Meanwhile Charles set out on a second expedition to Norway, in the month of October, 1718. He had taken all his measures with so much prudence and precaution, that he hoped he should be able, in the space of six months, to make

* Here M. Norberg accuses the author of treating crowned heads with too little respect; as if this faithful account contained in it anything injurious, or as if we were obliged to relate aught but truth of departed kings. Does he imagine that history should resemble a sermon preached before a sovereign, in which the flattering orator loads his royal hearer with unmerited praises?

himself master of that kingdom. He rather chose to go and conquer rocks amid ice and snow, in the depth of winter, which kills the animals even in Sweden, where the cold is less severe, than to recover his beautiful provinces in Germany. These he expected he should soon be able to retake in consequence of his alliance with the Czar; and, in any event, it was a much more tempting object of ambition to wrest a kingdom from his victorious foe.

At the mouth of the river Tistadaelf, near the Danish channel, and between the towns of Bahus and Anslo, stands Frederickshald, a place of great strength and importance, and considered as the key of the kingdom. To this town Charles laid siege, in the month of December. The soldiers, benumbed with cold, were hardly able to break the ground, which was so much hardened by the frost that it was almost as difficult to pierce it as if they had been opening trenches in a rock. But nothing could resist the resolution and perseverance of the Swedes, while they saw their king at their head, and sharing in all their labors. Never, indeed, did Charles undergo greater fatigues. His constitution, strengthened by eighteen years of severe labor, was hardened to such a degree that he slept in the open field in Norway in the midst of winter, covered only with a cloak, and without doing the least injury to his health. Several of the soldiers on duty dropped down dead with cold; and though the rest were almost frozen to death, yet as they saw their king sharing in all their hardships, they dared not utter a single word of complaint. Having heard, a little before this expedition, of a certain woman in Scania, called Johns Dotter, who had lived for several months without any other nourishment than water, he, who had all his life studied to inure himself to the worst extremes that human nature can support, resolved to try how long he could fast without fainting. Accordingly he fasted five whole days, without either eating or drinking; and on the morning of the sixth rode two leagues, and then alighted at the tent of the Prince of Hesse, his brother-in-law, where he ate heartily, without feeling the least disorder, either from his long fast of five days, or from the plentiful meal which now succeeded.*

---

\* Norberg alleges, that it was to cure a pain in his breast that Charles submitted to this long abstinence. Confessor Norberg is surely a most wretched physician.

With such a body of iron, inspired by a soul so bold and inflexible in every condition, he could not fail to be formidable to all his neighbors.

On the eleventh of December, being St. Andrew's day, he went at nine in the evening to view the trenches; and not finding the parallel so far advanced as he expected, he could not help expressing his surprise and displeasure. Mégret, a French engineer, who conducted the siege, assured him that the place would be taken in eight days. "Well! we shall see," said the King, and went on with the engineer to survey the works. He stopped at a place where a branch of the trenches formed an angle with the parallel. He knelt on the inner *talus*, and resting his elbow on the parapet, continued for some time to view the men who were carrying on the trenches by starlight.

Circumstances, in their own nature trivial, become important when they relate to the death of such a man as Charles XII. I must therefore take upon me to say, that the whole of the conversation, reported by so many writers to have passed between the King and Mégret the engineer, is absolutely false. The following account I can affirm, upon the best authority, to be the real truth of the matter.

The King stood with almost the half of his body exposed to a battery of cannon pointed directly against the angle where he was. He was attended by two Frenchmen only; one of whom was M. Siquier, his aid-de-camp, a man of courage and conduct, who had entered into his service in Turkey, and was particularly attached to the Prince of Hesse; the other was this engineer. The cannon fired upon them with grape-shot, to which the King, as he stood behind them, was most exposed. A little behind them was Count Schwerin, who commanded the trenches. While Schwerin was giving orders to Count Posse, a captain of the guards, and to one Kaulbar, his aid-de-camp, Siquier and Mégret saw the King fall upon the parapet, with a deep sigh. They ran to him; but he was already dead. A ball of half a pound had struck him on the right temple, and made a hole sufficient to receive three fingers at once. His head reclined upon the parapet; his left eye was beaten in, and the right one entirely beaten out of its socket. Though he expired the moment he received the wound, yet by a kind of instinctive motion, he had grasped the hilt of his sword in his hand, and still lay in that posture. At the sight of this shocking spectacle, Mégret, a man of a singular turn of mind, and of great indifference of temper, said, " Come, gentlemen, the play is ended, let us now go to supper." Siquier ran immediately and informed Count Schwerin of what had happened. They all agreed to conceal the news of his death from the soldiers till such time as the Prince of Hesse should be acquainted with it. The body was wrapped up in a gray cloak. Siquier put his hat and wig on the King's head; and in this condition Charles was carried, under the name of one Captain Carlberg, through the midst of his troops, who thus saw their dead king pass them, without ever dreaming that it was his Majesty.

The prince gave instant orders that no one should stir out of the camp, and that all the passes to Sweden should be strictly guarded, that so he might have time to take the necessary measures for placing the crown on his wife's head, and to exclude the Duke of Holstein, who might lay claim to it.

Thus fell Charles XII, King of Sweden, at the age of thirty-six years and a half, after having experienced all the grandeur of prosperity, and all the hardships of adversity, without being either softened by the one or the least disturbed by the other. Almost all his actions, even those of his private life, border on the marvellous. Perhaps he was the only man, most certainly he was the only king, that ever lived without weaknesses. He carried all the virtues of the hero to such an excess as rendered them no less dangerous than the opposite vices. His resolution, hardened into obstinacy, occasioned his misfortunes in the Ukraine, and detained him five years in Turkey. His liberality, degenerating into profusion, ruined Sweden. His courage, pushed to the length of temerity, was the cause of his death; and, during the last years of his reign, the means he employed to support his authority differed little from tyranny. His great qualities, any one of which would have been sufficient to immortalize another prince, proved pernicious to his country. He never was the aggressor; but, in taking vengeance on those who had injured him, his resentment got the better of his prudence. He was the first man who ever aspired to the title of conqueror, without the least desire of enlarging his dominions. His only end in subduing kingdoms was to have the pleasure of giving them away. His passion for glory, for war, and revenge, prevented him from being a good politician—a quality, without which the world had never before seen anyone a conqueror. Before a battle, and after a victory, he was modest and humble; and after a defeat, firm and undaunted. Severe to himself as well as to others, he too little regarded either his own life and labors, or those of his subjects; an extraordinary rather than a great man, and more worthy to be admired than imitated. From the history of his life, however, succeeding kings may learn that a quiet and happy government is infinitely preferable to so much glory.

Charles XII was of a tall stature and portly figure; he had a fine forehead, large blue eyes full of sweetness, and a well-formed nose. But the lower part of his face was disagreeable, and too often disfigured by a frequent laugh, which scarcely opened his lips; and as to hair and beard, he had hardly any at all. A profound silence reigned at his table. Notwithstanding the inflexible obstinacy of his temper, he always retained that bashfulness which goes by the name of false modesty. He was but little qualified to make a figure in conversation, because, having addicted himself entirely to war and action, he was utterly unacquainted with the pleasures of society. Till the time of his residence among the Turks, which furnished him with a good deal of leisure, he had read nothing but "Cæsar's Commentaries" and the "History of Alexander." It is true he had written some remarks on the art of war, and particularly on his own campaigns from 1700 to 1709. This he owned to the Chevalier Folard, but said that the manuscript had been lost at the unfortunate battle of Poltava. Some people would make us believe that Charles was a good mathematician. That he was possessed of great depth and penetration of thought cannot be denied; but the arguments they produce to prove his knowledge in mathematics are by no means conclusive. He wanted to alter the method of counting by tens, and to substitute in its place the number sixty-four, because that number contains both a square and a cube, and, being divided by two, is reducible to a unit. This, if it proves anything, only shows that he always delighted in what was difficult and extraordinary.

With regard to his religion, though the sentiments of a prince ought to have no influence on other men, and though the opinion of a monarch so illiterate as Charles is of little consequence in these matters, yet in this, as well as in other particulars, we must gratify the curiosity of mankind, who are anxious to know whatever relates to a prince of his character. I am informed by the gentleman who has furnished me with the greater part of the materials which compose this history that Charles XII was a serious Lutheran till the year 1707. Happening then to be at Leipsic, he there met with the famous philosopher, Leibnitz, a man who thought and spoke with equal freedom, and had already instilled his notions into more princes than one. I cannot believe what is commonly reported, that Charles XII conceived an indifference for Lutheranism from the conversation of this philosopher, who never had the honor to talk with him above a quarter of an hour; but I have been told by Fabricius, who lived with him in great familiarity for seven years successively, that having seen, during his abode among the Turks, such an infinite variety of religions, he became more lax in his principles. This fact is likewise confirmed by Motraye in his voyages. The same, too, is the opinion of Count Croissi, who has often told me that of all his old principles, Charles retained none but that of absolute predestination, a doctrine that favored his courage and justified his temerity. The Czar was of much the same way of thinking with regard to fate and religion, but talked of these subjects more frequently, as, indeed, he did of everything else with his favorites, in a very familiar manner; for he had this advantage over Charles, that he was a good philosopher and an eloquent speaker.

Here I cannot help taking notice of a most uncharitable suspicion, too readily embraced by the weak and credulous and too industriously propagated by the malicious and ill-natured, to wit: that the death of princes is always owing to poison or assassination. It was then the current report in Germany that Siquier was the man who killed the King of Sweden. That brave officer was long grieved at this injurious aspersion; and as he was one day talking to me on the subject, he said, "I might have killed the King of Sweden; but, had I been capable of forming such a barbarous resolution, so great was my veneration for that illustrious hero, that I could not have had the courage to carry it into execution."

I know, indeed, that Siquier himself gave occasion to this heavy charge, which, even to this day, many of the Swedes believe to be well founded. He told me that being seized with a violent fever at Stockholm, he cried out that he had killed the King of Sweden; and that, in the height of his frenzy, he even opened the window and publicly begged pardon for the regicide. When he was informed, in the course of his recovery, of what he had said in his illness, he was almost ready to die with grief. This anecdote I did not choose to publish during his life-time. I saw him a little before he expired, and think I can safely affirm that, far from killing Charles XII, he would have suffered a thousand deaths to save the life of that hero. Had he actually committed such a horrid crime, it must have been to serve some prince, who no doubt would have liberally rewarded him for such a piece of treachery; but he died in France so extremely poor that he even stood in need of my assistance. If these reasons are not thought sufficient to vindicate his memory, let it be considered that the ball by which Charles fell could not have come from a pistol, and yet that Siquier had no other way to give the fatal blow than by a pistol concealed under his garments.

The King was no sooner dead than the siege of Frederickshald was raised, and a total change took place in the government. The Swedes, who considered the glory of their sovereign rather as a burden than an advantage, applied their whole attention toward concluding a peace with their enemies, and suppressing that absolute power which Baron Görtz had so much abused to their ruin. The States, by a free and voluntary choice, elected the sister of Charles XII for their Queen, and obliged her, by a solemn act, to renounce all hereditary right to the crown, that so she might hold it by the suffrages of the people. She bound herself by the most sacred oaths never to attempt the re-establishment of arbitrary power; and at last, sacrificing the love of royalty to conjugal affection, yielded the crown to her husband, who was chosen King by the States, and mounted the throne on the same conditions as his royal consort.

Baron Görtz was taken into custody immediately after the death of Charles, and condemned by the Senate of Stockholm to lose his head at the foot of the common gallows—an act of revenge, perhaps, rather than of justice, and a cruel insult to the memory of a king whom Sweden still admires.